The Watchman Fell Asleep

SUNY series in Israeli Studies
Russell Stone, editor

Praise for *The Watchman Fell Asleep*

"Uri Bar-Joseph has written an extraordinarily detailed yet efficient account of what went wrong inside the Israeli government. This is no small accomplishment ... Bar-Joseph's analysis is not just some arcane story written for intelligence specialists and history buffs. It is an important tale of a deterrence failure and the inability of policymakers to recognize, despite overwhelming evidence, that their deterrence policy was failing."
— *The Journal of Strategic Studies*

"The value of Bar-Joseph's hour-by-hour account is to see how the 'conception' locked intelligence officers, military planners, and policymakers into an intellectual straitjacket, functioning as a barrier to information sharing and effective analysis until it crumbled at the last minute."
— *The Journal of Military History*

"This is a stimulating book that attempts the most detailed analysis yet undertaken of the disastrous failure on Israel's part to prepare for the 1973 war."
— *International Journal of Middle East Studies*

"Bar-Joseph's volume ... is sure to become the standard account of Israel's intelligence fiasco on the eve of the Yom Kippur War. It contains much new and interesting information for those who seek a better understanding of Israeli decision making in the run-up to the war."
— *Israel Affairs*

"Bar-Joseph provides a remarkable and depressing hour-by-hour account of the intelligence failings as they unfolded during the key days of October 1 to October 6."
— *Shofar: An Interdisciplinary Journal of Jewish Studies*

"This landmark study is certain to become the classic analysis of the October War. It ranks with Roberta Wohlstetter's famous study of the Japanese attack on Pearl Harbor. Bar-Joseph's account draws on many important new sources, which he weaves into a dramatic account of the intelligence failure."
— Alexander L. George, Stanford University

"The 1973 surprise was traumatic for Israelis and instructive for strategists everywhere, so it has spawned a large literature. Uri Bar-Joseph's book and stands out as the latest and most definitive of these works."
— Richard K. Betts, Director, Saltzman Institute of War and Peace Studies, Columbia University

"...a fascinating ... study ... of ... the event that is considered as the most traumatic in Israel's history."
— *Yedioth Ahronot*, in praise of the Hebrew edition

"Uri Bar-Joseph's study is the most important study ... published so far on the War of Yom Kippur."
— *Haaretz*, in praise of the Hebrew edition

"*The Watchman Fell Asleep* ... presents a chilling picture of a nation's fate almost gambled away by a handful of brilliant men unable to conceive that they might be wrong."
— *The Jerusalem Post Magazine*, in praise of the Hebrew edition

The Watchman Fell Asleep

The Surprise of Yom Kippur and Its Sources

Uri Bar-Joseph

STATE UNIVERSITY OF NEW YORK PRESS

Cover photo: Shlomo Arad

Published by
State University of New York Press, Albany

© 2005 State University of New York
All rights reserved

Printed in the United States of America

No part of this book may be used or reproduced in any manner whatsoever without written permission. No part of this book may be stored in a retrieval system or transmitted in any form or by any means including electronic, electrostatic, magnetic tape, mechanical, photocopying, recording, or otherwise without the prior permission in writing of the publisher.

For information, contact State University of New York Press, Albany, NY
www.sunypress.edu

Production by Mike Haggett
Marketing by Susan M. Petrie

Library of Congress Catloging-in-Publication Data
Bar-Joseph, Uri.
   [Hatsofeh she-nirdam. English]
   The watchman fell asleep : the surprise of Yom Kippur and its sources / Uri Bar-Joseph.
     p. cm.—(SUNY series in Israeli studies)
   Includes bibliographical references and index.
   ISBN 0-7914-6481-4 (hardcover : alk. paper)—
   ISBN 0-7914-6482-2 (pbk. : alk. paper)
   1. Israel-Arab War, 1973—Causes. 2. Israel—Politics and government—1967–1993. 3. Military Intelligence—Israel. I. Title. II. Series.
DS128.1.B36613 2005
956.04'8—dc22   2004016830

10 9 8 7 6 5 4 3 2 1

For Michal

Contents

Acknowledgments ... ix

Introduction ... 1

Part I. The Egyptian War Decision and Its Implementation

Chapter 1. The War Decision ... 11

Chapter 2. Planning the Next War: Past Experience and the Main Problems ... 15
    Problem I: The Crossing of the Canal   17
    Problem II: Egyptian Air Inferiority   19
    Problem III: Inferiority in Armored Fighting   23

Chapter 3. The Egyptian Deception Plan ... 25
    i. The Role of Deception in Egyptian War Planning   25
    ii. Passive Deception   26
    iii. Active Deception   27
    iv. Assessment of the Egyptian Deception   30

Chapter 4. The Egyptian-Syrian War Coordination ... 33

Part II. Israel Prepares for War

Chapter 5. The Balance of Forces—the Israeli View ... 39

Chapter 6. The Intelligence Conception and Its Sources ... 45
    i. The Conception   45
    ii. The Empirical Evidence   47

Chapter 7. The Strategic Warning and Its Role in Israel's War Plans ... 53

Chapter 8. The Next War Scenarios ... 59

Chapter 9. The War Estimate: October 1972–August 1973 63
    i. October 1972–April 1973   63
    ii. April–May 1973   66
    iii. June–August 1973   73

Part III. The Dynamics of an Intelligence Fiasco

Chapter 10. August–September 1973 81

Chapter 11. Monday, October 1, 1973 103

Chapter 12. Tuesday, October 2, 1973 113

Chapter 13. Wednesday, October 3, 1973 119

Chapter 14. Thursday, October 4, 1973 133

Chapter 15. Friday, October 5, 1973 141

Chapter 16. Saturday, October 6, 1973, 0400–1400 187

Chapter 17. Surprise 201
    i. The Cabinet   201
    ii. The Canal Front   202
    iii. The Golan Front   211
    iv. The Air Force   218

Chapter 18. The Cost of Being Caught Unprepared 225
    i. The Material Losses   225
    ii. The Psychological Impact of Surprise   228

Chapter 19. The Causes of the Intelligence Failure 235
    i. Obstacles Unique to the Warning-Response Process   236
    ii. Bureaucratic Obstacles   240
    iii. Groupthinking   243
    iv. Psychological Obstacles at the Individual Level   246
    v. The Human Factor   248

Notes 253

Bibliography 289

Index 299

Acknowledgments

When the Yom Kippur War broke out, at 2:00pm, October 6, 1973, I was at home, reading a book. About 20 hours later, I arrived, together with a few soldiers of my reserve unit to Hatzav, the base camp of the 9th tank Regiment of the 14th Armor Brigade, some 25 kilometers east of the Suez Canal. The camp was deserted. The doors of the regimental store-keeping were wide open and a radio was still playing on. We loaded machine guns, ammunition and additional equipment to our two jeeps. In the rush to the front we lacked the equipment and the time to properly prepare the vehicles for combat. A few days later I learned that the 9th Regiment was almost totally destroyed in the fighting that took place during the first hours of the war. And only years later I found out that between our two jeeps and the entire Egyptian 18th Infantry Division there were hardly any IDF forces.

Like most Israelis who experienced the shocking surprise of that Yom Kippur, I too wanted to know why and how it happened. Unlike most, however, I was lucky enough to have Professor Michael Handel as my teacher at the Hebrew University in Jerusalem. Michael, probably the most serious scholar of the Yom Kippur surprise and a wonderful teacher, ignited my academic interest in this subject. He passed away in June 2001, shortly before the Hebrew edition of this book was first published. I was also lucky to have Professor Alexander George as my mentor during my PhD studies at Stanford University. It was in the framework of his course "Decision making and Strategic Interaction" that I wrote my first academic paper about the 1973 intelligence debacle and the theory of strategic surprise.

Many of the documents that are included in this study were provided to me by persons who, for obvious reasons, prefer to remain anonymous. These documents have enabled me to present the distorted intelligence picture as it was provided, on the eve of the war, to Israel's military and civilian policymakers. In order to understand how this picture was constructed, I interviewed most of the officers who were involved in its making. As far as I can judge, the interviews reflect the honest opinions of these officers as they tried to describe, as accurately as possible, the sequence of events that preceded the war. Some of them have asked to remain unidentified — a request which I have honored. The names of the rest are included in the bibliography of this book. I thank them all for their help.

My student Dima Adamsky provided me with excellent material from Russian sources about the Soviet aspects of the coming war. My friend Shuki Teicher suggested some excellent insights to the Hebrew edition of this book. I would also like to thank my colleagues in the Division of International Relations at the School of Political Science at Haifa University and Dr. Michael Rinella and Michael Haggett of SUNY Press for their help in the publication process of the book. Lastly, I would like to thank my family for their support during this period.

Introduction

On the wall at the entrance to the office of the Director of Military Intelligence (DMI) of the Israeli Defense Force General Headquarters (IDF GHQ) in Tel Aviv, on the wall of his head of the Research Department, in the offices of the analysts of the Directorate of Military Intelligence (AMAN), in AMAN's training bases, and in nearly any office of this agency, hangs a sign that quotes the words of the prophet Ezekiel:

> The word of the LORD came to me: "Son of man, speak to your countrymen and say to them: 'When I bring the sword against a land, and the people of the land choose one of their men and make him their watchman, and he sees the sword coming against the land and blows the trumpet to warn the people, then if anyone hears the trumpet but does not take warning and the sword comes and takes his life, his blood will be on his own head. Since he heard the sound of the trumpet but did not take warning, his blood will be on his own head. If he had taken warning, he would have saved himself. But if the watchman sees the sword coming and does not blow the trumpet to warn the people and the sword comes and takes the life of one of them, that man will be taken away because of his sin, but I will hold the watchman accountable for his blood.'"[1]

In 1973, on the holiest Jewish day of Yom Kippur, the watchman saw the sword and did not blow the trumpet. And the sword took many lives. The watchman did not blow the trumpet since for almost a year by then, he was asleep.

The sudden Arab attack of Yom Kippur 1973 is the most traumatic event in Israel's stormy history.[2] The success of the Egyptian and the Syrian armies, during the war's first day, in occupying the "Bar-Lev" defense line along the Suez Canal as well as considerable portions of the Golan Heights, and the loss of 300 out of the 500 tanks that defended Israel when the war started, posed the most serious threat to Israel's existence since the 1948 War. In the words of Defense Minister Moshe Dayan in the morning hours of October 7, "the 'Third Temple' was in danger."

The Arab accomplishment was the direct outcome of AMAN's failure to provide the political and military echelons with a high-quality strategic warning of the impending attack. Such a warning, which according to the nation's security doctrine was expected to be given at least 48 hours before the breakout of war, was a necessary condition for the mobilization and deployment of Israel's reserve forces—about 80 percent of its ground army. Although the IDF ultimately won the war, the heavy losses that it suffered and its failure to attain a decisive victory that would erase Arab achievements at the initial stages of the war, left Israel's security doctrine badly shaken. Consequently, since 1973 Israel has been searching for a new doctrine that will better respond to the threat of surprise attack.

In the intelligence failures class of events, the 1973 fiasco is certainly one of the most significant, equal to that of Pearl Harbor and Barbarossa. But in contrast to the case of Pearl Harbor, prior to the war Israel had an almost perfect picture of Arab attack plans, military deployment, and the intention to launch a war. And, unlike in Barbarossa—where the Soviets had excellent information about German military preparations but were misled by a sophisticated deception plan—the Arab deception plan in 1973 was rather primitive. A few days before the war, Israeli experts had already identified it as a deception. Consequently, the variance in the causes of surprise on Yom Kippur makes it a very important case also for the development of theory of strategic surprise.

* * *

For more than forty years now, since the publication of Roberta Wohlstetter's classic study on the American fiasco of Pearl Harbor,[3] the dominant thesis among students of the subject is that intelligence failures are not the product of insufficient information or of negligence or stupidity by intelligence producers and consumers. Rather, these failures are the result of inherent pathologies of the warning-response process that affect "honest, dedicated, and intelligent men."[4] The experience gained since the early 1940s repeatedly confirms this thesis. The most recent proof (for the time being) is the intelligence failure of September 11, 2001.[5]

The many studies of intelligence organizations' failure to provide a timely and accurate warning prior to sudden attacks have identified, described, and analyzed a large number of inherent obstacles in the warning-response process. Some of them are more typical to the specific interaction between the surprise initiator and its victim. They include, among others, concealment, which aims at preventing the victim from obtaining information about the initiator's intentions and capabilities to attack ("signals," by Wohlstetter's terminology); deception, aimed at increasing misleading information about the initiator's intentions and capabilities ("noise," in Wohlstetter's terminology); the "cry-wolf syndrome," which is the outcome of repeated futile warnings that erode, in the long-run, the victim's receptivity to warnings; compartmentalization, which artificially, though unintentionally, obstructs the flow of relevant information; the tendency of intelligence agencies to indulge in best-case and worst-case scenarios; and the structural disadvantage that is embodied in the victim's delayed response to incoming warnings.[6]

A problematic relationship between intelligence officers and policy-makers can add another source for an eventual failure. The tendency of policy-makers to serve as their own intelligence officers might lead them to reject solid intelligence estimates. On the other hand, policy-makers may also tend to automatically accept the intelligence product—a phenomenon that can lead to the creation of a dogmatic and monolithic estimate about the likelihood of war. Overcommitment of policy-makers to their own political agenda (e.g., the White House commitment to the invasion of Iraq in 2002–2003), might hamper their receptivity to intelligence products that are inconsistent with this agenda. Furthermore, the tendency of some intelligence officers to interfere with the political process and of policy-makers to intervene in professional intelligence work might further disrupt the ability of the intelligence agency to provide a timely and accurate warning.[7]

A third source for warning failures is general pathologies of information processing. Here, students of surprise attack use theories from fields such as cognitive and social psychology, organizational studies, and cybernetics in order to analyze the impact of specific pathologies that obstruct effective information processing in the warning–response process. Such obstacles may include cognitive dissonance,[8] confirmation bias,[9] and heuristic judgment,[10] which disrupt the individual's ability to perceive reality accurately. The first two obstacles explain the tendency in the individual to ignore incoming information that contradicts the belief that a sudden attack is unlikely. The third explains why the estimation process of complicated situations may fall victim to judgmental errors, and situations prior to sudden attack are always complex.

At the small-group level of analysis, Irving Janis's theory of groupthink, which analyzes the dynamics within a small and cohesive group with a strong tendency to conformity, is crucial for understanding why the collective estimation process produces in so many cases a gross misperception of reality.[11] Finally, at the organizational level, features such as hierarchy, centralization, the tendency toward the use of standard operating procedures (SOP), or bureaucratic politics, produce additional explanations for the incompetence of intelligence agencies to produce high quality warnings at times of crisis, and of military organizations in properly responding to them.[12]

Two facts make the surprise of Yom Kippur an excellent case to test the validity of these theoretical explanations: First, the persons involved in the making of this fiasco were all experienced and intelligent, and the mistake that they made in assessing the Egyptian and Syrian war intention was an authentic one. Unlike the case of Pearl Harbor where numerous conspiracy theories claim that Roosevelt or Churchill knew ahead of the Japanese attack, and unlike the popular conspiracy theory suggested in recent years by Suvorov to explain the surprise of Barbarossa,[13] hardly any such theory exists in the Israeli case.[14] Second, Israel had excellent information about the Arab military preparations and the Egyptian and Syrian intention to launch the war. On the basis of this information, it could be concluded that the attack was highly likely. Given these facts, it is no wonder that at the focus of the academic study of this fiasco stands the attempt to explain why the main persons involved believed until the very last moment that Egypt did not perceive itself as being capable of launching war and that Syria was not ready to launch one without Egypt.

Some of the answers that have been given to this riddle cover a wider spectrum than others. Michael Handel, for example, identified three "noise barriers," which distorted the signals that had to pass through them. The first of the three involved various other sources of threat in the international and regional systems as well as a too quiet international environment (e.g., the *Détente*), which averted the victim's attention from the real threat and destroyed its ability to correctly assimilate the signals of the coming attack. The second barrier was created by the initiator's attempt to conceal its plans and to mislead the victim with regard to its real intentions. The last barrier was the noise generated unintentionally by the victim, which farther hampered the proper assimilation of the signals of the impending threat.[15] Not surprisingly, the interaction between the three barriers led Handel to conclude that "surprise can rarely be prevented."[16] More than ten years later, he repeated this conclusion, adding that this was so "because at the root of the problem—the weakest link in the intelligence process—is human nature."[17]

Most studies of the 1973 case focused on Handel's third barrier. Avi Ben Zvi, who compared the Yom Kippur surprise with other intelligence failures, concluded that the source of the problem in 1973 was the Israeli inclination to grant more importance to strategic assumptions—primarily that the risk of war was too high from Arab perspective—than to information at the tactical level that indicated that they were preparing for war. Comparing Pearl Harbor and the Yom Kippur attack, more than twenty years later, Ben-Zvi did not change much of his conclusion: The main mistake of Israel's war assessment was the underestimation of Egypt's ability to launch a limited strike while using its newly acquired Scud missiles to deter Israel from attacking its rear.[18] Richard K. Betts reached a similar conclusion in his excellent study of surprise attack: Overreliance on a strategic conception that Egypt did not intend to launch war led to the underestimation of tactical information that indicated that the strategic assumption might be wrong.[19]

Other students of the subject have focused on the causes for the Israeli adherence to the conception that war was unlikely. Avi Shlaim explained the fiasco by a number of organizational and psychological obstacles that he identified in Israel intelligence, military, and political environments.[20] Janis Gross Stein used the first edition of the excellent biography of Lt. Gen. David Elazar, the IDF Chief of Staff during the war,[21] to point out a number of symptoms of groupthink in Israel's decision- and intelligence-making processes. Later she emphasized as a major cause for the failure the unsophisticated way by which Israel perceived its ability to deter Egypt from war, primarily the use of the balance of military forces as the main means to estimate the effectiveness of deterrence while ignoring the balance of interests.[22] Two veteran AMAN officers emphasized the psychological milieu in which the estimation process took place. Zvi Lanir, who focused his study on the distinction between fundamental and situational surprise, found that "the shock on Yom Kippur was primarily caused by the Israelis' discovery that they misconceived themselves, their military, social, and, to some degree, their moral image."[23] Yoel Ben-Porat, who served as a senior officer during the war, maintained that pretension and arrogance on behalf of intelligence officers, who believed that they could correctly grasp the complex strategic calculus of leaders such as Anwar Sadat and Hafez Asad, contributed significantly to the 1973 fiasco.[24] A third Israeli student of the debacle (with ample professional background as well) compared the 1973 case with the 1954 intelligence fiasco known as "the unfortunate business"—and concluded that crude violation of norms of behavior between intelligence producers and consumers contributed significantly to the debacle in both cases.[25]

Despite the evidence to the contrary, a number of studies maintain that the root of the Yom Kippur failure is to be found, nevertheless, in the intelligence information that was available to Israel on the eve of the war. Here, a distinction should be made between those who reached this conclusion due to insufficient knowledge of the evidence and those who are highly familiar with it. An example for the first is the work of Alex Hybel, who compared the cases of Pearl Harbor and Yom Kippur and concluded that Israel failed to reach the critical information necessary for a reexamination of the thesis that war was unlikely. This failure was, to a large extent, the outcome of a successful Syrian and Egyptian deception campaign.[26] Aharon Levran, a high-ranking AMAN officer during the war, maintained that at the root of the intelligence failure was the "curse of the wealth of intelligence sources"—primarily the fact that AMAN relied on one specific high-quality source to provide a war warning. As long as this source—Dr. Ashraf Marwan, a close aide to Sadat, whose identity had been disclosed recently[27]—did not provide a warning, AMAN's analysts were reluctant to change their "low probability" assessment.[28] Eliot Cohen and John Gooch used Levran's explanation when concluding that the Israeli fiasco was caused not only by analytical mistakes but also by overreliance on one source that disappointed at the most critical time.[29]

While Levran assumed that Israel's prime source did not alert his handlers since he did not know all the details of the Egyptian plan,[30] AMAN's director in 1973, Major General (res.) Eli Zeira claimed that Marwan—whom he calls "the information" in his war memoirs—was an Egyptian double agent whose task was to deceive Israel with regard to Egypt's war plans. According to Zeira, Marwan was the source of the information that validated the Israeli assumptions regarding Egypt's necessary conditions to launch war, but he was also the source of a number of false warnings that were intended to decrease Israel's war awareness. Thus Zeira claims, in the summer of 1973, Marwan informed the Israelis that war would start, if at all, at the end of the year.[31] Consequently, Zeira regarded the possible deception by Marwan as "the jewel in the crown of Egypt's deception operation . . . and Egypt's biggest success in the War of Yom Kippur."[32] Other students of Handel's second barrier were more prudent when estimating the value of Egypt's deception. John Amos concluded that Egypt's deception hampered Israel's ability to properly assess the meaning of the war indicators that were collected by its intelligence agencies.[33] And Aharon Zeevei—at present AMAN's Director—who is also the most prominent student of the Egyptian deception, concluded, "The concealment and deception measures taken by Egypt and Syria, especially Egypt, successfully hid from the eyes of Israel's intelligence community, and even from that of the United States, their intentions to go to war."[34]

* * *

The many explanations for the Yom Kippur intelligence blunder are insufficient to bridge the wide gap between the excellent information that was available to AMAN on the eve of the war and the poor quality of strategic warning it produced. Hence, this book focuses on the action taken by Director of Military Intelligence Zeira and his chief estimator of Egyptian affairs, Lt. Col. Yona Bandman, who were the main (though not only) persons responsible for providing the policy-makers with a distorted intelligence picture—one that artificially gave more weight to calming rather than to alarming information. In the case of Zeira, and to a lesser extent Bandman, the bias toward a reassuring estimate was a motivated one. As a result of this behavior, the decisions taken by Defense Minister Moshe Dayan and the Chief of Staff did not reflect the graveness of the situation and did not meet even the minimal IDF deployment plans for a possibility of war. Why Zeira and Bandman acted the way they did is addressed in the last chapter of this book.

* * *

Much of the evidence that this book uses to trace the process that led to the Israeli surprise comes from two types of previously undisclosed primary sources. One is documents—primarily intelligence reports but also protocols of discussions—that provide the most comprehensive description available to date of the way AMAN assessed the situation prior to the war. This source also sheds new light on additional relevant issues, such as the role of strategic warning in Israel's military doctrine between 1967 and 1970. Many of these documents were given to me privately and are publicly unavailable. As far as I can judge, they are all authentic and they provide a balanced description of the intelligence on the eve of the war. Notably, since this book (in a more detailed version) was published in Israel in September 2001, it has not provoked questions about the validity of the documental data.

The second primary source used here are interviews that I conducted with most of the relevant intelligence and military officers who were involved in the fiasco. This type of source is naturally more problematic, particularly because the 1973 intelligence debacle is still such a traumatic event in the Israeli collective history and, even more so, in the private lives of the persons who were involved in its making. To the best of my judgment the verbal evidence I received reflects the authentic memoirs of the interviewees. Some of them used records that they had kept since 1973 in order to refresh their memory; others consulted friends. In any event, I tried to limit the use of these testimonies to cases where the information that they provided could be sustained by at least another source. Despite the difficulties involved in using this type of source, it cannot and should not be ignored. Many of the persons I interviewed had never been called to testify before the Agranat Commission—the only official investigation of the Yom Kippur War. Others had never been asked the questions that I asked them. Their testimony is critical; the documents tell us what AMAN's estimates were, but the verbal evidence explains how they were born. Any attempt to trace the Israeli intelligence failure without getting into the "black box" in which the intelligence estimate was created is doomed to fail from the start.

Part I

The Egyptian War Decision and Its Implementation

Chapter 1

The War Decision

The principal Egyptian decision to go to war was made on October 24, 1972. On the evening of that date President Anwar Sadat convened Egypt's Armed Forces Supreme Council at his Giza residence to declare his decision to end the no peace–no war status quo that had lasted since early August 1970, when the War of Attrition ended.[1] Explaining his decision, Sadat said:

> The June 1967 defeat has made both enemy and friend doubt that we would ever fight again. Consequently, all the solutions I am presented with are based on this logic. Our commitments are being tested. I am not prepared to accept defeatist solutions or surrender. I will not sit at a table with Israel while I am in such a humiliating position, because that means surrender. In the face of our people, our enemies, and our friends, we must prove unemotionally and with careful planning that we are capable of sacrifice and can stand up and fight and change the situation with whatever means are at our disposal. . . . The time for words is over, and we have reached saturation point. We have to manage our affairs with whatever we have at hand; we have to follow this plan to change the situation and set fire to the region. Then words will have real meaning and value.[2]

Many of the participants—among them War Minister Mohammed Ahmed Sadiq and his deputy, Abdel Khader Hassan, and senior army officers such as Gen. Abdel Ali Khabir (the commander of the central district), Gen. Mohammed Ali Fahmy (commander of the navy), Gen. Saad Mamounn (commander of the Second Army), and Gen. Abdel Muneim Wasel (commander of the Third Army)—expressed reservations about the feasibility of

Egypt's war option. They were mainly concerned with Israel's air superiority, Egypt's vulnerability to deep penetration raids, and the challenges involved in the crossing of the Suez Canal and the establishment of defensible bridgeheads on its eastern bank.[3] Sadat declined these reservations, emphasizing instead his resolve to go to war even under highly unfavorable conditions:

> We are confronted with a challenge. "To be or not to be." A partial solution has been presented to me [the U.S. peace proposals] and is still waiting for my approval. But, I am not going to accept it. We will simply have to use our talents and our planning to compensate for our lack of some kinds of equipment.[4]

Two days later Sadat dismissed his Minister of War, his deputy, and the Commander of the Navy. Sadiq's replacement was Gen. Ahmad Ali Ismail—an old foe of the Chief of Staff, Lt. Gen. Saad el Shazly. Ismail had a dubious military record and a poor health condition due to cancer. But, he had one major advantage: Unlike his predecessor, he supported Sadat's decision to launch a war and he envisioned it in the same way that Sadat and Shazly did. Consequently, for the first time since the defeat of June 1967, the President, his War Minister, and the Chief of Staff reached a consensus not only about the need to resort to war, but also regarding its goal and its operational dimensions.[5]

During the October 24 meeting, Sadat defined the goal of the war simply as "Breaking the ceasefire."[6] On this basis the war planners defined its concept:

> ... a comprehensive "local" war in which only conventional arms would be used. The strategic aim was to upset the prevailing balance in the region and to challenge Israel's concept of security and the principles behind its military strategy. This would require time to allow for the participation of other Arab nations, the most important factors being the creation of a united Arab stand and exploring the possibility of using oil as a weapon of political pressure to influence the outcome of the war. The strategy, therefore, was an offensive military operation to liberate the occupied land in consecutive stages according to the capabilities of the armed forces, and to inflict on Israel the greatest possible number of losses in men and weapons in order to convince it that an indefinite occupation of our land was too costly to bear.[7]

This modest and very limited war conception reflected Egypt's strategic dilemma since the defeat of June 1967, and, even more so, since the end of the War of Attrition in August 1970. On the one hand, stood the Egyptian desire to erase the outcomes of the Six-Day War—outcomes that were "culturally, psychologically, and politically unacceptable."[8] On the other, was Egypt's pessimistic view regarding its ability to win a victory in the battlefield—a lesson gained in the 1967 and 1969–1970 wars and the outcome of a sober analysis of the Egyptian–Israeli balance of forces by the end of 1972.

Chapter 2

Planning the Next War: Past Experience and the Main Problems

Much of the Egyptian skepticism regarding the ability to win (or at least not to lose) the coming war, was rooted in the course and the outcomes of the War of Attrition of 1969–1970. Nasser initiated that war, despite the heavy risks involved, in order to raise the morale of the Egyptian public and the Egyptian army, and as a means to demonstrate Egypt's resolve to restore by force the pre–1967 War situation. In planning it in 1968, Egypt's war planners attempted to optimize their advantages in static warfare, in order to cause Israel as many casualties as possible. But, when it ended, the Egyptian army was closer than the IDF to defeat and could show only limited military achievements.

During most of the fighting, Israeli ground and air forces proved to be superior to their enemy. A 17-month Egyptian effort to shed Israeli blood—primarily by heavy bombardment of the IDF's defense line along the Canal, and commando ambushes on the routes to the Israeli strongholds—yielded 260 Israeli soldiers dead. Even by the standards of a small society such as Israel was in 1970, this was a bearable cost. As the IDF Chief of Staff, Lt. Gen. Chaim Bar-Lev noted in referring to this issue, the number of Israeli road accident casualties in 1970 was 529.[1] The exact number of Egyptian losses, on the other hand, is unclear but was far higher. Shazly speaks of 2,882 soldiers and civilians,[2] but this figure contradicts Egyptian reports of about 4,000 casualties in the spring of 1970 alone.[3] Israeli estimates of Egyptian losses in the war are around 15,000, and an American expert assesses them to be around 5,000.[4] Even if we take the minimal figure as the real one, the Egyptian-Israeli casualties' ratio would be 10:1—an unacceptable ratio by any standard. Moreover, in almost each confrontation between Egyptian and Israeli units, the Israelis gained the upper hand. Although the Egyptian army initiated a large number of commando raids behind Israeli lines, their results—with only a few exceptions—were rather disappointing. This became even more clear when compared to the IDF's sophisticated and almost always successful special operations during the war.

The Egyptian-Israeli capability gap was even more evident in the air. Although the planes loss ratio, according to Israeli reports, was 1:7 in favor of the Israeli Air Force (IAF),[5] Egypt's inability to protect itself against Israel's air raids was most vividly expressed in early 1970, when, after ten months of fighting, Egypt was left defenseless against Israeli deep-penetration raids that threatened to topple Nasser's regime. In contrast, the Egyptian Air Force (EAF) lacked any real capability to attack in the Sinai, and except for some hit-and-run raids against Israeli targets along the front, it was hardly a factor in the war. Shazly's conclusion regarding the air situation well reflects the pessimistic Egyptian view: "In effect, the enemy air force was ten years ahead of ours."[6]

Despite this gloomy picture, Egypt did have some accomplishments. The most important one was the advancement, immediately after the cease-fire entered into effect, of its air defense layout toward the front and its deployment along the Suez Canal. This move had put the entire front sector up to about ten kilometers east of the canal within the range of its SAM-2, SAM-3, and, later, SAM-6 missile batteries. In operational terms, it enabled the Egyptian army, for the first time since 1967, to effectively limit the IAF freedom of action over the theater of operations—a necessary though insufficient condition for launching a war. Furthermore, the mere fact that Soviet combat units were presently positioned in Egypt constituted an advantage. As Nasser saw it, the Soviets could both deter the Americans from increasing their role in the conflict and pressure them to compel Israel to accept a peace agreement at a reasonable cost for Egypt.[7]

But the Soviet presence created problems as well. The most important issue involved the mere political feasibility of an Egyptian war initiative. Soviet participation in an Egyptian war initiative to reoccupy the Sinai was highly unlikely, and the Egyptian leadership was well aware of this. During Soviet–Egyptian talks after Nasser's death, Sadat was told that the USSR expected that its combat units in Egypt would be replaced prior to any decision to renew hostilities.[8] In this sense, the Soviet military presence in Egypt limited not only Israel's freedom of action but also that of Egypt.

The same was true with regard to another Egyptian achievement—the improvement in the army's combat ability. On one hand, the War of Attrition gave the Egyptian soldier and the Egyptian officer ample combat experience, self assurance, and a closer understanding of the Israeli military tactics.[9] On the other hand, in light of the extensive casualties that Egypt suffered in the war, especially due to insufficient anti-aircraft defense, one may wonder if the simple soldier's fear barrier, primarily from IAF attacks, was really broken.

Despite this unpromising state of affairs, the Egyptian army continued its preparations for war after the end of the War of Attrition. On the basis of planning, which had already started in 1967, it continued conducting a series of exercises called "Tahrir" ("Freedom") that had begun in the summer of 1968. At their core stood various canal-crossing scenarios by five infantry divisions, the occupation of five bridgeheads on the eastern bank of the Suez, the repulse of Israeli counterattacks, and the exploitation of success in order to break through into the Sinai.[10] After the end of the War of Attrition and the deployment of the SAM layout near the canal, Nasser instructed his army to prepare the "Granite 1" plan—a crossing plan and an armored break-through toward the Gidi and Mitla Passes. In contrast to earlier plans, which had been practiced only as a skeleton or staff exercises, "Granite 1" was fully practiced by three mechanized divisions, two armored divisions, three independent tank brigades, three reconnaissance battalions, a marine brigade, and airborne forces.[11] In the summer of 1971, Gen. Muhammad Ahmed Sadiq, who was nominated in May as War Minister, instructed the planning of a more ambitious war plan, "Granite 2," to occupy the whole of the Sinai. Later, under the title of "Granite 3," the plan was further expanded to include the occupation of the Gaza Strip as well.[12]

But, in light of the Egyptian-Israeli balance of military capabilities, these ambitious plans were rather infeasible. No one understood it better than Lt. Gen. Saad el Shazly, who was nominated in May 1971 to be the Chief of Staff of the Egyptian army. His main concern was neither the occupation of the Gaza Strip nor of the whole of Sinai, but rather the first and the most complicated phase of any future war—the crossing of the Suez Canal. It involved three interrelated problems: the mere crossing of the canal; the need to counter Israel's air superiority over the theater of operations; and the ability to repulse the IDF armored counterattacks.

Problem I: The Crossing of the Canal

The Egyptian crossing plan identified four main obstacles on the road to the buildup of five stable bridgeheads on the eastern banks of the Suez Canal: a sharp tide and low ebb combined with water banks made of stone steps, which made it difficult for amphibious vehicles to get to the water and climb to the bank on the other side; a 10- to 20-meter-high embankment on the Israeli side, which had to be breached; the Bar-Lev defense line made of thirty-five strongholds and the 360 tanks of the IDF regular tank division positioned in the Sinai; and the water ignition system that Israel had installed in the canal, in order to set any crossing force on fire.[13]

It is unclear why the plan did not regard the linear structure of the canal as a significant obstacle. The Bar-Lev line planners estimated that the main Egyptian problem would be an assault crossing of a linear water obstacle—each section of which was fully controlled by the defending force.[14] On the other hand, two of the obstacles outlined in the Egyptian plan were found, post-factum, easier to overcome than expected. The Bar-Lev line strongholds were planned from the start to have a limited role in blocking a full-scale crossing. In 1973, primarily because of lack of strategic warning, only sixteen of them were staffed and they were manned by third-rate soldiers. During the first and the most critical hours of the war, they turned out to be a liability more than an asset, since the tanks of the Sinai Division (Division 252) had to defend the strongholds rather than ward off the enemy. The Egyptian planners seem to have understood the limited ability of the strongholds to play a critical part in case of an all-out crossing. Hence, they concluded that their encirclement would lead to their fall. The war instruction that was distributed shortly before the war emphasized: "You should avoid delaying too much and wasting effort in fighting to take over the strongholds."[15]

The project of setting the Suez Canal ablaze—codename "Or Yekarot" ("great light")—was mostly a deceptive project, aimed at deterring the Egyptians from launching a war. On February 28, 1971, a real experiment in setting a small section of the canal on fire took place. The goal was to demonstrate to the Egyptians the dangers involved in a large-scale crossing attempt.[16] In this sense it was successful: When ending his tenure as a Chief of Staff in December 1971, Chaim Bar-Lev estimated that "Or Yekarot" stands as a "highly successful deceptive move . . . that has occupied the Egyptians until now."[17]

Following Sadat's decision to launch war with the available means, the army, under Shazly, started investing far more energy in overcoming the problems described in Instruction 41—the order that outlined in detail the crossing phase. Some of the preparations involved meticulous and systematic staff work. Under the supervision of Gamasy, the Egyptian planners located the most suitable conditions for the crossing. The parameters used included, inter-alia, weather conditions, tide and ebb conditions, the water speed in the canal, sunrise and sunset hours, and moon rise. The most suitable dates were coordinated with Syria. Then, the Egyptian planners looked for the most inconvenient dates for Israel—primarily holidays. On the basis of this staff work, Sadat was provided in early April with a number of possible D-days in May, August, and September–October.[18]

By March 1973, the Egyptian army completed the buildup of a number of crossing battalions, each equipped with 144 boats, enabling the transfer of 32,000 infantry soldiers to the eastern bank of the Suez Canal.[19] In addition, by the spring the Egyptians received from the USSR three PMP assault bridges (the fourth was supplied during the war), which enabled the fast reinforcement of the infantry force with tanks and additional heavy equipment.[20]

As well as getting the necessary water-crossing equipment, the five infantry divisions that were to cross the canal started, toward the end of 1972, a series of intensive crossing exercises. This training aimed at both improving the ability of the soldiers to carry out the complicated mission, and—in light of the military defeats in earlier confrontations with the IDF—to enhance their belief in their ability to carry it out.[21] In order to make the problematical crossing stage more manageable, Instruction 41 detailed the complicated operation into a small and relatively simple set of tasks, each of which were repeatedly rehearsed by the crossing forces. Thus, for example, according to Instruction 41, each soldier had to know not only the number of his crossing wave or his boat but also the names of the soldiers on his left and right. Moreover, each of them knew very well not only the amount of ammunition that was available to him but also how many rounds he was allowed to use at the assault stage and the holding defense stage, and how many bullets he was permitted to shoot against enemy planes.[22] By the fall of 1973, after rehearsing this phase of the crossing dozens of times, the Egyptian soldiers could act almost automatically. Indeed, many of them did not grasp until the very last moment when fire started, that this time it was not merely another exercise but rather the real crossing of the Suez Canal.

Problem II: Egyptian Air Inferiority

If the 1967 war demonstrated the vulnerability of the EAF to a sudden air attack, the War of Attrition showed that even under more favorable conditions the EAF was no match for its Israeli rival. But Egypt's vulnerability to IAF raids was reduced when, in the aftermath of the War of Attrition, its antiaircraft layout moved closer to the front line, thus providing air defense for the Egyptian army in the theater of operations at the first stage of the war. Neither side, however, was certain that the new deployment caused an actual radical shift in the balance of forces in the crossing sector. A sole test to the new situation took place in September 1971 when—in response to the shooting down of an Israeli C-97 Stratocruiser that was on an air photography mission 22 kilometers east of the canal—Israeli F-4 Phantom planes launched 12 air-to-ground (AGM) Shrike missiles against the radars of Egyptian SAM batteries. One of the missiles hit the cement base of a warning antenna and caused some damage. The others totally missed their targets.[23] On the basis of the experience gained in the war in Vietnam, the Egyptians turned off the radars, leaving the missiles without a target to home on. The Israelis concluded from this incident that in order to save the radars they had to be turned off and, thus, they became vulnerable to attacks by other means.[24] The Egyptians concluded from the incident that they also had the means to suppress the threat of the IAF on the eastern bank of the canal.[25] Consequently, on the eve of the war they reinforced their anti-aircraft layout at the front, increasing the number of SAM batteries along the 150 kilometers of the canal from 46 to 62.[26] But, as they must have known, the feasibility of this defense system had yet to be tested and was far from perfect.

Beyond this source of potential weakness, the Egyptians faced three other problems. The first was the dependency of their air-defense on Soviet soldiers. Since the spring of 1970, when, in the framework of "Operation Kavkaz" a Soviet air-defense division arrived in Egypt to assist in defending the country against the IAF raids, critical segments of their air defense system had been manned by Soviet personnel. In the summer of 1971, the Soviets operated 30 percent of the Mig-21 fighters positioned in Egypt, 20 percent of the SAM batteries, and most of the electronic equipment.[27] The equipment operated by the Soviets was of the most advanced type—systems such as the SA-3 and SA-6—which proved to be the most effective means against the Israeli planes. Following the July 1972 expulsion of the Soviet personnel from Egypt, Egyptian soldiers—some of whom had been under training in the USSR for more than two years—started operating the SA-3 systems that the Soviets left behind. Shortly afterward they also began to man the SA-6 batteries, and by the end of 1972 this process was completed.[28] As Shazly put it, quite proudly: "Long before the October assault . . . our air defense was well established over the crucial strip six miles to the east of the canal."[29]

A second and a highly critical problem involved the ability to provide air defense for areas other than the crossing sector. The War of Attrition vividly showed that the F-4 Phantom planes that Israel started receiving in 1969 provided the IAF with an excellent capability to attack targets deep within Egypt's interior. The deployment of the Soviet air-defense division in spring 1970 caused the immediate ending of these raids, primarily out of an Israeli interest to avoid a direct confrontation with the USSR. But, once the Soviets left, the main barrier for the deep-penetration raids had been removed. By the end of 1971 the IAF had already had 78 F-4 Phantoms and 126 A-4 Skyhawks[30]—each with a sufficient range to hit any target within Egypt. By Egyptian calculations, in 1972 the IAF could deliver a payload of 2,500 tons of high explosives per day while the combined air forces of Egypt, Syria, and Jordan could carry only 760 tons.[31] Consequently, preventing the IAF from bombing Egypt's interior remained a critical problem that demanded a real solution. The construction of an air-defense system, which would cover all strategic locations, was one solution—but one that was too expensive in terms of hardware and manpower. The attainment of capabilities to hit targets within Israel, in order to deter the IAF from assaulting targets within Egypt, was another. From Cairo's perspective this, indeed, was the more promising though not perfect answer.

Egypt's request for Soviet-made long-range attack planes, especially to attack the IAF airfields, was first presented to the Kremlin during President Nikolai Podgorny's visit to Cairo two weeks after the end of the 1967 War.[32] But, in the Soviet arsenal there was no answer for the Egyptian demand. During the 1950s and 1960s the USSR developed strategic bombers and advanced fighters, but none of the fighter-bombers were a match for the U.S.-made F-4 Phantom or the A-4 Skyhawk. Gen. Ahmed Baghdady, the EAF commander, expressed his frustration with the situation in early 1972, saying, "What I need is a deterrent aircraft. A fighter-bomber, about Mach two, with a good payload and the range to reach the enemy's interior."[33] In late 1972, the EAF started receiving the Soviet-made SU-17 attack plane—an improved version of the SU-7—but even this aircraft was no match for the Phantom. In October 1973, Egypt had only 20 SU-17s.[34]

Another source of support was provided by some Arab countries. Since spring 1973 Egypt had started receiving Western-made attack planes, primarily Mirage 3E and Mirage 5 from Libya and a squadron of older Hawker Hunters from Iraq. The Hunters were flown by Iraqi pilots, while the pilots of the Mirages were mostly Egyptians.[35] But, though the longer-range Mirage gave the EAF, for the first time since 1967, the ability to attack Israel in a low-low-low operational profile, the small number of available planes—25 on the eve of the war—was far from meeting the critical mass needed to hit Israel effectively.

Without suitable planes to counterbalance the Israeli advantage, the Egyptians had to resort to more available means from the Soviet arsenal. Two weapon systems were found to meet their demand, but only minimally. The first was the AS-5 Kelt air-to-surface missile which entered Soviet operational service in the mid-1960s. It was carried by the TU-16 medium-range bomber, which was used by the EAF, and had a range of 180–230 kilometers and a payload of 1000–1500 kilograms. The Kelt was powered by a rocket engine and was guided by an active radar or anti-radar seeker to its target, at high subsonic speeds. But, with a length of 9.5 meters and a wingspan of 4.6 meters, flying at high altitude and in a straight line to its target, the Kelt constituted a large, vulnerable target. The likelihood that it would penetrate Israel's air-defense system was rather low. On the other hand, its cheap cost and the fact that it needed no pilot made it a rather attractive option. The second possible deterrent system was the Scud B (SS-1B) surface-to-surface missile with a range of 280 kilometers. With a Circular Error Probability (CEP) of about 900 meters, the Scud was not accurate enough to hit Israeli planes in their bases, but since there was no defense against them, the Scuds could threaten Israeli cities, thus deterring the IAF from hitting targets in Egypt's rear.[36]

The Soviets were reluctant to sell the Egyptians such systems, mainly for political considerations. As Brezhnev told his audience in his secret speech in the Crimea in July 30, "We organized our military shipments for [Egypt and

Syria], so as to help for the consolidation of their defense, but not to give reasons for adventurous moves."[37] Egypt had first requested the Kelt and the Scud-B systems during Sadat's visit to Moscow in March 1971. But the Soviets agreed to supply the Kelt only on condition that it would be used against Israel with their consent. Sadat refused and the deal was put on hold.[38] The Scud deal did not reach even this stage. In October 1971, the Kremlin agreed to sell the Kelt system without any limitations, but the deal was delayed.[39] The first Kelt systems arrived in Egypt in early 1973 and a first launching test from a Tu-16 bomber took place in May.[40] In March 1973, the Soviets also agreed to sell the Egyptians a Scud-B brigade. The missiles and the launchers arrived in Alexandria in early August, and intensive training under Soviet instruction started immediately.[41] Despite this effort the Scud Brigade was not fully operational when fighting started in early October.

By October 1973 the Egyptians estimated that the combination of the available Mirage attack planes—though in small numbers—the Kelt systems that had become operational, and the presence of a Scud brigade on Egyptian soil gave them a certain ability to deter IAF from hitting their rear. As will be shown later, the Israelis saw it quite differently. This estimation gap was one of the main causes for Israel's intelligence failure.

The third problem, which derived from Israel's air superiority, was the limited ability of the Egyptian army to defend itself against Israeli air raids in the Sinai, beyond the 10 kilometer compartment of terrain that was covered by the SAM sites west of the Suez Canal. This problem had put the Egyptian planners on the horns of the dilemma: On one hand, any advancement of ground forces out of the range of the air-defense layout would have exposed it to effective air attacks. On the other, the occupation of a too-narrow strip along the canal could be insufficiently significant from a political perspective and too risky from a military one. Many senior Egyptian policy-makers, including the War Minister until October 1972, Gen. Ahmed Sadiq, estimated that such a limited move would leave the attacking force both without the defense of the canal and dependant on supply lines stretched over the canal, which could be an easy target for ground and air fire.[42]

In confronting this challenge the Egyptians relied on two types of solutions. At the operational level they purchased massive quantities of mobile anti-aircraft systems—primarily the SA-6 mobile batteries capable of crossing the canal, portable SA-7 anti-aircraft missiles carried by the infantry, and the mobile ZSU-23–4 radar guided anti-aircraft guns (Shilka), which were highly effective against low-flying aircraft. By October 1973 the Egyptian air-defense system included fifteen SA-6 batteries, 5,000 SA-7, and a large amount of the Shilka systems.[43] At the strategic level, the decision to limit the goal of the war to the occupation of a narrow strip along the canal solved much of the problem. As the course of the war shows, the combination of these two solutions enabled the Egyptian army—at least until the last stage of the war—to defend itself, quite effectively, against the IAF attacks.

Problem III: Inferiority In Armored Fighting

The Egyptian ability to confront the IDF ground forces in the Sinai involved two main problems: First, would the crossing forces be able to cross the canal at all? Here, the main obstacle was expected to be about 300 Israeli tanks deployed in pre-prepared positions that enabled them to cover the canal water by direct gun fire and to launch local counterattacks against any infantry force that succeeded to cross. Second, even if the crossing stage was completed successfully, could the Egyptian army develop a successful attack toward the Mitla and Gidi Passes? The main obstacle in this respect was the IDF's reserve divisions, which enjoyed superiority in equipment, training, and doctrine, as well as effective air support.

Since the Egyptians had decided almost a year before the start of the war to avoid a breakthrough into the Sinai because of their weakness in the air (and also on the ground), they did not need to find practical answers to the second question. Hence, confronting the superior Israeli armored corps at the crossing stage was their main source of concern.

The Egyptian plans assumed that local tank counterattacks could be launched within fifteen to thirty minutes after the crossing and that the regular Sinai (252) Division, with more than 300 tanks, could reach the crossing forces two to three hours after the beginning of the crossing stage. The Egyptian planners assumed that by this stage they would accumulate sufficient forces to repulse the divisional counterattack.[44] The eight reserve brigades that had been allocated, according to their intelligence, for the defense of the Sinai were, their main concern. According to Egyptian estimates Israel was expected to know about the war three days before it broke. And, since they assessed that the IDF needed ninety-six hours to mobilize and deploy its reserve force, the counterattack would be launched at H+24. A more pessimistic estimate—which according to Shazly was prepared by the head of the Defense Intelligence Department—anticipated that the Israeli intelligence would know about the war fifteen days ahead, and that eighteen IDF brigades would deploy in the front prior to the break of the war. According to this scenario, the main thrust of the IDF counterattack could be launched at H+6 to H+8—four to six hours before significant armored forces could cross to the eastern bank of the canal and participate in the battle.[45]

If this was, indeed, the picture on which the Egyptian war plan was drawn, it reflects a rather poor understanding of the Israeli capabilities. First, according to the 1968 Israeli plan, some of the forces that were to reinforce the regular forces in Sinai, such as regular tank brigade No. 460 (the Armored Corps School brigade, positioned in southern Israel), were expected to deploy for war within twelve hours from warning. Most of the reserve forces were scheduled to do so within thirty-six hours. A complete deployment was to take place forty-eight hours from warning.[46] This was half the time of the Egyptian estimate.[47] Second, as we shall see, the Israelis assessed that they would be able to locate the Egyptian preparations for war four to six days before its eruption. In this sense, the Egyptian assessment that Israel would know about the war only three days ahead tended to be too optimistic, while the fear of a fifteen days' warning span was, by far, over pessimistic. And finally, the assessment that Israel would deploy eighteen tank brigades for defense was highly inaccurate. According to the Israeli plans, in addition to the three brigades regularly deployed in the Sinai, six additional reserve tank and mechanized brigades were to take part in the fighting. This, indeed, was the order of battle in the Sinai front during the war.

In order to meet the threats from the IDF ground forces, the Egyptian planners resorted to a number of means. First, the crossing was to take place by five infantry divisions along the whole front, without creating a specific concentration of forces. Thus, it exploited the Egyptian numerical superiority in manpower and equipment and created a difficulty for the Israeli armored forces, which were better trained in fighting in bigger frameworks. It also left the IAF without specific attractive targets.[48] Second, in order to enable the crossing infantry soldiers to confront the Israeli tanks, they were massively equipped with personal anti-tank weapons. This was done at the expense of the second and third echelons, whose anti-tank weapons were delivered to the first crossing wave.[49] The result was an impressive concentration of such weapons—72 Sagger AT-3 anti-tank guided missile launchers, and 450 anti-tank grenade launchers—in each divisional crossing sector. In addition, the Egyptian army deployed large quantities of anti-tank weapons—about 54–57 artillery pieces or anti-tank guided missile launchers per kilometer on the western bank of the canal, in front of the crossing sectors.[50] Third, the Egyptians used massive helicopter-borne commando units to block the main routes to the front line in order to isolate the theater of operations by delaying the arrival of the IDF reinforcements to the crossing sectors.[51]

And yet, the main means to prevent Israel from effectively confronting the invading force was neither in the realm of anti-tank weaponry, nor in the isolation of the battlefield from reinforcements. Rather, it was the use of various means to cover the preparations for war in order to deceive Israel's intelligence community into estimating that the unusual Egyptian military activity on the eve of the war was the outcome of a routine Tahrir exercise.

Chapter 3

The Egyptian Deception Plan

1. THE ROLE OF DECEPTION IN EGYPTIAN WAR PLANNING

"All warfare is based on deception," wrote Sun Tzu, author of *The Art of War,* but the Egyptian deception plan in 1973 was rather modest. As far as it is known deception did not stand at the center of the plan of war and the Egyptian leadership avoided making the achievement of surprise a necessary condition for launching a war. Sadat intended to go to war in October, with or without surprise and, as it has been noted already, the Egyptians' most optimistic assessment was that Israel would know about the coming war three days before its eruption. Following the gloomy assessment of the chief of the Defense Intelligence Department, Gen. Fuad Nasser, that Israel was likely to understand the big secret once preparations for war started fifteen days before D-day, the deception plan was improved in the hope that the Israeli warning-span would be limited to five days.[1] In the Syrian case, and in contrast to some claims,[2] one can hardly find any evidence for a systematic deception. Here, the focus was on covering the real intention behind the Syrian military preparations. Against this background, the Egyptian amazement, that less than forty-eight hours before war breakout Israel still did not suspect anything, is understandable.[3]

Though it included certain elements from the Arab culture,[4] the Egyptian deception plan, which was completed around January 1973, was based on the Soviet concept of "maskirovka"—which embodies the achievement of surprise at the strategic, operational, and tactical levels. At the center of the Egyptian plan stood the attempt to convince the Israelis that the information about military preparations they were likely to collect was connected to the "Tahrir 41," a large-scale routine crossing exercise—one in a series of exercises conducted twice a year, since 1968. The conduct of an exercise as a cover for a large-scale operation became a method for the Warsaw Pact armies in the early 1960s, and the Soviets used such exercises to cover their preparations for the invasion of Czechoslovakia in 1968. As in the case of any successful deception plan, it was based on two main elements: passive deception (concealment) and active deception.[5]

ii. Passive Deception

The main means to reach a high level of concealment was compartmentation. The commanders of the Second and Third Armies learned that Tahrir 41 was merely a cover for the real war that would start five days later only on October 1, the date that the exercise started. Their division commanders learned about it on October 3 and the brigade commanders a day later. The battalion and company commanders received this information only on October 5. Only minutes before taking off, helicopter pilots who were to carry commando units into the Sinai were informed that their mission was not an exercise.[6] The Egyptian political echelon was also kept in the dark. In briefing his National Defense Council on September 30, Sadat avoided any indication that war was to start within a week.[7] Even his Foreign Minister, Muhammad Hasan al-Zayat, who was in New York for the United Nations annual assembly, did not know about it.[8] Notably, the Syrians—who avoided using active deception—took even more extreme measures of compartmentation. Their battalion commanders were informed of the war on October 6, only hours before it started. They were told to let their company commanders know about it an hour before fire broke out and their platoon commanders only minutes before H-hour.[9]

As far as it is known, the Egyptians avoided informing any Arab country, including their closest allies, about the coming war—although according to one source the PLO forces in Lebanon were put on alert on October 5 for a war that would start a day later.[10] Their source was probably Syrian. Informing the USSR was an even more problematic issue. On one hand, given Egyptian and Syrian dependency on Soviet military and diplomatic aid, the Kremlin had to receive an official message before war started. On the other, a too-early notification could yield Soviet pressures to avoid the war and various steps that might indicate to the USA—and thus also to Israel—that there was an imminent threat. In early October, Sadat and Asad informed Moscow that war was to start soon. The precise D-day and the H-hour were delivered to the Soviet ambassador in Damascus only on October 4. His colleague in Cairo learned about it only after the Egyptian flag was raised on the eastern bank of the canal.[11] The KGB station chief in Cairo reveals in his memoirs that he was aware of Egypt's war preparations but also admits that the Kremlin finally understood that war was unavoidable only two days before it started. Then, the USSR immediately started the emergency evacuation of its residents from Egypt and Syria.[12]

iii. Active Deception

The active measure taken to convince Israel that Egypt's military preparations were not for war but for an exercise were carried out by delivering three main types of false messages to the Israelis. The first aimed at annulling the value of the early warning (EW) indicators that were collected by Israel, by increasing the effect of the cry-wolf syndrome. As we shall see later, since indicators and warnings about Egypt's intention to launch war had been received in Israel before the war, especially in the spring of 1973, without the breakout of war, this syndrome played a destructive role in Israel's ability to correctly assess the situation before war did come in the fall of 1973. As far as it is known, the earlier cases of tension were not part of an Egyptian deception plan but rather the outcome of a real intention to launch war (spring 1973) or an attempt to create a crisis in order to gain political concessions (late 1971 and late 1972). More relevant are the means intentionally taken by the Egyptians in order to erode Israel's readiness for war. Four such types of means can be identified:

- *The Tahrir exercises:* Since 1968 these exercises had been carried out routinely. Some were skeleton exercises, others tactical or staff exercises, and some were combined exercises. Though their prime target was to prepare the army for war (and in some cases to back up Egyptian war threats), they were also conducted to get the Israelis used to Egyptian accumulation of offensive forces near the front line.[13]
- *The mobilization and demobilization of reserve soldiers:* Since early 1973, 22 exercises of mobilization and demobilization of reserve units had been conducted. This enabled the Egyptians both to effectively mobilize and to get the Israelis used to this process. Three mobilizations, in which 120,000 reserve soldiers were called to arms, took place during the last ten days before the war.[14]
- *The advancement of forces to the front line:* The bulk of the force that was to carry out the crossing—five infantry divisions—had been routinely deployed in positions since 1970. The deployment of additional forces as from late September 1973 was highly exceptional in many of its dimensions but was not totally irregular since in earlier Tahrir exercises emergency deployments took place as well.
- *Repeated alert exercises of the EAF:* Starting September 22, when the Egyptians started moving forces to the front, the EAF conducted a series

of emergency deployment exercises. According to Egyptian sources, the IAF reacted by increasing its state of alert. The Egyptian exercises aimed at testing the Israelis' response to such a move and also to get them used to the irregular activity of the EAF.[15]

A second type of deceptive message aimed at creating a business-as-usual atmosphere in Egypt. Some of the most typical messages in this framework involved the following:

- Tahrir 41 will be over on October 7. On October 9 the Egyptian army will return to routine activity, including the renewal of courses in the War College and in the School of Staff and Command.[16] The residents of Alexandria were informed that trains were ordered in order to bring back the brigade that was routinely deployed in their town.[17]
- The Egyptian media reported on the demobilization of reserve soldiers that were mobilized on September 27, but only 20,000 went home. The rest, who were more essential for the war effort, remained in service.[18]
- The Defense Ministry made a public announcement, a few days before the breakout of war, about the beginning of the registration of soldiers for the pilgrimage to Mecca at the end of the month.[19]
- The creation of a routine activity atmosphere along the front line was achieved by special groups of soldiers (nicknamed by the Israelis the "lazy ones") who used to walk near the canal without weapons, half dressed, swimming in the water and fishing. The Egyptians also avoided closing the Morgan oil field on the western side of the Suez Bay before the war, despite the possibility that it would be attacked.[20]
- Routine military and diplomatic activity was maintained. The Chief of Staff and other senior officers lived "in two worlds" in the days before the war; the cabinet ministers paid the War Minister a routine GHQ visit,[21] a public announcement reported a scheduled meeting between the Egyptian and Rumanian War Ministers in Cairo on October 8; a number of ministers, including the Foreign Minister, were abroad when the war started; and President Sadat told a foreign minister who visited him that he intended to participate in the UN General Assembly during October.[22]
- Calming explanations for irregular military activity were presented. Diplomats in Cairo were informed that the army was preparing for a possible Israeli strike in light of Syrian-Israeli tension. The daily *al-Ahram* published similar reports. The movement of Egyptian destroyers, which were to block the Bab al Mandab straits on October 6, was

explained in the media by friendly visits of the Egyptian navy to Port Sudan and Aden.[23] The Arab media, primarily the Egyptian Middle East News Agency, reported on a growing tension in the Golan front, thus explaining the Syrian concentration of forces there.[24] In a rare use of active means of deception, the Syrian media reported that President Asad intended to pay a nine-day visit in eastern Syria, starting October 10.[25]

The third category of deceptive messages that were delivered by the Egyptians involved pieces of information that portrayed their army as being unprepared for war. This was a classic method of deception for two reasons: first, it reflected the genuine Egyptian assessment until late October 1972, and second, it strengthened the rather dominant Israeli estimate that Egypt did not perceive itself as having the capability to win a war. And yet, for various reasons, the Egyptian deception plan made only a limited use of this type of message.

The clearest expression of the Egyptian attempt to strengthen the Israeli estimate that Egypt was unprepared for war can be found in public expressions of the time, especially in the speeches of Sadat. In the weeks before the war, Egyptian delegates in international forums were instructed to moderate their belligerent tone.[26] An analysis of Sadat's speeches shows that since June 1973 a more appeasing tone replaced the threats that were usually used against Israel. Thus, for example, instead of the regular threat that "what has been taken by force has to be regained by force" the Egyptian leader spoke in July about activity in the UN as a means to put an end to the results of the aggression.[27] The clearest example of the new and deceptive messages was the speech that he gave on the third annual day of Nasser's death, on September 28. In contrast to past practice, Sadat ignored the issue of war and gave, instead, a speech that his Chief of Staff defined as "low-key, restrained, and very different from his fierce speeches of the past few months."[28]

It is less clear whether the Egyptians deliberately attempted to create an impression that their army was unprepared for war. Information about it appeared in the Western press, especially between December 1972 and April 1973. Thus, according to a UP Agency news-item of December 11, 1972, a secret report that was distributed in Cairo said that only 40 percent of the army's weaponry and 60 percent of the EAF planes were in operational status. The *Financial Times* reported on December 16, that the Egyptian army not only lacked offensive capabilities but it also did not have the ability to defend the country against an Israeli attack. The French *Le Figaro* carried on February 8 a description of the corruption of senior officers, and the *Washington Times* assessed on March 26 that following the Soviets' expulsion, Egypt remained without the expertise and some of the more sophisticated hardware needed for an effective anti-aircraft defense against the IAF raids.

In light of the performance of the Egyptian army during the war, such reports clearly overemphasized its weaknesses. And, since they also served the Egyptian need to calm Israeli fears of a war they seem to be a part of an intended disinformation campaign.[29] But this conclusion might be wrong. First, if these types of press reports were part of a genuine deception campaign, the Egyptians should have increased their volume toward the war. But they ceased to appear in the spring. Second, in Egyptian memoirs they are not mentioned as part of the deception campaign. Given that the Egyptians are highly proud of the methods they used to deceive the Israelis, ignoring the press reports would be rather strange. Third, some of the reports seem to be genuine and reflect the real operational status of the Egyptian army. Thus, for example, before becoming a War Minister, Ismail prepared a secret report that described the poor state of the Egyptian war machine. Similarly, reports about the lack of ability of the army not only to launch an offensive but also to defend Egypt against an Israeli attack seem to echo Sadat's words in a discussion at his residence on October 24. There he said: "How could we hope to launch an offensive when we're not even prepared for defense?"[30] Lastly, given the effort invested by the Egyptian leadership in raising the morale of the soldiers and the people toward war, such a disinformation campaign might have had a negative and dangerous impact on the popular morale, thus being counterproductive.

At the same time, it seems that deceptive information regarding Egyptian-Syrian disagreements had been distributed in the Arab media near the beginning of the war. Here, the Egyptians played upon a conventional Israeli wisdom—a belief that the Arab world would never unite for war—in order to strengthen the impression that in light of current disagreements Egypt and Syria would not be able to coordinate their military activity.[31]

iv. Assessment of the Egyptian Deception

The end result of the Egyptian deception plan is clear. As Zeevi, a highly prominent student of this subject, put it, "The strategic surprise that the Egyptian forces achieved as a result of the deception plan drastically changed the balance of forces in the front during the first days of the war. The deception enabled the Egyptians to reach an operational-strategic surprise, decreased Egyptian casualties, and increased the relative combat efficiency of the attacking forces." But it is still questionable whether this outcome was the product of the high quality of the plan and its performance, or of poor performance on the Israeli side.

While Egyptian writers describe in superlatives their success in deceiving Israel, a more sober analysis of the plan shows many of its weaknesses. Its main theme—Egypt's military inferiority and its incapability to launch an all-out war against Israel—was very logical since it correlated not only with the dominant Israeli assessment but also with the Egyptian one. Consequently, the use of Tahrir 41 to cover for the preparations for war was logical as well. On the other hand, the way that the deceptive information was delivered to Israel reflects some of the plan's deficiencies. In general, the victim always regards information that is obtained by sensitive sources as more reliable than information that is gained through less secure channels. Hence, a high-quality deception operation seeks to use the most secure channels available in order to transmit the deceptive information to the opponent, so that it is less suspicious. A good example is "Fortitude South"—possibly the most successful deception operation in modern history. In this case, the Allies used various means of human, signal, and photographic intelligence in order to deceive the Nazis that the invasion of Normandy was not the main invasion of Europe in June 1944 and that their main effort would be launched a few weeks later in the area of Pas de Calais. The operation was so successful primarily because of the "Double Cross System"—MI5's success in catching all the German spies in the British islands and turning them into double agents, who informed their handlers that the Invasion of Normandy was merely a decoy. Combined with SIGINT and VISINT (signal intelligence and visual intelligence) deception, this led the Germans to deploy much of their forces in Pas de Calais until the critical stage of the invasion was over.

When compared to "Fortitude" and even lesser operations, the Egyptian deception operation seems to be rather primitive. Its messages were delivered mainly by means of the open media: The Egyptian press reported the text of Sadat's calming speeches; Western media carried the reports (if indeed they were part of a planned deception) about the deficiencies of the Egyptian army; information about Syrian–Egyptian disagreements was published by the Lebanese press (notoriously known for being a channel of disinformation); and the Egyptian media reported about the mobilization and demobilization of reserve soldiers. In some cases, deceptive messages had been transmitted by military means of communication, but in such instances (e.g., the Tahrir 41 orders) it was done through unsecured or low-level secured means that the Egyptians could be quite certain that the Israelis monitored.[32] Other messages, such as the registration for pilgrimage to Mecca, were first transmitted by military communications and then—perhaps because of fear that the Israelis might not receive it—also in the open media. Other means of deception, such as the use of the "lazy ones" or the continued operation of the Morgan oil field, were also unsophisticated since they were clearly visible from the Israeli side. Providing foreign diplomats with false explanations for the massive deployments in the Golan and the canal fronts is another example of the use of unrefined means to deceive the Israelis.

Indeed, as far as it is known, the Egyptians did not use any sophisticated means—such as the use of double agents or secured codes that were known to have been broken by the Israeli intelligence—that could give their deceptive messages a higher level of credibility. The fact that the Egyptians avoided using such channels reflects, above all, their low level of comprehension regarding the Mossad and AMAN's penetration into their secrets. As we shall see later, Israel had excellent human and signal intelligence (HUMINT and SIGINT) means of collection in Egypt, and AMAN had received ample evidence regarding the looming threat on the southern front, at least since September 30. Had the Egyptians possessed good knowledge about the level of Israeli penetration, they might have been even more pessimistic regarding their ability to achieve a strategic surprise. But, since they lacked such knowledge, the only way by which they could ensure that Israel would receive their misleading messages was the use of open or semi-open means of transmission. They succeeded so well not because of the qualities of their deception but because of grave deficiencies in the Israeli analysis of available war information.

Chapter 4

The Egyptian-Syrian War Coordination

A critical dimension in the Egyptian war plan was that simultaneously with the offensive in the south the Syrians would launch a war in the north. As the plan became more realistic, this coordination became more operational.

Since coming to power in late 1970, President Asad had strived for a coordinated Egyptian-Syrian military initiative to regain the Golan and Sinai.[1] The coordination took place at two levels. Politically, following a series of secret talks, Asad and Sadat reached in late 1971 an agreement on a number of issues—the nomination of the Egyptian War Minister to command the two fronts, the neutralization of Libyan leader Muammar Gadhafi from participation in the war planning, and the need to better coordinate the war strategy.[2] Militarily, senior officers from both sides had conducted talks since 1970 about the operational dimensions of the coordinated war, and they had reached, toward the end of 1972, a considerable point of progress. Though additional talks were still needed, the main question at this stage ceased to be military and became political (i.e., a decision to go to war).[3] In late 1972, however, the Syrians assessed that their army lacked the ability to confront the IDF.

The Syrians estimated in 1972 that the IDF's regular order of battle in the Golan consisted of two infantry brigades and one tank brigade, five gun and mortar battalions, and additional forces that amounted to three battalions. This force was to be reinforced at times of tension.[4] According to this estimate, in case of a Syrian offensive the IDF's counterattack was to be carried out by fourteen to nineteen brigades—of which five to six were armored and four mechanized—and approximately twenty-five gun and mortar battalions.[5] A more updated and realistic intelligence estimate forecasted that the main Israeli effort would be carried out by two to three armored brigades and two additional brigades. The IDF would either attempt to outflank Damascus from the south, or advance directly from Kuneitra through Sa'asa to the Syrian capital, with a secondary effort taking place through northern Jordan.[6] The Syrians assessed that the IAF would use 200–250 fighters and attack planes in the Golan sector and that it would carry out its opening strike against their air bases and SAM sites. At a later stage, the IAF would be used in order to isolate the theater of operations and to destroy artillery, command posts, and other forces at the front.[7]

Unlike the Egyptians, who regarded the acquisition of strategic capabilities to hit Israel's depth as the key to any war decision, the Syrian concern was more minimal, primarily the ability to provide effective air defense for the ground forces that were to occupy the Golan Heights. In the summer of 1973, following a series of large-scale arms deals with the USSR, they reached this ability.[8] On the eve of the war, Syria had 360 SAM launchers, out of which sixty (fifteen batteries) were of the mobile SA-6 type.[9]

The Egyptian war decision of October 1972 and the accelerated Syrian arming process that had begun during the second half of 1972 turned the question of war into a more practical issue. The first discussion of operational dimensions seems to have taken place during the visit of the Egyptian War Minister in Damascus in February 1973. According to one source, Asad agreed to take part in the Egyptian initiative but demanded to reschedule it from May to a later period, due to the Syrian need to find an effective solution to Israel's air superiority.[10] More significant negotiations took place during the Asad-Sadat summit of April 23–24, at Sadat's presidential residence in Burg el Arab, west of Alexandria, when the two leaders agreed on the principal lines of the coming war. Asad came out of his talks with Sadat convinced that the Egyptian operational goal at the first stage of the war was the attainment of the Gidi and the Mitla passes and that at the second stage the Egyptians would attempt the occupation of the whole of Sinai. Both leaders agreed that the Syrian war goal would be the occupation of the Golan Heights.[11]

According to Asad, he concluded that war in the coming May was infeasible after talking with the Egyptian War Minister, who had to admit that his army was not ready yet.[12] Sadat, in his memoirs, avoided (for obvious reasons) defining his territorial goals. Instead, he emphasized that both he and Asad had agreed to launch war, implicitly in October, and that they had decided to establish a joint Syrian–Egyptian Armed Forces Supreme Council to supervise the continuation of operational coordination.[13]

The Council convened for the first and the last time, four months later, on August 22–23, at the naval headquarters in Alexandria. The participants included the Egyptian and the Syrian War Ministers, their Chiefs of Staff, and a few other senior officers. Under a heavy veil of secrecy they agreed on the timetable for their forces' deployment for war and the way to do it. They also decided on two possible date ranges for the war's initiation: September 7–11 and

October 5–10. Asad and Sadat were to inform them, at least fifteen days ahead, of their decision about D-day.[14]

Following the end of the discussions, Syrian Defense Minister Mustafa Tlas, and the commander of the EAF, Maj. Gen. Husni Mubarak, left for Syria, where Asad and Sadat were scheduled to meet August 26–27. Following a briefing on the results of the Council's meeting, the two leaders agreed to opt for war in early October. The selection of October 6 as D-day took place on September 12, in a secret meeting that the two held in Cairo during a public summit with King Hussein of Jordan.[15] On the morning of September 22, the military echelon was informed about the selected D-day. It seems that at this stage, or around it, the joint war plan received its official name—operation Badr—named after the first victory of the prophet Muhammad in 624. The Syrian army had already initiated its war deployment in late August. The Egyptian army started carrying out its deployment procedure only on September 22. At this stage they had not resolved their disagreement concerning H-hour. The Syrian war plan was to start at sunrise; the Egyptians planned to begin at sunset. This decision would be finalised, as we shall see later, only three days before the start of the war.[16] But, apart from these details, by late September 1973, Egypt and Syria had reached their highest level of cooperation.

Part II

Israel Prepares for War

Chapter 5

The Balance of Forces — the Israeli View

Very much like the Egyptian estimate, the Israeli view of the military balance in the aftermath of the War of Attrition tended to regard the IDF as superior to the Egyptian army. Nevertheless, despite a high level of consensus among Israel's policy-makers that the way in which the war ended reflected this superiority, there was also awareness concerning the existence of some operational problems.

IDF Chief of Staff Chaim Bar-Lev emphasized in a highly classified report at the end of his tenure in late 1971:

> In June and July 1970 the Egyptians and the Soviets learned that their "War of Attrition" would bring them nothing. The IDF did not move from the Canal and was not deterred by the Soviet intervention. When they were faced with the opportunity of an "American peace initiative" [the Rogers plan], they accepted it and, thus, shifted their efforts from the battlefield to the diplomatic theatre.[1]

Estimating, especially after the advancement of the SAM layout, that Egypt was likely to renew fire after the end of the 90-day cease-fire, Israel took immediate and intensive measures to strengthen the Bar-Lev line and to prepare the Sinai for a new war. Though the rate of these works slowed down later, toward the end of 1971 the Chief of Staff estimated that the IDF was ready for war:

> Today we can certainly say that as far as fortifications, roads, obstacles, positions, water supplies, communications, air bases, and everything needed for fighting is concerned, the Sinai is well fortified and organized. Jet planes can use the Etzion air base. The supply of air

bombs and other air munitions has reached a reasonable level. The air system, as a whole, has consolidated a technique to take care of the concrete problems we face—the SAM layout, defended airfields, etc. All these have been improved and exercised again and again. In order to deter the Egyptians from the renewal of fire, we applied some means of deception, which gave them a lot of headaches and problems. The most successful of these is "Or Yekarot" ["great light"], which has been keeping the Egyptians busy until now.[2]

Despite this reassuring estimate, the Israelis were aware of one major challenge that they faced. The War of Attrition showed that even the use of the world's most advanced attack plane, the F-4 Phantom, could not prevent heavy IAF losses in its attempts to destroy Egypt's modern and highly dense air-defense system. In the aftermath of the war, this challenge had become even more demanding, since the advancement of the SAM layout to the canal limited the IAF freedom of action not only over Egypt's airspace but also over part of the eastern bank of the canal. Considerable technical improvements in the system's effectiveness had made the task of its destruction even more complicated.

The IAF intelligence analysts estimated in the early 1970s that the Egyptians' SAM system had become a real threat. This was the outcome of both the experience that had been gained in the War of Attrition and the risks that the operators were ready to take in order to hit Israeli aircraft, including the possibility of shooting down their own planes. While they estimated that the integrated Egyptian air defense system might suffer severe operational problems during wartime, they nevertheless concluded that at the single-battery level the Egyptians had reached a rather proficient combat capability.[3]

The IAF's main concern was the mobile SA-6 systems that started arriving in Egypt after the cease-fire entered into effect. The new system presented two operational problems: First, being a small target and a mobile one, its destruction had become more difficult. In the past, a reconnaissance mission that revealed the location of the fixed SA-2 and SA-3 batteries had enabled an immediate attack within hours. Now, the localization of the sites prior to attack was of a little use, since the mobile SA-6 batteries had the capability to start moving within ten minutes from order and to start firing within twelve minutes after arriving at its destination.[4] Second, the SA-6 could hit targets flying at 300 feet and above.[5] Until the introduction of these systems a very low flight was the main strategy that the IAF pilots used to evade the missiles. The deployment of the SA-3 in the spring of 1970 limited their freedom of action significantly. The introduction of the SA-6 limited it even more.[6]

To meet the new challenge—especially a scenario in which the Egyptian ground forces would cross the canal under the umbrella of the SAM layout and then start moving into the Sinai under the cover of the SA-6 batteries, which would cross the canal as well—the IAF had started preparing since late 1970 an operation called "Tagar" ("Challenge"). Aimed at the destruction of the Egyptian missile sites at the outset of the war, Tagar's planning involved intensive cooperation with the USA, primarily in the field of electronic warfare.[7] Although the effectiveness of some of the American means, such as "Shrike" air-to-ground missile (AGM), proved to be limited, the IAF still estimated, at least since 1971, that it had a suitable answer for the SAM challenge.[8]

Tagar—on the basis of which the IAF would later build the "Dugman" ("Model") plan for the destruction of the Syrian anti-aircraft layout in the Golan—combined a massive operation of ground and airborne electronic means of warfare with the use of iron bombs to destroy the missile sites. It was to last six hours and to be carried out in four phases. The first flight—preparation—aimed at suppressing the anti-aircraft guns and isolating the battlefield from enemy planes. The second phase—the main one—was the bombing and the destruction of the missile sites themselves. The third flight aimed at destroying the surviving batteries. The last flight was to take out missile reinforcements, which were expected by this stage to start advancing from the rear. The success of the plan was dependent not only on good weather but also on the use of all available electronic means of warfare, air photographs that were to be taken just before the start of the attack, and the use of ground artillery for shooting chaff and shelling nearby batteries.[9] Repeated exercises and detailed planning led the IAF commanders to conclude that though the operation might cost significant casualties, its chances of success were high and it would allow the IAF freedom of action over the combat zone.[10]

The IDF war conception was based on the assumption that the next war's goals would be two: preventing any Egyptian achievement, and reaching a cease-fire as soon as possible. But, in contrast to the prolonged War of Attrition, the IDF High Command estimated that a quick and decisive victory was now feasible due to the emergence of four new factors: the fragility of Sadat's political stature that would make it difficult for him to withstand heavy military pressure for a long period of time; lack of Soviet interest in a new war and, hence, a more limited readiness on the part of the Kremlin to provide Egypt with military and political support; greater American support for the use of massive power by the IDF, especially if Egypt initiated the war; and the strengthening of the IDF's power, especially in the air, which enabled a wider freedom of action vis-à-vis the Egyptian army. These factors facilitated a war conception that was based on:

> A start in "high tones" from the first day of the war. This will surprise and shock Sadat and the superpowers and will yield an immediate

cease-fire. Our plans include also the crossing of the canal, an operation that can be done. Yet, it should be remembered that this action is costly and the decision to carry it out should be taken according to concrete conditions.[11]

This optimistic estimate of the situation relied not only on past experience that showed Israeli superiority in almost any military confrontation, but also on what was considered at the time as a good acquaintance with the qualities of the Egyptian soldier. Following tests conducted by Israeli psychologists on Egyptian POWs from the 1967 war, IDF experts concluded that since 1956 the level of competence of Egyptian officers had declined and that 60 percent of them would not have passed the IDF officers' tests. Such findings led Chaim Bar-Lev to conclude in late 1970: "The Arab soldier lacks the necessary qualities for modern war. Sophisticated weapon systems and modern warfare doctrines demand a high level of intelligence, adaptation, fast response, technical skill, and, above all, the ability to perceive the situation realistically and to tell the truth, even when it is a bitter and difficult one."[12]

Four additional factors added to the Israeli sense of self assurance. One concerned the territorial dimension. The 1967 war moved Arab armies away from Israel's hinterland, putting, instead, the capitals of Syria, Jordan, and Egypt under the threat of the IDF air and ground forces. A second factor involved the improved quality of the IDF's armament. In the early 1960s, the USA agreed to sell Israel certain weapon systems, but up until 1967 the IDF had continued to rely mainly on French arms. After the war, partly because of the French embargo, American arsenals had become far more accessible. Since the end of the 1960s, the IDF had been receiving highly advanced weapon systems, including the F-4 Phantom attack plane, the M-60 Main Battle Tank (MBT), modern artillery, and sophisticated electronics. Consequently, the quality gap between the IDF and its Arab counterparts had been widened.[13] Third, the experience that had been gained in the history of the Israeli-Egyptian conflict convinced the Israelis that the Egyptian army had a very limited ability to conduct an offensive war.[14] And, finally, the outcomes of a number of significant clashes with Arab armies further convinced the Israelis of their military superiority. The most significant event did not take place in the Egyptian front but in the Golan. In June 1970, following Syrian provocations, two tank battalions of Brigade 188 (the "Barak" Brigade) managed to occupy the southern sector of the Syrian defense line in the Golan within two hours. The Syrian losses amounted to thirty-six tanks, twenty artillery pieces, and fifty destroyed bunkers. Three Israeli tanks were damaged but were returned to service. Beyond this numerical result, the operation itself demonstrated the Israeli ability to easily—and without the use of surprise—destroy the Syrian line of defense and outflank Damascus from the south.[15]

Along with these professional factors, the post–1967 period was also characterized by an atmosphere of boastfulness and the belief in brute force as the sole means to solve Israel's security problems. Such an atmosphere had certainly facilitated the tendency of Premier Golda Meir to neglect the diplomatic options that had become available to Israel following the war.[16] It also influenced the way Israeli generals mistakenly calculated the necessary balance of forces at the frontline during the war's opening stage once it started in October 1973. But the way Chaim Bar-Lev, or his successor David Elazar, estimated the IDF's ability to reach a decisive and quick victory was a far cry from the way others thought about it. Thus, for example, following his retirement from military service less than three months before the outbreak of the 1973 war, Maj. Gen. Ariel Sharon said in an interview:

> Militarily, Israel ranks one rank higher than a medium power. If we accept the division according to strength, that at the top there are two superpowers—the USA and the USSR—and, then, at the second echelon come France, England, and others, then Israel belongs today to this echelon of powerful nations and not to that of the medium-size powers. We have an exceptional military might.[17]

On the basis of this estimate, Sharon also described the cost that Egypt would pay if it went to war:

> A horrible, horrible cost. A cost Egypt won't be able to stand. In the Six Days [War] the Egyptians could withdraw to the canal. And, so it was also in the [1956] Sinai Campaign. In the next war the Egyptian withdrawal line would be Cairo. They don't have another line. And it would involve a horrible destruction of Egypt. A total destruction. I deem it as unnecessary. We don't need it. But, we'll never return to a war of attrition, though we won it. The Egyptians would suffer a horrible strike.[18]

Such arrogant expressions genuinely reflected the dominant Israeli atmosphere prior to the war; they must have impacted the way the intelligence estimate regarding the likelihood of war was formulated. But, at the foundation of this estimate stood a more sober analysis, based on highly reliable evidence.

Chapter 6

The Intelligence Conception and Its Sources

i. The Conception

Conception—a thinking framework that allows order and significance for pieces of information relevant for a proper perception of a concrete problem—is an essential tool in intelligence work. The partial report of the Agranat Commission, which was publicly released in 1974, concluded that at the root of Israel's intelligence failure was "the persistent adherence of intelligence officers to what they termed as 'the conception.'"[1] Indeed, the members of the committee identified the source of the intelligence failure correctly, though they failed to explain it properly.

It is difficult to say when the conception was actually born. The Agranat Commission, which was established after the war to investigate the causes for the IDF's unpreparedness on the eve of the war and its failures during the war's first three days, noted that it had existed in AMAN since 1971,[2] but it seems that at this point it erred. The operational logic behind it can be traced to the IDF GHQ discussions of late 1968. Then, the Chief of the General Staff—Staff Branch, Maj. Gen. Ezer Weitzman (who was the IAF commander from 1958 to 1966), and Brig. Gen. Benny Peled of the IAF (who served as the IAF commander in the 1973 war), categorically argued that since the EAF could not hit the IAF's air bases in Israel, the Egyptians were confronted with two options: either to avoid a large-scale crossing of the canal, or to launch such an operation and face defeat.[3]

Whether the Israelis were aware of it or not, the Egyptians thought similarly and, as already described, had invested considerable efforts in reaching the capability to hit the IAF in its bases. The Israelis were aware of the Egyptian failure to obtain this goal. This, combined with the results of the War of Attrition, bolstered their belief that Cairo would avoid any attempt to cross the canal before obtaining a reasonable ability to neutralize Israel's air superiority. AMAN was aware of the possibility that from the Egyptian perspective the deployment of the anti-aircraft layout along the canal limited the IAF's freedom of action over the main battle zone. Even so, the defenseless Egyptian rear remained an Achilles' heel that should have prevented the initiation of an all-out war.

After Nasser's death and his replacement by Sadat, this way of thinking evolved into a more coherent intelligence conception. At its basis stood three assumptions: First, the Egyptian leadership reached the conclusion that war was the only way to get Israel out of the Sinai. Political pressure and diplomatic negotiations would not suffice. Second, another War of Attrition would not advance this goal. The Egyptians had not been satisfied with the outcomes of the last war, and it was concluded that the goal of their next war should be the occupation of some territory in the Sinai in order to use it as a political leverage leading to an Israeli withdrawal. Third, the Egyptians had a problem of air power. The last two wars had proved their acute weakness in air offense and defense, and, therefore, they attached utmost importance to improving their capabilities to hit the IAF bases. It was clear that they needed more advanced aircraft and they regarded their acquisition as a necessary condition to launch a war—even a local one.[4]

An additional dimension of this conception involved the way that Egypt's new leader, Sadat, was perceived. Since he came to power, he had been seen as a temporary replacement for Nasser—a peculiar, unstable, sometimes even a ridiculous leader, who employed empty declarations and made baseless threats. In contrast to Nasser, who had enjoyed an image of a serious and responsible leader despite the disasters that he brought on the Egyptian people, Sadat—rightly or wrongly—received the reputation of a reckless fantasizer. The bold and successful measures he took, such as the destruction of the opposition to his rule in May 1971 and the expulsion of the Soviets in July 1972 did not reflect, according to this view, an impressive ability to make effective decisions under pressure. Usually these measures were ignored; alternatively, they were perceived as sheer luck. This view was also shared by others in Egypt and the USA. Its contribution to the shaping of the Israeli conception regarding Sadat's ability to go to war was highly significant.[5] And yet, it is important to note that this low estimate did not play a formal role in analyzing Egypt's war threats and had never been an integral component of the conception that merely assessed Egypt's minimal conditions to initiate a war.

In addition to focusing on Egypt, Israel also tried to assess the probable war intentions of other Arab states. The most natural candidate to join an Egyptian war initiative was Syria, which had lost the Golan Heights during the 1967 war. Since President Hafez Asad came to power in late 1970, AMAN estimated that Syria would join the war and that it would agree to allow the war timing to be decided by Egypt. In light of the Israeli-Syrian balance of forces, AMAN saw it as improbable that Syria would launch a war by itself. While there was a wide consensus among AMAN's analysts about this issue, there were disagreements concerning the stage at which Syria would join the war. The analysts of Branch 5 (Syria, Lebanon, and Iraq), headed since the summer of 1971 by Lt. Col. Aviezer Yaari, estimated that Syria would launch the war simultaneously with Egypt. Others in the Research Department, including its head, Brig. Gen. Arie Shalev, estimated that the Syrians would wait to see how the war in the south developed before deciding whether to join it or not. But this had no impact on the conception that, in essence, said: "Syria will not launch an all-out attack against Israel unless it is taken at the same time with Egypt."[6]

Another potential participant in the next war was Jordan. But, in light of the tight Israeli–Jordanian dialogue during that period, the traumatic experience of King Hussein from the 1967 war, and the way Israel helped him to withstand the Palestinian and the Syrian attacks during September 1970 ("Black September"), the likelihood that Jordan would join a Syrian–Egyptian war initiative seemed very low. In early 1972, for example, Dayan estimated during a cabinet meeting that "Jordan will not take part in the war."[7] In addition to relying on Jordanian public statements and intelligence information, this assessment relied on direct talks with the king and his aides. This assessment continued to dominate the Israeli strategic thinking until the breakout of the war and even during the war.

Thus, at the focus of Israel's conception on the next war stood the assumption that Egypt would be the axis of any future war decision. The war decision would be a function of Egypt's estimate about its chance to reach tangible military achievements. Its operational criterion was the acquisition of the capability to hit targets in Israel's depth as a means to neutralize the IAF. Syria would join the war, but only as second fiddle. Notably, the anchoring of the war initiative exclusively to an Egyptian decision made AMAN's analysts responsible for estimating Egypt (Branch 6) the dominant factor in assessing the likelihood of the next war. Due to some personal circumstances, this would have a major impact on the way Israel perceived the situation in October 1973.

ii. The Empirical Evidence

Although the sources of the conception can be traced to operational assumptions that were based on the logic of the post–1967 situation, its new and more detailed form relied on hard evidence as well—information that was received from a top Mossad source, well placed within Egypt's elite. The source, who Zeira titled in the first edition of his war memoirs as "the information," was Dr. Ashraf Marwan, the son-in-law of President Nasser.[8]

Born in 1944, Marwan married in the 1960s Nasser's third (and most beloved) daughter, Muna, and became the president's roving ambassador. Under this title he had become a personal courier for special missions, first for Nasser and, then, for his successor, Sadat. Some of these missions involved delicate arms deals with the Saudis. Others were of a more personal nature. Thus, for example, when Gen. Shazly resigned from the army in protest to Nasser's decision to nominate Ahmed Ali Ismail as Chief of Staff in March 1969, it was Marwan who served as the go-between for the president and Shazly (who ultimately agreed to return to his post).[9] According to some sources, Marwan also served, at least part of the time, as Sadat's bureau chief and as a coordinator on behalf of the president with the Egyptian intelligence services.[10]

In 1969, Marwan contacted the Israeli embassy in London and offered his services to the Mossad. Although his accessibility to Egypt's top secrets made him a most desirable source, the fact that he was a "walk in," as well as his identity and certain aspects of his behavior, created the suspicion that he was, in actuality, a double agent. His authenticity was approved, however, by repeated checking, before and after the 1973 war.

The information that Marwan provided included written documents and verbal reports. The documents involved political, economic, and military information, such as Egypt's war plans, Egyptian–Soviet arms negotiations, and protocols of talks between Egyptian and Soviet leaders. Typical examples were the protocols of Nasser's secret talks in Moscow in January 1970 in which he demanded Soviet intervention in the War of Attrition, and a top-secret message that Sadat sent to Brezhnev on August, 30 1972, requesting, once again, long-range aircraft.[11] They were, as Zeira defined it, "confirmed reports that were the dream of any intelligence service in the world."[12] Some of this information was passed on by Prime Minister Golda Meir to foreign factors; they independently reviewed the information and concluded, like the Israelis, that the material was absolutely authentic.

Marwan's verbal reports—information and his own personal assessments—lacked the same high quality of the written documents but were nevertheless highly valuable. Yet, some AMAN analysts treated the source suspiciously, primarily since he was a "walk in." Most important among them was Lt. Col. Yona Bandman, the head of Branch 6 (Egypt, Sudan, and North Africa) and AMAN's prime analyst of Egypt's war intentions.[13]

Only a few in Israel's intelligence community received Marwan's reports. In AMAN these few included the DMI, the head of the Research Department and his two assistants, the head of Branch 6 and his assistant for political analysis, and the head of Branch 3 (superpowers). Zvi Zamir, the head of the Mossad, Rehavia Vardi, his head of HUMINT collection department ("Tzomet"), and a few others were in on the secret in the Mossad. In a rather exceptional manner, a number of political consumers such as Golda Meir,

Moshe Dayan, and Minister without Portfolio Yisrael Galili (Meir's closest advisor) received the information in its raw form. So did the Chief of Staff. Zamir acted in this manner because he believed that having direct access to information that intimately described the way the Egyptian leadership analyzed the situation was of prime importance. An attempt to put an end to this procedure was vetoed by Dayan.[14]

A detailed analysis of the contribution of Marwan's information to the buildup of the conception is presently unattainable. But, on the basis of a number of sources, it seems that his reports enabled AMAN to provide a high quality picture of Egypt's strategic dilemma since the end of the War of Attrition: on the one hand, the desire to go to war in order to regain the losses of 1967; on the other, the military weaknesses, first and foremost in the air. This does not mean that prior to receiving this information Israel was unaware of the dilemma, but that Marwan's reports confirmed the assumptions that had earlier been based on circumstantial evidence. In this sense, his reports served as a compass indicating how right or wrong Israel's intelligence estimates of Egypt's war intentions were.[15]

Despite the evidence to the contrary, public claims of recent years maintain that Marwan was a double agent and the most important asset of Egypt's deception campaign. The main proponents of this assertion are Eli Zeira in his memoirs, and Dr. Ahron Bregman's various accounts of Israel's history.[16] In addition to relying on Marwan's status as a "walk in," they base their case on a number of points:

1. Marwan provided Israel with various documents—such as the protocol's of Nasser's secret visit to Moscow in January 1970 or Sadat's August 1972 message to Brezhnev—which showed that obtaining the means to attack Israel's depth was a precondition for launching war. When Sadat changed this policy in late October 1972, Marwan did not report it despite the fact that he knew about it.[17]
2. Twice before the war, in December 1972 and April 1973, Marwan warned that Egypt had decided to launch war. In both cases the warning was given weeks before the expected D-day—i.e., they enabled Israel to take the necessary measures to meet the threat. In both cases the warnings proved to be false. The warnings had been provided in order to lessen Israel's apprehension of war (i.e., to increase the effect of the cry-wolf syndrome).[18]
3. Ten days after the meeting of the joint Syrian-Egyptian Armed Forces Supreme Council (August 22–23), in which the possible dates of the war were agreed upon, Marwan misled his handlers by informing them that Sadat decided to delay the war until the end of the year.[19]

4. Marwan's war warning was given 40 hours before H-hour. Such a warning, according to Egyptian calculations, did not provide the IDF with sufficient time to prepare for war. The warning that was provided on Friday night repeated the earlier one but included a specific timing for the outbreak of the war. Here, the Mossad was misled about the H-hour, which was 1400 rather than 1800.[20]

Most Israeli intelligence officers who are familiar with this case tend to reject the double-agent theory, which they do for many good reasons. To start with, Marwan did not intentionally cultivate the Israeli conception about Egypt's precondition for war. This was a genuine precondition for war from Nasser and Sadat's perspectives and Sadat decided to give it up as a last resort from an unacceptable status quo. Since by December 1972 Marwan had already warned that Egypt had decided to go to war, it must have become clear to the Israelis that Sadat was willing to initiate fighting without meeting this precondition. Indeed, the Israeli Defense Minister, his Chief of Staff, the head of the Mossad and other senior officials estimated during the first half of 1973 that Egypt intended to launch war even if this precondition was not met. Sadat, moreover, threatened in 1971 and 1972 that he would launch war unless a political process started. Letting the Israelis and the Americans know, by his own agent, that these threats were actually empty ones (since he did not intend to launch war without acquiring long-range fighter bombers or Scud missiles), was a clear-cut case of a counterproductive and illogical strategy.

The claim that Marwan provided two false warnings in order to intensify the impact of the cry-wolf syndrome does not hold water either. Israel also received these warnings from a number of genuine sources, including King Hussein. The warnings, moreover, were not false. The one from December 1972 reflected Sadat's war decision of late October, the practical military preparations for war that followed the October decision, and an urge to launch war as soon as possible. The April warning reflected a genuine decision by Sadat to launch a war in mid-May—a decision that was postponed due to Syria's insufficient war readiness. To claim that Marwan intentionally delivered to Israel two false war warnings before October 1973 makes no sense as well, since more than eroding Israel's war awareness, such an action could erode his own credibility. If he was, indeed, a double agent and had Sadat intended from the start to launch war only in the fall of 1973, a far more useful course of action would have been to inform the Israelis that the war noise they might hear in late 1972 and in spring 1973 did not reflect a genuine decision to go to war. Thus, when it would have become clear that war did not erupt, Marwan's credibility as a serious source for war warning could be strengthened. And then, on the eve of the war, he could use this credibility in order to mislead his handlers to believe that the war noises they might collect from Egypt were caused by the Tahrir

41 exercise or Egyptian fear of an Israeli attack. Such action could be, indeed, very useful in deceiving the Israelis. But it was not taken.

Marwan's warnings prior to the war constitute another proof that he was genuine. Delivering a message in early September that war was not to be expected soon (if this, indeed, was the content of the message) could serve no practical purpose since it was not followed by similar messages aimed at deceiving Israel about the real cause for the war indicators that she was supposed to collect when the Egyptian army started gearing for war. Delivering the two genuine war warnings would have been an even less reasonable act had Marwan really been a double agent. First, there can be no explanation for why the warnings were delivered at all. On October 4 the Egyptians knew that the Israelis did not realize yet that war was coming.[21] Using their own agent in order to inform them about it is, simply, too absurd. After all, even if the Egyptian war planners estimated that the IDF needed five days to fully deploy for war, they certainly knew that 40 hours warning was far better than nothing. Second, the H-hour of 1400 was decided, as recalled, less than three days before war started. Marwan could not know about it. Third, as we will later see, Marwan gave his handlers in their meeting on the eve of the war, the real Egyptian war plan, a plan that had been kept secret even from those in Egypt who knew about the coming war and of which the Syrians had not been aware of at all. The plan could have given the Israelis a major advantage when fighting started. The fact that they did not use it effectively has nothing to do with Marwan's credibility and a lot to do with AMAN's poor performance at the beginning of the war.

Marwan was a complex person, and the motivation behind his decision to serve the Israelis is yet unclear and will probably remain so forever. He could certainly warn the Israelis about the coming war earlier than he did and in a more decisive tone. But in light of his earlier warnings that did not materialize, he might have been more cautious in the fall of 1973. This, however, does not qualify him as a double agent. Had he really been one, Israel's surprise could have been even greater.

Chapter 7

The Strategic Warning and Its Role in Israel's War Plans

Since the early 1950s, Israel's national security doctrine defined a warning of an all-out war (a strategic warning) as one of the three pillars—along with deterrence and battle decision—on which the nation's security relied. At the top of the intelligence community's priority intel requirements stood the threat of an Egyptian war initiation, and the worst-case scenario, known as "Mikreh Hakol" ("the case of all"), was that of a surprise attack by Egypt, Syria, and Jordan—backed by other Arab countries.[1]

Until 1967, providing such a warning was a relatively simple task, since the Egyptian army deployed west of the Sinai peninsula. Between 1957 and 1967 it conducted two emergency deployments in the Sinai: once in February 1960 in an event known as "Rotem"—a crisis that was diffused peacefully[2]—and then in May 1967 in the deployment that ultimately led to the Six-Day War. The territorial outcomes of the war led to a new geo-strategic situation, where only 200 meters of the Suez Canal water instead of 200 kilometers of the desert sands separated the IDF from most of the Egyptian army. Under these new circumstances, when five Egyptian infantry divisions deployed constantly along the water line, the number and the quality of early warning indicators available for the intelligence community was drastically reduced. Chief of Staff Chaim Bar-Lev was well aware of this problem, as reflected in his comments upon entering office on January 1, 1968: "We know well that the correlation between our success in war and our intelligence corps' warning system cannot be dismissed. The more we moved forward territorially, the state of our intelligence did not improve."[3]

In 1968, AMAN's director, Maj. Gen. Aharon Yariv, nominated a committee to review AMAN's strategic warning capabilities vis-à-vis Egypt, Syria, and Jordan. Though the committee concluded that AMAN had a reasonable ability to obtain a warning in each of these countries, its members also noted that attaining it in the south had become far more difficult "since the Egyptians do not need to transport masses of forces for long distances prior to the start of attack/canal crossing."[4] In 1968, Yariv demanded massive resources in order to build "two warning sources in Egypt" and the reinforcement of manpower to cover this issue.[5] A year later, he estimated that following the previous year's investments AMAN's ability to provide a strategic warning had improved. He nevertheless demanded additional budgets to make it better.[6]

In addition to signal intelligence (SIGINT), AMAN also used visual intelligence (VISINT) means of collection—primarily air photographs, which revealed the deployment at the canal line, and ground observations posts, which reported the activity on the water front—in order to detect war preparations. But the use of these means involved some problems. The advancement of the Egyptian air defense to the east in August 1970 limited the IAF freedom of flight over the front and necessitated the use of sophisticated aerial photography equipment—sometimes unavailable to the Israelis—to keep developments in the depth of the front under surveillance. In the summer of 1973, when the Syrians deployed a parallel air-defense system in the Golan, AMAN faced a similar problem in the north as well.[7]

Despite constant improvements in AMAN's warning capabilities, Director of Military Intelligence Yariv, a cautious intelligence officer, avoided creating the impression that he could provide a strategic warning with certainty. Instead, he preferred to emphasize the difficulties involved in this task. Thus, in an IDF GHQ discussion in November 1968, he said: "The Egyptians have the possibility to do it [launch a surprise attack] more than ever in the past."[8] The Chief of Staff accepted his DMI's cautiousness. Responding a few weeks later to one of the generals who asked that Yariv clarify the chances of receiving a strategic warning, Bar-Lev said: "AMAN's Director says he will do everything to get a warning, but he cannot be certain."[9]

The need to provide a war warning dominated Israel's intelligence agenda even more in the aftermath of the War of Attrition. In early 1972, the Chief of the General-Staff Branch, Maj. Gen. Yisrael Tal, asked AMAN to assess, in writing, its strategic warning capability. The document, titled "The collection layout's capabilities for the main warning situations in Egypt and Syria," was prepared by AMAN's Collection Department and was submitted in mid-June 1972. At its core stood the assertion that necessary Egyptian logistic preparations would yield a twenty-four-hour warning in the case of a small-scale operation "and at least 4–6 days before the execution of a large-scale action." Since the EAF's state of readiness would have to be raised at least 6–7 days before a large-scale action, it was assessed that AMAN may obtain an even better warning. AMAN, according to the document, improved its warning capabilities for the Syrian front as well, and warning indications could now be available also in the north. Despite this general sense of optimism, AMAN's experts emphasized the limits to their warning capabilities, especially in the south. First, they noted, a limited action that "does not necessitate large-scale preparations and in which the communication systems could be blocked," might take place without prior warning. Second, in situations of "a general tension accompanied by lengthy logistical preparations, or against the background of large-scale exercises of the Egyptian army which would include the advancement of massive forces" the cause behind the Egyptian action might remain unclear.[10]

Thus, it is clear that prior to the war AMAN's ability to provide a strategic warning was built on the basis of early warning war indicators. Information about the status of these indicators would be obtained by SIGINT and VISINT means of collection. The document did not refer at all to the role of warnings from human intelligence (HUMINT) sources, at least in part since these sources belonged mainly to the Mossad. As we shall see later, the best warnings about Arab war intentions on the eve of the war would come from these sources. But, even without taking them into account, AMAN's experts had been quite confident in their ability to provide a strategic warning.

A vivid illustration of AMAN's reliance on early warning indicators was given during a discussion in mid-April 1973 at the Prime Minister's residence, when DMI Zeira, who replaced Yariv on October 1, 1972, promised Golda Meir: "I am sure that if Egypt intended to launch a massive crossing of the Suez Canal we would know about it in advance, and we would be able to give a warning, not only a tactical one but also an operational one, i.e., a number of days in advance."[11] When asked by the Premier how this would be known, Zeira replied: "We would see commanders' patrols and advancement of forces, a reinforcement of the anti-aircraft layout, and we would see that the neglected trenches along the canal were being cleaned. . . . And, generally, when the Egyptian army enters into action—we know about it."[12] In her memoirs Golda Meir, noted that this answer satisfied her concern about a sufficient warning.[13]

Unlike Yariv, who as a cautious DMI had never committed himself to provide a strategic warning with the assurance of certainty, his replacement tended to be far less hesitant in this regard. This was reflected not only in his reassuring answer to the Prime Minister's question but also in his undertaking in the Knesset's [Israeli parliament's] Foreign Affairs and Security Committee, whose members were worried about the same issue: "We check the situation day by day, hour by hour. . . ." he told them. "We feel that our intelligence system is such [a good one] that Israel will not be surprised by any development."[14]

Zeira's commitment to provide a warning was highly significant since such a warning had become the point of departure for strategic thinking after the end of the War of Attrition. As Chief of Staff, David Elazar explained after the Yom Kippur War:

> We had this conception for years, and in my mind it was the right one, that we should not keep a too high and too expensive state of readiness, which might exhaust us for years, before the real test came. Hence, we had this conception of the regular army, which is a means you hold in any event in order to prevent a catastrophe. This was not a desirable approach. . . . [but] it was selected as something we could do without a warning.[15]

According to this conception, the strategic warning's main role was to alert policymakers regarding the need to mobilize the reserve army—a mobilization that would create a reasonable balance of forces at the front. In this sense, the belief that an adequate war warning would be provided in due time had become both highly dominant and a necessary condition for the conduct of a successful war. As the Agranat Commission concluded, the IDF "had no detailed plan for a case of an all-out enemy surprise attack."[16]

The key issue here is the definition of the term "due time." The IDF basic war conception combined defensive and offensive elements. Defensively, the task of the Israeli forces along the Bar-Lev line and in the Golan was to prevent the Arab armies from successfully crossing the canal in the south and breaking the first line of defense in the Golan. The possibility of letting the Egyptian forces cross the canal and advance into the Sinai outside the parameter of their air defense, and then contain and destroy them, was rejected by the Chief of Staff on professional but also on political grounds.[17]

The IDF main defense plan, "Sela" ("Rock"), was born in 1968. Its execution demanded the reception of a high-quality strategic warning—i.e., a warning that would provide sufficient time to mobilize and deploy the reserve forces before war started. According to plan Sela, three tank divisions—the Sinai regular division (252), and reserve divisions 143 and 162—were to assemble west of Bir Gafgafa. The 300 tanks of division 252 were to deploy in pre-prepared positions along the Bar-Lev line, so that they could cover the canal by fire and destroy the Egyptian forces while they were still in the water. Divisions 143 and 162 were to deploy behind, in order to carry out a counterattack at the end of the defense stage. If the need arose, the reserve forces could reinforce the regular units and take part in the defense battle as well. The IDF order of battle (OB) for plan Sela was to reach 1,036 tanks, 216 artillery pieces, and additional forces. Its complete implementation necessitated five days' warning.[18] Given the size of the Syrian army, the IDF OB for a war in the north was smaller. It reached only two divisions—mostly made up of reserve forces. And, given that the distance they had to cover from their reserve stores units to the front was shorter, the warning time span in the case of a war with Syria was only 36 hours.[19]

While AMAN promised four to six days' warning and the complete deployment plan in the south demanded five, the possibility that war would break out within a shorter notice was taken into account as well. On May 9, 1973, the Chief of Staff presented the Prime Minister with the main war plan and the assumptions on which it was based, but he added that there were plans for war on a short notice: "For me," he told her, "a short notice is forty-eight hours. I take a worst-case scenario into account on purpose, so that we will be ready even if we have only forty-eight hours to go into the war, as we should do, properly and ready."[20]

The defense plan that was based on a short-notice scenario in the Sinai, "Shovach Yonim" ("Dove Cote"), was originated in late 1970. Initially, it was planned as a response for limited challenges: "a. the renewal of fire along the line. b. attempts to get a hold on the eastern bank of the canal. c. enemy commando action in the Sinai."[21] The IDF's working assumption was that the regular forces of Division 252 would suffice to meet these challenges. But in January 1973, the Southern Command received a new version of the Dove Cote order, according to which "this plan would also provide an initial answer to [all] the enemy's courses of action."[22] In other words, since early 1973, Dove Cote—which relied almost solely on regular forces—was to meet not only limited action but also larger-scale Egyptian moves. This was a precautious measure that took into account the possibility that an all-out crossing attempt could come, in contrast to earlier expectations, with hardly any warning. The OB of Dove Cote was three hundred tanks, eighty-eight artillery pieces, two high-quality infantry battalions, and additional forces.[23] Even this modest plan required a minimal warning: twenty-four hours to deploy two additional tank brigades at the front line and to replace the reserve forces that regularly occupied the Bar-Lev line with high-quality infantry troops. Its complete implementation necessitated forty-eight hours' warning.[24] The execution of plan "Gir" ("Chalk")—the northern equivalent of plan Dove Cote—called for a minimal order of battle of one tank division, combined of regular and reserve brigades, and some additional forces. It demanded a minimum of twenty-four hours from the moment of warning.[25]

Although the IDF under Elazar planned for a war that would break with a minimal warning, it had never planned for a situation in which war might start with no warning at all. As the Chief of Staff put it after the war, "We really never planned that [the call up of the reserve soldiers] would be identical to H-hour. ... In other words, we never planned ahead ... that we wouldn't have a warning. ... We always had this assumption that there must be some early warning. ..."[26] Both he and his deputy, Yisrael Tal, described a situation in which war could break out with no warning at all as a "catastrophe." "We thought," testified Elazar, "that the regular army and the air force was a force for holding defense in case of a surprise ... a case of catastrophe."[27] His deputy spoke in a similar tone:

> We viewed such a case, where there is no warning, as a catastrophe. You cannot make a plan for such circumstances except for a conception.

Because when there is no warning you cannot know ahead where the forces will be. In such a case—we conceived that all the IDF regular elements would run to the front to hold defense, we saw the IAF as carrying most of the burden, and a public mobilization of the reserve army.[28]

Elazar's confidence that war could not start with no warning at all relied probably on three pillars: First, a good acquaintance with Israel's means of collection—first and foremost certain SIGINT means as well as the Mossad's excellent source in the Egyptian leadership—that were likely to yield a high-quality warning in due time, if Egypt decided to launch war. Second, past experience showed that Egypt and Syria had difficulties in maintaining a proper level of secrecy before initiating large-scale moves against Israel.[29] Third, there were AMAN's written commitment and Zeira's verbal ones that a strategic warning would be delivered in due time to conduct an organized call and deployment of the reserve army. On the basis of these assumptions, the IDF prepared for the coming war.

Chapter 8

The Next War Scenarios

Although Israel's main concern since August 1970 was a war on two fronts, this was by no means the only war scenario with which the IDF had to deal. Indeed, during this period AMAN considered various alternatives, mainly for the Egyptian army. An all-out crossing of the canal in an attempt to occupy the Sinai was only one of them. A forty-page intelligence review of Branch 6 of the Research Department (released April 16, 1972) summarized these options.

At the center of the review stood the Egyptian crossing plan. The Egyptian OB for this operation was conceived to be made up of five infantry divisions (Divisions 2, 7, 16, 18, and 19, which had been positioned along the canal since 1970), two to three independent infantry brigades (Brigades 119, 135, and 212), two mechanized divisions (Divisions 6 and 23), two armored divisions (Divisions 4 and 21), and two to three independent armored brigades (Brigades 15 and 25). The artillery order of battle included 1,800 artillery pieces and heavy mortars. In addition, the document detailed other participating forces, including two bridging brigades and an impressive use of special forces incorporating three paratrooper brigades, thirteen to fifteen commando battalions, and three to four marine battalions.

AMAN anticipated that the Egyptians might use one of three courses of action. The first, defined as "small fighting action," included various operations conducted by small units—at the squad to a company-plus level—against various Israeli objectives at the Bar-Lev line and beyond it. If these acts were successful, they would escalate to include air and naval attacks as well as ground attacks into the depth of the Sinai. A second course was a surprise renewal of fire along the canal, using the available artillery, and its reinforcement at a later stage. The likelihood of receiving a warning prior to such an act was not too high and depended, primarily, on conjectural circumstances such as the state of alertness of the observation posts along the line, or the conduct of a reconnaissance flight within the forty-eight hours that the Egyptians needed in order to bring their forces to combat readiness. As recalled, AMAN estimated that under certain circumstances it was possible that no warning would precede the Egyptian action.

The third, and the most significant course of action, was a ground attack across the canal into the Sinai. Here, AMAN's analysts made a distinction between three types of action. The minimal one was an attempt to occupy a limited section, between the strongholds, by a force of up to an infantry brigade, supported by artillery and tank fire from the Egyptian bank of the canal. The intelligence estimate was that such an operation—which had only political implications—did not necessitate any significant changes in the Egyptian routine layout and, implicitly, could be carried out without an early warning. A second, and more complicated course of action, involved an Egyptian attempt to take over large sections of territories along the canal at the depth of a few hundred meters and up to a kilometer inside the Sinai. This act was to be carried out by forces from each of the five infantry divisions that were routinely positioned at the front line. Artillery from the depth, tanks on the ramps, and light antitank weapons were to provide the crossing forces with a defense against the IDF counterattack. AMAN estimated that in the Egyptian view such an act could be undertaken without any need to occupy the Bar-Lev line strongholds.

The third ground option was an all-out offensive aimed at the occupation of the whole of Sinai. Deploying the forces for such a move was to take, by AMAN's estimate, between a week and a fortnight. According to the Egyptian war plan that the Israelis had, the first phase of the war, which was to last twenty-four hours, included the crossing of the canal by five infantry divisions in five different sectors, the occupation of the crossing zones and their flanks, the transfer of armored forces to the eastern bank of the canal, and the occupation of an area up to the Israeli second line of defense—some ten to eight kilometers east of the canal. This phase could take place day or night, but AMAN estimated that since the IAF was less efficient at night, a night crossing was more likely. In order to isolate the combat zone, the Egyptians planned to use special forces. Seven to nine commando battalions were to be helicopter-borne to block the axis of movement on the eastern side of the Mitla and the Gidi passes. A debarkation of a marine brigade made of two infantry and one tank battalions on the Romani shore, and its reinforcement by another brigade, was to stop IDF reinforcements from using the northern axis of movement. AMAN analysts estimated that the Egyptians might also carry out an amphibious operation through the Great Bitter Lake and Lake Timsah. On the second and the third days of the war the Egyptian forces were to advance to the east and reach the Mitla and the Gidi passes. The last stage of the war involved the complete occupation of the whole of Sinai.[1]

As we now know, this war plan—probably the Granite 2 plan that was prepared before Sadat's October 1972 decision to launch a war with limited territorial goals—was not in effect in late 1972. But, the new Egyptian war plan, to which only a few in the Egyptian leadership were aware, was unknown to the Israelis. In this sense, it seems that AMAN's detailed knowledge of the more ambitious Egyptian plan facilitated the assessment that it was militarily infeasible and that Sadat and his generals thought so too. This assessment received a vivid expression in AMAN's verbal and written war estimates, especially since Zeira had become the Director of Military Intelligence.

Chapter 9

The War Estimate:
October 1972–August 1973

i. October 1972–April 1973

On October 1, 1972, Maj. Gen. Aharon Yariv ended his eight years' tenure as Director of Military Intelligence and was replaced by Maj. Gen. Eli Zeira. Prior to becoming DMI, Zeira served as the bureau chief of Chief of Staff Moshe Dayan and then, as the commander of a paratrooper brigade, head of AMAN's collection department, and the IDF Military Attaché in the USA. Zeira was a far more self-assured DMI than his predecessor, as was vividly reflected in his commitment that AMAN would provide a high-quality warning prior to war. Yariv, as recalled, refused take upon himself such a commitment.

Since Zeira entered office, AMAN had started voicing not only this commitment but also its war estimates in a far more confident tone. Under Yariv, AMAN's assessment regarding the likelihood of war was cautious. Yariv personally estimated that although Sadat was well aware of his military weaknesses he had nevertheless maintained a certain military option. In early 1972, for example, after Sadat's "year of decision" ended without the presentation of any challenge to the status quo, he said that despite the Egyptians' military inferiority and the decrease in the tone of belligerency in Cairo's declarations, the Egyptian army continued preparations for war—a possibility that could not be ruled out.[1] Typically, AMAN's last annual estimate under that of Yariv was carefully phrased:

> It is highly likely that the present situation will remain with no major change also during the next year. We estimate that until the beginning of April 1973, and possibly beyond it, Egypt will not reach the necessary conditions to carry out a calculated military option. But, the

Egyptian regime continues striving for such an option, even a limited one, and can deem it possible in spring 1973, although probably not before mid-1973.[2]

This tone went through a radical shift once Zeira replaced Yariv. In early December 1972, the new DMI told Golda Meir and her close advisors, who were worried because of the arrival of reliable information about Egypt's intention to renew fire, that: "The chance that Egypt would initiate war is not high.... The probability that they will try to cross the canal is close to zero."[3] The new tone was also reflected in AMAN's official documents. The semiannual intelligence estimate of January 1973, the first of its kind under Zeira, assessed that the possibility that Egypt would renew fire in an attempt to cross the canal and occupy part of the Sinai "was now far away more than ever before."[4] This decisiveness reflected no new information concerning Egypt's decision to relinquish the military option. Indeed, the opposite was true; following Sadat's decision to go to war, AMAN started receiving a growing number of warnings, primarily from Mossad sources, concerning the Egyptian decision and its implementation. Hence, the change of tone was the outcome of the new atmosphere created in AMAN under Zeira—mainly his belief that clarity was the most important quality of the intelligence product. As he told the Knesset's Foreign Affairs and Security Committee members five months before the war:

> The Chief of Staff has to make decisions and his decisions should be clear. The best support that the DMI can provide him with—if this is objectively possible—is to provide an estimate that is as clear and as sharp as possible. It is true that the clearer and sharper the estimate is, then, if it is a mistake, it is a clear and sharp mistake—but this is the risk of the DMI.[5]

Professionally, Zeira tended to count on Yona Bandman, a bright and experienced officer, who became the chief estimator of Egypt's war intentions when nominated in the summer of 1972 to head Branch 6 of AMAN's Research Department. Very much like Zeira, Bandman perceived his task as providing consumers with sharp and clear estimates, mainly in black and white, without getting too deeply into the gray areas of uncertainty. And, very much like Zeira, Bandman was also an ardent believer in the "conception." Indeed, it was the irony of history that approximately at the same time that Sadat decided to launch a war, a sheer coincidence had brought to key positions two officers who assessed that since the necessary conditions for launching an attack had not been met yet (and were not likely to be met in coming years), war was highly unlikely. Many in AMAN thought differently. And yet, the dominance of Zeira and Bandman combined with their stubborn belief in the validity of the conception (despite growing evidence to the contrary), had created since late 1972 a widening gap between AMAN's estimate of the likelihood of war and the reality of Egyptian and Syrian war preparations.[6] This gap received a vivid expression in AMAN's semiannual estimate of January 1973.

The departure point of this document continued to be Sadat's difficult situation: On the one hand, the "no peace nor war" deadlock threatened the stability of his regime. On the other, he lacked effective means to break this situation. A limited military option aimed at gearing a diplomatic process was too risky, since Israel had made it clear that it would make no distinction between a small or a large military move and would react in full force to any renewal of fire. And, since Egypt perceived itself as incapable of withstanding an all-out war, it was deterred from any use of force. Hence, and though Sadat already proved that he could make mistakes, AMAN estimated that "the probability that Egypt would renew fire is very low. The probability of sporadic acts is low as well."[7]

AMAN's analysts assessed that the lack of a military option combined with an unwillingness to put forward more reasonable political offers, left Sadat with the continuation of the present status quo—a situation he had to "live with." Consequently, they assessed that in the coming months no dramatic changes in the situation were likely to take place, though Egypt might show some diplomatic activity in the Arab, international, and American arenas in order to try to isolate Israel and enhance Sadat's domestic posture. In the long run, Sadat would have to choose between one of two options. One route was that of "extended struggle"—i.e., a delay in the attempt to solve the "1967 problem" until Egypt received the necessary means (long-range aircraft and Scud missiles). Meanwhile, the regime could make use of various measures to improve the economic situation in order to reduce popular pressures. Alternatively, Sadat could agree to additional concessions in order to promote a diplomatic process. AMAN experts estimated that he would avoid the second option. Implicitly, at least, they estimated that Sadat would select the first option and would shelve the conflict with Israel for a number of years.[8]

Syria confronted a similar problem. AMAN's analysts estimated that by the end of 1972 Asad's regime faced a difficult dilemma: the need to continue the armed struggle against Israel in order to regain the territories lost in 1967, on the one hand, and Syria's military inferiority, on the other. But, unlike the Egyptians, who were ready to combine military and diplomatic means in order to attain their goals, Syria opted only for the military option emphasizing that solving the "1967 problem" was a matter for a long-term struggle. Hence, until the Arab world attained the military might that would let it regain by force the territories that had been lost in 1967, as well as the rights of the Palestinians, it should at least obtain the ability to defend itself against Israel.

AMAN evaluated that this tough Syrian position had left Damascus with two problems. First was the possibility that Egypt and Jordan would reach separate agreements with Israel, thus leaving Syria completely isolated in a struggle that it had no chance of winning. In order to cope with this threat, the Syrian leadership emphasized the need for a pan-Arab cooperation in the struggle against Israel—especially in the framework of the Egyptian–Syrian–Libyan Federation that was established in 1970. The analysts of Branch 5 assessed that for this reason the Syrians pressured the Egyptians to initiate military action at the Suez front and demanded the rejection of American pressure for separate agreements. The Syrians' second, and more pressing, problem was how to react to Israel's massive military pressure, which started in late 1972, to limit the Syrian support for Palestinian terrorism and to end sabotage acts from Syrian territory.[9] AMAN's analysts were right in assuming that from the Syrian perspective the new Israeli policy was considered as a one-sided attempt to change the rules of the game.[10] In mid-January when the document was composed, the Syrian response was unclear. Later, when it became evident that Asad had ordered the Palestinians to stop acting in the Golan, the Israelis took it as a proof of Syria's recognition of its own military inferiority.[11] In the coming months, this conclusion had obvious ramifications on AMAN's estimate of Syria's readiness to join forces with Egypt against Israel.

ii. April–May 1973

During the second week of April, Israel's intelligence community received a number of war warnings. They came from different Mossad sources in Egypt and voiced similar motifs: Egypt was disappointed by Kissinger's response to Sadat's diplomatic initiative of late February, and the political deadlock left no alternative but war. Some of the messages reported dates for the planned war—the most reliable of them spoke about May 19. According to the warnings, the present war plan was different from the one described by AMAN a few months earlier. The war's goal was defined as the occupation of the area between the canal and the Gidi and the Mitla Passes, with no territorial goals beyond it. This task was to be carried out, at the initial stage, by the five infantry divisions that were to cross the canal and occupy the Bar-Lev line. Helicopter-borne commando forces were to land on the main axis of movement to the front in order to block Israeli reinforcements. Commando units were supposed to attack Sharm el Sheik as well. Once a stable bridgehead was established, the armored forces were to cross the canal and start advancing to the passes. The warnings also reported other targets: the blocking of the Bab el Mandab straits; hitting oil installations in the Sinai and within Israel; and air attacks against military targets in Sinai and infrastructure targets within Israel by Iraqi Hunters and Libyan Mirage-5s, which had started arriving in Egypt.

The war plan that the Israelis had at this point was identical to Operation 41, whose codename was changed to "Granite 2" in 1972. In April 1973, as part of the scheme to attract the Syrians to take part in the war, its name was changed to "Granite 2 — Updated," and it was the war plan that the Egyptians presented to the Syrians. Israel probably did not receive information concerning the more limited plan that the Egyptians actually planned to carry out.

April's war warnings also included information about the Syrian war plan. At its center was a breakthrough by Infantry Divisions 5, 7, and 9 along the line into the Golan Heights and the occupation of a zone of 8 to 10 kilometers west of the frontline. Armored Division 3 — one of the two Syrian armored divisions — was to exploit this success in order to complete the occupation of the Heights.

While the information about the war plans was detailed, the number of warning indicators regarding military preparations to carry it out was small. It included, primarily, the departure of Iraqi Hunters and Libyan Mirages to Egypt, the arrival of some Arab token forces in Syria, and considerable artillery reinforcement in the canal front, which had been detected by air photographs. Throughout April and May, Syrian forces reinforced the line in the Golan, and then returned for training in the rear. Simultaneously, dramatic war noises were heard from Cairo. This included public announcements about cabinet meetings in the army's war room ("Center 10"), radio broadcasts (since April 23) of war slogans, civil defense and partial blackout exercises, and the mobilization of volunteers for popular defense. But, since the orders of battle in the canal and the Golan fronts had never reached a critical mass that would enable the launching of a war, the Israelis were not worried. An Israeli estimate that was delivered to the USA on April 20 asserted that the signs on the ground did not indicate an intention to take immediate action. On April 29, DMI Zeira reported to Dayan and Elazar that "nothing special" had been observed in the field. The members of the Knesset's Foreign Affairs and Security Committee received from him a similar report.[12]

This process of insufficient war preparations, on the one hand, and the arrival of strategic warnings, on the other, validates in a certain way the assumption that Sadat had decided to launch war on the third week of May but postponed it in light of the secret talks he held with President Asad on April 23–24. As we know, the accumulation of Egyptian forces for the war was to start two weeks before D-day. On the Syrian front it was a far longer process, but then in May the Syrians had no intention to start it at all. Hence, the decision to postpone the war at least three weeks before D-day may explain the arrival of strategic warnings at an early stage and also the lack of warning indicators. But this is a post factum interpretation. At the time the events took place, they were assessed differently.

The first reaction to the warnings, which started arriving a few days earlier, was given by DMI Zeira in a meeting called on April 13 by Defense Minister Dayan to estimate the situation. Zeira assessed that the warnings, as well as the arrival of attack aircraft from Iraq and Libya, did not indicate that the Egyptians intended to start a war, since, as he put it, "they are not so stupid to think that they have a chance to win it." Instead, he emphasized that it would be a mistake to "create vis-à-vis the Americans the sense that we are 'super-worried' about war . . . because this is the Egyptian intention . . . to create a sense, in the US and among us, that something should be done here in order 'to prevent a war.'"[13] The way that AMAN treated the incoming information was similar. The Research Department gave the warnings—most of which came from Mossad sources—only a minor expression or no expression at all. And, when presented in AMAN's documents, they were assessed to be an echo of Sadat's public war threats and the war atmosphere in Egypt or, at most, an expression of the Egyptian desire to launch war.

The Defense Minister and the Chief of Staff estimated the warning in a more serious light. In the April 13 meeting, Dayan noted that he started reading the raw material (as recalled, Marwan's reports were delivered to him and a few others in its raw form). He added that he found in it "ramifications and hints that generally strengthen very much this thing of war." The Chief of Staff said in the meeting: "instinctively I feel that this time it is more serious than the other warnings. . . . I am certain [probably because of the information given in the warnings] that this [war breakout] won't be less than a month from today, so we have [sufficient] time to be ready."[14]

AMAN gave its estimate of the situation in a document it issued on April 18. Generally, the document assessed that the likelihood of a war initiated by Egypt was low. But, the intelligence analysts pointed out correctly, and they continued to do so until October, that between the three available options—helicopter-borne commando assaults in the Sinai, renewal of the war of attrition, and an all-out canal crossing—Sadat saw the last option as the most promising one and as risky as the other two. Hence, they concluded that the probability for the all-out crossing option was the highest, although the probability for any Egyptian use of force remained very low.

The document also analyzed the likelihood of a war in the north. Syria's military weakness and the Syrian lack of belief in the ability of the Egyptian army to contend with the IDF led AMAN's experts to assess that if Asad took action in the Golan, it was likely be static, at the same time, or shortly after a war would start in the south. By static warfare, AMAN meant artillery fire on targets in the Golan and civilian targets across the Jordan River, air attacks on targets in the Golan and within Israel, and small-scale ground attacks. If Egypt made significant military gains, the Syrians might carry out a divisional attack in the Golan, which might expand if it proved to be successful.[15]

Branch 3 of the Research Department assessed that the Soviets had no interest in an Arab war initiative, since it was likely to lead to an Arab defeat that would jeopardize the stability of the regimes of Asad and Sadat. Furthermore, it would damage the image of the USSR as a reliable superpower that was ready to take risks in order to support its clients. The main risk in Soviet eyes was an undesirable confrontation with the USA. To avoid such a situation, the Soviets may have delivered information to the Arabs about the risks involved in a war. And, at a later stage, in order to express their dissatisfaction with such a move, they could delay arms shipments or take their naval units out of Egyptian ports.[16]

* * *

On the same day AMAN distributed this document, Prime Minister Golda Meir convened a small group of policy-makers and advisors to discuss the situation in her Jerusalem residence. Known as "Golda's kitchen," the forum included at this time Defense Minister Dayan, Minister Without Portfolio Yisrael Galili, the Chief of Staff, the head of the Mossad, DMI Zeira, and assistants.[17]

Dayan opened the discussion by asking the participants to estimate the likelihood of war and to suggest what could be done about it. Zeira, in his capacity as the national estimator, was the first to speak, and he repeated, in essence, AMAN's assessment of the same day. Noting that in comparison to the "show" of November–December 1972, there were now more indications of concrete preparations, Zeira emphasized that any logical analysis of the situation would show that the Egyptians would err if they launched a war, and if this logic was accepted, there was no need for a discussion. Zeira also ruled out the possibility that there was a real operational cooperation between Syria and Egypt. "The Syrian President," he said, "knows that if the IAF wants, it can destroy the Syrian Air Force within two hours." Hence, when the Syrians tell the Egyptians "Our army is under your command and we are ready for a coordinated plan if war breaks," they don't really mean it. The Soviets, he added, have no interest in war, and if it breaks, they will push for its fast conclusion. The American stand might be different: Nixon may not fear a war in which the Soviet clients would be beaten despite the possibility that it might provoke an anti-American sentiment in the Arab world, demonstrations, and damage to American property. If war erupts, Zeira estimated, "The United States will pressure us to finish it quickly and will help us to delay cease-fire until we reach a more logical line."

The head of the Mossad, Zvi Zamir, carried no formal status in the domain of intelligence assessment. His view, as expressed in this discussion, constitutes a rare opportunity to see the difference between his and Zeira's war estimates. He started by saying:

> I must say that I view the situation as a little bit more grave than Zeira. I am not certain I can give prophesies. I don't say that there is

certainty this would happen.... We know the thesis of preconditions for war: lack of ability to react in the rear, a reasonable air-defense, bridges to cross the canal, and electronic equipment.... If we analyze the state of readiness of the Egyptian army, then Sadat is stronger than ever before. If he did not want war, what would have been easier for him than accepting the suggestion of the Libyan leader, Muammar Gadhafi? Then, he could cut the army in half and establish a five-year plan.[18]

Zamir added that according to information from his agency's sources, the recent arrival of 18 long-range Mirage planes in Egypt was a determining factor in deciding the timing of the war. He summarized: "If we conclude from facts, there is now a better chance, and this is not only our estimate but also an estimate of people who know the Egyptians well, and therefore—there is a chance of war...." Zamir was also more concerned than Zeira about the Syrian involvement: the Egyptian logic says "that if the Syrians have any chance [to regain the Golan Heights], it exists only if they join us [the Egyptians] in war. There is some logic about it."

The Chief of Staff viewed the situation similarly:

I do not want to estimate in percentages, but of all the warnings I remember—this is the most serious one. Our departure point should be that it [war] can happen. I do not analyze the situation differently from the men of AMAN, there are many illogical elements here and their chances of success are dubious and not solid—but there is an internal logic towards war here. The number of years [of "no war no peace" situation] also becomes a quality factor. They can build a conception that war can get them out of a dire situation.

Since there were no concrete signs for preparations for war, Elazar added, there was no need for urgent military moves or the mobilization of reserve forces. What the IDF needed to do was to complete preparations and update its plans for a possible war. And if war occurs, he concluded, "What we need to do is to hit them so badly for a week or ten days that they will need five more years to raise their head again.... If he [Sadat] starts fire, I would like to reach a situation where we achieve a significant decision."

Dayan regarded the likelihood of war as even higher than Zamir and Elazar. "If I'm asked whether they go now for war or not—I believe they go for a war." Though it was known that Dayan thought highly of Zeira, the DMI's thesis about why Egypt could not launch a war had a limited impact on his way of thinking, since "all wars had begun when we later needed very basic studies to explain why they started at all." His estimate that war was likely relied on a number of factors. One involved the Syrians and the vulnerability of the Israeli settlements in the Golan: "They [the Syrians] feel that they can really do it when they stand there with 1,500 tanks and an anti-aircraft layout given to them by the Soviets and with the readiness to sacrifice." Another consideration was the impact of the Israeli deterrence. In contrast to the conventional wisdom, Dayan thought that the fear of Israel's military superiority might lead the Arabs to an opposite conclusion:

> Recently, it [deterrence] has not had a cooling effect and it almost reached an opposite outcome. . . . All this does not deter them but leads them to conclude that they have nothing to lose. Therefore, if an Arab war initiation does not yield military outcomes, it would bring about a change in the political setting. They build on the Soviets and the Americans and their oil more than on their commando.

Lastly, Dayan became convinced that the Egyptians would opt for war since "they do not roll in the opposite direction of peace and long-term plans. And, when you have half or three-quarters of the soldiers [that are needed] and you don't opt for another outlet, then there may be a commutation of renewal of fire." When fire starts, Dayan concluded, it won't be a small-scale action but "fire all over the canal."

The Prime Minister, who summarized this part of the discussion, presented in her simple words the dilemma and her answer: "A few dozen people [AMAN analysts] say it is illogical but can happen. And, if we act according to this—that it might happen—then we have to do something." She was mainly concerned with American pressures and the domestic political front, and the discussion now turned in these directions. But, the diplomatic, military, and domestic aspects of the possible war are less relevant here. For our subject, the most important point is that in mid-April 1973 the Israeli leadership concluded that Egypt and Syria were likely to launch war soon. Zeira's estimate was rejected. Accordingly, various steps were taken to meet the incoming challenge.

* * *

On April 19, the Chief of Staff informed the IDF GHQ that in the next few months the army would take measures to meet the challenge of a war on two fronts. He also warned Egypt, publicly, against the initiation of war. Similar warnings were issued during the following days.[19] During the coming weeks the IDF started updating its war plans. On May 9, the Prime Minister visited the IDF underground war room and, there, she was briefed on the situation. DMI Zeira, as clear as always, described the situation in Egypt and in Syria:

> On the other side of the hill, we know with complete precision the amount of weapons and their location. At the canal zone—about 1,200 tanks and more than 1,000 artillery pieces of various kinds.

Around Cairo—about 700 tanks and more than 300 artillery pieces. The Red Sea Command—about 100 tanks and more than 100 artillery pieces. The Egyptians have more than 600 fighters and bombers.

The Syrians, he added, have at present 700 tanks and 600 artillery pieces at the front and an additional 400 tanks and 300 artillery pieces around Damascus. The Syrian air force is equipped with more than 300 fighters and attack planes. The DMI described, then, the Egyptian and the Syrian war plans and concluded his presentation with an estimate on the likelihood of war, which, as usual, he saw as very low. But, in contrast to the estimates of his agency's Research Department, he assessed that if the Egyptians decided to act—"it would be, at most, a war of attrition." With no apparent reason, he gave the outbreak of a large-scale war the lowest likelihood.[20] AMAN's estimate, as recalled, was that if the Egyptians decided to start a war they were more likely to opt for an all-out one.

The Chief of Staff, who then presented Golda Meir with the IDF war plans, had a very different war estimate from that of Zeira. Elazar started his presentation by telling the Prime Minister: "From this moment onward, I talk about a war that will take place. All preparations are for war. . . . I speak about the scope of this summer."[21] From this standpoint, that the IDF was making preparations to meet a real threat rather than the imaginary one that the Director of Military Intelligence spoke about, he continued his talk.

In the coming days AMAN's low-probability war estimate remained in effect. It relied, primarily, on information regarding the continuation of routine in the Egyptian and Syrian armies. Though AMAN detected some Syrian moves—such as a partial mobilization of reserve soldiers and an intensification of training in ground and air force units—no concrete warning indicators had been detected.[22] In addition, there was a calming estimate derived from new information that had arrived from the same Mossad sources that provided war warnings during the second week of April. Now they reported that for various reasons Egypt had decided to delay the initiation of war.[23]

Despite the calm atmosphere, Defense Minister Dayan met the IDF GHQ twice, on May 14 and on May 21, to discuss the coming war. As he told the generals on May 14, the Arab's intensified war preparations combined with the lack of a diplomatic outlet, created dynamics that must inevitably lead to an explosion. He believed that the Egyptians had no illusions about their ability to occupy the Sinai but that the initiation of war was a reasonable military move—though, probably, an expensive one—in order to pave the road for the beginning of a political process. Zeira, who presented the intelligence estimate, repeated his assessment that in the coming months the Egyptians would not go to war. If they nevertheless act militarily, he said, they were more likely to opt for a limited move than an all-out crossing of the canal.[24]

A week later, Dayan convened the IDF GHQ again. Summarizing the two discussions, he presented his intelligence assessment and instructions in eight points. The first three described his war assessment:

1. To take into account that the war will be renewed during the second half of this summer.
2. That the war will be renewed by the initiation of war . . . by Egypt and Syria.
3. That in the war . . . Egypt and Syria, not Jordan, would take part. There is no disagreement that in the territory of Egypt and Syria there would be a participation of other states, such as Libya, Iraq, and Sudan.[25]

Following Dayan's instructions, the Chief of Staff spoke. At one point he said that the IDF was preparing war plans in accordance with the Defense Minister's guidelines and that the army even had plans for a case in which Jordan would join the war. Dayan reacted immediately, in a way that left no doubt that he regarded the war as a very real threat rather than an abstract one:

> You, the IDF GHQ, make plans throughout all the days of the year. I am talking about this summer. I talk now as a representative of the government, and also on the basis of information. We, the government, tell the IDF GHQ: Gentlemen, please prepare for war, and those who threaten war are Egypt and Syria. Jordan doesn't announce that it will open war. . . . This is what we ask the GHQ to be ready for war this summer, which will start in a month.[26]

In between the two discussions, Dayan authorized the Chief of Staff to raise the state of alert of the IDF and to take the necessary means to prepare for war. On May 17, the IDF declared the "blue–white" state of readiness.

Dayan's clear-cut instructions to prepare for war that would be initiated during the second half of the summer (before September 22) constitute a rare type of accurate forecast in the history of strategic surprises. Tragically for Israel, and for him personally, Dayan's estimate of the situation would go through a radical shift within a few weeks. Meanwhile, however, the IDF started preparing for war.

iii. June–August 1973

In the Israeli myth of the Yom Kippur War, the "blue–white" state of readiness involved primarily the costly (IL60,000,000) and unnecessary mobilization of the reserve army for a war that did not take place. In reality, however, "blue–white" was, primarily, a codename for a plan to enhance the IDF's ability to win the next war. Indeed, the army raised its state of readiness and kept a ready force of 515 tanks throughout this period. A number of reserve units had been mobilized for this purpose, but they were kept training for the coming war. Most of the money was spent on war preparations. It included the intensification of the IDF capabilities to cross the canal by the buildup of two units of assault bridging and the completion, earlier than scheduled, of the IDF's first roller bridge; the earlier building of a new division (No. 210), a move that was supposed to take place only in 1974; and the build up of the headquarters of an additional division (No. 440), which was supposed to take place only after 1977. Other divisions were reinforced by more than ten tank, artillery, and reconnaissance battalions. The rest of the money was spent on the advancement of reserve stores units closer to the front—a move that enabled the reserve forces to get to the battlefield faster once war started—as well as in improving avenues of approach for tanks and artillery and in fortifications. The Deputy Chief of Staff noted after the war: "Thanks to the 'blue-white' plan, the army that entered the Yom Kippur war was stronger than the routine plans for October 1973. The IDF was even stronger than the army that was planned for 1974 and 1975."[27]

The intensified buildup process was not, however, without faults. Some of the equipment that was used for the buildup of the new units was taken from existing ones, and when the war broke out these units had insufficient equipment. Similarly, some of the reserve stores that were advanced to the front were disorganized when the Arab attack started. Even so, Maj. Gen. Avraham Adan, who described these deficiencies, admitted also that because of "blue-white" the army was relatively ready for war—better than in 1967.[28]

However, while the preparations for the coming war were still in full gear, the other dimension of "blue-white"—the increased state of alert—started to fade away. On June 8, less than three weeks after ordering the IDF GHQ to prepare for a war that would take place within a few months, Dayan accepted the Chief of Staff's suggestion to reduce certain elements of readiness.[29] From this point forward, a gradual process began to unfold. It ended on August 12, when the Deputy Chief of Staff ordered the IDF to return to a normal state of readiness. Nevertheless, certain precautionary measures were taken. According to a standing order, the minimal number of tanks in the Sinai was to be 300; 210 of them were to be allocated by Division 252 and another 90 by Division 162. Despite this safety measure, it appears that neither the Chief of Staff nor the Minister of Defense were fully aware of the fact that the rather dramatic orders of the spring had ceased to have any operational meaning by the beginning of the second half of the summer.[30]

This change was not the result of any new information concerning the Egyptian decision to avoid going to war. It was the outcome of the fact that as time passed by, all known dates for war had gone while routine was kept within the Egyptian army. Post factum, we know that this was a product of three factors: The Egyptians had already completed most of their war preparations in the spring; an Egyptian plan to raise tension in order to trigger a diplomatic process had become useless since the decision to go to war had already been made; and the Egyptian strategic interest in calming Israel's fear of war toward the real attack. But this was unknown to the Israelis in the summer of 1973.

For DMI Zeira and many of AMAN's analysts, the relaxed atmosphere was more proof (which they hardly needed), that their spring estimates were valid. From Elazar's viewpoint, and even more so from Dayan's perspective, it put a significant question mark on the validity of their estimate from the spring.

Zeira did not change his war estimate throughout the summer. On June 12, he appeared before the members of the Knesset's Foreign Affairs and Security Committee and explained to them that the USSR and Libya were now the region's main moderating forces: The USSR, for fear that a new war and another defeat of its clients would create additional threats to its status in the Middle East, and Libya, for Gadhafi's fear that a too early embarkation for war would end in another Arab defeat. Approximately one month later he assessed at the same forum that the minor reference to the Middle East in the Nixon–Brezhnev summit at San Clemente (June 25) reflected a decrease in the value of the region to the superpowers. "Consequently," he added, "Egypt's blackmail ability to get the superpowers to compel an agreement has faded away."[31] On his August monthly briefing to the committee members, he described the Egyptian and Syrian military buildup, especially in the domain of anti-aircraft defense. Though Zeira avoided nullifying its significance, he explained that these arsenals did not create a potential for immediate threat but "for a threat that may arise three years from now." At present, he explained to his audience:

> Egypt has no doubt at all that the balance of forces and the political global situation do not allow a logical move to open fire.... There is very good information that the main reason Egypt does not start fire is that it will be impossible to limit it, and the fear of an Israeli response, which would always be massive and total.[32]

When presenting Egypt as having no war option at all, Zeira probably relied on Sadat's public speeches. An early August AMAN document, which analyzed these speeches, reached the conclusion that they reflected an Egyptian intention to shelve the conflict with Israel for years to come and to focus, instead, on solving domestic problems.[33]

The reduction of war threats from Egypt had an impact on the Chief of Staff's estimate as well. Since entering office in early 1972, Elazar assessed that the likelihood of war during his tenure was high. In the spring his confidence that war was likely to erupt soon increased even further. When it appeared that the situation was calm, he started to consider the possibility that he was wrong and that AMAN and Zeira were right. He said so privately, and this was the atmosphere in his secretariat. He expressed it publicly when saying, for example, in late June that he expected the coming summer, at least until the annual UN assembly meeting was over, "to be normal."[34] But, unlike Zeira, Elazar assessed that the war threat had not disappeared. This was clearly reflected in an answer that he gave to a question by the IDF journal correspondent who asked him in a Jewish new-year interview about his expectations for the next year. The Chief of Staff said:

> First, we have to know that the threat of war is not over yet. When I follow what is said in the Arab world, I can still see great and authentic ambitions to solve the problems between us and the Arab states by means of war, by a military decision of the state of Israel. Therefore, it is too early to forecast optimistically that perhaps next year we will make another move toward relaxation, since the threat of war still exists. We can prevent it, we can deter the enemy from war, but only by having a force that cannot be decided in the battlefield.[35]

While the Chief of Staff continued to perceive war as a real threat, Dayan's public statements during the summer of 1973 reflect the impression that the calm atmosphere since late May had led him to radically shift his war estimate. Before the summer he judged the likelihood of war by the Arab motivation to launch it. An analysis of the growing Egyptian frustration from the lingering status quo led him to conclude that Sadat might initiate war—even one which he was likely to lose—in order to get out of this dead end. Since the spring warnings bore no results, he adopted AMAN's analysis of the situation, which assessed the likelihood of war not on the basis of the balance of motivations but according to the balance of forces. Here, the situation was far more calming.

This approach was vividly expressed in Dayan's speech in the IDF Staff College on August 9. Though he noted that the occupied territories "provide Egypt, Jordan, and Syria a maximal motivation to fight us," he added that a different factor would determine the end result: "The overall balance of power is in our favor, and this—the determining and the decisive factor against all other Arab factors and motivations—blocks the immediate renewal of the war." As Dayan had put it, this was not a passing situation:

> The [Arab] weakness is the outcome of many factors that I do not think will change soon: their soldiers' low level of education, technology, and integrity; the Arab world's disunity, that it unites occasionally

but superficially and only for a short while; and the decisive weight of the extreme nationalism that nips in the bud any compromise and recognition of Israel."[36]

Dayan concluded that in light of its military superiority, Israel could now invest less in security. He promised that the regular military service would be reduced next year by three months and noted that the reserve service had already been shortened by 31 percent. In 1977, Dayan forecasted, Israel will invest in security 14.7 percent of the state budget, compared to 40 percent in 1970.[37]

Dayan's optimism was expressed in many other ways during that summer. In an interview with Time magazine in July he predicted: "The next ten years ... will see the borders frozen along present lines, but there will not be a major war."[38] A few weeks before the war, he said in a speech to the workers of the Security Ministry: "I do not forecast a war for the coming ten years, but, if war erupts before that, I'll come to explain to you why it happened."[39] In the ear of an American diplomat, Dayan likened the Arab armies to rusting ships, slowly sinking in the harbor.[40]

This confidence had certainly had an impact on Dayan's beliefs that Israel could now make unilateral changes in the occupied territories, such as the buildup of a deep-water harbor in northern Sinai, between Rafah and El Arish. General elections were to be held in Israel by the end of October. Less than a month before the war, in the middle of his Labor Party election campaign, Dayan declared: "Today we can say that the fundamental [Arab] demand would never take place. Gaza will not be Egyptian, the Golan will not be Syrian, Jerusalem will not be Arab, and there will be no Palestinian state."[41]

Such declarations reflected Israel's self-assurance and satisfaction about the situation and contributed to it. The belief that war would unlikely be soon was shared by members of the ruling party, such as Dayan and Yigal Allon, and also by the right-wing opposition. Less than three weeks before the war and shortly after retiring from the army, Ariel Sharon, who had become a new leader in the Likud Party, declared: "Israel stands now before quiet years, from the security perspective, and we should use them in order to take care of other disturbing problems. We are now at the best security situation and, with the present borders, we actually have no security problems."[42] The boastful aspects of this atmosphere received vivid expressions in declarations by known Israelis, such as a senior member of the legendary PALMACH, the elite Jewish military force during the British mandate years, who declared: "I belong to those who think that there is no need to be frightened by Egyptian war hysteria, even if they start fire. They will not try to cross the canal. Not only do they not have the courage to do it, they don't have the power and the ability to do it."[43]

In such an atmosphere, with hardly any external control of the security establishment, considerable security fiascos such as the downing of the Libyan passenger plane (February 1973), or the embarrassing failure of the Mossad's attempt to assassinate a Palestinian terrorist in the Norwegian town of Lillehammer (July 1973), received no criticism by the tamed and loyal media. The papers, the radio, and the Israeli TV, still regarded in that summer the IDF, AMAN, the Mossad or the Security Service (SHABAK) as "sacred cows." And, in this popularly authentic atmosphere—whose main theme was that "our situation had never been better"—Israel entered the month of September, at the beginning of which the first indications of war could already be seen.

Part III

The Dynamics of an Intelligence Fiasco

Chapter 10

August–September 1973

According to the timetable that was determined during the secret meeting of the Joint High (military) Council in Alexandria on August 22 and 23, Sadat and Asad were to inform the military echelons about D-day at least fourteen days in advance in order to ensure a well-timed military deployment. In actuality, it appeared that at least in the Syrian's case, the military hourglass preceded the decision on the political level. The reason is clear. Much of the Egyptian formation, including the five infantry divisions that were scheduled to cross the canal, had been in position for years. The Syrians, on the other hand, removed the majority of their forces from the front in the spring, so as to enable them to train for war. Now they had to redeploy them.

In late August, AMAN gained the first indications that irregular activity was taking place in the Syrian sector of the Golan Heights. It involved, primarily, the anti-aircraft layout. The major indication was a conspicuous reinforcement in the number of SAM batteries. On August 20, during a GHQ meeting, DMI Zeira reported that the Syrians had deployed thirty SAM batteries in the area between Dar'a and Dumair (the Golan Heights front), fifteen of which were the SA-6 type. This formation was similar both in quality and quantity to the one that had been built by the Egyptians at the canal front, but it was more densely positioned.[1] In addition, the Syrians brought their anti-aircraft formation as close as possible to the border, though outside of the IDF's mortar range. During September a third warning indicator would be added: The rate at which the batteries were moved between the sites, which had been constructed to protect them, increased. In the past, the SA-2 and SA-3 batteries had been rotated every two weeks, but toward the end of September this movement was sighted at more frequent intervals.[2]

Zeira's explanation for the Syrian move gave no reason for concern, even though the way that the SAM layout was built covered not only the area of the Golan Heights but also some territory in Israel itself. He estimated that its purpose was defensive and that it was motivated by the Syrian apprehension about Israeli air attacks, such as the heavy assaults that they had suffered at the beginning of 1973.[3] Air Force intelligence specialists agreed, explaining that the deployment (the major part of which was based on batteries that had arrived over the last few months from the Soviet Union) was intended to defend Syrian forces in the area between Damascus and the Golan Heights. The new layout also offered protection to important sites in Damascus and the Damascus Basin. The fact that it also covered large areas that were under Israeli command attracted less attention.[4]

In contrast to this calming approach, the IDF Deputy Chief of Staff, Maj. Gen. Yisrael Tal, presented a more concerned position. By his logic, since the new anti-aircraft deployment threatened the IAF's freedom of operation over the Golan, and since the IAF was the primary barrier to a Syrian breakthrough westward, one of two precaution moves were to be implemented: reinforcement of ground forces on the Heights with an additional regular division (that the IDF did not have), so that defense could rely on ground forces alone, or initiating a war against Syria in order to destroy the newly built anti-aircraft layout. Hence, Tal demanded to continue with the regular flight patterns and to warn Syria that any attempt to attack Israeli planes would bring about destruction of their SAM sites. At the same time, he thought Damascus should be required to pull back the batteries into the depth of Syrian territory. Tal also suggested that Israel should exploit the first opportunity to open war and to obliterate the Syrian anti-aircraft layout. His suggestions were rejected.[5]

During tranquil times the Syrian deployment at the Golan front had included three infantry brigades, approximately 400 to 450 tanks, and between 40 and 45 artillery batteries.[6] This deployment was reduced even further in the summer of 1973, because of the withdrawal of forces during the spring. Therefore, the Syrians began, at a relatively early stage, to reinforce their ground forces. It appears that this had already begun on August 7, but it only gained momentum following the Sadat–Asad meeting in Damascus (August 28–29), during which it was decided to open war on October 6. The summation of the weekly report of AMAN's Research Department for the first week of September, reported that on the 3rd of the month, the level of readiness of Syrian air and land forces was increased and that the front line had been reinforced with a considerable number of intermediate-range artillery batteries. A few days later, AMAN reported that on the night between September 7 and 8, the level of readiness of the Syrian Air Force was raised to a higher standard; presumably, this was also the case with ground forces at the front. In addition, one brigade in the front line was reinforced. AMAN had no prior information concerning Syrian intentions to take such moves, and the information on reinforcement of the front line was gained in real time from ground observation posts. A reconnaissance flight, taken on September 11, showed that the Syrians continued reinforcing their front line units. At approximately the same time, a source, whose identification is not clear, reported that President Asad had agreed to join an Egyptian initiation of war at the end of the year, after Soviet experts told him that a joint assault would enable the Syrian army to "completely conquer the Golan in thirty-six hours."[7]

AMAN's explanations for these moves were relatively calming. At first, the front line's reinforcement was connected to preparations for terrorist activity, and the raised state of alert was explained by the scheduled visit of President Asad to Algeria. Then, on September 9, the IDF GHQ met to discuss various aspects of the Syrian deployment. DMI Zeira estimated that the reinforcement of the front line toward the fall—a period during which forces were normally reduced—took place since Syrian training exercises had started later than usual that year. Nevertheless, the Chief of Staff decided to take cautious means, including limitation of both military and civilian flights over the Golan Heights.[8] As far as is known, AMAN gave neither a verbal nor a written estimate of the report according to which Asad agreed to join the Egyptian war initiative.

Against this background of a gradual increase in Syrian military readiness and the calming explanation that AMAN gave it, came the incident of September 13. It began as an Israeli attempt to execute a reconnaissance flight along the shoreline in northern Syria—an area in which anti-aircraft defense had been considerably reduced because of the transfer of SAM batteries to the Golan front. The flight was conducted by two Phantom planes, which approached the Syrian shore north of Lebanon, with a cover of four Mirage planes flying at high altitude. The interception of the Israeli planes by eight Mig-21s resulted in an escalating air battle and the shooting down of nine Mig-21s and one Mirage. A Syrian attempt to prevent the rescue of the Israeli pilot who had parachuted over the Mediterranean, culminated in bringing down four more Mig-21s.[9]

In hindsight, the September 13 incident had a significant effect on the way in which Israel evaluated the Arab preparation for war during the following weeks. Indeed, it increased concerns regarding threatening developments in the northern front and sharpened the attention of the decision-makers to the possibility that the Syrians would attempt to take revenge. During a cabinet meeting on September 16, Defense Minister Dayan said that they would react, and that the weakest type of response would be the shelling of Golan settlements. The Chief of Staff agreed but was particularly concerned about the shooting down of an Israeli plane by the newly built SAM layout. In contrast, AMAN's estimation was that the incident increased Israel's deterrent posture and that Damascus would be more hesitant now before initiating similar confrontations. But the main effect of the incident was devastating, since it channeled Israeli estimates regarding the ongoing Syrian force buildup to a totally misconceived direction: Instead of suspecting that the buildup was aimed at preparing a war in coordination with Egypt, the incident supplied a convenient explanation—that the Syrians had prepared a local military response to the incident. Thus, for example, Zeira reported on September 17 on further reinforcement of Syrian positions in the first line of defense. He explained it by a Syrian concern that started at the end of August and intensified following the air battle. In a similar manner, he reported the same day that the Egyptian Air Force had entered into an offensive state of readiness, estimating that it had been done in light of Egyptian apprehension that Israel had initiated the incident in order to warn the Arabs against the re-establishment of the "eastern front."[10]

* * *

AMAN's tendency to explain the incoming war signals in every possible form but for war can be better understood in the context in which the organization estimated the likelihood of any war in coming years. This assessment was best reflected by DMI Zeira in a GHQ discussion held on September 17. It was the first in a series of three meetings—the other two took place on September 24 and October 1—which aimed at evaluating the strategic directions of the IDF development in coming years. Zeira started the discussion by estimating the probability of war in the next five years. He based his estimate solely on the anticipated Arab procurement of weapon systems, primarily in the air. According to the well-established parameters, in order to initiate war, the Arabs would need to:

    a. Purchase planes that were technically and operationally capable of attacking targets deep within Israel.
    b. Get surface-to-surface missiles (SSMs) that were capable of hitting targets in Israel's depth.
    c. Improve air defense of Arab states.[11]

The scenario built by Zeira tended toward the worst case, i.e., a situation in which the Arab oil producers would be ready to finance, more generously than in the past, the military requirements of Egypt and Syria, and the weapon suppliers—not only the USSR but also West European countries and the USA—would be willing to supply more freely than before weapon systems to regional powers. On this basis, he estimated that a qualitative and quantitative improvement was likely to take place in Egyptian and Syrian air defense in the next five years; that their capability to strike civilian and large-scale military targets in

Israel's depth by Scud and "Frog" SSMs would improve; that the purchase of modern fighter-bombers would enable the Egyptians, perhaps by 1975, to attack targets deep within Israel; that remote Arab states, such as Libya, would develop capabilities to hit Israeli naval targets far from Israel; and that the absorption of modern tanks would improve Arab land-warfare capabilities.[12]

Zeira estimated that these developments would not cause a major change in Cairo's war willingness. In his opinion, the only new factor added to the Egyptian arsenal would be "the ability to carry out deep strikes while such an ability does not in any way exist today." But, even if Egypt gained such capabilities, it would nevertheless face operational problems due to the difficulties involved in attacking well-defended targets in long-range strikes, by planes capable of carrying only a limited load of arms. Adding to Egypt's problems, the DMI assessed that Israel was likely to maintain its advantages in the technological realm, in man power, and in air systems. His conclusion was clear:

> It does not appear that the Egyptians are likely to assume that they are capable of defeating the IAF in its bases or to neutralize it in a way that would minimize its ability to seriously endanger Egypt so that the Egyptians would be able to occupy Sinai or part of it, which means an all-out confrontation with Israel. Our assessment is that they will estimate that their striking capabilities in our depth will not give them the ability to win a decisive victory but only a limited offensive option.[13]

After removing, both in theory and in practice, the possibility that Egypt would launch a major war against Israel in the next five years, the DMI turned to assessing the chances of more limited moves. Here, he was more cautious. His point of departure was the present situation: "The Egyptians understand that, today, they cannot present any real military threat." Within a few years, however, gaining some offensive capabilities combined with a limited deterrent power, may lead to an attempt to use their military cards, not only in the diplomatic realm but also through the use of limited military strikes.[14] Concluding his remarks, Zeira made it clear that the Egyptian threat would remain very limited for the coming five years:

> Egypt will have the technical-operational option to strike in Israel's depth, and this is where the situation will be different from today's. Taking into account the comprehensive balance of power, we estimate that it will be limited and will not let the Egyptians assess that they have a decisive capability vis-à-vis the IAF. However, it might give them options for a limited action under appropriate political conditions, and if they feel their situation improved, they may take a greater freedom of action than in the past.[15]

As far as it is known, this professional assessment met no objection from any participant in the meeting, including the Defense Minister.[16] In this sense, it seems to reflect also the state of mind of Israel's security elite, less than three weeks before the outbreak of the war.

For our subject, three additional comments are in place: First, the prediction regarding the development of the Arab–Israeli balance of forces, especially in the air, withstood the time test and correctly forecasted (in addition to the affect of war and the profit of the Arab oil producers) the principle directions of Arab force buildup in the years to come. In this sense, Zeira's estimation of capabilities was highly reasonable.

Second, AMAN's conclusion from this prediction was completely erroneous. Even today it is difficult to understand why its chief analysts in 1973 adhered solely to the element of in-depth striking capabilities, ignoring other inputs that shaped the Egyptian strategic calculus, primarily the uncompromising desire to regain the territorial losses of 1967, and the growing frustration over the continuation of the status quo. This question becomes an even shriller cry in the light of the fact that, as far as it is known, since November 1972, reliable information that the Egyptians were still considering the acquisition of in-depth strike capability as a precondition to launch, a war ceased to arrive. The opposite was true. The best sources reported that Egypt was heading for war soon. All this information, which completely contradicted the thesis that Zeira presented in the GHQ meeting, received no attention in his estimate.

Finally, the third point is the most important for our subject: Zeira, who maintains so decisively that the Egyptians understand that they have no military option at present and are likely, at most, to have had very limited military options five years ahead, is hardly able, if at all, to accept the possibility that he is entirely mistaken and that his assessment—primarily about the near-term future—is entirely invalid. In this sense, the gist of Zeira's long-term assessment in mid-September lays in its accurate description of the frame of mind of AMAN's most influential analysts—the head of Branch 6, the head of the Research Department, and he himself. The voice of others' analysts, such as the head of Branch 2, or the head of Egypt's political section—who were experienced analysts of Egyptian affairs and who believed that Sadat intended to go to war soon—were not heard.[17]

The rigidity of this evaluation was even more noticeable on the background of another event. In mid-September, AMAN was preparing its annual intelligence estimate. In a conversation with the Chief of Staff, Zeira pointed to two central research errors of the past year: the assessment that the USA would initiate a new diplomatic initiative, and the estimation that the USSR would refuse to supply its clients with new weapon systems, primarily Scud missiles. By September 1973, it was known that Egypt had started receiving them in August.[18] Awareness of these mistakes should have created concern regarding the validity of the thesis that Egypt was not ready to go to war. After all, the political deadlock motivated Sadat to break it by means of force, and the supply of the Scuds made such a move more feasible. There are no indications, however, that these factors played any role in shaping AMAN's annual evaluation.

* * *

On September 22, another reconnaissance flight was taken over the Golan front. It showed that the Syrian army was deployed in full emergency layout along the first line of defense, including its rear; that the deployment of artillery was significantly reinforced, and that the tank reserve units of the three infantry divisions that were now deployed in the front line had been advanced to their rear.[19] Two days later, the second GHQ meeting on the IDF development in coming years took place. At its center stood the possible procurement of the F-15 fighter for the IAF. But, when the turn came for Maj. Gen. Yitzhak Hofi, the commander of the Northern Command, to speak, he referred to the situation in the north rather than to the IDF's long-term force buildup:

> I would like to first emphasize something that is well-known, but, in my opinion, is serious, perhaps even very serious—that we have no warning at all in this sector. The Syrians have lately got out of their layout and returned to it, and we did not know. . . . There is here a danger of a sudden attack. . . . In my opinion, the conclusion from all that we have seen is that the Syrians constitute a greater risk to Israel than the Egyptians. [Though] Not in the long-term of fighting.[20]

To this disturbing picture, Hofi added more facts that increased the dimensions of the Syrian threat: the absence of any ground obstacle capable of blocking the advance of Syrian tanks westward; the lack of strategic depth, which left the civilian settlements on the Heights exposed to a ground attack; limited warning space for the Air Force; and significant limitations on the IAF's ability to support the ground forces to hold defense, because of the Syrian SAM layout that now covered most of the Golan Heights' airspace.[21] Hofi's remarks were primarily based on intelligence material that was collected by ground observation posts. According to the SOP of that time, raw intelligence from other means of collection was not distributed to the commands. The only additional intelligence information that was provided to Hofi and his colleagues was in the form of documents that had been written at the Research Department, which combined only parts of the relevant information with its assessment.[22] Consequently, neither Hofi nor the commanders of the Central and Southern Commands had the essential means to build their own independent intelligence estimate.

The Commander of the Northern Command's remarks did not go unnoticed. Although the discussion returned to its original agenda, toward its end Dayan engaged with the problem, stressing that the threat must be addressed:

> If, indeed, it is true that the Syrians can, without prior warning, advance tanks and take two or three settlements in the Golan Heights, perhaps even more—this would be an unprecedented catastrophe.... I cannot afford myself to go to a break until after the New Year [September 26–29] without knowing that the situation is dealt with. There must be another assumption of the GHQ, or your assumption, the Chief of Staff, that the situation is different, or that you have an answer to such a situation.[23]

The Chief of Staff's response indicated a certain dislike of Dayan's alarmist tone. "I do not accept," Elazar said, "the assumption that the Syrians are capable, today, of conquering the Golan Heights." In answer to Dayan's question of whether he meant that a sudden attack was impossible, Elazar gave a more detailed answer:

> Under no circumstances is a sudden attack possible.... [although] our warning in the case of Syrian ground forces is worse than in the case of others and less than what we would like it to be.... But our general warning regarding the Syrians, in those areas without which one cannot go to war, is a good one and, therefore, I do not think they can prepare a surprise attack without our knowledge. Secondly, we have in the Golan Heights enough force that can, within a reasonable amount of time and according to this warning, block an attack. And thirdly, perhaps most importantly, the Syrians have built a considerable SAM layout, and we are careful not to enter it for a reconnaissance flight, or if we need to attack an artillery battery.... [But] if the question is a question of war, then, in my opinion, this layout will make no change in the ability of the Air Force to finish off Syria in half a day.[24]

This exchange is important for two reasons. First, the Chief of Staff expressed complete confidence that despite the problematic intelligence coverage in the Golan, AMAN would provide a high-quality warning that would prevent a strategic surprise. Second, the exchange sounded like a dialogue between the deaf. Dayan's concern, as it was clearly expressed following Hofi's remarks, and as he expressed it until October 6, was not of an all-out Syrian attack aimed at the occupation of the Heights but rather a limited move, such as a strike by a tank battalion, which could break through the weak Israeli defense line, take over a settlement or two, and kill its inhabitants. Even if, ultimately,

Syria would pay dearly for such action, Israel would pay highly as well. The Chief of Staff did not address such a problem but only referred to an all-out war scenario. In this sense, the exchange reflected their different order of priorities: Dayan was worried only about a small-scale strike, since he estimated that Syria could not go to war. One cannot negate the possibility that Dayan's concerns were motivated by a political factor — the price that the Labor Party and he himself would have to pay if such a disaster took place at the height of the election campaign. Elazar's prime concern, on the other hand, was general war, which in contrast to Dayan, he still considered to be possible, though not in the immediate future.

Immediately after the meeting, Dayan requested the Chief of Staff to provide an answer to the small-scale strike scenario. Elazar said that he was looking into the situation with the Northern Command's commander. In spite of his estimate that "it is not logical, it is idiotic, completely unreasonable to assume that Syria will go to war alone," he arranged such a discussion for the next morning.[25]

Details about the situation in the Golan were conveyed to Golda Meir, who for quite some time expressed similar concerns. She consulted Dayan on whether or not she should go to the meeting of the advisory forum of the European Council that was planned for September 29. Dayan's answer was calming, but he advised her to discuss the tension with King Hussein, who was to arrive for a meeting with her the next day.[26]

* * *

Since his warning on May 9 about a coming war, King Hussein had delivered at least two additional warnings. The first was transferred through the Mossad on July 17, in the aftermath of a series of Jordanian–Egyptian–Syrian talks, in which the king had heard allusions to an expected war. The reports coming from Jordan indicated the possibility that Egypt and/or Syria would open fire on July 26 — the opening day of the Security Council Assembly on the Middle East. According to this information, the Egyptians estimated that an immediate call for a cease-fire by the Security Council — to which Egypt and Syria would respond positively — would prevent them from suffering a devastating defeat. In August, Hussein and Golda Meir met again. This time the King was more reserved about the possibility of war in the near future, but he nevertheless warned that Sadat's internal problems could force him to an act out of desperation.[27]

The meeting that took place on the evening of September 25 was not a routine one. The King had urgently requested it two days earlier and it required changes in Golda Meir's agenda. It took place in a Mossad guest house near Tel Aviv. Hussein, who came with his Prime Minister, Zayd al-Refai, and other officials, appeared, according to Golda Meir's secretary Lou Kedar, nervous and anxious.[28]

The talk dealt primarily with bilateral and other common issues. The King described, at length, the September 10–12 meeting that he had held in Cairo with Sadat and Asad, emphasizing that both had made it clear that they could no longer accept the "neither war nor peace" situation. He stressed that he was also in agreement, and expressed hope that "before the patience of the Arabs expires completely, something will happen to prevent war." He also said that the two checked with him his readiness to renew the eastern front. His reply was "leave me alone," adding that "he had already paid a high price for such a partnership in 1967." Then, the King brought up the tension in the north:

> ... from a very very sensitive source in Syria, that we have received information from in the past and passed it on ... all the [Syrian] units that are meant to be in training are now, as of the last two days or so, in position for a pre-attack. ... That includes their aircraft, missiles, everything else ... in pre-jump positions [to attack Israel] ... Whether it means anything or not, nobody knows. However, one cannot be sure. One must take this as a fact.

The Prime Minister asked, "Is it conceivable that the Syrians would start something without the full cooperation of the Egyptians?" The King replied, "I don't think so. I think they are cooperating."[29]

It is not clear whether the Israelis knew the identity of the Jordanian "very very sensitive source," but it seems that it was a Major General of the Syrian army who had been recruited for their service two years earlier. At the end of August or the beginning of September, he delivered the Syrian war plans that were approved by the Egyptian–Syrian high command, probably in the Alexandria meeting of August 22–23.[30]

The warning impressed Meir. Around midnight, she called Dayan at his home and reported what the King had said, expressing her own concern. Dayan responded by saying that he was personally aware, along with the IDF, of the situation and intended to reinforce the northern front the following day. This relaxed the Premier. She returned to the conference room and continued discussions with the King until the meeting was over.[31]

At the same time that the two heads of state met, another, more professional discussion, took place. The Israeli representatives were the head of the Mossad, Zvi Zamir, and the DMI's assistant for operations, Col. Aharon Levran. Their Jordanian counterpart elaborated upon the Syrian war preparations and expressed concern about it. However, Col. Levran was skeptical about this information, and his disregard did not encourage the continuation of a dialogue in this channel in the days to come.[32]

The Hussein–Meir talk was watched by some other individuals from the Prime Minister's office, the Mossad, and the IDF. One of them was the Head of Branch 2 (Jordan, Iraq, and the Arab Peninsula) of AMAN's Research Department, Lt. Col. Zusia ("Zizi") Kaniazher, who was there as AMAN's representative. Being highly involved in the department's internal debate about the meaning of the Syrian buildup, Kaniazher became immediately aware of two new and important elements in the King's words. First, the King said that the Syrian army was "in pre-attack" positions. AMAN's experts (as well as Dayan, Elazar, and others), had estimated until then that the Syrian force buildup aimed at a limited strike rather than an all-out war. Second, the King noted, though in response to the Premier's question, that the Syrian war preparations were coordinated with Egypt. So far, AMAN had no indication of such a coordination. And, since the common wisdom was that Syria would avoid a war without Egypt, the possibility that the force buildup in the north was designed for war became more likely.

When the meeting ended, Kaniazher called the head of the Research Department, and reported these two points. A more detailed account was to follow in the morning. Then, Kaniazher made an unprecedented move that was beyond his realm of responsibility. He called his colleague, Lt. Col. Avi Yaari, the head of Branch 5, who for some time had contemplated what stood behind the Syrian military activity, and told him that according to a senior ranking source—Yaari would know its real identity only years later—the Syrian preparations were for war and they were coordinated with Egypt. He acted this way since Yaari was not in the need-to-know group of AMAN's officers who knew about Hussein's visit, and yet the King's warning was highly relevant for his ability to carry out his professional tasks. But Kaniazher was also motivated by the fact that Yaari and he himself constituted the main opposition in the Research Department to the dominant thesis, according to which Egypt and Syria had no intention to launch a war in the foreseeable future.[33]

Indeed, until then, Yaari and his colleagues in the Branch had difficulty understanding what caused the Syrian massive reinforcement at the end of the summer. On the one hand, it indicated preparations for war; on the other, they, like everyone else, were certain that Syria would avoid launching a war without Egyptian participation. And, since the head of Branch 6 categorically rejected the possibility that Egypt would launch war soon, they could not explain the Syrian conduct. Now, for the first time, they could combine two elements of the problem into a single coherent answer.[34]

The following morning, armed with information that he had just received from Kaniazher, Yaari came to Shalev's office demanding to know all the relevant information concerning Syrian intentions to go to war. Shalev admitted that there was information that he could not share with his prime Syrian expert. He added that the same procedure would also be maintained in the future. This was unacceptable for Yaari, and their voices escalated. The head of Branch 5 maintained that he could not carry out his task properly, without having access to all the relevant information. Consequently, he continued, when highly sensitive and relevant information is not distributed through the appropriate channels, it is transmitted by unsecured phone line.[35]

The stormy exchange between Yaari and Shalev had an immediate effect on the content of the planned meeting between Shalev and Kaniazher, which took place a little later. Instead of analyzing the King's message, Shalev focused on reprimanding Kaniazher for his unauthorized distribution of sensitive material to Yaari. In the heated exchange that developed, Kaniazher (who previously served as the head of the Egyptian military section and acting head of Branch 6) forcefully insisted that Egypt was gearing for war and that Shalev and Bandman did not understand what was taking place there. He added that since the distribution of relevant information for the assessment of Syrian intentions was banned, he used his discretion to report it to Yaari. Shalev, for his part, raised his voice to remind Kaniazher that he was in charge of Jordanian rather than Egyptian affairs and that, hence, the developments in Egypt were not his concern. In addition, he charged him for being an "alarmist" who unnecessarily generated panic.[36]

This incident's most significant outcome was that Kaniazher was neutralized from taking part in the highly classified discussions on the King's warning that were to take place that day. Thus, his conclusion that the King warned that Syria was gearing for war, and that it was done in coordination with Egypt, did not climb beyond the level of the Research Department. And, since Shalev used the time to rebuke Kaniazher rather than to listen to his analysis, it made no impact on him either.[37] The Commander of the Northern Command—the would-be beneficiary of the King's warning—had no knowledge of it.[38]

* * *

September 26 was New Year's Eve and, consequently, a short working day, but the King's warning triggered a series of intensive discussions and activities. One was held at Shalev's office. The participants (whose identities are unclear) concluded that the King's words could not be taken as a warning against a concrete action.[39] A second discussion took place at the Chief of Staff's office at 0815. In his opening remarks, Elazar spoke about a warning from a "serious source" that the Syrian army was ready for war, though it was unclear whether this was done in cooperation with Egypt. DMI Zeira, who then spoke, described newly arrived warning indicators: an additional raise in the state of alert of the Syrian army, the call off of leaves, the mobilization of civilian vehicles, and the call-up for active duty of reserve soldiers. This information sufficed for AMAN's experts to conclude that at least technically the Syrian army was now capable of starting hostilities on a short notice. Zeira was, however, more reserved with regard to the "serious source" warning. He maintained that the quality of the warning was not high and that AMAN's thesis that Syria would not go to war without Egypt and that Egypt did not perceive itself as capable of going to war was still valid. As far as it is known, the DMI did not make any link between the unusual Syrian deployment and information that started to trickle down two days earlier about massive military movements from the Cairo area to the Canal Zone.

The Chief of Staff agreed that the Syrian deployment was not for war. But the combination of a three-day holiday, in which thousands of Israelis would visit the Golan, and the apprehension of a limited Syrian strike that might, under such circumstances, cause very heavy damage, led him to take some precautionary measures. He ordered the reinforcement of the Golan sector with one 175mm artillery battery and two tank companies from Tank Brigade 7. In addition, the state of alert of the IAF, of Brigade 188 (the Golan's Tank Brigade) and one artillery battalion, was raised. As a result, the tank order of battle in the front was to reach 100, confronting 800 Syrian tanks. This force ratio was fine with the Chief of Staff. The same day, he issued the Northern Command an order, saying: "From today until further notice, the state of alert will be raised towards a possibility of a Syrian attack at the Golan Heights." The order detailed the decisions made by Elazar in the morning meeting.[40]

At 0900 the third discussion at the Ministry of Defense office started. Earlier Dayan was briefed by Levran on the meeting with the King.[41] The present discussion included also the Chief of Staff, his deputy, the Defense Minister's assistant, Maj. Gen. (res.) Zvi Zur, DMI Zeira, the Commander of the Northern Command, and assistants. At the focus of the discussion was the previous night's warning, but the name of the king was not mentioned. Elazar's opening remarks reflected vividly his state of mind:

> I don't think it is a serious matter.... We know that the Syrian army is deployed in an emergency deployment, and it is a deployment from which you can attack and do other things—it is true. But ... it seems to me, that we do not face a war with Syria. I think that nothing can be more idiotic, on behalf of Syria, as attacking alone. I think that we have all the indications that there is not going [to be] a war of the two of them, and, hence, I would not make war preparations in order to prevent a war in the Golan Heights.[42]

This assessment, perhaps the most decisive of Elazar's throughout the period before the war, reflected his impatience toward Dayan's apprehension of a Syrian act and his pressure to take immediate steps to prevent it.[43] Very much like the discussion two days earlier, it was evident that while Dayan was worried about a limited strike that could be taken without additional preparations, Elazar's main concern was an all-out war. He nevertheless related also to a small-scale attack, assessing its probability as low as well. "This [a sporadic attack] can happen," he said, at the same meeting. But, "we assume it to be very unlikely—they know that it won't end with their shelling. They learned already that as far as we are concerned, there are no geographical limitations."[44]

It is quite clear why Elazar so easily annulled the King's warning. Generally, he tended now to relate a lower probability to war, believing that he was wrong in the spring. Hence, he was more inclined to accept AMAN's assessment. Specifically, he seems to have been influenced by the sources who had reported to him about the meeting. One was Zeira, who probably received his report from Levran, who was skeptical about the warning that he had received together with Zamir through back channels. Both Levran and Zeira believed that no war was likely—a worldview that led them to null the Jordanian warning. Elazar's second source was the head of the Operation Department in the G Branch, Brig. Gen. Yaacov Stern, who had listened to the exchange between Hussein and Meir along with Kaniazher and some others. He, too, believed that no concrete warning was delivered, and he told Elazar so.[45] At these morning hours, the text of the exchange was not ready yet. Elazar, just like Dayan, based his assessment on secondary, biased sources. It is quite probable that if he had been briefed by Kaniazher and had heard his interpretation—that ex post facto was the right one—he would have been more cautious. But, by this stage—either because of his earlier clash with Shalev, or because his estimate contradicted his superiors', or because the IDF's SOP dictated a more ordinary chain of reports—Kaniazher was out of the picture.

Dayan agreed that Syria would not launch a war without Egypt, but his main concern—a strike against a civilian settlement—continued to haunt him. "We must remember," he said, "that [in the Golan] there is no Suez [Canal] that you need to cross, and what they have to do is to cross the no man's land and get in with tanks..."[46] Hence, while accepting the steps taken by the Chief of Staff as sufficient for the time being, Dayan decided to visit the Golan, analyze its defenses, and deliver a warning to Syria. Elazar did not like the decision, fearing that it would raise concerns among the settlers.[47]

Dayan left for the Golan immediately after the meeting was over. He was briefed there by Hofi about the Command's present activities, including the digging of a new anti-tank ditch and the laying of additional minefields that could delay a Syrian advancement. However, he also learned that the Command's warning span was very limited. Warning against a Syrian shelling was based on ground observation posts, which were supposed to locate the removal of the artillery camouflage nets. And, warning against a ground offensive was dependent on long-range observations, which were to identify Syrian preparations for attack. At night, so Dayan learned from Hofi, the Syrians could manage a total surprise.[48]

Dayan's message to the settlers and the journalists, who were called to meet him in Ein Zivan, reflected his concerns. He opened by noting, "On the Syrian side of the border, there are hundreds of tanks, hundreds of artillery pieces in operational range, and a SAM layout similar, in its density, to the Egyptian layout west of the Suez." To this he added the special situation in the Golan, where no ground obstacle existed between the Israeli settlements and the Syrian Army. Hence, he said, special attention should be given to the strengthening of the settlements.[49] Specifically, Dayan warned the Syrians that any action to revenge their losses in the air battle of September 13 would bring about a painful response. And yet, fearing that his warning might be interpreted as a preparation for an Israeli attack,[50] he dictated to one reporter: "I don't see any special reasons in recent time for warning. There is no reason to view a growing tension, but no reason for relaxation." Nevertheless, after these calming words, he explained once more his worries, in light of the Syrian massive buildup of ground and anti-aircraft layout.[51]

* * *

The next three days, the two holidays of the New Year and the Sabbath that followed, constitute a sort of intermezzo in the intensive activity that started after the GHQ meeting of September 24. The Israeli policy-makers spent the holiday in different places. The Chief of Staff went with his family to Sharm el Sheik; Dayan was at his home in Zahala; and Golda Meir spent time with her family in Kibbutz Revivim in the Negev.

But these three days were not uneventful. The most public among them was the terrorist overtaking of an immigrant train on its way from Czechoslovakia to Austria. The agreement of Bruno Kreisky, the Austrian Chancellor, to close the immigrants' transit camp at Schannau in exchange for the release of the hostages was perceived in Israel as a shameful surrender to terror. Kreisky's Jewish origins combined with Austria's Nazi history added to the emotional frustration. Backed by massive public support, Golda Meir defined Kreisky's behavior as a clear antithesis to a "proper Zionist answer" to terrorism. On Saturday night the government convened for a special meeting, confirming Meir's plans to urgently meet Kreisky in Vienna. The meeting, which took place on October 2, delayed the Prime Minister's return to Israel from her European trip, precisely when her presence in the decision-making center was needed most.

Below the surface, however, other events—far more relevant for Israel's security—took place. During the holiday, new information arrived concerning a raise in the state of alert of the EAF, the ground forces at the Canal sector, and naval forces of the Red Sea theater. Simultaneously, AMAN received more indications concerning heavy military movements, including that of amphibious armored fighting vehicles (AFVs) and the possible advancement of a division from the Cairo area to the 2nd Army sector at the Canal. The interpretation that was given by Branch 6 of these events was very clear:

> Egyptian fears of an Israeli offensive action, which started after the air battle of September 13, when thirteen Syrian Mig-21 planes were shot down, continue. These fears were intensified because of the annual anniversary of Gamal Abdul Nasser's death (September 28), and possibly the Ramadan feast. In light of these apprehensions, the state of alert was raised in all arms of the Egyptian army.[52]

The basis for this interpretation is unclear. It is possible that Branch 6 had some information—perhaps the product of Egypt's deception campaign—that linked the raised state of alert and alleged Egyptian fears of an Israeli attack or special circumstances in Egypt. But the decisive manner in which it was explained was not supported by any solid information.[53] As in other cases, the assessment was presented as based on hard evidence—while, in fact, it was based on the personal assumptions of its writer, the head of Branch 6. It reflected his belief that the duty of the intelligence officer was to present his consumers with the clearest intelligence picture, even when it was not so clear. As we will see, this form of presentation reached its height toward the eve of the war. For the time being, it sufficed to calm the apprehension of most of its consumers.

* * *

On the night of September 29–30, AMAN received a CIA report based on "highly reliable" sources, warning that from the end of September a large-scale Syrian offensive to occupy the Golan Heights was expected. According to this information, the Syrian army had already initiated its battle procedure. The information also included the Syrian attack plan, which was similar to the one reported by Branch 5 a few months earlier. The attack was to start at twilight by three infantry divisions (5, 7, and 9), which were expected to occupy a strip of 8 to 10 kilometers during the night. At the second phase, Armored Divisions 1 and 3 were to develop an offensive that was aimed at reaching the Jordan River and taking over a bridgehead at its west bank.

Usually, such information would have shaken the intelligence and security establishment, but this was not the case this time. As AMAN's experts knew well, behind the term "highly reliable" sources stood King Hussein, who delivered the Americans a similar warning as that provided to the Israelis on September 25. AMAN's chief analysts did not give much weight to the fact that the most important intelligence agency in the free world delivered such a rare war warning or that the warning was far more concrete than that which was described to Dayan and Elazar by Levran and Stern in the aftermath of

Golda Meir's meeting with Hussein four days earlier. But the analysts of Branch 5, who throughout this period tended to assess more seriously the Syrian threat, used the opportunity to issue a special intelligence review on the Syrian war plan. The top echelon of the Research Department added a calming assessment to the document, saying that AMAN did not consider the present layout as reflecting a Syrian intention to attack, thus neutralizing the value of the warning.[54]

* * *

Sunday, September 30, was the first regular working day after three and a half days of holiday. It started routinely. The state of alert in the Golan, which was raised on New Year's Eve, returned that morning, in part, to normal. AMAN's analysts turned their attention now to Egypt. For five days, Branch 6 received various reports on irregular activity of the Egyptian army, and now it learned that a large-scale Tahrir exercise was scheduled to start. The planned military activity was reported by AMAN:

> Between October 1–7, 1973, a large-scale staff exercise on the occupation of Sinai is going to take place. Its participants will probably be the headquarters of the air, anti-aircraft, and naval arms, and the headquarters of the armies, the divisions, and the special forces. Because of the exercise, the state of alert will be raised (as of October 1) to its highest in the air force, and all the units which are to participate in the exercise, and all leave will be called off.[55]

After providing details about the mobilization and planned release of reserve soldiers, the head of Branch 6 assessed its meaning:

> The information about the expected exercise and the call of reserve soldiers for a limited time, implies, therefore, that the advancement of forces and additional preparations that are under way or will be done in coming days, such as: completion of fortifications, mobilization of civilian fishery boats, and check of state of readiness of the units, which allegedly can be seen as alert signals, are, in actuality, solely connected to the exercise.[56]

This assessment was an exception even by Branch 6's standards. Usually, Bandman (as some of his colleagues) had the pretension to provide clear-cut estimates about past events. This time, and in the most crucial matter, he gave a decisive estimate about future events. Notably, the recent military developments in Egypt came on the background of a growing tension in the north, less then twenty-four hours after the CIA had made it clear that it regarded the possibility of a Syrian attack as serious, and a few days after King Hussein, who met earlier with Sadat and Asad, warned that such an attack would be coordinated with Egypt. Nevertheless, AMAN decisively determined that the various war indicators on the Egyptian front that were expected to appear in coming days implied exercise rather than preparations for war.

* * *

At 1800 the same day, a special discussion on the situation in the north took place in the Chief of Staff's office. It focused on the weekend's developments, including the CIA's warning that the Syrian military preparations were almost completed. At the beginning of the discussion, DMI Zeira reported on the most recent events: On September 28, two squadrons of Sukhoi attack fighters left their base at T-4 in northern Syria and deployed to Dumair airfield, about 90 kilometers from the frontline, where they had no shelters. Tank Brigade 47 was underway from its bases near Homs to the frontline. To the best of AMAN's assessment, the whole Syrian army was now deployed in an emergency deployment. According to Soviet doctrine, Zeira noted, such a deployment enables attack without further preparations.

While the information presented by the DMI was alarming, the interpretation of it was far more calming. Zeira assessed that Syria would avoid going to war without Egypt, and even if Egypt launched a war, there was no certainty that Syria would immediately join it. It was more likely that Damascus would wait to see the results of the Egyptian initiative and would join only if they were successful. And, since Egypt was under no pressure to go to war, it did not mean to do it. Consequently, he summed up, the Syrian preparations were not for war. Instead, he suggested, there were two explanations: the creation of a false momentum that might satisfy the army, or fear of an Israeli attack.

The head of the Research Department, Arie Shalev, followed suit. He explained unusual military activity in Egypt by a fear of the IDF, preparations for the Tahrir 41 exercise, and the feast of Ramadan. He, too, assessed that in the Syrian view the cost of war with Israel would exceed its value, and hence they were not likely to start one. Both Zeira and Shalev estimated that there was a low probability, at most, for a Syrian limited move, though the latter assessed that an attempt to occupy an Israeli stronghold on the frontline was more likely than the occupation of a civilian settlement.

The Commander of the Northern Command presented no reservations about this assessment but emphasized the problem of insufficient tactical warning in the Golan. Ideally, Hofi said, an additional tank brigade constantly deployed on the Heights would have solved the problem. But everyone realized that due to financial constraints this was not a realistic solution. Very much like

Hofi, most of the others who were present in the discussion tended to accept AMAN's calming assessment. "We give the Syrians too much credit," said one of the participants, expressing the discussion's atmosphere.

The exception was, again, the Deputy Chief of Staff, Yisrael Tal, who maintained that the problem was not "revenge for the thirteen planes . . . but the threat of a Syrian offensive." His arguments carried weight. First, he maintained, if the Syrians rejected an Egyptian proposal to go to war in May because they lacked some equipment, they had closed this gap, primarily by receiving bridge layer tanks. Second, the completion of the anti-aircraft and the ground deployments gave them the capability to go to war. Adding the buildup along the Suez sector and reminding that according to some information the Syrians were more certain now that they could occupy the Golan, Tal concluded that IDF had to prepare for war. In light of the possibility that bad weather and Syrian massive air-defense buildup would limit the IAF's ability to assist in blocking a Syrian attack, he suggested reinforcing the front line with one tank brigade, a battalion of M-109 artillery, and the mobilization of a reserve force that would enable the buildup of this formation.

Tal's assessment was rejected by the Chief of Staff. Elazar agreed, nevertheless, to reinforce the Golan by more units of Tank Brigade 7, in addition to the two platoons that were sent there five days earlier. As a result of this and some other moves, the artillery force in the Golan was doubled, and the number of tanks reached 113 (and an additional thirty-three with full kit but no teams) in comparison to sixty-nine in routine.[57]

The rejection of his assessment compelled Tal to take an unusual move. He went to the DMI's office and presented his alarmist estimate to Zeira and Shalev once more. This time, however, his main emphasis was on the disproportionate balance of forces in the Golan. The Chief of Staff, so he explained, knew only too well that the IDF could not block an all-out Syrian attack with such an order of battle. But Elazar accepted the intelligence estimate according to which war was unlikely. Hence, he avoided additional necessary reinforcements. The only way to change the situation was if Zeira and Shalev changed their estimate. Both refused.[58]

* * *

Tal was not the only GHQ member who thought that AMAN's estimation was wrong. The Intelligence Department of the Israeli Navy (IN) had followed the activities of the Egyptian navy for quite some time. During the holiday it gained a number of indicators on war preparations, including information about changes in the deployment of the Egyptian navy and certain preparations that had taken place in naval units along the coast of the Red Sea. But, for Col. Rami Luntz, the head of the IN Intelligence Department, the most important indicator was minefield clearing along the canal line, as observed by ground observation posts. He rejected AMAN's explanations according to which the Egyptians refresh the minefields. By his logic, such an activity, in parallel with the exercise, exposed the Egyptians to an Israeli attack.

On Sunday morning Luntz conducted an update discussion. On the basis of the intelligence that was presented to him, he said, "AMAN says an exercise and I say war." He repeated this assessment immediately afterward in a discussion with IN Commander Maj. Gen. Benjamin Telem. The latter accepted this assessment and issued the IN the necessary commands. The day after, Telem requested an urgent meeting with Zeira, in which he presented his intelligence officer's estimate. Zeira rejected it, noting that AMAN had better information than the navy.

Luntz's independent assessment derived, at least partially, from the fact that his department played only a minor role in the making of the dominant thesis about Egypt's minimal conditions to go to war. Hence, Luntz was less committed to this thesis. He also estimated, for years, that unless a diplomatic breakthrough took place, Egypt would go to war. Hence, he was more open to warning indicators in this direction. Finally, his background was as an operational officer, and he thought as one. Hence, political considerations were less relevant for him. When he gained a critical mass of war indicators, he gave a war warning. And since, *ex officio*, he was in charge of alerting the IN rather than the state of Israel, he invested most of his energy in this domain, giving up, a priori, any attempt to change the national estimate.[59]

* * *

AMAN too had officers who objected to the dominant estimate. The operation officer of SIGINT Unit 848, Lt. Col. Shabtai Brill, who *ex officio* read all the material that had been collected by his unit, was one of them. For him, the most significant indicator for Syrian offensive intentions was the advancement of the two Sukhoi squadrons on September 28. This move stood in clear contrast to the SOP as known since 1967. The Six Days War taught the Syrians to keep their most valuable aircraft, at times of tension, in rear airfields as a means to protect them. Their advancement to the combat area enabled them to attack Israel but, similarly, exposed them to Israeli destruction, especially since the airfield of Dumair (in contrast to T-4 in the north), lacked fortified hangers.

This Syrian move, combined with additional warning indicators that had been collected by Unit 848, led Brill to a series of professional debates with the Unit commander, Col. Yoel Ben-Porat, who refused to accept this information as a war warning.[60] Brill decided to bypass his commander. On September 30, he conducted a few hours tête-à-tête talk with Brig. Gen. Zvika Lidor, the DMI's deputy for Organization and Management, in which he described and analyzed the available information, which clearly indicated war. Lidor, who *ex officio* had no access to the information collected in AMAN, became convinced that something should be done about it. On October 2, he met with Arie Shalev and pointed out a number of indicators that implied war. Shalev rejected his estimate. Then, Lidor, together with the head of AMAN's Collection Department, Col. Menahem Digli, went to speak with Zeira, who was sick at home. Their attempt to convince the DMI to change his assessment failed as well. All that Lidor succeeded to do was to advance a reconnaissance flight in the canal sector — a move that would become highly significant.[61]

* * *

On the evening hours of September 30, additional warning indicators arrived: the Syrians continued to reinforce the front line with more tanks and SAM batteries, the emergency deployment included now also the second defense line, and all leave in the army was called off. Branch 5's document that reported this information stated: "The present emergency deployment is unprecedented." And yet, next to this, came a more calming section, added by the Research Department's command:

> Despite the additional reinforcement, our estimate that the reinforced deployment was taken because of Syrian apprehensions of an Israeli attack, remains. . . . We do not assess that this might imply an independent Syrian military initiative, despite this morning's information that indicated such a possibility. Such an initiative is possible only if taken in parallel with an Egyptian one. Though there is a state of alert in the Egyptian army, it is not connected, as far as we know, to an offensive initiative, but to Egyptian apprehension of an Israeli initiative, and a large-scale staff exercise in the Egyptian army.[62]

* * *

The process that began in late August intensified during the beginning of October, when the Egyptian Tahrir 41 exercise commenced. The intensive events that took place in the following days demand its discussion on a day-by-day basis.

Chapter 11

Monday, October 1, 1973

On the late evening hours of September 30, a message from a Mossad agent who was considered reliable arrived in AMAN's Research Department. It said that on October 1 a large-scale Egyptian Canal crossing exercise would start, that it would end in a real crossing, and that the Syrians would also join the war. Egypt's War Minister was to be in charge of the operation. Its goal was the crossing of the canal and the occupation of the territory up to the Gidi and the Mitla Passes. Its opening phase included air strikes against airfields and oil facilities in Sinai, aimed at triggering a superpower intervention to start diplomatic negotiations on Israel's withdrawal from the Sinai. Additional information indicated irregular activity in the Egyptian army: promotion examinations for thousands of officers, which were to take place in early October, were postponed; reserve soldiers, including soldiers who finished their regular service in July, were called to service; a massive movement to the front of mechanized divisions, bridging units, and paratrooper and airborne units, was underway; Egypt's anti-aircraft layout had been reinforced; Cairo's international airport was closed without explanation a day earlier [probably September 29]; and senior Egyptian officials hinted that war might break out.[1]

Ex post facto, it is evident that all this information was true: On October 1, the Tahrir 41 exercise—the main means to deceive Israel about Egyptian war plans—had begun. The start of the exercise constituted, from the perspective of Egypt's war planners, the beginning of offensive operations. The war plan, as reported by the source, was that of "improved granite-2"—the plan to reach the passes east of the canal—which was the real operational plan as far as most Egyptians that knew that war was under way were concerned. The war's target was, indeed, to inaugurate the conditions for a diplomatic process. And, as AMAN knew also from other sources, mobilization of reserve soldiers and a massive force advancement toward the front, had already started. The reports about the postponement of promotion examinations and the closure of Cairo's international airport were of special interest. Obviously, the staff officers who prepared the Egyptian army's working plan were aware of the fact that the date of the examinations fell on that of Tahrir 41. Hence, there was no reason to assume that the mere conduct of a routine exercise was a sufficient cause for this postponement. The opposite was true. Only a far more important and irregular event could break the army's SOP, postpone the examinations and, thus, delay also the promotion of thousands of officers. The airport's closure indicated another exceptional activity, though its nature was less clear. Perhaps this was the reason why AMAN did not report only this but also similar events.[2]

Since the information came from a source with a good record, and since the interpretation given to it was that the Egyptian attack was scheduled to start the next morning, the message caused concern in AMAN. The head of the Research Department, who received it upon its arrival, immediately called the head of Branch 6, and the head of the Research Branch in the IAF's Intelligence Division, Lt. Col. Yehuda Porat, to check the combat-readiness status of the Egyptian army and air force. Both came back reporting that there were no indicators for an immediate action. Hence, Shalev concluded that the warning was groundless. He nevertheless ordered Bandman to report it to the head of Branch 5, Lt. Col. Avi Yaari, to add that it was analyzed on the background of an Egyptian state of readiness, and that there were no signs the army was ready for war.[3] Bandman informed Yaari that the specific source warned that the Egyptian military preparations were for war in cooperation with Syria, and that war would start, under the cover of an exercise, on the morning of October 1. According to Yaari, Bandman added that it did not change the Research Department's assessment that the preparations were for exercise and not for war.[4]

Shalev also informed his superior, DMI Zeira, about the new warning, and after his experts told him that Egypt was not ready to launch war immediately, he informed Zeira about it. But, in light of the source's quality, he suggested the DMI report to the Chief of Staff about the warning. He also suggested advising him to raise the state of readiness in the Suez and Golan front lines, and in the air force, toward a possible attack at dawn.[5]

Zeira declined. Throughout this night he did not tell his superiors that a reliable Mossad source warned that the next day Egypt and Syria would launch war. He reported to Elazar about it only when meeting him in the corridor, when both made their way to Dayan's office for the third (and last) discussion in the series of strategic discussions that started on September 17. In a joking tone, he told Dayan, Elazar, and their assistants about the source that warned that war would start on that day, and about the havoc that it caused (see below) in the Northern Command. Zeira also emphasized how his correct assessment that no war would break out saved his superiors's sleep.[6] When the three men entered the meeting hall, the Commander of the Northern Command got hold of the Chief of Staff Military Assistant, Lt. Col. Avner Shalev, inquiring why the Chief of Staff was not in his office during the late-night hours. To Shalev's question regarding why Elazar was expected to be there, Hofi explained that he had received a warning that war might break out in the morning hours and that he wanted to discuss it with the Chief of Staff.[7]

* * *

The warning that Hofi received made its way through informal channels, since the formal ones had been blocked by DMI Zeira. The process was triggered by the head of Branch 5. Upon receiving the warning and the assessment that it was groundless, Yaari reported it, by his own initiative, to the intelligence officer of the Northern Command, Lt. Col. Hagai Mann. Emphasizing the linkage between the Egyptian intention to launch war and the Syrian decision to join it, as well as the possibility that it might start the next morning, Yaari added that in his opinion the Command should raise its state of alert. Mann reported this information to Hofi. The latter decided, by his own initiative, to use a surprise mobilization exercise of reserve tank Brigade 179, which took place that night, as a means to increase the Command's order of battle. Consequently, the reserve soldiers, who were to be released within hours, remained near their tanks throughout the night. In the morning, Hofi spoke with DMI Zeira, who told him that AMAN had not issued a war warning. It was only then that he released most (but not all) of the reserve soldiers.[8]

Yaari's initiative carried a personal cost. Upon learning about it, Zeira instructed Shalev to rebuke him for expressing, outside AMAN, an estimate that contradicted the authorized assessment. According to Shalev, he rebuked Yaari for his unauthorized proposal to raise the Northern Command's state of readiness. Whatever the reason for it was, the incident had a clear result: It lessened Yaari's motivation to stick to his estimate that Syria might be gearing for war. Another event that took place on that day must have had a similar effect. At the end of a discussion in the DMI's office, the head of Branch 6 said, in a decisive tone, that the positive outcome of the previous night's events was that everyone realized now that the military activity in Egypt was solely connected to the Tahrir exercise.[9] It is doubtful if everyone present accepted this stand. But it is certain that such attitude did not encourage open discussions in the Research Department.

* * *

Zeira's decision to avoid the immediate dissemination of the warning caused a reaction, at least from the Minister of Defense. Dayan's assistants felt that since this was not the first time that Zeira had made such a move, something should be done about it. Accordingly, Dayan sent a note to Zeira during the GHQ staff meeting, demanding to know why he had not received the warning on time. Zeira responded as follows:

Moshe,
1. I received the message by phone at 0230.
2. The message was a first version and, so far, we do not have a complete version.
3. Throughout the night we made an assessment, checked all the information that arrived last night and in recent days ... and toward the morning hours we reached the conclusion that the message was baseless and that it was an exercise.
4. Hence, I did not report anything to the Chief of Staff and the Defense Minister. In order to avoid telling you: "There is information but I don't trust it" (by the way, in recent days we have had a number of such messages).
5. I reported the information this morning, during the General Staff meeting, and distributed it through regular channels.
6. In principle, I do not think that information, which by our assessment is baseless, should be disseminated during the night. This can be done in the morning, together with its assessment.[10]

Zeira's response is a telling story of his perception of his functional responsibility. After all, the source was considered as "a highly serious one." The information that he had provided went far beyond a mere war warning and included good indications that unusual military activity was taking place in Egypt. And others in AMAN—not only Yaari, but also the head of the Collection Department, Col. Menahem Digli, and the commander of the agency's SIGINT section, Unit 848, Col. Yoel Ben-Porat, who received a telephone briefing on this warning during that night—took it very seriously.[11] The Mossad considered it serious as well. Its headquarters sent the information that same night to the head of Golda Meir's office, Eli Mizrahi, who personally brought it at about 0330 to Yigal Allon, the Prime Minister's replacement while she was abroad.[12] And, AMAN's No. 1 analyst, Arie Shalev, thought, even after concluding that it was wrong, that Zeira should call the Chief of Staff and advise him to raise the IDF's alert.

In contrast to all these, the DMI—the sole linkage between AMAN, whose prime task was to provide Israel with a war warning, and the policy-makers, who had to act on the basis of such information—avoided disseminating this critical information. By his own account, he did so in order to "save" the night's sleep of the two persons whose prime responsibility was to ensure that Israel would not be surprised. The fact that neither of them took harsh measures in response tells a great deal also about Israel's organizational culture and normative behavior in the most sensitive domain of the nation's security.

* * *

Zeira's confidence that war was unlikely was also expressed during the General Staff meeting that took place on Monday morning. He reported that a Tahrir exercise was to start that morning and last until October 7, and he mentioned that according to some sources the exercise was a cover for war. He "definitely" rejected this possibility, partly on the basis of the experience that had been gained in April, when similar action was taken and war had not broken out. "The Syrian deployment," Zeira added, "is the largest we have seen during last year, and, today, we learned that another brigade was on its way to the front."[13] Zeira admitted that according to important sources (i.e., King Hussein), this deployment was built for war. But, since Syria would not launch war alone, and there were no indicators that Egypt geared for war, the best explanation for the Syrian preparations was fear of Israeli action. In response to a question, Zeira noted that the Egyptians and the Syrians cheated each other about their war intentions; each knew that the other cheated but they nevertheless continued their discussions about war.

The Chief of Staff focused on the northern front. He accepted AMAN's estimate that a Syrian independent war initiative was illogical, adding:

> Is it plausible that Syria will wake up one morning and, without Egyptian assistance, will occupy the Golan Heights? I don't think this is plausible. I think that for us the result would be unpleasant at the first stage, and there will be casualties in the settlements along the border. It will be unpleasant, but the final outcome could be catastrophic for the Syrians since, if this is not a planned war but a one-time Syrian outburst, it will take us 24–48 hours to destroy the Syrian army and cause havoc in Syria, and this is so obvious that it voids any [Syrian] illusion. Therefore, I estimate a sudden Syrian attack in the Golan as improbable.[14]

But, the source of the problem in the north was insufficient tactical early warning and the lack of an antitank obstacle. Hence, despite the low probability for a Syrian general offensive, there was no other choice but to strengthen the Golan with additional forces. Elazar noted that a move in this direction had been taken already and that he was ready to send two additional tank battalions if any new warning arrived, in order to "prevent a catastrophe." Having no early warning meant that even such a large order of battle might be insufficient to prevent a Syrian attempt to occupy a military stronghold or a civilian settlement near the border. Ending his estimate of the situation, Elazar added that the Syrians had avoided such action since 1967. This endnote did not calm Dayan. His main worry continued to be the possibility that the "Syrians would enter our settlements and this would be a disaster." Accordingly, he instructed the IDF command to look for a better solution to the problem of a local attack without any prior warning.[15]

In continuation with the Chief of Staff's order a day earlier, the G (general staff) branch GHQ issued on October 1, "Ashur" ("Assyria") order No. 1. According to this order, twenty additional tank crews of Brigade 7 were deployed in the Golan. The total reinforcement amounted now to forty-two tank crews that manned the tanks of Brigade 179. Additional reinforcements, including a 155mm gun battalion, were to follow. A tank battalion of Brigade 179 (that was mobilized during the previous night's exercise) was to stay on alert until replaced by the crews of Brigade 7. Arrangements were made to reinforce the Golan front with additional units, including a second tank battalion from Brigade 7.

The October 1 reinforcement was the second of its kind — the first took place on New Year's Eve. From now on, until the third reinforcement that would take place on October 5, military activity in this sector would focus on extensive mine-laying and the buildup of an antitank ditch.[16]

* * *

October 1 saw an increase in the state of alert in other IDF units as well. Most important among them was Unit 848, whose commander, Col. Yoel Ben-Porat, has defined as "AMAN's central warning unit." The raise in 848's state of alert was an outcome of the "summer/winter" SOP, which was built on the basis of the experience that had been gained during the Soviet invasion of Czechoslovakia in August 1968. Since all preparations for the Soviet operation were disguised as an exercise, AMAN initiated a new procedure, according to which, whenever a large-scale exercise near the Israeli border began, the units of 848 along that border were to enter a state of war readiness. This SOP served two goals: to create conditions that would allow units to function effectively if war erupted, and to improve their collection capabilities by transition to more intensive working shifts.

Col. Ben-Porat — who planned to accompany the same day the IDF ombudsman, Maj. Gen. (Res.) Chaim Laskov, on a visit to Um Hashiba (code name "Babylon"), the unit's central base in Sinai — called his staff officers for an early-morning work meeting. By his account, it was a tense and dramatic meeting, an outcome of the war warning that had arrived a few hours earlier. Other participants remember a calm and a rather routine discussion, focused on the unit's raised state of alert because of the Tahrir 41 exercise rather than the war warning, of which they were not aware at all. This contrast involves other issues as well. While Ben-Porat describes how the "Babylon" base was at a full state of war alert, others remember that on the very same day they saw a routine exchange of commanders in some central units of 848. One of them involved the commander of "Babylon," who returned to Tel Aviv with Ben-Porat and Laskov. Obviously, if Ben-Porat had been certain that war was coming, he would not have replaced the experienced commander of his most important base in Sinai with a less experienced officer.[17]

Some initial measures to increase the state of alert in the Southern Command were taken as well. Here too, the trigger was the warning of the night before, which made its way by informal channels to the Command's Commander, Maj. Gen. Shmuel Gonen. Gonen ordered the cancellation of leave for tank and artillery crews. The head of the Operation Department in the G Branch, Brig. Gen. Yaacov Stern, who had to approve the order, was reluctant to do so. He issued the order only after Gonen made it clear that he would wake up the Chief of Staff if his demand were not met.[18] Consequently, the order of battle in the Southern Command reached now 187 tanks and seven artillery batteries. Arrangements were made to reinforce the number of tanks to 300 and the artillery by two additional battalions.[19] Another indicator for the concern in the south was an approval given by the Chief of Staff to carry a reconnaissance sortie in the canal sector. The mission was delayed by two days because of heavy clouds and the low priority that had been accorded to it by the IAF.[20]

* * *

As if to justify the decision to raise the state of alert in the Southern Command, another warning arrived the same day. The unidentified source reported that Egypt had decided to launch an operation whose goal was to occupy the Suez Canal and reach the Gidi and Mitla Passes, in order to stimulate a superpower intervention, which would bring about the opening of the canal and the initiation of a political process. The source reported that all the units, including bridging units, were moving from the Cairo area to the front line, and that gaps had been opened in the western bank of the canal in order to enable the laying of bridges. According to the source, however, no decision had been made yet about the operation's D-day.[21]

Even this warning, which mainly confirmed that of the previous night, was insufficient to cause a crack in AMAN's solid assessment of Egypt's war intention. The officer responsible for this estimate, Lt. Col. Yona Bandman, explained years later that he did not relate any significance to such warnings since he regarded them as a distorted echo coming from sources who saw military preparations for an exercise and thought that they were for war. The head of Branch 6's political section, Mr. Albert Sudai, thought differently. For quite some time he had been certain that Egypt saw no alternative to war. On the basis of the available information, he reached the conclusion—which he told to anyone ready to listen—that Egypt was gearing for war and that war would start on Yom Kippur. The head of the military section in Branch 6, Maj. Yaacov Rosenfeld—an experienced analyst of Egypt's military affairs who became the section's head only days before the war started—was less decisive than Sudai. But, in the coming days, he would become increasingly convinced that war rather than exercise was the true cause for the Egyptian activity. Yet all attempts, especially by Sudai, to insert into AMAN's documents an assessment that was different from the dominant one, ended in failure.[22]

In this sense, the warnings fell victim to a tragic combination between the beliefs of AMAN's prime analyst of Egyptian (and indirectly also Syrian) war intentions, and incoming information that contradicted them. On the one hand, there was Bandman's persistent estimate that the Egyptians did not perceive themselves as capable of launching a war. This view fit very well his tendency to rank HUMINT sources, in general, as of very low quality and to always doubt their credibility.[23] On the other hand, there was the fact that the high-quality warnings about Arab war intentions came, mostly, from human sources. The outcome was the nullification of the warnings. Combined with Bandman's high status in the Research Department, it partially explains why much of the relevant information that had been collected on the eve of the war, was lost.

* * *

AMAN did not save its calming assessment solely for itself or for its Israeli consumers. In response to the CIA dispatch about Syria's military layout and war intention, which arrived September 29–30, AMAN's analysts confirmed that they had similar information but rejected the possibility that Syria was gearing for war. Instead, they defined the Syrian war plan as a "master plan," which implied a Syrian general interest in the occupation of the Golan but no concrete preparations in this direction. The logic behind this estimate—as explained to the CIA—was simple: The Syrians know that they cannot launch a war by themselves and that Egypt is not going to join them. Hence, the alarmist information might indicate, at most, preparations to carry out a limited attack.

* * *

The series of rather stormy events of Monday, October 1, yielded mixed results. On one hand, the warning that arrived the night before, which (unlike

Hussein's warning) had received wide distribution though mostly through informal channels, increased the number of officers in AMAN and in the IDF who were now aware of the possibility of war. It initiated a process that would lead to a significant increase in the state of alert on the canal front on the eve of the war and contributed to another reinforcement in the Golan. On the other hand, the interpretation that had been given to this warning, that war was to start the same day, combined with the fact that war did not break out, led to a complete erosion of its value. This end result—a typical outcome of the cry-wolf syndrome—also influenced the balance of forces between those in the Research Department seen as alarmists and their opponents. Those who believed that war was not imminent felt that, again, they were right. Some alarmists were now less confident than before about the validity of their judgment. And, this had a negative impact on AMAN's ability to properly digest the war information that arrived in the following days.

Chapter 12

Tuesday, October 2, 1973

Tuesday, October 2, was calmer than the previous day. It saw only one warning concerning Egypt's war intentions. In essence, it said: There is an intention to attack Israel; the Egyptian army is in full emergency status; the operation will start as an exercise, but according to all available indications it will turn into war. The message was not disseminated to the Minister of Defense or the Prime Minister.[1] It is unclear whether the Chief of Staff received it.

At noon, the Research Department distributed its daily review of the situation:

Egypt
A. Activity in the canal front is regular. Between October 2–4, advancement of ammunition, supply, and equipment to the forces of the northern sector of the Red Sea Command is expected. It is possible that this is to be done in the framework of a logistic exercise.
B. On the night of October 1–2 about 120 vehicles carrying crossing equipment moved from west of Cairo to the east. About 25 vehicles carrying crossing and bridging equipment were located at the Port Said sector. A few days ago, about 40 vehicles with similar equipment moved from the Helwan area to Cairo. It is possible that these activities are being carried out in the framework of an exercise of the GHQ bridging brigades.
C. The War Minister authorized officers to participate this year as well in the pilgrimage to Mecca during the last week of Ramadan (the second half of October), so, at this stage, routine at the Egyptian army is kept.

Syria
A. On the night of October 1–2 the following moves were located:
  1. The GHQ bridging battalion or part of it, probably left its regular base in Homs and is underway now.
  2. Armored Brigade 47 continues its movement. According to one piece of information it might have reached Sweida.
  3. Units from Armored Division 3 are on the move from their deployment area in Kteifa.
B. In general, routine activity was kept in the front line. Notably, Syrian soldiers in light battle order were observed in the northern sector, and in the central sector camouflage nets were removed from some of the medium-gun batteries.
C. 14–18 "Sukhoi" planes moved today from T-4 airport to Blay, and it is possible that some or all of them are of the "Sukhoi SU-20" type. The advancement of the Sukhoi planes to Blay and Dumair enables them to attack targets in northern Israel, in a low-altitude profile. We estimate that this move was taken as part of a defensive state of alert—whose goal is to prepare a means to attack Israeli targets in response to a possible Israeli action—and also for warning purposes. Air ammunition was supplied to bases.[2]

In addition to this review, the Research Department disseminated two additional documents. The first reviewed works to improve descents to the canal in the 3rd Army sector. It summarized reports from observation posts along the front on preparations of about forty out of the eighty-five descents—primarily the break of sandbag walls, which blocked the way to the water. The report mentioned similar works that were carried out in the northern sector and explained that they "aimed to create a quick and convenient approach to the water and prevent the sinking of vehicles into the sand during the crossing operation." Then, the document explained what stood behind this intensive activity:

> It is possible that the "awakening" in the issue of crossing descents in the 3rd Army sector (in parallel to extensive preparations that had been taken recently and which continue to be taken in the 2nd Army sector—adding ramps and descents to the canal and the laying of new approach roads), is being carried out in the framework of the inter-arm exercise that is taking place now in the Egyptian army.[3]

If, in the domain of Egyptian affairs, the calming assessment was formulated by the head of Branch 6 in coordination with the head of the Research Department, assessment of Syrian war intentions involved significant disagreements between the head of Branch 5 and his superiors. The document disseminated on October 2 vividly reflected this conflict. Based on the CIA warning that arrived three days earlier, it described the Syrian war plan—similar to the plan that Branch 5 had disseminated six months earlier—and assessed its probability. But the assessment of Branch 5 went through significant changes by the Division's top echelon. When the document's consumers received it, it included three points that nullified its warning value: First, the Syrians do not believe that they can, by themselves, conduct a successful offensive to occupy the Golan, due to their military weakness, especially in the air. Second, there is no sign of Egyptian readiness to renew fire—a necessary condition, from the Syrian perspective, to achieve a significant military success. Third, there are no domestic or external pressures for a Syrian offensive, though a response for their defeat in the September 13 incident is a different case.[4]

* * *

In a discussion that took place in the Research Department the same day, the dominant thesis was attacked from various angles. One involved information that implied that the Egyptians had advanced 1,500 tons of live ammunition from emergency storage near Cairo to the front. This enormous logistical effort, which employed 300 lorries, was dangerous not only because of the nature of the cargo but also because the lorries were overloaded. Moreover, a follow-up of the convoy's track showed that in contrast to regular practice and patterns of an exercise, checkpoints along the route of the convoy did not pre-receive information about its coming. The head of the Research Department, one of the more decisive supporters of the dominant thesis, raised a number of questions about this convoy, but he received no satisfactory answers. Others who were more worried about the possibility of war, such as Unit 848's Operations Officer, Shabtai Brill, regarded the convoy as a clear warning indicator for war preparations.

Other question marks involved the Syrian front. The report that Brigade 47 left its base in Homs and was underway southward, reminded Maj. Amos Gilboa of the Basic Department, which accidentally participated in the discussion, that this relatively new Brigade was planned, according to the Syrian war plan, to join infantry Division 5 and attack the Golan's southern sector. On the basis of this and some other pieces of information, he tried to undermine the validity of the dominant thesis. Here, he met a sharp response from Arie Shalev, who had extensive experience in Syrian affairs. Gilboa's attempt failed. The head of Branch 5, who could support his estimate, was not present in the discussion.[5]

Another issue, which due to unclear reasons, did not receive the attention it deserved, involved the volume of the wireless traffic in the framework of the

Tahrir 41 exercise. In earlier exercises, Unit 848 received hundreds of messages a day—a typical traffic for a large-scale exercise to cross the canal and to occupy Sinai. But, the volume of traffic in the present case was far smaller—a few dozen messages a day. This issue of "the dog that did not bark" was raised in internal discussions in 848 as an additional proof that the information from the canal front did not suit the known patterns of an exercise. The unit's commander, Col. Ben-Porat, argued post factum that he instructed the head of Branch 10, Lt. Col. Yossi Zeira, who represented 848 in the Research Department's discussions, to report to Arie Shalev on this issue and some other warning indicators. Only after the war did he learn that Zeira (a cousin of DMI Eli Zeira), did not say a word about it to Shalev.[6] One may wonder, however, why Ben-Porat did not act more aggressively. In his memoirs, he claims that he had been certain, at least since Sunday night, that AMAN's dominant thesis was invalid. His senior position entitled him the means to express this view to his commanders, but even by his own account he did so only forty hours before war broke. This fact and some other patterns of his unit's operations in the coming days indicate that at this stage Ben-Porat was far from certain that the Arab military activity was for war.

* * *

The internal conflict in AMAN left no mark on the discussion that the Chief of Staff and the Defense Minister held the same day in the latter's office. As far as they were aware, AMAN's official assessment, as reflected in the documents that they had received and the reports that they had heard, was sharp and clear. Elazar expressed it at the beginning of the discussion when presenting his intelligence estimate:

> We checked it again and concluded—and we can say it definitely—that what we have in Egypt is an exercise.... In Syria, despite [the alarmist information] there are no signs that they plan to open fire. There have been changes in the deployment of the air force, which we can regard as a war deployment or a better deployment. I don't have an explanation for this deployment. Either they are afraid that we will initiate [hostilities] or they plan to, and my assessment is that they are not going to open fire.[7]

At least partially, Elazar's certainty that Egypt did not gear for war relied on an inspection that he had held earlier that day of the operational status of AMAN's special means of collection. These means were built to yield clear indications for war in case preparation for it was under way. Elazar knew these means well. On Tuesday, perhaps even on Monday, he asked DMI Zeira if

AMAN activated these specific means. Zeira answered in the affirmative.[8] His answer, however, did not reflect reality. The special collection means had not been activated yet, and Zeira knew it very well.

We shall return to this highly significant issue in order to understand the tragedy of Yom Kippur. At this stage, however, it is important to understand that Elazar's certain answer to Dayan relied also on the belief that the means, which on some occasions had been referred to as "Israel's national security policy" were operational and that, hence, surprising Israel became far more difficult.

The Chief of Staff estimated that the recent reinforcement in the Golan—which brought the armored force there to 111 tanks—combined with three battalions, which were ready to be flown from Sinai to the Golan to man the equipped tanks of Brigade 179, sufficed to meet any Syrian challenge short of war. He also estimated, as he told Dayan, that "it is impossible that we won't know if the Syrians intend to occupy the Golan."[9]

Dayan was more suspicious about Syrian intentions, perhaps since his main concern was a Syrian limited move. This time, however, he did not ignore the possibility of war. He raised a number of questions about the Syrian emergency deployment and the information that said that they intended to launch war. He ended by asking the Chief of Staff to prepare a document presenting his estimate of the situation on the war's probability. Specifically, he wanted answers to a number of questions:

> Can Syria go to war without Egypt, and do weather conditions at this time of the year allow such a war initiative? What is the [Egyptian and Syrian] deployment, and what is the difference between their present and past layouts, in terms of artillery, air, and tanks? What is the essence of the available information including its sources? And, also, our deployment including reinforcements, e.g., do we lay mines and do other things?[10]

Answering Dayan's last question, Elazar said that large-scale mine laying works had already started in the Golan and the digging of an antitank ditch would start soon. From the fact that Dayan noted that under the present circumstances the government was likely to approve additional steps, including the paving of an essential road,[11] it is clear that while he saw the present threat as an immediate one, he was also concerned with finding a fundamental solution to the problem concerning lack of warning in the Golan.

Dayan's request for an independent estimate of the situation was legitimate though untypical for the patterns of working relations between the Chief of Staff and himself. It certainly reflected his concern about the situation. But Dayan wanted the document ready by next morning, prior to a discussion with the prime minister, who returned from her traumatic meeting with the Austrian

Chancellor. This intensive timetable did not allow Elazar to conduct an orderly independent staff work. Moreover, in order to do it properly, the Chief of Staff had to read, by himself, a large quantity of raw material, which, at the time, he did not have on his desk. And, in any event, AMAN had to decide which material would go to Elazar and which would not. It is rather probable that the same biases that influenced AMAN's analysts to aim their estimates toward a certain direction would have influenced them when selecting the material for the Chief of Staff. Hence, though an independent estimate of the situation was vital at this stage, the fundamental conditions dictated another solution. Consequently, Elazar's assistant, Avner Shalev, and the head of the Research Department, Arie Shalev, prepared the same night, by cutting and pasting from various AMAN documents, a new document entitled "The deployment of the Syrian army and our forces in the Syrian front."

According to the document, the Syrian deployment, at that time, was exceptional in comparison to the past: 750–850 tanks (of which 600 in the first line of defense) compared to 250 tanks in May; 550 artillery pieces (of which 370 in the first line of defense) compared to 180 pieces in May; and thirty-one SAM batteries between Damascus and the front, compared to two in May. The document related high probability to the possibility that this deployment was built because of a growing Syrian apprehension of an Israeli strike. Lower probability was given to the possibility that it was aimed at a Syrian response to the September 13 incident. As far as it is known, the document did not relate at all to the possibility of a general war in coordination with Egypt. The Chief of Staff signed it off-hand. It was submitted to Dayan on the morning of October 3.[12]

The Agranat Commission criticized Elazar for failing to build an independent estimate of the situation through an independent analysis of raw intelligence material, a more critical analysis of AMAN's documents, and personal visits to the front lines.[13] Though the commission's criticism was on target, one cannot ignore the fact that the Chief of Staff was totally dependent on the intelligence that he received from AMAN. Ex post facto, he would complain that most of the warnings did not arrive at his desk. He was certainly right about this, which explains why he was not aware that a grave situation was developing in the south. But the stream of intelligence raw material did not shrink during the days before the war; it started one year earlier, when Zeira entered office. The Chief of Staff had ample time to change this pattern, but he did not. And this was his own responsibility.

Chapter 13

Wednesday, October 3, 1973

Two main events highlight Wednesday, October 3. The first was the meeting between Egyptian War Minister Ahmad Ismail and Syrian President Hafez Asad in Damascus, during which they reached an agreement with regard to the war's opening hour. The second was the discussion that was held at Golda Meir's residence upon her return to Israel. This was the first time that the nation's top political and military echelons gathered to discuss the situation. Information concerning Egyptian and Syrian military deployment and intentions continued to flow throughout the day.

* * *

The Egyptian delegation that arrived on Wednesday morning in Damascus included the War Minister and General Bahi al-Din Naufal, the General Secretary of the Supreme Commission of the Egyptian and Syrian Armed Forces—the same body that was convened secretly in Alexandria on August 22–23 in order to furnish the operational coordination of the war. Immediately upon arrival they convened with Syria's War Minister Mustafa Tlas and Chief of Staff Yusuf Shakour. During the meeting, the Syrians explained that they were not ready to start the war on October 6 and demanded that it be delayed for forty-eight hours.[1] According to Heikal, they were surprised by Egypt's intention to go to war within three days and maintained that they needed five days in order to empty the oil tanks of Homs[2]—a strategic target that now, when the SAM batteries that protected it had been moved to the front line, had become more vulnerable.

The H-hour constituted another bone of contention. The Syrian Chief of Staff wanted to start fire at sunrise, while the Egyptians preferred the late afternoon or twilight time. No doubt, each side wanted to fight when the Israeli defenders were blinded by the sun. The Egyptians, moreover, wanted to initiate fire as close as possible to the night hours—timing that would enable their forces to cross the canal under the cover of darkness and, thus, to neutralize the IAF's efficiency.[3] According to Heikal, Ismail and Naufal raised a number of arguments why a late H-hour was desirable. The most interesting one was that the morning fog might prevent the Syrian pilots from hitting the IAF's bases of Ramat David and Ekron.[4] This is an interesting argument, since it indicates that the Syrians exaggerated when they described their first strike plan to their allies. Syrian planes did not attack any IAF base—during the war's opening strikes, or later.

Both sides agreed to work out their disagreements in a meeting with President Asad. During the meeting, Ismail made it clear that delaying D-day might considerably hamper the chance to achieve surprise, especially since Egypt's Middle East News Agency had reported, by mistake, that the state of readiness of the Second and Third Armies in the canal front had been raised.[5] At the same time, however, he agreed to reach a compromise about H-hour. He suggested that it be 1400. Asad accepted the Egyptian stand on both issues.[6]

Three important issues can be derived from this account. The first involves the level and the quality of the Egyptian–Syrian coordination for war, which, by Egyptian accounts, was highly fragile. The notion that the Egyptian army would give up its prime means to cover its war preparations—the Tahrir 41 exercise that was scheduled to end on October 7—and would launch war on the 8, thus losing the element of surprise, was groundless. Nevertheless, the Syrians suggested (and for unclear reasons) that this should be done. The delay in fixing the coordinated H-hour until three days before the war, especially when both sides were aware of their disagreement about it, is another indication of a low level of coordination. Indeed, the diplomatic and military conduct of Egypt and Syria during the war shows that apart from their coordination of the joint inauguration of war, they failed to synchronize even one additional operational move.

The second point has to do with the last-minute change of H-hour. This change, as we will later see, had a major impact on Israel's lack of readiness once war started. According to the Egyptian plans in possession of AMAN, firing was to commence toward the evening, as a means to reduce the threat of the IAF during the war's first and most critical hours. The fact that it started four hours earlier added another dimension of chaos to the already dire situation in which the IDF found itself on Yom Kippur. In this sense, from the Egyptian perspective, the unplanned last minute change in H-hour was actually a blessing in disguise. In contrast, it seems that it had a negative impact on the Syrians' ability to achieve their operational goals according to their original plan.

And, finally, the mistaken public report that the state of readiness of the 2nd and 3rd Armies had been raised—a report that Ismail used to convince the Syrians how important it was to adhere to the original timetable—is also of interest. The Egyptians, according to Heikal, regarded this disclosure as a dangerous development that might expose the looming threat to the Israelis.[7] In actuality, it reflects how wrong they were in understanding Israel's intelligence capabilities. The fear that a message in the open press would be the missing link that would enable Israel to grasp the imminent strike indicates the Egyptian underestimation of Israel's collection capabilities. The Mossad and AMAN provided, as we now know, far better information about Egyptian and Syrian war preparations. In this sense, the Egyptians clearly overestimated Israel's ability to grasp, on the basis of available information, Arab war intentions. Here, at least, they had a chance to see how their military preparations were assessed in Israel. Under the headline "No tension was observed yesterday on the banks of the Canal," the daily *Haaretz* reported on October 3 on the military situation in the south. The imprint of AMAN's analysts can be clearly seen in this piece:

> Despite the message from Cairo that a call for a state of readiness had been made yesterday in the Egyptian army units along the Suez Canal, no tension was observed and no change took place on either of the banks of the Canal. The estimation is that the Egyptian announcements were aimed at assisting Syria, which had recently concentrated her army in her border with Israel, because of an unexplained fear of an Israeli action. AP news agency reported from Cairo during the morning hours that the Middle East News Agency had announced a state of alert in the Egyptian army positioned around the Suez Canal. The announcement pointed out that this state of readiness was declared after Israel mobilized army units. Military sources denied yesterday that the IDF concentrated forces along the border with Egypt. Despite the Egyptian announcement, no tension was felt yesterday along the Canal and it seems that no changes in the deployment and state of alert took place there. The Egyptian soldiers were observed to be behaving routinely. The estimate in Israel is that the Egyptians leaked the information about the readiness of their army, in order to provide the Syrians with "moral support." Last week, the Syrians conducted changes in their deployment of military units, which were advanced to their border with Israel. In light of this, the Minister of Defense warned Damascus against provoking Israel. It seems that following this warning and publications about Israel's alert in the Golan, Cairo decided to announce that her army is also ready.[8]

* * *

The participants of the meeting that was convened at the Prime Minister's home in Jerusalem were, in part, more concerned. Dayan, who initiated the meeting along with Golda Meir's confidant, Yisrael Galili, made it clear that he wanted to share responsibility, especially with regard to the civil population in the Golan.[9] It seems that Dayan did not consider the Prime Minister's deputy, Yigal Allon, who replaced her while she was abroad, as an appropriate partner for sharing this responsibility.

In addition to Meir and Dayan, the other participants were Allon and Galili, the Chief of Staff, the commander of the IAF, the head of AMAN's Research Department (who stood in for DMI Zeira, who was sick), and their assistants.[10] Dayan, as the one who asked to convene the meeting, opened by explaining that his demand was because "of changes in the fronts, primarily in Syria and, to some extent, in Egypt." In his sharp tone, he explained the source of his concern: In Egypt there is an enemy, but between this enemy and the settlements there is the Suez Canal and the desert. In Jordan, there are settlements, but no enemy. "In Syria, we have an enemy and we do not have [such] an obstacle. In any event it is not a serious one, and we have settlements there," he said. "Therefore, this is a constant and special source of concern." Consequently, Dayan wanted the discussion to focus on three issues: the Syrian, but also the Egyptian, military deployment; the available information about their intention to renew fighting; and Israel's military preparations.[11]

The head of AMAN's Research Department presented the intelligence estimate. Shalev opened with a reminder of (though not by name) Hussein's warning of about a week earlier and then described the Syrian plan "to occupy the whole of the Golan, by five divisions, five infantry brigades, and two armored brigades." Then, he mentioned "concerning information about Egypt: There is one piece of information from one source that arrived on September 30 that on the morning of October 1 Egypt plans to attack in Sinai when the Syrians will act, simultaneously, in the Golan."[12] Here, he added a somewhat unclear statement: "In the material that has been received from reliable source, it doesn't say 'war' but an exercise."[13] It is possible that Shalev related to AMAN's interpretation of a follow-up debrief of the source, which implied that he did not mean to say that war would start on October 1, but that the exercise might, under certain circumstances, turn into a war. At this point, Shalev turned to describe the Syrian deployment:

> On the Syrian front there is an emergency deployment. It is a deployment in which large parts of the Syrian army are positioned between Damascus and the front. Part of it was deployed in early September and it gained momentum after September 13. . . . I would

like to point out some differences in comparison to September 1972 and February–March 1973.
1. Two Sukhoi-7 fighter squadrons were deployed in front airfields.
2. A bridging battalion was advanced to the front.
3. An unprecedented large amount of GHQ artillery has been moved to the front.
4. The SAM layout on the front is far more serious than in the past. This is the outcome of Syria's overall strengthening in missile batteries. While in January 1973 they had one battery south of Damascus, today they have 31 batteries, which cover the air zone of the Golan Heights.[14]

At this stage, Dayan intervened in order to emphasize that this antiaircraft layout endangers any Israeli plane that would fly over the Golan. He then added:

The almost sole meaning of such an internal division is that they want to strengthen their line so much, and their ability to act in the Golan Heights under the missiles' umbrella, that the Heights is covered better than Damascus. This is not a normal defensive move.[15]

Following this interruption, Shalev continued covering the developments in Egypt. Focusing on the exercise that was taking place there, he emphasized that it was a regular event. To prove his point, he mentioned that a similar exercise was held during Ramadan two years earlier, that leaves in the Egyptian army were to be renewed on October 8, and that the war minister issued an internal directive that officers who want to go to Mecca would be able to do so during the third part of the month of Ramadan.[16] At this point, the head of the Research Department moved to AMAN's assessment:

We have here two phenomena: (1.) Emergency deployment in Syria. (2.) Exercise in Egypt. I think that we have to choose between an assessment that each has independent causes to act the way it acts, and between the possibility that they have something in common, and what that may be. The common, is the worst possibility—an all-out war in Syria out of the present emergency deployment, which is basically defensive, but also enables going for the offense without additional buildup. This possibility of war—is it possible [that] under the disguise of an exercise in Egypt [they prepare war]? To the best of my knowledge and my estimate, on the basis of a sense that relies on a lot of material that we have received in recent days—Egypt still assumes that it cannot go to war. I think that the probability of such a move, without referring to political and other aspects that can lead to success, is low; otherwise it would have acted upon it, but Egypt estimates that it still cannot go to war. This view arises out of the possibility of knowing and feeling the way that they think about themselves, and that the possibility of a combined war—Egyptian and Syrian—does not seem probable. Since there is no change in their estimate of the [Israeli] forces in Sinai that can go fight the Egyptians, I have reached the conclusion that, basically, it is an exercise, [and] that on the 10th of the month they will let the reserve force go. The Minister of Defense was right in his demand to mainly analyze Syria.[17]

Following Shalev's analysis, a short discussion concerning possible Arab courses of action began. The Prime Minister asked, "If the Syrians started—could the Egyptians, with what they have now, immediately deploy for an attack, and be of any help to Syria?" Shalev responded, "Operationally, they certainly can go for the offense out of this layout." This raised a number of comments, including another one from Meir, who now attacked the issue from another angle: "Couldn't it be just the opposite, that the Egyptians would attract our attention, when the Syrians would like to do something in the Golan?" Shalev explained that the probability of this option was low, since Asad knew his limits, and the Syrians "are aware of Israel's regional strategic superiority.... in the air." The Egyptians, Shalev added, are also worried about Israel's air superiority. Despite his certainty, Shalev had to admit that the situation, this time, was different, since Asad has "a feeling that the subject of air defense is better now ... [though] he is well aware of Israel's strategic superiority ..." Shalev was more concerned about a limited Syrian move in the Golan, though the probability of such a move was also low, since, as he put it, the Syrians knew that Israel would not limit its response.[18]

The Chief of Staff's estimate of the situation was based not only on intelligence evidence but also on experience that had been gained in similar situations:

I'll start with the conclusions, though I cannot prove everything. I don't think, at this stage, that we face a combined Egyptian–Syrian attack, and I think that Syria, by itself, does not intend to attack us without cooperation with Egypt. There are combined designs. They had it all the time. And we, occasionally, knew about [specific D-day] dates. What we knew on previous dates was sometimes more practical than what we know now. In other words, in periods where we knew about Sadat's dates, I think that they had more ... desire to attack immediately, which is more than what we see today. A combined attack is, of course, possible but it is a function of a political and military situation, and it might happen one of these days. I don't see the threat as concrete in the near future. This means—not as a function of the present estimate.[19]

The comparison made by Elazar between the present situation and similar situations in the past is interesting, since it indicates a different logic of assessment from that of AMAN analysts. In contrast to the past, especially the events of spring 1973, in which good information, including specific dates for launching war, became available, this time no such date was known. Though some reports from good sources spoke about the possibility of war in the near future, none of them—with the exception of the September 30 warning about a war that was allegedly to start the next day—included a specific date. One can understand, then, Elazar's logic: In the past, when there might have been the intention to go to war but it did not materialize, Israel gained excellent information about it, including specific D-day dates. Hence, it was reasonable to assume that prior to actual war, which would demand large-scale preparations, Israel would gain even better indications. In this sense, in contrast to AMAN, whose prime analysts believed that they could assess Sadat's intentions correctly, the Chief of Staff weighed the present information in comparison to the past and concluded, on the basis of what he knew at that moment, that the present situation was less threatening.

The key question here is: What did the Chief of Staff know? In his testimony before the Agranat Commission he said: "For me, this week in the Southern Command, between October 1 and 6, was considered most normal. I did not observe anything extraordinary."[20] Indeed, an analysis of Branch 6's reports on the situation in the front, in comparison to the information that had been gathered—especially reports from IDF observation posts along the canal—shows that a large amount of warning indicators were not reported in AMAN's documents. Those that were, such as the October 2 review of irregular activity along the bank, were accompanied by a calming evaluation that diminished much of its warning value. The same morning, moreover, Elazar received a CIA reassessment of the causes for the Syrian emergency deployment. Earlier, as recalled, the CIA warned Israel, on the basis of information from Jordanian sources, that Syria was gearing for war and AMAN's response of October 1 mitigated the value of this warning. Now the CIA analysts, probably under the influence of their Israeli counterparts, expressed a more calming tone. Their new interpretation was that the Jordanian warning was an echo of an order of general readiness in the Syrian army—an order that was phrased in an aggressive tone and was mistakenly interpreted by the Jordanian source (i.e., King Hussein) as real preparations for war. The strengthened Syrian layout was explained, this time, as motivated by the regime's need to create internal dynamics of tension as a substitute for a real attack, or as a function of the process of escalation that led to a Syrian fear of an Israeli attack. Elazar's following comments continued the same logic. After reminding that the Egyptian and Syrian armies are comprised of a regular force that is usually deployed in the front, and that according to the Soviet doctrine a defensive deployment can be used for offense as well, the Chief of Staff added:

> This is true with regard to an all-out war with both of them. It is even more so when it comes to the Syrian army. The Syrian army is deployed in the Golan Heights in such a large potential that it can technically cross the line and occupy—and if it does so, it can obtain local achievements. This has been true for some years now. I must admit that this time an attack is somewhat more probable than in the past, because of the SAM layout, since this gives them more security, that they will have defense also in the Golan Heights. . . . [But] in case Syria would go for something more fantastic, we will have to know. We have good . . . information. And, when you operate a big machine, it is likely that you'll have leakage. [21]

Elazar's trust in Israel's collection capabilities is the key to understanding his concept of the optimal way to confront the threat in the north. He explained it to the Prime Minister:

> We face the question: What is the concept of our deployment [in the Golan]? It can rely on the present system, with some reinforcement. We [usually] have between 60 and 70 tanks, and today we have more than 100. So far, we have held it with four artillery batteries and today we have eight there. Hence, our concept can be that we hold this layout somewhat reinforced, as it is now, or that we move to a different system, of holding a maximal force, in order to prevent Syrian partial success, if they try to do it.

Elazar estimated that the measures taken so far sufficed to meet the Syrian threat and gave the IDF several courses of action in response to a Syrian offensive move:

1. We have the ability to broadly hit northern Syria, since they do not have missiles there, and their air defense system cannot defend it.
2. We can hit the Damascus area.
3. We can go and destroy the SAM layout and obtain a freedom of action in the front.
4. We can respond to immediate threats and act in the Golan Heights. Here, I want to make it clear, that when we say that they have a SAM air defense system, it does not mean that they hermetically

closed the airspace. We will fly and attack ... and we might lose two or three planes.[22]

Here, the Prime Minister asked what could be done, nevertheless, to strengthen the defense in the Golan. Elazar explained that it was possible to move regular forces from the southern to the northern front, but then the south would remain without sufficient forces. Alternatively, units of the reserve army could be mobilized for long-term service, and, thus, it would be possible to constantly reinforce the Golan with another brigade. At the same time, it was possible to raise the IAF's state of readiness. Then, he summarized his stand:

> All this is built on estimate and not a sealed proof, since I do not have a definite answer to the present Syrian deployment. They have built such an emergency deployment, without a good reason, many times in the past, for defensive purposes. It is possible that it is defensive today as well, and that they did not understand, until now, what happened to the 13 planes [lost on September 12]. It is possible that they think we planned something bigger, and they might expect another move, and want to be ready with an immediate response. It is possible that we let the Egyptians [should be the "Syrians"] hold us in tension, since I must admit that it makes them angry to have 600 tanks against 60 of ours. They have 500–600 artillery pieces while we have 12. . . . Domestic problems may have their own impact. . . . It might be a combination of all these reasons, but I don't have a clear intelligence answer, and, therefore, I said that this was my estimate.[23]

The Chief of Staff's conception of the IDF's correct deployment in the north (and also in the south), was, thus, the function of two factors: the threat potential (i.e., the opponent's military power that could be used for offensive purposes); and the probability that this threat would materialize. Obviously, he did not believe that a ratio of 10:1 in tanks or 50:1 in artillery was a reasonable ratio. Hence, he accepted Dayan's demand to partially close this gap. But, he essentially believed—and for a good reason—that "in case Syria would go for something more fantastic [i.e., an all-out war], we will have to know." The head of AMAN's Research Department, who set next to him, did not object. Consequently, it seems that from Elazar's perspective the most important factor in determining the level of Israel's defense was the quality of the intelligence warning. In the early days of October, he did not see a need for further reinforcement, not because he mitigated the Syrian military potential, but because he estimated, like everyone else, that Syria would not launch war without Egypt. And, since AMAN so clearly reported that all was quiet on the southern front, the Chief of Staff was under the impression that the situation in the south was "most normal." Hence, he was also less worried about the situation in the north.

The approach that was presented by the Defense Minister is interesting as well. Since the tension started, Dayan was worried about a Syrian small-scale attack. Now, for the first time, he also related to the possibility of an offensive to occupy the whole of the Golan and regarded to it as a rather possible move since the newly built SAM layout covered the Golan front better than Damascus and enabled the Syrian army to advance eastward under an effective anti-aircraft umbrella. Trying to assess the logic behind such a move, Dayan added:

> If they succeed in taking over the Heights, they stabilize a line that is similar to the one that we have in the Suez.... The Soviets have explained to them that they can occupy the Golan Heights, and here Syria stands in a situation where everything that it lost in the Six-Day War can, theoretically, be occupied in a single move under the defense of the SAM and artillery layout that they have today. And then, they have a defense line of a relatively good natural obstacle—the Jordan River—and they would solve all their national problems by liberating the Golan Heights from our hands.

Adding now the Egyptian factor, Dayan explained why a similar move by Egypt was illogical:

> If the Egyptians crossed tomorrow, in one blow, the Suez [and advance] ten–twenty kilometers, [or even] forty kilometers, to the Mitla [Pass], then they would have to advance their SAM batteries, at first stage to the canal and, then, beyond it.... If the Egyptians think about such a move, they'll find themselves in a very unpleasant situation after the first one. They'll have to pay dearly for crossing the canal and, then, they would have to fight in an endless area, while we come at them from all directions.... The Egyptians' situation would be that they wouldn't solve any problems and later they would face a more difficult situation than the present one, where the Suez defends them. If they cross the Suez they are exposed and they expose themselves so badly that there are many people, who are far from being stupid, who say: if only they would come—all the tanks would strike them, etc.[24]

Dayan's logic was impressive. And yet, like everyone else, he fell victim to the same fallacy of estimating Asad's intentions as a function of Sadat's, rather than the other way around. In other words, precisely since Dayan felt that the structure of the Syrian deployment did not fit AMAN's calming assessments, he could have concluded that Syria's deployment was an indication not only to its intention to go to war, but—since Syria could not launch war without Egypt—also for Egypt's war intentions. The fact that Dayan, the most individualistic and most experienced among Israel's policy-makers, did not reach such a conclusion, is another indication of the strength of the belief that Egypt was unprepared for war.

Indeed, the consensus among the participants in the meeting was that the main threat came from the north. Following Dayan's words, Allon asked how long it would take the reserve forces to reach the Golan, and whether there was a possibility to deliver a warning to the Syrians. Galili suggested examining what could be done in order to reinforce the defense of the settlements. Golda Meir, who had asked repeatedly whether there was any military equipment that should be acquired now, returned to the distinction that Dayan had made between the northern and the southern fronts:

> I would like to ask Moshe [Dayan]: Let's say that the objects move and a war starts. I fully accept this concept, of the difference between Egypt and Syria. I don't think that there should be any debate about it. The Egyptians can cross the canal—but they will be further from their bases. Ultimately, what will it give them? The situation is totally different with Syria; even if they want the whole of the Golan, even if they take a few settlements, for them, every move beyond the line—if they succeed in holding it—it is in their hands.[25]

The Prime Minister's words were almost the final accord of this discussion—the most organized and detailed of its kind before war broke out. Golda Meir accepted Allon's suggestion to conduct a cabinet discussion about the situation on Sunday[26]—the clearest indication that she did not regard the present situation as an emergency. Upon leaving the room she gave another expression for her mood. She shook the hand of Arie Shalev, adding, "thank you; you calmed me down."[27] In her simple words, she summarized the discussion in her memoirs: "Nobody in the meeting thought that it was necessary to call up the reserves, and nobody thought that war was imminent."[28]

* * *

Some observers identified in the way that this discussion was held—when, despite the alarming information, no one stood up to challenge the thesis that the Egyptian and Syrian military preparations were not for war—clear symptoms of the "groupthink" syndrome.[29] Indeed, the sharp contrast between the alarming information and the fact that war did break out, and the relatively calm consensus that dominated the discussion, indicates that certain symptoms of groupthink did indeed influence the behavior of the participants. But the main source of the consensus was AMAN's assurance that Egypt did not perceive itself as capable of launching war, and the impression that the decision-makers had—on the basis of AMAN's reports—that no irregular activity was taking place on the canal front. To this one can add the tendency of Israel's political echelon to accept, especially after the Six-Day War, the assessments and the recommendations of the professional military and intelligence echelons.

This situation is reminiscent, to some extent, of the dynamics that took place between President Kennedy, his assistants, and CIA officers on the eve of the Bay of Pigs operation. In that case, too, a group of highly sophisticated policy-makers had approved a rather infeasible and an extremely risky plan to overthrow Fidel Castro. In both cases, the groupthink syndrome had had its effect on the social dynamics that took place and led to a situation in which policy-makers avoided an attempt to doubt the estimates and operational plans of the intelligence officers. In both cases, moreover, they tended to act this way since the intelligence data and the assessment with which they were provided were carefully built to meet the intelligence organization's agenda. And, in both cases, the political echelon avoided raising questions about these assessments, at least in part because of the professional echelon's high prestige.[30]

The one person who could, perhaps, destabilize the estimate that war was not imminent, was the head of the Mossad, Zvi Zamir. In the spring, very much like Dayan and Elazar, he estimated that the continuation of the political deadlock was leading to war and he continued to be more worried about it than his colleague in AMAN. Zamir was in charge, ex officio, of the Tzomet ("Juncture")—the Mossad's HUMINT collection—and was well aware of the war warnings that had been arriving in recent weeks from a number of its sources. He was also familiar with information from AMAN's SIGINT and VISINT means of collection. On the same day the meeting took place, he met Golda Meir to discuss the situation and expressed the opinion that Egypt and Syria were gearing for war. She asked him to meet Dayan and present him with his estimate. Dayan was not impressed and told Meir, after his meeting with Zamir, that he accepted AMAN's estimate rather than that of the Mossad.[31] By some claims, Zamir was not decisive enough when expressing his estimates, especially when, a day later, his feeling that it was war received another impetus.[32] One has to remember that prior to the war the Mossad had no analysis section and no formal status in this domain. Hence, and though Golda Meir appreciated Zamir's advice, the head of the Mossad lacked the means to challenge AMAN's institutional assessment and the personal professional prestige of DMI Zeira. Zamir, moreover, was not certain about the inevitability of war. Unlike AMAN's official stand, he estimated that it was possible and that the way the IDF deployed along the border did not correspond with the graveness of the war warnings.[33] Very much like Maj. Gen. Tal, he tried, but failed, to present an alternative to the dominant thesis. In contrast to Tal, who after September 30 gave up his struggle, Zamir would also continue his efforts later.

* * *

Despite the fact that on Wednesday no new decisions were made about the IDF's state of readiness, the implementation of previous orders continued. The GHQ branch in charge of mobilization and readiness issued orders to the relevant units to check alert arrangements and arrangements to mobilize the reserve army, but to keep it in a low profile. This procedure was to end by 0900, October 5. Simultaneously, the Northern Command received orders to lay more than 4,000 mines, dig a six-kilometer antitank ditch, and build additional tank ramps between October 3 and 9.[34]

The IDF's improved state of readiness skipped, however, its most important element. In 848, which was considered to be Israel's prime warning unit, the state of readiness was decreased on Wednesday. According to 848's chief, this was done because of a direct order from AMAN's command. Opposite evidence is provided by the unit's operation officer, who maintains that during Wednesday's morning staff meeting, Ben-Porat made it clear that if, so far, he had had doubts about the information collected by the unit, now he was ready to accept the Research Department's estimate. Accordingly, he authorized a Yom Kippur leave for more than one-third of the soldiers and the officers of the unit's forward bases. Among them were the commanders of the Sinai region, and of the Babylon central base in Sinai, as well as other base commanders. Some of them, such as the commander of the Sinai region, were called back to service on Thursday night, when information about Soviet emergency evacuation from Egypt and Syria started arriving. Others returned to duty only on Saturday.[35]

Chapter 14

Thursday, October 4, 1973

If until October 3, AMAN's official assessment had been that there was no likelihood of war at all, the events of October 4 started to cast a shadow on this estimate. Three events are most relevant for our subject: the morning discussion at the office of the Minister of Defense about additional means to defend the Golan settlements; the afternoon reconnaissance sortie and, later, the air photograph interpretation that revealed the unprecedented dimensions of the Egyptian army deployment in the canal sector; and the information, which started arriving in the early evening hours, about the emergency evacuation of Soviet personnel from Egypt and Syria. The night between Thursday and Friday saw the first version of Marwan's warning about Egyptian war preparations, but since the head of the Mossad received it only after midnight, it will be discussed in the framework of Friday's events.

* * *

The participants in the morning meeting that was convened by Dayan included the Chief of Staff, his deputy, the Commander of the Northern Command, the head of AMAN's Research Department, and assistants. At the focus of the discussion were Dayan's words at the beginning of the meeting. His address clearly reveals his state of mind forty-eight hours before war broke out:

> I have a trauma, not of the Heights, but of the settlements there.... I think it is necessary and worthy for the state of Israel, for the IDF, to invest a lot of money and a lot of work and a lot of money and a lot of work ... to create a situation in which [the Syrians] cannot start to

move, and which they'll just have to deal with. If we have three days, if we can delay them, if we can mobilize the reserve, even one day, so that there is no surprise—we'll take care of it. . . .

In order to solve this problem, Dayan urged the participants to come with new ideas—be it mines, fish ponds, or any other obstacles—which might hinder a sudden Syrian attack. Without such means, he said, the buildup of civilian settlements in the Golan should be reconsidered since their protection would count on strategic warning that may or may not be obtained. But Dayan also expressed the belief that doubling the tank force in the Golan from 77 to 150 would solve the problem if the IAF could focus its efforts in this front. Accepting the estimate that "Egypt does not [mean] to fight now," Dayan summarized by assessing the present situation:

> The general assumption is that they will not go for any action without the Egyptians, and that the Egyptians will not go. Let's assume, nevertheless, that they do. This month we will not make drastic changes. After this month, winter starts. In the winter it is clear that a serious war won't start. . . . I summarize: What can be done during this month should be done. What can't be done—make a plan to see how much it should cost. . . . [1]

Three points arise from Dayan's analysis: First, he seems to have shared the Chief of Staff's perspective that that week in the southern front had been utterly normal. Second, he estimated that the reinforcement of the Golan Heights at that time sufficed to meet a Syrian attack, as long as Egypt did not participate and that the IAF could be fully deployed against the Syrian army. Third, Dayan did not convene this meeting in order to discuss an immediate threat of a Syrian attack but in order to find long-term solutions for the Syrian threats to the Golan civilian settlements. Whether he meant it or not, he also concluded during this meeting that the security cost of these settlements outweighed any benefit.

* * *

On Thursday, at noon, the IAF attempted, for the third time that week, to carry out a reconnaissance sortie at the Canal Zone. As recalled, on October 1 the Chief of Staff authorized a sortie, but it was not conducted because of a cloudy sky and low preference in the IAF order of priorities. For unknown reason, no attempt was made on October 2. On October 3, probably also under the pressure of Brig. Gen. Zvi Lidor, who had received alarming reports from 848's operations officer, Shabtai Brill, a sortie was conducted, but the camera's shutter failed to open and the photography failed. On Thursday, the sortie was successful. It covered the Suez sector up to 30 kilometers west of the canal. Immediately upon landing, the central air photograph interpretation unit started its work. At midnight, similar units in AMAN's headquarters and in the southern command started interpreting the same photographs. Their findings, which showed that the Egyptian army was "deployed in an emergency deployment unlike anything we have ever seen in the past," would be disseminated to consumers on the early hours of the next day.[2]

The fact that for four days Israel's most efficient means of collection was not properly utilized to cover the southern front is another indication that the situation there was perceived as normal. A clear indication for this is the fact that Maj. Gen. Shmuel Gonen, the commander of the Southern Command, spent the night of October 4–5 with friends in Haifa.[3] Obviously, had he felt that the situation was not normal he would have stayed at his Command. But, unlike Elazar and Dayan, whose estimates relied exclusively on AMAN's calming reports, Gonen had an independent means of information—reports from observation posts along the front. And they told a very different story.

During the last days of September, the observation posts along the canal started reporting about events that could hardly be linked to the Tahrir 41 exercise: massive vehicle movement and an increase in the number of officers' visits to the front; massive reinforcement of tank and artillery units; preparations of declines to the water; and mine removal near the water line.[4] This information was reported in the Command's daily intelligence reports, but very much like the interpretation that had been given to them by Branch 6, they were colored in calming tones by the intelligence officer of the Southern Command, Lt. Col. David Gdalia. This was not accidental. Though Gdalia received the reports, he did not estimate them independently—as he should have done—but did it on the basis of the assessment that he had received from Branch 6. As recalled, Yona Bandman, the head of Branch 6, informed on October 1 that the warning indicators that would be collected during the coming week should be linked to the exercise. Hence, at the command level, the information that was collected by the observation posts was interpreted as "irregular indicators in the framework of the exercise," rather than warning indicators for war.[5] For the same reason Gdalia also corrected an intelligence document that had been prepared by his deployment officer, Lt. Binyamin Siman-Tov. The document pointed out eight warning indicators that did not correspond with the exercise thesis and which could only mean war. Siman-Tov concluded that the Tahrir 41 explanation was used to disguise war preparations. The changes that were inserted by Gdalia nullified the document's warning value.[6]

The damage caused by Gdalia was even more acute, since communication between other intelligence officers in the Southern Command and Branch 6 had been defective. As a result, the Branch's officers avoided visiting the Command

and the canal area and, consequently, had no means to get a direct impression of the situation at the front.[7] Moreover, the head of Branch 6 did not relate any importance to intelligence at the tactical level. Hence, even when he received reports from the front that indicated irregular activity, he avoided incorporating them into the final intelligence products that were provided to consumers. By his own account, he acted this way because "he was dealing with policy."[8]

The final outcome of this coincidence was twofold: First, the intelligence collected at the Southern Command level had no impact on the production of the intelligence estimate at the national level. Second, the Commander of the Southern Command received estimates that solely reflected those of Bandman. The fact that the Command's intelligence branch did not make any real contribution to Gonen's awareness of irregular military activity at his front was vividly expressed by the fact that during the week before the war Gonen visited the front line only once. The record of his intelligence officer was no better: He, too, visited the front only once, on October 2, when accompanying Gonen.[9]

The interpretation of the air photographs of October 4 sharply changed this situation. If until this stage the situation in the south was perceived as "normal," the new evidence about the massive front line deployment dictated a far more threatening situation. This change, however, would take place only during the early hours of the next day. Until then, a new and highly significant warning indicator would be added.

* * *

Even today, it is not yet clear if, and to what extent, the Soviet military personnel who were stationed in sensitive positions in Egypt, and even more so in Syria, understood that their clients' military preparations were for war. Generally speaking, the Kremlin was well aware of the fact that the situation in the Middle East was explosive. In his secret July 1973 report to Communist leaders during their annual meeting in the Crimea, General Secretary Brezhnev estimated "The hatred toward the [Israeli] conquerors in the Arab world continues to grow and at any moment it can find an outlet in the form of military outbreak."[10] According to the memoirs of Gen. Vadim Kirpichenko, the KGB's "resident" in Egypt during the war, Soviet intelligence officers in Cairo and Damascus identified the military preparations, and once they became convinced that they were for war, the evacuation of Soviet personnel and their families was initiated.[11] The Soviet ambassador in Egypt, Vladimir Vinogradov, became suspicious after he saw a long military convoy, carrying water-crossing equipment traveling through Cairo, and Egyptian military officers walking around in combat gear.[12]

If these were, indeed, the indications that led the Soviets to realize that Egypt was planning to go to war, it would be evidence of their low-quality collection capabilities there. But, it is also possible that the Kremlin had no interest in knowing ahead that its two clients were gearing for war. After all, such knowledge would have put Brezhnev and his colleagues on the horns of the dilemma, between the need to alienate the military initiative in order to preserve the detente achievements, and the need to support it, thus risking their relations with the USA.

The Egyptians, on their behalf, avoided a formal notification of their intention to go to war—in violation of the 1971 Soviet–Egyptian friendship and cooperation treaty. On September 22—the day on which the military echelons in Egypt and Syria were informed that war would start on October 6—Sadat met Vinogradov and hinted that he might launch war soon.[13] On October 3 the two men met again. According to Sadat, he formally informed the ambassador during that session that Egypt and Syria had decided to go to war. According to the ambassador's account, Sadat merely complained about Israel's arrogance and provocations, which might compel Egypt to react. Both accounts agree that Sadat avoided discussing operational parameters of the war and did not mention any specific D-day, though Vinogradov notes that he was asked to stay in Cairo for the time being.[14] Since October 2, moreover, the senior Soviet liaison officer in Egypt, General Samachodsky, had been receiving information according to which the Egyptians were worried about an Israeli military initiative.[15]

As agreed earlier between Sadat and Asad, the latter reported to the Soviet ambassador in Damascus on October 4 about the planned military initiative, including D-day.[16] Even if Asad avoided naming the exact H-hour, it was already known to the Soviets. During the early evening hours, Foreign Minister Andrei Gromyko convened an emergency meeting. The participants included, among others, his first deputy, Vasilii Kuznetsov; the head of the US department, Georgi Kornienko; the head of the Middle East department, Mikhail Sytenko; and senior ambassador Victor Israelyan, who served as a member in Gromyko's staff. Gromyko informed the participants that war would start on Saturday, October 6, at 1400. He then said that the Kremlin had decided to evacuate all Soviet civilian personnel and their families from Egypt and Syria immediately. Ensuring their safety, he added, outweighed the concern that such an evacuation would give away the secret of the impending attack to the United States and Israel.[17]

From the Egyptian (and probably also Syrian) perspective, the Soviet decision was a source of grave concern. The Chief of Staff of the Egyptian army explained in his memoirs: "So far, to our amazement, the enemy had not guessed the truth. If anything could now persuade him, this panicky action would."[18] The estimate among Gamasy's assistants was just the same. They knew that there was no possibility to call off, disguise, or cover the evacuation. The Americans and the Israelis would know about it and regard it as a clear indication of the imminence of war.[19] This was also the reaction of the Soviet "resident" in Cairo.[20] Sadat was disappointed upon receiving the information about the Soviet move. More than being concerned that it would give away his big secret, he was worried by this Soviet demonstration of mistrust in Arab ability to initiate a successful military move. He nevertheless agreed to assist the evacuation operation.[21]

The Egyptians were right in assessing the implications of the sudden evacuation. Indeed, it was the clearest indication that Israel had received so far that the Arab preparations were for war. But, even such a dramatic change did not suffice to shatter AMAN's dominant thesis that Egypt did not perceive itself as being capable of launching war.

* * *

Communications intelligence (COMINT) elements in Unit 848 started getting indications that a sudden evacuation of families of Soviet military and civilian personnel was under way in Syria during the late afternoon hours. At this stage, the Soviet citizens were taken by buses to Latakiya port. At about 2200 first reports about an airlift of the Soviet airline Aeroflot to Egypt and Syria started to arrive. A little after midnight it became evident that a change in evacuation plans from Syria had taken place and that evacuation by air had replaced naval evacuation. Shortly afterward the number of planes taking part in the airlift became clear: eleven altogether, out of which five went to Syria, three to Egypt, and another three to an unknown destiny. Shortly afterward, it became known that they also flew to Egypt.[22]

The estimate that was offered by Branch 3 (superpowers) of AMAN's Research Department for the Soviet move was indecisive. At this stage it was unclear if the evacuation also included experts and advisors or only their families. The distinction was significant: evacuation of the families alone indicated concern for the lives of women and children. A more inclusive evacuation could point to a crisis in relations. The estimate mentioned Lebanese press reports from recent days about tension in Soviet–Syrian relations but also glorification of this relationship in the Syrian press. Consequently, AMAN's analysts offered two possible explanations for the move:

1. A Syrian decision to expel the Soviet experts and advisors, as Egypt did [in July 1972].
2. An emergency evacuation of Soviet women and children from Syria, in light of a Soviet assessment/information that a military clash between Syria, and possibly also Egypt, and Israel is expected. This possibility gains strength from [recent] information (which had not been verified yet) about a flight of 5 "Aeroflot" planes to Egypt, in parallel to the flight of the planes to Syria.[23]

The wording that was chosen by AMAN's analysts, even when highly irregular events indicated the imminence of a severe crisis, is evidence that they still looked for a compromise between incoming information that indicated a growing likelihood for war and a belief that war was not likely. But Thursday's events were, nevertheless, the beginning of the end of the dominant thesis. A few more hours would pass before AMAN's political and military consumers would receive the information about the Soviet evacuation and digest its implications. For the first time since Syria and Egypt started their war preparations, warning material would reach the critical mass that would compel policy-makers to start taking the necessary steps to meet the possibility of war on two fronts.

In AMAN, the change in the atmosphere was already felt on Thursday night. Throughout that night analysts of the Research Department were busy discussing and debating the possible causes for the evacuation. The confidence of many analysts in the validity of the dominant thesis started to shake. According to one account, this also included Yona Bandman, the most dominant believer in the conception.[24] Some changes also took place in Unit 848. According to its commander, they began when his staff started intercepting information about the evacuation and when the first reports of the interpretation of the air photographs of the Egyptian military deployment started to arrive at about 1900. Ben-Porat maintains that at 2200 he made a call—one of a series of calls—to DMI Zeira, telling him categorically that the imminence of war was the only explanation for the evacuation. Simultaneously, he issued his unit orders to prepare itself for war.

Others in Unit 848 remember Thursday night's events differently. They accept that the level of activity was raised and that some officers who were on leave were called back for duty. But, they say, Ben-Porat's personal assessments were not translated into concrete orders. As a result, the unit kept the same level of readiness that it had maintained since October 1, rather than entering a war state of readiness. Consequently, some of its officers remained on leave until Saturday morning, female soldiers were not evacuated from bases near the front until war started, and the preparation of main bunkers in Sinai and the Golan to operate under fire started only in the early hours of Saturday, when information that war would break the same day, arrived.[25] And, even by Ben-Porat's account, he avoided calling DMI Zeira again about the possibility of war, after his attempts to change his commander's estimation had failed on Thursday night.[26]

Prime Minister Golda Meir.
IDF archives.

Defense Minister Moshe Dayan.
IDF archives.

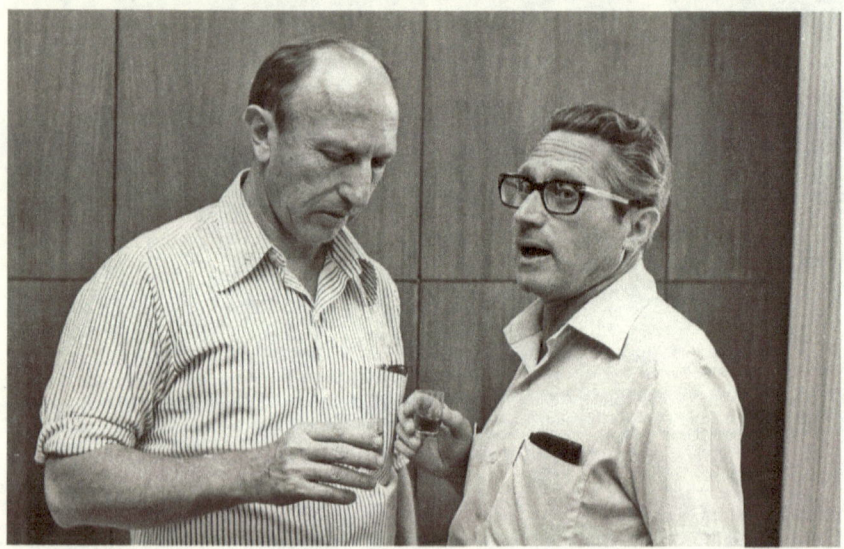

Zvi Zamir (left) and Aharon Yariv in a ceremony to mark the end of Zamir's tenure as the chief of the Mossad.
Private collection.

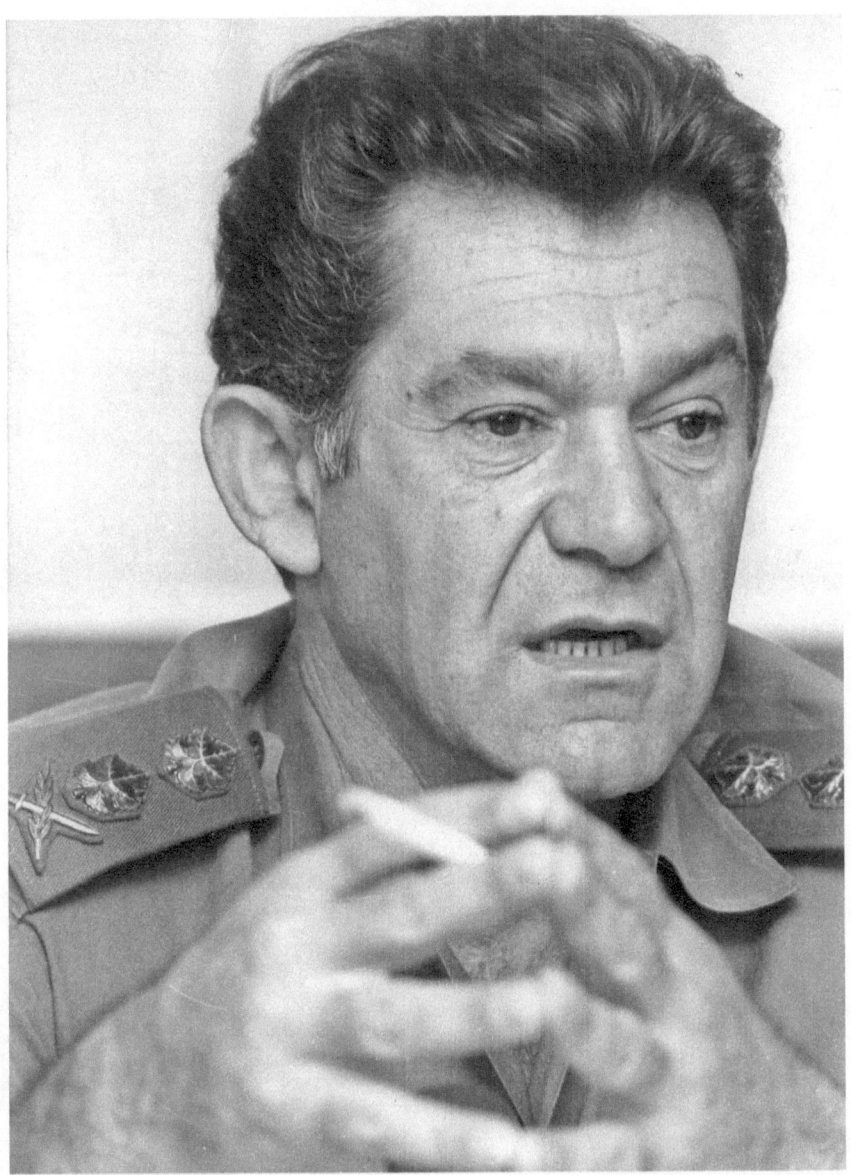
The IDF Chief of Staff, Lieutenant General David Elazar.
IDF archives.

Change of guards: Eli Zeira replaces Aharon Yariv as DMI, October 1, 1972.
IDF spokesman.

Director of Military Intelligence, Major General Eli Zeira, reviews a parade.
IDF spokesman.

The head of the Research Department of Military Intelligence, Brigadier General Arie Shalev. IDF spokesman.

A meeting of the branch heads of the Research Department: sitting next to the table on Shalev's right, Avi Yaari and next to him Zusia ("Zizi") Kanizher. On the far left, with a pipe: Yona Bandman.
IDF spokesman.

A meeting of the branch heads of the Research Department: Shalev at the head of the table and Levran on his left.
IDF spokesman.

President Sadat and War Minister, Ismail Ali, observing an Israeli post in the front four months before the war.
Associated Press.

King Hussein, President Asad, and President Sadat in the Cairo Summit, September 12, 1973
Associated Press.

Reserve soldiers prepare their tanks for battle in an army base in the north, during the late hours of Yom Kippur, October 6, 1973.
The State of Israel, National Photo Collection.

An armored column climbing the Golan Heights, October 7, 1973.
The State of Israel, National Photo Collection. Eitan Haris.

Defense Minister Moshe Dayan receives a briefing from Maj. Gen. Gonen at the command post of the southern command at Um Hashiba, October 7, 1973.
The State of Israel, National Photo Collection. Shlomo Arad.

Planning the counteroffensive in the north: sitting, on the left, Maj. Gen. Yitzak Hofi, standing next to him, Defense Minister Moshe Dayan, standing next to Dayan, Maj. Gen. David Elazar. IDF spokesman.

Chief of the IDF Staff David Elazar and his Egyptian counterpart Mohammed Abdel Ghani al-Gamasy leaving the tent at km 101 after signing of the disengagement agreement that ended the war, January 18, 1974.
The State of Israel, National Photo Collection.

Chapter 15

Friday, October 5, 1973

The upper echelons of the Israeli security and intelligence system found themselves facing several obstacles when trying to correctly evaluate the threatening information that was quickly gathering during the days before the war. This process reached its peak on the eve of Yom Kippur, Friday, October 5. The chain of events began on the night between of October 4 and 5, when a war warning from Israel's best HUMINT asset, Ashraf Marwan, had been received. It continued with the interpretation of the air photographs that were taken in the sortie on the canal front, which revealed that the Egyptian army was deployed there in an emergency array that had not been spotted before. Later on, it became clear that the Soviet emergency evacuation had intensified in other aspects.

Even part of the information that had accumulated was enough to bring the Chief of Staff to decide during the morning hours to raise the state of alert of the regular army to its highest level and to call for preparations to mobilize the reserve soldiers. The gathering information was also the basis of a series of emergency meetings that took place until the early afternoon hours, in which the top civilian echelon and the members of the IDF General Staff were brought up to date on the current state of affairs. Another piece of warning information that reached AMAN during the afternoon and which, on its own, would probably have convinced Elazar to have demanded the mobilization of the reserve army on Friday evening, was not reported to him. As a result, this decision was delayed until the morning of Yom Kippur.

* * *

Around midnight, October 4, a message arrived at Mossad headquarters in Tel Aviv. Marwan's case officer reported that his agent had contacted him and informed him that he wished to meet with the head of the Mossad as soon as possible. Marwan used the pre-arranged code word for talking about war, but did not mention specific details or a specific D-day. The message was forwarded to Freddy Einy, Zamir's bureau chief. Considering its importance, as well as the fact that it entailed the potential immediate travel of the head of the Mossad, Einy reported the message to Zamir at around 0230. Zamir estimated that the message relayed no immediate war warning. He knew that the source had specific code words to communicate such a case, but he did not make use of them at this time. However, he authorized Einy to arrange for a flight to London the following morning in order to meet the source there. Zamir decided to do it not only because he regularly met and handled Marwan, but also because he assessed that in light of the tension, which led him to believe that war was likely, this meeting had a special value. In addition, he had no other urgent matters to tend to at that time.

A short while later, Zamir was awakened by another call, this time from AMAN's director. Zeira told him about the rushed evacuation of the Soviet families from Syria and apparently from Egypt as well. The fact that he decided to pass on this information to his colleague in the Mossad, and at such a late hour, was a clear indication of the fact that he did not feel that matters had remained the same as they were just a day earlier. Zeira, nevertheless, said that the evacuation did not change his assessment that war was unlikely. Zamir responded with what he had already been saying for some time—that to make such a definite estimate on the basis of the available information was too risky. In the conversation itself, Zamir did not refer to the report that he had just received from Einy. But, a few minutes later, Einy called again. Zamir told him what the DMI had said about the evacuation, and Einy responded by saying that this information went hand-in-hand with Marwan's message in which he requested to meet Zamir in relation to war. This time Zamir was more impressed. He ordered his bureau chief to report this in the morning to the Prime Minister's military secretary, Brig. Gen. Yisrael Lior. He himself called Zeira to tell him about Marwan's request to meet regarding the possibility of war and about his intention to set out for that meeting in the morning. Zeira asked Zamir to inform him as soon as possible of the outcome of the meeting.[1]

The head of the Mossad left for the meeting in London during the early hours of Friday morning. His bureau chief, who would later testify in the Agranat Commission that Marwan's message had no precedent, tried to locate the Prime Minister's military secretary on Friday morning but without success. Consequently, he only left him a message to call him back, an act that contradicts his later claim regarding the importance of this information. It is also unclear whether the message was disseminated by the customary routes. Indeed, the Marwan material was habitually disseminated to the Prime Minister and the Defense Minister as well as to a restricted number of recipients in the intelligence community. But, since it involved mainly administrative matters this time—the source's request to meet Zamir without the use of the specific codeword for imminent war—it is likely that it was not disseminated outside the Mossad. It seems, therefore, that the only person outside the Mossad who knew about Marwan's message on Friday was the DMI. In the discussions that were held by Dayan and Meir, the matter was presented by Zeira, but not in clear words.

The head of the Mossad set out Friday morning to meet the source in Europe. His meeting with Marwan took place in the late-night hours of that day. We shall get back to it later.[2]

* * *

Teams of air-photograph interpreters in Tel Aviv and the Southern Command labored the entire night to interpret the results of the sortie of the day before and to draw them up on the maps. The head of the military section in Branch 6 stayed up all night to prepare an immediate intelligence review of the subject. He distributed it at 0545. The document presented the first updated picture of the Egyptian military deployment in the front since the September 25 air-photograph sortie. Following a short introductory section, it said:

2. The air-photograph sortie of October 4 at the Canal Zone front covered at least 30 km west of the Canal. From the findings it can clearly be deduced that the Egyptian army on the Canal front is in an emergency formation, the magnitude of which has never been seen before.
3. The most important findings are:
    a. Fifty-six additional artillery batteries (308 artillery pieces), including mainly field artillery (52 batteries/276 artillery pieces), were located. Altogether, 194 artillery batteries (mortars of 120mm and up) were located on the Canal front zone (from Port Said to Suez) that is 1,110 artillery pieces compared to 138 batteries/802 artillery pieces that were found in the last sortie of September 25, 1973. (A more or less similar order of battle was located there throughout the last year.) The additional field artillery was divided almost equally between the two armies. The number added corresponds to that of two complete divisions and even more. At the same time, all five infantry divisions deployed along the Canal are fully manned according to the known table of organization and equipment.
    b. The revetments for crossing/bridging equipment had been partially occupied. GSP self-propelled pontoons (a total of about 30) have been located with high probability in at least five concentrations of

revetments, one in each infantry divisional sector. Vehicles had not been located in the other concentrations.

c. In the "yards" of most tank firing ramps along the Canal a tank platoon (2–3 tanks) was detected, whereas in the past only a handful of tanks were located on the ramps along the Canal.

d. The brigade-plus dug-in layout north of Katzetzin, which had not been occupied in the past, is now occupied by armored fighting vehicles (AFVs) — partly identified as armored personal carriers (APCs) and mortars. In addition, vehicle concentrations were located in the rear of the array. At this stage it is impossible to estimate the size of the force deployed in this area. It is possible that the disposition is being occupied by forces of a mechanized division, about whose forward movement from Cairo to the 2nd Army sector we had information.

e. A tank brigade and a battalion of SU-100 tank destroyers were forwarded to the area of Agrod (about 25 km west of the Suez). Concentrations of three tank battalions were identified in that area — a total of 87 vehicles and another 22 SU-100.

f. The tank concentrations of the independent tank Brigade 15, which had been routinely located in the Abu Zweir area, are not there. On the other hand, three tank battalion concentrations were located in the Zalhiya area. These are probably the concentrations of Brigade 15 that had redeployed.[3]

In contrast to routine practice, the review carried no assessment. This was not an accident: Though his superiors attempted to add a paragraph with a more reassuring evaluation, the head of the Egyptian military section vigorously rejected it.[4] Indeed, the report needed no additional interpretation. Dayan, its most experienced reader, gave it the best interpretation, perhaps, when saying: "You can get a stroke from just reading the numbers."[5]

* * *

In the early-morning hours, DMI Zeira held a discussion with a number of senior analysts in the Research Department. They suggested various explanations for the Soviet evacuation and the unprecedented Egyptian deployment. During the discussion the question of whether or not to operate AMAN's special means of collection was raised, but no new decision was taken. Zeira reiterated that he thought the probability of war was very low. The disturbing piece of news for him was the Soviet evacuation. It did not fit with the dominant thesis, according to which the threatening deployment was the outcome of a training exercise in the south and a Syrian apprehension of an Israeli attack in the north. He was less disturbed by the Egyptian formation. As far as it is known, Zeira did not mention a word in this forum regarding Marwan's warning or the fact that the head of the Mossad had gone abroad to meet with him. A demand was made to activate AMAN's special means of collection, but it was rejected. The head of Branch 5 demanded to conduct another air photograph sortie over the Syrian front, and his demand was accepted.[6]

* * *

At 0825 the Chief of Staff called for a short meeting in his office. The participants included his deputy, Yisrael Tal, DMI Zeira, and IAF Commander Benny Peled. It was a purposeful discussion, but apparently with an incomplete protocol, which may be the reason why many accounts of the war tend to ignore it.[7] But the decisions that were made during this meeting were the most important ones taken since the start of the tension in mid-September. Elazar's mood, after he heard the reports of the Soviet evacuation and an updated picture of the Egyptian formation along the canal (but, apparently, not of the warning Zamir received during the night), was clear:

> If I were a military commentator or a member of the Knesset, I would say this is not an attack. But, since I am neither a commentator nor an MK, I need to look for proof that we are not going to be attacked. I don't have enough evidence that all these signs do not signal an intention to attack.[8]

Accordingly, he issued a series of orders: all furloughs on the northern and southern fronts were to be cancelled; the IAF was to be in full alert with no furloughs; the entire 7 Brigade would reinforce the Golan Height's front; an armor brigade would be flown to the Sinai; and, for the first time since the Six-Day War, a "C State of Alert" (meaning, mobilization of the entire personnel needed to mobilize the reserve forces) was declared, in preparation for a possible mobilization of the IDF reserve forces. The military secretary of the Prime Minister was informed about the information that had been received during the night regarding the Soviet evacuation and the dimension of the Egyptian deployment.[9]

* * *

The meeting of the Chief of Staff's forum was carried out in a rushed manner because the Minister of Defense's forum was to hold its weekly meeting at 0900 and all those present at the first meeting were to attend the second one. They were joined by Dayan's assistant, Lt. Gen. (res.) Zvi Tzur, the General Director of the Ministry of Defense, Yitzhak Ironi, and assistants. The Chief of Staff opened the meeting by briefing those present about the short meeting that had just ended in his office, and added:

> The main issues are these: they are reinforcing their forces; the Soviet families have been evacuated; there are changes in the deployment of the Syrian Air Force. All these can mean an intention to attack. They could also be signs of defense. One interpretation says that the Russians' departure is an act of protest on their part that they are against this, because they received a warning through the Americans. Going for the worst-case scenario, I would say there is [no] proof that this is a diplomatic rift.[10]

Dayan interrupted here to say that the reason for the evacuation "is not a diplomatic rift." Elazar agreed, saying, "Another sign tells me that this is not a political rift, because it is with the Syrians and the Egyptians at the same time." And the Defense Minister added, "A diplomatic rift is not with women and children, it is with men. This could be a result of their fear that we will attack."

Elazar continued, adding to the warning signs the possibility that the Syrian army advanced its armor concentrations to the front line. He concluded by saying:

> We have no indisputable validation for an intention to attack, but it does not prove the other hypothesis either. As a result we are taking a few measures:
> 1. All furloughs on both frontiers are cancelled.
> 2. Furloughs in the Air Force are canceled. The Air Force will remain with all the pilots in the bases, and on full alert.
> 3. I want everything that can be reinforced to be reinforced, to take advance measures, and not only on the front. I mean everything that can be considered as a reserve. This is a holiday where people sit at home. It won't cause a great panic; I am inclined to declare a serious state of alert.[11]

DMI Zeira, who spoke next, presented his estimate of the situation. He regarded the Soviet evacuation as "the most serious and problematic" development. "If the Soviets had done nothing," he said, "the indicators would be that the Egyptians and the Syrians are not going to attack but are rather anxious about our moves—and we have done a series of things lately that could cause them anxiety." After mentioning some of these Israeli acts, he turned to assess what could be standing behind the Soviet move. The more logical explanation was:

that the Russians know that the Syrians and the Egyptians are about to attack. They estimate that our counterattack will be successful and that it will hit the hinterland and the families, and that is why they want their people out. Or they want to tell the Egyptians and Syrians: Look, we know you are going to attack, we are getting the families out, and we want you to know that we are not with you on this one.[12]

Zeira proposed two more explanations for the Soviet evacuation: fear of an Israeli attack, and a crisis between Moscow, Syria, and Egypt. He admitted that both explanations had faults. But he also added that he still did not have "positive proof" yet that an evacuation was indeed taking place. "The bottom line," he concluded, "is that I don't have an explanation why the Syrians are doing this."[13]

Zeira's analysis of the motivation behind the Soviet evacuation was reasonable. What was striking was his complete ignorance of the new information about the deployment along the Suez. Again, one must keep in mind the circumstances. There had not been a successful air-photograph sortie in that area since September 25 and, as a result, AMAN did not have a clear picture about the situation on this front. Throughout the preceding week, AMAN's experts had told their consumers that nothing irregular was taking place there. Consequently, the Chief of Staff believed until Friday morning that the situation in the south was "utterly normal." The calming estimate of the situation in the south determined also the estimate of the situation in the north. While the Syrian formation was perceived to be more threatening due to its magnitude and its closeness to civilian settlements, the consensus among policy- and intelligence-makers was that Syria would not launch war without Egypt. Now it became clear that the magnitude of the Egyptian formation in the south surpassed anything that was expected. Moreover, the way it was deployed—especially the deployment of large quantities of crossing equipment on the water front—indicated offensive intentions. Yet, Zeira totally ignored these issues when assessing the situation.

There may be a few explanations for the DMI's behavior. To start with, Zeira had nurtured the thesis that Egypt did not see itself as having the capability to launch a war, and he had cultivated this view for over a year in his role as the national estimator, turning it into a kind of dogma. At this stage, his belief in this thesis remained unshaken. Zeira, moreover, trusted the assessment of the head of Branch 6. Undoubtedly, the fact that the latter stuck to this thesis with determination enabled the DMI also to continue holding fast to it without questioning its validity. In addition, Zeira was, consciously or not, personally committed to the adamant assessment that Egypt was not about to go to war—at least not in the next two years. He was most identified with this assumption in the forum of civilian and military decision-makers, and only three weeks earlier he had explained in the GHQ meeting why the situation was likely to remain unchanged during the coming five years. In that meeting he confidently dismissed the possibility that Egypt would go to war any time soon, saying, "The Egyptians understand that they cannot present any real military threat at this point in time."[14] Admitting now that there were flaws in the intellectual superstructure that he had constructed, and behind which he stood unwaveringly, was emotionally very difficult. Ignoring it was a more convenient outlet. And, finally, like many others in Israel's top echelon, Zeira shared the belief that in determining the likelihood of war the Arab factor became after 1967 less dominant than the Soviet one. Hence, he was automatically inclined to attribute more importance to the Soviets' moves, although they did not represent a direct threat to Israel, and to assign less importance to an unprecedented level of Egyptian deployment, which directly threatened Israel's security.

Dayan, who was more sensitive to what was happening on the southern border, asked Zeira whether "there was anything unusual in the 'traffic' over the Egyptian [communication] lines." For more than a week, Zeira had been urged by AMAN's head of the Collection Department, Col. Menahem Digli, and the head of unit 848, Col. Ben-Porat, to activate the special means that had not been used since the end of the "blue-white" state of alert in August. Zeira's answer to both officers was unequivocal: You will gather information, not do research. But, when the head of his Research Department demanded the same, he refused him as well.[15] As recalled, on October 1 or 2 the Chief of Staff asked Zeira whether he had activated these special means, and Zeira confirmed that he had. Now he gave a similar answer to Dayan:

> Everything is quiet. There is a lot of material concerning the luggage [of the Soviet families] and the exercise. I have a dilemma about the exercise as well. Is there a tactical exercise without troops? Is there a telephone battle? Is there an exercise with all the forces? Thus far we have no indication what kind of an exercise it is. In most areas they are not moving forces.... There are situations for which we have no explanation. I think the situation today is such that we have no explanation; there are assumptions, [but] we don't have a serious and founded explanation at this point, at 9:15 a.m. Maybe there will be more information in an hour or two.... The way I see it, the basic evaluation of the situation remains unchanged. I don't see Egyptians or Syrians initiating an attack, despite the Russian exercise. But, I now have doubts, and it is entirely justified to do everything the Chief of Staff mentioned.... Zvika [Zamir] received last night some information from one of his sources, and it's a good source. The source gave a warning that something was about to happen, and he asked

Zvika to come and meet him immediately. Tonight at 10:00 p.m. he'll see him. We prepared a list of questions.[16]

Three points arise from Zeira's words here. First, when he told Dayan that "Everything is quiet," he also calmed Dayan's worries without a real foundation. The special means had been prepared to enable Israel to cope with exactly the kind of surprise that it encountered on Yom Kippur of 1973. Dayan and Elazar knew their potential, and allowed themselves to relax, being confident that if indeed preparations for an attack were taking place, these means would most probably produce indications to this effect. But, they did not know that just an hour or two earlier Zeira had sat with a few of the senior analysts and together they had debated whether to activate them. In other words, Dayan and Elazar were misled in thinking that these resources did not produce war indications because such indications did not exist. In reality, they did not produce such indications because they were not activated in the first place.

The Agranat Commission saw this matter—one of the most secret issues of the entire investigation—as being of grave importance. This is indicated in the commission's public report, published as early as 1975, which affirmed that "the confidence of the Minister of Defense in AMAN's estimate . . . grew after the DMI told him in response to his question on the morning of October 5 that he was making use of all possible sources of information."[17] Parenthetically, the Commission added: "This answer may have resulted from a misunderstanding on the part of the DMI, but it was objectively misleading."[18] It is unclear whether the Commission knew that throughout that week senior officers in AMAN had requested Zeira to activate these means—although, as far as it is known, they testified to the Commission on this matter.[19] But, it is rather clear that since Zeira discussed the activation of the means earlier that morning, this issue was high on his agenda and one can hardly accept that he misunderstood Dayan's questions. As far as it is known, he gave orders to activate the special means only on the night between Friday and Saturday, and his order reached the unit only on Saturday morning.[20]

The second point relates to the available information about exercise Tahrir 41. At this stage, analysts in the Research Department already had some doubts about the real nature of the exercise which, according to the information collected by Unit 848, was very different from similar exercises that had been held in the past. The most remarkable difference involved the volume of the wireless traffic of the exercise, which was considerably smaller than in the past. In this sense, although the exercise was already four to five days old, there were no indications that it was actually taking place. And yet, when asked about it, Unit 848's representative, Lt. Col. Yossi Zeira, who participated in the discussions in AMAN's Research Department, maintained that his unit's experts estimated that an exercise was taking place.[21]

The DMI was correct in mentioning to Dayan that there were questions about the exercise, but he did not clarify that some of AMAN's experts maintained at this stage that there was no exercise at all.[22] His answer demonstrates that he did not take into account the gap that had now grown even wider between the exercise—about which there were now many doubts—and the military deployment that looked like war preparation more than anything else. But Zeira had many accomplices here, including the Minister of Defense and the Chief of Staff. They could have asked questions about this gap, and they did not.

The third point involves the way in which Zeira presented Marwan's warning. That morning he was the only one in Israel who had heard directly from Zamir about the warning and who had also participated in the meetings where the national estimate of the situation was formulated. The Prime Minister was not informed about it by the head of the Mossad, and her military secretary had not yet heard of it from Zamir's bureau chief. Zeira had conveyed the warning in mild, nonchalant terms. Had he said what he had been told—that Zamir received information during the night that his best source (one that would most likely know of an Egyptian intention to go to war) had asked to meet with him urgently in order to speak about a possibility of war—he might have made a real contribution. But, Zeira did not do so for his own reasons and thus alleviated his listeners of another worry. During that entire day, the Chief of Staff was unaware that Zamir was to meet Marwan over a war warning that the latter had delivered a day earlier.[23]

Following Zeira's estimate, a dialogue developed between the Minister of Defense and the Chief of Staff. Dayan accepted the measures that Elazar had taken, saying, "Everything you did for this Yom Kippur is fine." He added that a helicopter should be prepared for his use and raised the question of whether something should be done to prepare the Israeli public for the possibility of a state of alert. The Chief of Staff explained that on Yom Kippur it is impossible to carry out a public mobilization since "during this holiday the entire country is dead." Dayan responded, "Forces should not be moved unless it will really start. The roads are empty today." The Chief of Staff, who was still bothered by the paralysis of the public mobilization mechanisms on Yom Kippur, mentioned that in the Staff headquarters they had considered operating the IDF radio to read Psalms every two hours. Dayan's answer revealed his priority at this point: "So we have to tell everyone now that they need to listen to the IDF radio? It will cause a great panic, and if we do, who will listen to Psalms? No one will turn on the radio."[24]

It seems quite clear that, for Dayan and the others present, the fear of creating tension about war without a war actually breaking out was a scenario no less troublesome than the concern over a surprise Arab attack. The trauma of the "duck night" still haunted everyone's collective memory, and surely

Dayan's personal memory. That public mobilization exercise of April 1959 was to test the Israeli call-up system and the reaction of the Arabs to the exercise. The exercise was carried out without Ben-Gurion's authorization and caused great tension in Israel and the region. In its aftermath the Chief of the General-Staff Branch, Maj. Gen. Meir Zorea, and AMAN's chief, Maj. Gen. Yehoshafat Harkabi, were dismissed. All those participating in the present discussion were reluctant to take responsibility for a similar development during the Jewish holiest day, and when an election campaign whose main theme was Israel's excellent state of security was under way.[25]

Of all those present, Dayan's assistant, Zvi Zur, was the one to draw attention to the real issue at stake: "Let's say [the Arabs] are really getting ready for war. They would probably want to surprise us and in quite an unusual manner. The fact is that we still don't know, and maybe they are really getting ready." When Dayan accepted that this was a real possibility, Zur suggested taking military and diplomatic measures in order to signal to the Egyptians that Israel was aware of their intentions. Dayan's response was partially positive:

> ... I think there is one thing we need to do. I think there is no other way but to have the Americans ask the Russians why they are going home. Did we say this to the Americans? Even if we did not ask them to, they would ask them [the Russians]. It is not a secret. Everybody sees it. And, I'm not only talking about the bus drivers. They know that all the women and children are leaving. Their neighbors know it. Eli [Zeira], won't the Americans ask the Russians why are they going home?"[26]

Zeira maintained that the Americans did not know about the evacuation and he opposed bringing them in on the secret.[27] It seems that he was guided here primarily by political concerns. When the Minister of Defense repeated that it was desirable "that the Americans tell [the Soviets] that Israel is one hundred percent not going to attack," Zeira responded that "it's like Israel communicating through the Americans to the Russians: Russians don't panic. Stay in Egypt."[28]

This reasoning did not satisfy Dayan. He decided recommending the Prime Minister communicate through the American Secretary of State, Henry Kissinger, a three-point warning message to the Soviets:

a. We are not going to do anything; they have gotten some crazy idea into their heads;
b. We know that they are doing it;
c. If they tell us anything different, they will find out that we are ready for that as well.[29]

Dayan also wished to avoid a situation in which Israel entered a war without informing its closest ally, especially after the CIA delivered a detailed warning just a few days earlier regarding the Syrian preparations for war. Therefore, he also thought the USA should be informed that "What we saw earlier in a less probable light, we now see as more probable, as being of higher probability."[30]

Earlier, Dayan had asked the relevant participants to join him in the next discussion with the Prime Minister. He now ended the discussion by making sure that all those present would be in Tel Aviv and the area during the holiday.

Three points are noteworthy in this exchange. The first relates to Zvi Zur's role. Although he had a rich military experience that included three years as Chief of Staff (1961–1963), in his present position he was the assistant of the Minister of Defense on matters of the economy and funds. Hence, he was not part of the small group that had been discussing the growing tension, especially in the north, for the past week. And yet, and perhaps because of it, Zur was the one to position the real problem at the center of the discussion—the possibility that the reasons behind the Egyptian and Syrian military preparations, as well as the Soviet evacuation and Marwan's warning, were one: Arab preparations for an unexpected attack. In this sense, his behavior resembles the Prime Minister's, who knew to ask her defense advisers naive questions that suggested that the emperor may be naked. Zur also knew how to throw light on the most critical issues. The fact that people who did not take part in earlier discussions acted like the child in Andersen's story, points to the possibility that a groupthink dynamic did indeed exist in these forums.

The second point relates to Zeira. He opposed Dayan's proposal to inform the Americans as an indirect way of sending a warning message through the Soviets to Egypt and Syria, for supposedly rational reasons. At the same time his position, most of all, represented the belief that it was still too early for such measures. This was true because Zeira's estimate of the situation was unshaken. The Soviet evacuation did, indeed, cause him some doubt, but such conduct was insufficient to alter it.

And finally, although the possibility that the Arabs were indeed preparing a sudden attack was brought up at the end of the discussion, nobody raised the issue of mobilizing the reserves. Dayan's discontent with the idea of mobilization, especially on Yom Kippur, no doubt influenced the other participants. In the context of the discussion, mobilizing the reserves would have served a double function: adding a last-minute measure of deterrence in an attempt to prevent a war, and ensuring the IDF's ability to cope with the Egyptian and Syrian attack if deterrence failed. But at this point—when everyone was still convinced that a war with no intelligence warning of any kind, even a warning of twenty-four hours, was inconceivable—a general mobilization seemed unwarranted. Therefore, the decision was made to deliver a warning through the

United States. It was so attractive because it answered the need for deterrence without having to pay the price that Dayan was not yet prepared to pay—a general mobilization on Yom Kippur. The vulnerability of this alternative was that it did not address the imbalance of forces on the front line in the event that a war actually broke out.

The Chief of Staff seems to be the closest of all those present to consider mobilizing the reserves since, by now, he did not exclude the possibility of war. What stopped him from doing so was his belief that a war was not possible without AMAN sounding the alarm. He expressed this belief on a number of occasions over the next few hours.

* * *

When the discussion at the Minister of Defense forum ended, Dayan, Elazar, Zeira, and their assistants gathered in the Prime Minister's office in the Kirya, the IDF's military complex in Tel Aviv. This discussion was meant mainly to inform Golda Meir of the latest developments. Dayan opened and then Zeira presented the intelligence picture. After a short description of what was known at this stage about the Soviet evacuation, he repeated his three explanations for this move.[31] His interpretation about what was going on in Egypt and Syria was the same as AMAN had presented throughout the entire tense period:

> The Syrians and Egyptians are afraid of our attack. The Egyptians are taking a lot of real security measures for the exercise: they added to the front [---]; the air force is in high alert; they moved their tanks up to the canal.[32]
>
> Syria: A winter [emergency?] formation for about a month. In the past few days we see much concern; they advanced [-] Sukhoi squadrons [---], an action that they have not taken before. In fact, this is an offensive move. It creates a state of mind commensurate with attack [--].
>
> What has happened to cause them to be concerned about us?
> 1. They are always concerned.
> 2. They saw the [September 13] aerial battle as a trap that we had prepared for them. When we are in a difficult situation, the world isolates us. An Eastern front is formed and we aspire to break it down.
> 3. Events on our side:-a) the paratroopers' exercise; b) a mobilization exercise [of Brigade 179] on the Golan Heights...; c) on the Syrian front we have reinforced quite extensively; d) the Defense Minister was on the Golan Heights on New Year's Eve; e) the Chief of Staff spoke at the paratroopers' convention [--][33]

Here, Zeira added: the possibility of an Egyptian-Syrian attack "is entirely improbable, but perhaps the Russians think that they are indeed going to attack because they do not know the Arabs very well."[34]

If there is one sentence that represents the hubris of the DMI as a person and of AMAN as an organization, close to twenty-four hours before the outbreak of the war, this is the one. Because here Zeira[35] actually told his superiors a simple thing: Indeed, the Soviets have trained the Egyptian and Syrian armies for years, Soviet military advisors work hand in hand with their senior commanders, and Moscow has been supplying these two countries with all their armaments for a generation now. In a time of war, moreover, they have and would turn to the Soviets to ask them to send forces to help them out and, officially, the 1971 Soviet–Egyptian Friendship and Cooperation Treaty includes an article that obliges the parties to consult each other in situations of danger to their security. And yet, there is no reason to be concerned. We in AMAN have better information than the Soviets and we know the Arabs better than they do. And, we know they are wrong if they think Egypt and Syria are about to start a war.

Ending his review, Zeira added that the head of the Mossad had received a warning from his source last night that "something is going to happen" and that Zamir had left to check out the information.[36]

The Chief of Staff, who spoke after Zeira, explained once again that although he did not estimate that the situation indicated preparations for an attack, he also affirmed, "We don't have positive information that it is not an attack formation" and "technically they can act. These dictate our actions." Here, he described to Golda Meir the measures of readiness that he believed were required, which included instituting a C State of Alert and reinforcing the Golan Heights and the Sinai with additional tank crews. Despite all this, he added, he still did not recommend mobilizing the reserves, which would have been a preliminary condition for the conduct of defense plans based on warning. He justified his stand by saying that "if they are going to attack we will receive better indications." In conclusion, he said, "From their point of view, it will be a success if we know only twelve hours prior to the attack, and therefore we will arrange for and hope to have an earlier indication. Additional air photographs were taken today of the Golan Heights."[37]

The Minister of Defense spoke after Elazar, expressing even less concern:

> Preparations have been made, all but mobilizing the reserves. We are not worried about the Egyptian front, and of the Golan Heights we are worried all the time. I suggest we tell the Americans that we have now more indicators that the possibility of an Arab attack is more real. We need to ask the Americans to turn to the Russians to make it clear to them and through them to the Arabs that we are not about to

attack. We need to warn them that if the Arabs start a war they will not be enthused about our response, and ask the Americans to get the Russians' reaction. If it's reassuring—fine. If not—we will ask for more equipment immediately.... During the night we gave them information except for the matter of the [evacuation of the Soviet] families. We have information that the probability [for war] is higher [now]. And, [the Egyptian formation] is the kind of formation that goes for crossing most definitely. If we could have said something to Kissinger, but Simcha [Dinitz, Ambassador to Washington] is here [for mourning].[38]

The Prime Minister was the last one to speak. She said it was possible to act through the delegate in Washington, Mordechai Shalev, and added a speculation of her own: "The [UN] General Assembly is sitting at the moment and everyone is coming down on Israel. It is possible that their warped mind is saying that the Assembly should be presented with a fact, that the region is not asleep but active." Then, she accepted Dayan's proposal to hold an emergency meeting of the government with all the available ministers. This meeting was set for 11:30.[39]

Two points are noteworthy about the way the Chief of Staff and the Minister of Defense presented the situation. First, Elazar's tendency to raise the state of alert not on the basis of estimation but on capabilities (especially as it became evident in the canal sector) was expressed again in a clear verbal manner. The Chief of Staff also mentioned clearly that the available information did not suffice to justify mobilizing the reserves. But, it is clear from his words that if such information had arrived, he would have demanded mobilization. Second, while the Chief of Staff demonstrated heightened concern, Dayan expressed an unclear duplicity. On the one hand, he was not too worried about what was happening on the canal. On the other, he assessed that the Egyptian formation on the canal was most definitely offensive. It is difficult to understand his reasoning, especially when we know that Dayan was not arrogant enough to believe that one Jewish tank could take on twenty Arab tanks. But, he was less worried about the situation in the south since he regarded the canal as an enormous obstacle preventing the Egyptians from crossing. Moreover, he was still unprepared to accept the possibility that war was just around the corner, and here he was possibly influenced by the fact that the DMI barely related to the Egyptian formation in his report of the situation. And, in any event, Dayan's uppermost concern was the fate of the civilian settlements. There were no such settlements near the canal and, therefore, he continued to dedicate the bulk of his attention to the settlements on the Golan.

* * *

At the same time the series of discussions was under way on that short Friday, warning indicators continued to accumulate in AMAN. Much of the new information involved unusual activity of the Soviet navy, which had began leaving the Egyptian ports. Until late morning, information was received about the departure or the preparation for departure of Soviet naval units that had been docked continuously in the port of Port Said since the fall of 1967, and of other Soviet ships from the ports of Alexandria and Marsa Matruch. AMAN's experts regarded this move as "irregular" and as of "special meaning at this point in time in light of the departure this morning (before 051000) [10:00 on October 5] from Egypt of four of the Soviets planes that arrived on the night between October 4 and 5. These planes arrived in an unusual manner to Cairo and are now apparently carrying families of Soviet personnel back to the Soviet Union."[40] Their evaluation of the reasons for the naval evacuation, like their estimation concerning the evacuation of the families, was indecisive:

> At this point we cannot determine why the Soviet vessels are leaving the Port of Alexandria, nor can we determine where they are headed. However, considering the military developments in Egypt and Syria as well as the information about the evacuation of the families of Soviet experts from Syria on October 5th, we can suggest two main possibilities:
> a. That this departure is part of extensive Soviet activity based on their assessments/knowledge that a war is about to break out in the region. In such an event, we can not eliminate the possibility that removing the vessels is part of a Soviet move to deter the Egyptians by making it clear to them that they better not get dragged into a military adventure and that the Soviet Union has no interest in getting entangled. It should be remembered that at the end of the "year of the decision" (1971), the Soviets did the same when they evacuated their vessels from the port of Port Said, most likely in order to deter the Egyptians from renewing the war.
> b. An Egyptian decision—perhaps coordinated with the Syrians— to get the rest of the military Soviet presence in Egypt out. This possibility is also based on the information regarding the four Soviet planes that left Egypt in the morning to the Soviet Union and Hungary. However, we estimate that the Egyptians have no real reason at present to demand the expulsion of the Soviet experts and vessels from Egypt.[41]

AMAN's written interpretation in the matter of the vessels was even more reassuring than Zeira's verbal estimate during the morning meetings. The DMI proposed and emphasized the possibility that the Soviet evacuation was due to their knowledge that their clients were about to attack. The document's estimate—which was certainly written by someone who did not think such an attack was about to happen—explained the evacuation in more general terms, such as "a war is about to break" (initiated by whom?), or, at worst, as an Egyptian military adventure. It is also difficult to see the reasoning behind the attempt to tie the evacuation to a supposed crisis in the relations of Egypt, Syria, and the Soviet Union. Even during the surprising acute crisis of July 1972, the Soviet departure was organized and lasted a few weeks. Only a good evidence that a war initiated by the Arabs was about to break out could explain this emergency evacuation. Moreover, Moscow did not turn to the United States. After all, had the Soviets believed that Israel was going to initiate a war, they surely would have turned to the White House to control its ally.

* * *

The ministers who gathered for an emergency meeting in the office of the Prime Minister at 11:30 a.m. knew very little about the Egyptian and Syrian threatening deployment and the Soviet sudden evacuation. Only those who were in the Tel Aviv vicinity at that time—Chaim Bar Lev (the IDF Chief of Staff until 1972), Shlomo Hillel, Michael Hazani, Shimon Peres, and Yisrael Galili—made it to the meeting. Dayan and his assistant, Zvi Zur, Elazar, Zeira, the director of the Prime Minister's office, Mordechai Gazit, and other assistants were also present.

Dayan opened the meeting on a somewhat minor key, explaining to the ministers why they were called:

> Recently there was a lot of information and signs from the field of reinforcement on both Egyptian and Syrian fronts. The reinforcement actually took place, and the information was as though they were planning the war on both fronts, only on the Syrian front, and so on. New information on this matter arrived last night or in the last twenty-four hours that slightly altered the negative assessment we had of this information. I wouldn't say that it has made our assessment of this information positive, but it was enough for us to gather you here.[42]

The DMI presented the intelligence picture. It was the most comprehensive review presented on that day, for some of the ministers were hearing this for the first time:

> The Syrians gradually went into an emergency layout beginning on September 5, and today they are in full emergency disposition across

the Israeli border and they are testing and exercising a certain plan, which is apparently their working plan for conquering the Golan Heights. This plan talks about the conquest of the Golan Heights by the whole Syrian army, within a short period of time—two to three days—and getting as far as the Jordan and beyond. They have also placed the entire Syrian army on an emergency layout. Simultaneously, they advanced two Sukhoi squadrons, from the T4 area, quite far from the front, to the border. At the same time, the Syrians have internally expressed serious concerns about an Israeli attack. And this disposition that we call an emergency layout is defensive, and according to Soviet doctrine it can be used for defense as well as offense. If I analyze this disposition, it is most suitable according to the Soviet doctrine—which is also the Syrian—for offense and defense. The Syrians built up this layout, practiced the attack, and they are very concerned about our attack....

During the last week they [the Egyptians] conducted a large-scale combined exercise of air, sea, and land forces, as well as anti-aircraft defense. This is a GHQ exercise at the army and division level. A similar exercise took place last year about the same time, so in terms of timing and size there is nothing out of the ordinary. But we also see a lot of indicators of real war readiness among the Egyptians, especially for defense, out of concern that we will make use of the exercise in order to attack them.

But again, this is a defensive disposition, which enables them also to launch an attack. They reinforced the front along the canal during the last few days and increased the number of artillery from 800 to 1,100, an addition of 300. This is, indeed, a substantial reinforcement. They positioned many tanks near the canal so that today they have the possibility to cover most of the canal. This is good for defense as well as offense. We received information in the past that in October they were thinking of a coordinated Syrian–Egyptian attack, and in fact today the Egyptian and Syrian armies are deployed in such a way that they can launch such attacks and defend themselves from the very same positions.

Tonight an odd thing happened, when out of the blue the Russians sent eleven passenger carriers to the Middle East—five to Syria and six to Egypt—and we assume that these airplanes were sent to evacuate something, not equipment of course and maybe people; we don't know exactly what and how many. Thus far, two airplanes took off on their way back—one from Syria and one from Egypt. In addition, almost all the Russian vessels positioned in Alexandria left the port, something that happened only once before when they were concerned that the

Egyptians would carry out what they called "the war of the year of the decision." That was in 1971. The meaning of that act was that the Soviets had reservations regarding an Egyptian attack.

I will repeat, all our information says that the Soviet Union is trying to influence Syria and Egypt not to attack Israel. However, we estimate that the Soviet Union's power to influence these two countries is (a.) small and (b.) diminishing.

I must add that in the last week many propaganda sources as well as Egyptian and Syrian military sources and radio and press sources spoke openly about our preparations for a war against Syria and Egypt, and the Russians and Syrians described the shooting down of the planes on the 13th of the month as subversive and a trap on our part aimed at destroying unity in the Arab world on the background of the Eastern Front and the world isolation of Israel, especially in the UN and at the conference of unaligned nations. The Arabs and the Russians interpreted this as an Israeli move against trends toward Arab unification and the efforts to isolate Israel.

A few things that have transpired during the past week could have increased Egyptian and Syrian concerns: the paratroopers' exercise in the Sinai and the mobilizing exercise on the Golan Heights, as well as moving tanks onto the Golan. At the same time, we still regard as highly probable that the Syrian and Egyptian states of emergency and alert result from their fear of us and at low probability that Egypt's and Syria's real intention is to carry out limited aggressive moves. However, the most unusual item in all this is the eleven airplanes that came to Syria and Egypt. We still have no explanation for this. This is where we see something irregular.

The Egyptians and Syrians are not optimistic about their possible success if they try something on a large-scale, especially considering their aerial inferiority....[43]

The intelligence picture that Zeira presented did reflect the disturbing events, but, as usual, he moderated their meaning through a reassuring evaluation. Whether consciously or not, the DMI employed a few mechanisms to bridge the gap between the alarming information and his calming estimate. Thus, while emphasizing that according to Soviet doctrine a defense deployment can be used for offense, he avoided mentioning that AMAN obtained Syria's defense plan ("Sumud"), as well Egypt's, and they were entirely different from the two armies' present layout. Certain indicative signs in both Syria (advancing attack fighters, deploying bridge-layer tanks near the front, and moving Brigade 47 to the Golan Heights front) and Egypt (especially advancing the bridging equipment to the canal water line) had only one interpretation: preparations for an attack. But Zeira ignored the indicators that could only mean offense and could not fit with a defense thesis. Tahrir 41 furthermore was far from being a routine exercise, both because of the Egyptian army's unprecedented deployment, which became clear that morning, and the information that indicated that no exercise was taking place. Zeira also avoided elaborating about the sources of the warnings in comparison to the reassuring information. The warnings came from King Hussein, the CIA, the best of the Tzomet agents, and the SIGINT sources of Unit 848. The reassuring information, according to which the Syrians and Egyptians were worried about an Israeli attack, came mainly from the Arab media. Finally, Zeira spared his audience the more serious and more probable interpretation for the Soviet evacuation, that the Arabs were preparing a war—an estimate he ranked as the most probable one at the Ministry of Defense forum just a short while before.

The Chief of Staff spoke next. He described the situation as it was:

> In my mind, AMAN's basic evaluation that we do not face a war is the most probable estimate. It is very possible, since the deployment and preparations we see are also characteristic of a defense formation. This could be a result either of a concern they have, whose nature we don't exactly understand, perhaps worry stemming from our actions. This is not the first time we have seen them worried, that they add up different pieces of information, the fact that we downed thirteen of their planes, or things we've said publicly, or the fact that we have reinforced our forces, our air photograph sorties, and that we have these kinds of operations all the time. Perhaps they want to increase the tension in the Middle East by a state of alert on both sides, or a limited action for a limited time as a retaliation for the thirteen airplanes or something like that.
>
> At the same time, I must stress that according to the Soviet doctrine, a defensive disposition is also an offensive one, and it is possible to move for the offense from this layout. Therefore, this disposition has all the necessary elements an army would need in order to attack. Since I'm not in the business of interpretation, I think it is still important to examine whether we have proof that this is not an offensive deployment. I must say that we do not have sufficient proof that they are not about to attack. We don't have adequate information that they do want to attack, but I cannot say, based on the information that we have, that they are not going to attack.
>
> I have to admit that this formation gives them the technical ability to attack. (A.) There is no proof that they don't want to attack. (B.) They can attack. As a result we took all measures of readiness. This means that during this holiday the IDF is in a high state of alert.

Furloughs in all units on the front lines were cancelled, especially in the air force, and the armored corps. I do not mobilize the reserves, and the state of alert is conducted just by the regular army. I assume we will receive more information [even if] they are going for some kind of attack in total surprise. When I say surprise—even if we know twelve or twenty-four hours earlier—that will also be a big surprise, and I assume that if we approach that phase, we will have more indications and information. If they seriously intend to do something, we will know more than what we do at the moment. I am saving the mobilization of the reserves and other measures for further indications.[44]

Three points stand out in Elazar's words. One relates to the contrast in the way that he presented matters as opposed to the way the DMI did. Zeira opened by presenting worrisome information and concluded with the reassuring estimation; Elazar began with a reassuring estimation and closed with worrisome conclusions. Zeira emphasized that according to the Soviet doctrine a layout that seems to be offensive is also intended for defensive purposes; Elazar clarified that a defense formation can also be used for offense. Zeira detailed all the indications supporting the estimation that the Arab military preparations were a result of fear of an Israeli attack; Elazar clarified that he did not have enough indications that the preparations were not for an attack. These contrasts reveal a clear picture of a very worried Chief of Staff as opposed to a more relaxed DMI.

The second point relates to the conclusions that the Chief of Staff drew from the ambiguous situation in which he found himself. That morning he ordered taking the measures that he felt were necessary on the basis of the information that he had at the time. Elazar clarified that his decision to avoid demanding the mobilization of the reserves was not because he thought that the regular army could halt the attack on its own, but because the balance between available warning indicators and AMAN's reassuring evaluation did not yet justify such a move. He believed, moreover, that AMAN had the necessary means to collect clear indicators for war if Syria and Egypt indeed intended to launch one. As recalled, less than two hours earlier he received another confirmation that the special means of collection had been working but did not, as yet, produce any war indications. And, he was also waiting for information from Zamir, who was about to meet his senior source at 10 p.m. that evening.

The third point emanates to a great extent from the second. At the beginning of that day Elazar appeared ready to put the entire regular army and the mechanism of mobilizing the reserves in a state of alert as the country moved toward Yom Kippur. Now he was ready to consider mobilizing at least a portion of the reserve army, and this became an essential topic of the discussion that ensued.

Galili led the discussion, suggesting to look into the issue of reserve mobilization should it become suddenly necessary. He asked whether the Minister of Defense and the Chief of Staff had legal jurisdiction to do so, or whether a government decision would be needed. The Prime Minister said that she lacked experience of this kind and seconded Galili's question. Their remarks clearly reveal that they did not want any legal obstacles regarding the mobilization or the operation of the army due to Yom Kippur.

Dayan responded by saying:

> If something happens on Yom Kippur—before the government meets on Sunday—the authorization of the Prime Minister will be enough on any matter, whether we call the reserves or initiate counterbombing. I do not imagine we can call a government meeting in the same rushed manner. I am assuming it would be okay and legal, etc.... We have no intention to initiate something but only to respond and to take care of any situation that will be forced on us. I hardly believe that there will be disagreements, and we will have only a short time to take care of it. Considering the preparations and equipment that the other side has, they have the possibility to start an operation within a few hours. They are near the canal and on the Golan Heights, and their pre-attack action may give a forewarning, but by the time we see it, the operation itself will be under way.[45]

Galili repeated the authority of the Prime Minister and the Minister of Defense to mobilize the reserves, and the ministers voiced no objection. He also mentioned that "on May 15, 1967 [on the eve of the crisis that preceded the Six-Day War], all the clairvoyants and astrologers said that we can count on having two years without a war and at the beginning of June it broke out.... There is something in the air that loosens the belt, and therefore there can be surprises."[46] These words opened a discussion about possible Arab courses of action. Although Dayan suggested avoiding such a discussion, Zeira responded by saying that the Egyptians faced four options: 1. To cross the canal and to advance to the Gidi and Mitla Passes; 2. Raids into the Sinai and across the canal; 3. Static shelling along the canal; 4. A combination of bombing and raids.

Here he added:

> All these are in low probability, and the lowest probable move is the crossing of the canal and the highest is raids and perhaps shooting here and there. Neither the Egyptians nor the Syrians are highly optimistic about their possible success if they try something on a large scale, especially because of their air inferiority. They are well aware of this inferiority, and as long as they feel that they cannot get a more

convenient situation in the air, they will not go for war, certainly not for a large one.[47]

This estimate was odd even by AMAN's standards. When Zeira gave it, AMAN was about to start distributing a summary review of the situation that included all the warning indicators for war. Under such circumstances, the DMI's estimate that the probability for war was low, but if something happened it would be a general war and not a limited move, was understandable. But, Zeira's assessment that the probability for an all-out war was the lowest was totally disconnected from the impressive body of evidence presented by the organ he himself headed.

The Prime Minister was the last to speak. Her words expressed a feeling of distress and an intuitive sense of threat, without having an answer to the problem:

> I would like to say one word: There is something, there are points that repeat themselves from the 5th of June 1967. There were, here and there, messages that the IDF was reinforcing the Golan. Now we have a piece in the Egyptian press that says that the IDF is deployed on the Golan and that Israel has concentrated more forces along the lines, under a constant air umbrella. The Syrian forces stand by, ready to repulse any attack. It reminds me so much of what we had at the end of May, or the beginning of mid-May, until June 5, that this should also tell us something. The Egyptian newspaper *al-Ahram* reports: "All signs are that the tension in the Syrian front reached such a degree that there is a great danger of a big confrontation along the lines any minute now. Syrian military sources emphasized that the enemy intends to carry out a large-scale attack and that the Syrian armed forces are ready to repulse it. The sources added that Israel has increased its military concentrations considerably vis-à-vis the Syrian front in the Golan Heights area, especially during the last hours." All this is written in today's edition of *al-Ahram*.[48]

The Prime Minister's press review was in place, and her gut feeling was correct. Her words reflected the highly explosive situation and her dissatisfaction about the uncertain situation in which she had to make decisions. But she did not ask the most reasonable question under these circumstances: Can the regular army block a possible attack, and should a reserve mobilization, even a partial one, be called? In such an atmosphere, the meeting ended somewhat after noon.

It is possible that had the ministers who participated in this discussion received AMAN's intelligence review that summarized the situation as of 1000, and had they read it carefully, they would have asked to discuss again the issue of mobilization. But the distribution of the review had not yet started. And it is unclear whether the ministers—even the more experienced ones—could fully grasp its implications.

* * *

The analysts of the Research Department completed writing the document at 11:00 a.m. and it was distributed at 1:45 p.m. It included forty-three paragraphs, of which thirty-seven described the state of military readiness in Syria and Egypt and the Soviet evacuation. The rest estimated the meaning of this information.

The review started with a description of the situation in Syria. The opening paragraph said: "Though during yesterday and tonight there was no urgency in Syrian activity, it was clear that there was tendency to complete certain preparations toward October 5 and 6." In this framework, the following activity was noticed:

a. The transfer of ammunition from depots deep in the country (Homs) to a central ammunition depot at the southern section of the front.
b. Urgent allocation and vehicle replenishment to a number of units (including divisional headquarters).
c. Replenishment of movement in some units.
d. Various sources report on an impression among Syrian soldiers and officers that large-scale fighting is expected, without an explanation of who would initiate it.
e. On the evening of October 4, Damascus officially informed of a Syrian decision to renew diplomatic ties with Jordan.[49]

After a description of Syrian military activity and reports in the Syrian press about border tension and "imperialist" attempts to separate Syria from the Soviet Union, came the report's assessment. It said that the goal of the press reports was to prevent or moderate a sense of crisis in Soviet–Syrian relations. AMAN's analysts (but not the analysts of Branch 5), fell victim to a primitive Syrian deception, when noting in paragraph 17:

> Our estimation is that since September 13, the relations between Syria and the Soviet Union started to become tense, on the background of Syrian demands to receive advanced weapons that would "save" Syria from repeated defeats by Israel. This tension was flamed by repeating reports, mainly in the Lebanese press, on a cooldown in the relationship between the two states. Consequently, the [Syrian] regime finds it more difficult than in the past to keep a stable policy with the Soviets.[50]

The foundation for this assessment is unclear. Certainly, the increase in Soviet arms shipments to Syria since the summer of 1972 did not justify it. And, until the sudden Soviet evacuation, some twenty hours earlier, AMAN did not report any significant tension in the Soviet–Syrian axis. Relying on the Lebanese press, which was notorious for being a channel of disinformation, certainly did not justify it either.

The way the document analyzed the developments in Egypt was even more strange. After reporting that "the highest state of alert in all branches of the armed forces continues," paragraph 20 said:

> Egyptian apprehensions of an Israeli intention to exploit the exercise and the Ramadan feast for an offensive air action, continue. These apprehensions increased toward the morning of October 5, 1973, probably following an air photography sortie that our planes carried out yesterday October 4 at the canal sector, similarly to sorties that were conducted on October 3.[51]

This explanation appears as sealed-proof data. And yet, as far as it is known, AMAN had no information indicating such Egyptian apprehension. It is evident from the document's next paragraph that Cairo's media — unlike its sister in Syria — did not carry any new reports about the state of readiness of the Egyptian army. Consequently, there were no new explanations for it. Moreover, there was no logical link between the way the Egyptian army was deployed — as was described by the morning report and the document's following paragraphs — and the explanation presented here. It is obvious then, that this section reflected, more than anything else, the beliefs of its writer — the head of Branch 6, Yona Bandman — who presented it in the form of hard data.

Paragraphs 22 and 23 repeated word for word the Egyptian deployment as described in the early morning report. As recalled, this description was based on the air photograph taken a day earlier. The next two paragraphs described the Egyptian activity along the banks of the canal. Paragraph 24 said: "Regular activity was observed this morning along the canal sector. The observation posts had been manned as usual, soldiers walk without battle-order and weapons, and works of heavy engineering equipment could be seen."

The impression that emerges out of this description is that nothing irregular took place along the canal on the day before the dissemination of this report, and that works of the "lazy ones" succeeded in totally misleading the IDF observation posts. But, the reports that these posts delivered tell a very different story. Thus, for example, the observation post in the Mafzea'ch stronghold in the canal's southern sector, located, on Thursday morning, heavy truck traffic and inspections of mining at the descents to the water points. On the night between Thursday and Friday it reported on the movement of at least 150 vehicles on the

Suez–Cairo road. The observation post in Purkan, in front of Ismailiya, reported on Friday morning on a large number of infantry in the area, and on officers' (including a brigadier-general) visits and observations. Botzer, on the banks of the Bitter Lake, reported on heavy reinforcements of front-line units on Wednesday, enormous convoys of vehicles, including tanks moving on chains that arrived at the front on the night between Thursday and Friday. South of Botzer, the Lituf stronghold reported on dozens of Egyptian officers, including commando officers, who visited the front line to make observations on the Israeli side of the canal. The Budapest stronghold, at the north, reported a blackout in the city of Port Said on the night between Thursday and Friday, and sounds of the traffic of heavy equipment, including tanks. One of the front-line battalion commanders testified after the war: "Toward Yom Kippur, the [Egyptian] line became full to capacity. The observation posts saw all this. The posts in the strongholds as well as the long-range observation posts."[52]

Post facto, the DMI, the Southern Command Intelligence Officer, and the head of Branch 6 would argue that these reports did not change their estimates, since similar events had taken place in the past, and because of the cover provided by the Tahrir 41 exercise and other deception activities. The Agranat Commission concluded that these explanations were groundless in the light of the available field intelligence reports.[53] It based this conclusion, among others, on findings of one of its investigation teams that compared the Egyptian deployment on the eve of the war to deployments in previous Tahrir exercises. This comparison yielded significant differences in a number of areas—"differences that invalidate the argument that similar deployments took place in the past."[54] It is quite evident, then, that the false picture presented by paragraph 24 was not a mistake in assessment but a distortion of raw material.

The following paragraph reported on some of the activity along the canal. As recalled, three days earlier AMAN disseminated a review of the intensive Egyptian works to prepare descents to the water. Then, Branch 6 estimated that this activity was connected to the exercise. Paragraph 25 in the present review avoided assessing the meaning of this activity and reported only the data:

> 25. During the last days the continuation of intensive works in the southern sector of the Canal, in which there has not been any activity in the last year, was observed. At the Janifah-Suez sector, 8 new descents to the water points were prepared and another 30 were improved. We can thus summarize that since mid-September '73, 70 out of 85 descents to the water points in this sector have been improved. In addition, west of Kantara (about 7 kilometers from the Canal) a new revetment for crossing/bridging equipment, containing about 120 revetments occupied with unidentified vehicles, has been located.[55]

If the highly irregular activity along the canal was unsuitably reported, the irregular activity in the Egyptian Air Force was correctly reported, but, again, came with an opening paragraph that nullified its warning value:

26. The apprehension and the high state of alert brought about certain moves [in the Egyptian Air Force]:
   a. The commanders of air brigades are to be, personally, at the operational centers as of first light, October 5, 1973.
   b. On October 4, courses in the Air Force were stopped. So far, we knew about the stop of courses in the Air Defense.
   c. Frequencies of ground-to-air communication had been changed in an irregular manner.
   d. Checks of operational telephone lines are done every hour (instead of every 12 hours).
   e. Regulation of controllers between control centers in order to strengthen the control of Bani Suwayf.
   f. Soldiers were allowed not to fast on the feast of Ramadan.

27. This morning, October 5, the Egyptian Air Force carried out transport and helicopter flights and fighter training flights in a number of bases.

28. About 17 Dulphin training planes were transferred to the airfield of Kawm Awshim, which is used as a storing base. The planes were transferred from the bases: Helwan (8), Nuzha (4), and Bilbays (5). It is possible that this movement was aimed at evacuation of the Dulphins in order to protect them, and that they would not disturb the activity of other planes from operational bases (Bilbays), or that might be filled up with plans (Helwan).

29. The Egyptians intensify the transfer of improved [personal surface to air] Strela missiles and other certain equipment from Libya to Egypt. The nature of the other equipment is unclear.

30. At this stage there are no signs for a concrete initiated action of the Egyptian Air Force, though the measures that had been taken improve its ability to move to operational activity.[56]

The description of Egypt's naval preparations suffered from a similar problem. Here, too, the report was opened by an assessment that was presented as evidence, though it was not based on data:

31. The identification of Israeli air and naval forces' activity during October 4 (in the framework of an Israeli naval exercise), caused for increased apprehension in the Egyptian Navy. In response, intensified security measures were taken. Shore defense and warning nets became fully operational.

32. In addition to patrols at the entrance to the bases, three submarines in the Mediterranean and one in the Red Sea became operational.

33. On the evening of October 4, an order to paint the houses' windows and, possibly, vehicle lights, was issued.

34. Red Sea:
   a. On the night of October 4–5 naval units conducted a patrol between the islands of Shaduwan and Ashrafi. This patrol was exercised twice already (7 April [19]73, and 7 July [19]73) by two torpedo boats P-183, one missile boat Komar, and one mine layer T-43. In the past we estimated that this exercise was aimed at locating an unusual track to enable:
      1. A covered transport of an Egyptian naval force from R'ar'daka to the Suez Bay.
      2. An ambush exercise, to intercept Israeli naval targets at the entrance to the Suez Bay.
   b. In the Suez Bay area a frogmen force, 22–28 rubber boats, and at least one Bartram boat, were located. We estimate that the purpose of this force is to transport commando forces by two boats (as recalled, we located in this area also a platoon of company 9: naval patrol).
   c. On the evening of October 4 the Egyptians started to reduce the presence of merchant vessels in the Bay of Suez. As of first light, October 5, they are allowed to move in the bay only with the permission of the naval headquarters.[57]

The last part of the report described and analyzed the intensified Soviet evacuation, which started the previous afternoon. It comprised three paragraphs:

35. At the same time that the 5 irregular flights arrived in Damascus, 6 Aeroflot planes arrived in an irregular flight to Cairo international airport. The planes are 4 Il-18 and 2 Il-62 planes (maximal capacity of 780 passengers). Four planes left already for the USSR—at least in part carrying passengers.

36. Possibly there is a connection between the flights to Cairo and the flights to Damascus, i.e.—the Soviets want to evacuate families of experts from both Syria and Egypt. At this stage we do not have information to this effect.

37. This morning 2 (a frigate and a landing-craft-tanks [LCT] that already sailed) out of 3 warships in Port Said, and 5 (a destroyer; a frigate; a mother ship for submarines; a rescue ship for submarines; and a towboat) out of the 11 Soviet war ships in Alexandria, and the minelayer that was in Marsa Matruch, were supposed to leave their ports. In fact, almost all the Soviet naval units departed from Egyptian ports, a totally irregular move. The following will remain in Egyptian ports:
   a. Port Said—an LCT
   b. Alexandria—6 auxiliary ships and one "P" submarine, which is possibly unfit for service.[58]

One can hardly ignore here the prudent phrasing of paragraph 36. Throughout the document it was reported in a matter-of-fact tone that certain irregular activity—such as orders to soldiers to break the Ramadan fast or the painting of windows and car lights in preparation for blackout, which correspond only with war preparations—is a result of the apprehension of an Israeli attack. In contrast, the phrasing that "possibly there is a connection" between the Soviet evacuation from Cairo and Damascus, was extremely prudent. Moreover, the section dealing with the Soviet activity avoided a clear linkage between the sudden evacuation of the families and the totally irregular evacuation of the naval units from Egyptian ports. At this stage, AMAN had no good explanation for the Egyptian military deployment and state of readiness, and the Soviet evacuation. Its analysts, however, estimated these developments in calming tones, portraying assessment as information. There is only one explanation for this behavior: linking the evacuation from Syria to the one from Egypt could only give a boost to the explanation that both states were preparing to go to war. Here again, the theory (or the "conception") dictated the selection of information and its assessment, rather than the other way around.

The Summary of the document reinforced this conclusion. It presented the authorized estimate of the Research Department and DMI Zeira regarding the causes of the dramatic developments of the previous twenty-four hours:

Egypt

38. At the Canal theatre a complete emergency layout, in dimensions that we have never seen in the past, had taken place. It is possible that

this deployment is one of the issues checked in the framework of the inter-arm exercise.

39. Since October 4 at noon, Egyptian apprehensions of an IDF intention to exploit the exercise and the Ramadan feast to launch an attack on targets deep within Egypt had been increased. As a result, the "real" state of alert at the Army's four branches was increased to the highest, as of midnight October 4–5.

40. Though the mere taking of an emergency disposition in the Canal front allegedly implies the existence of warning indicators for an offensive initiative, to the best of our knowledge no change took place in the Egyptians' estimate of the balance of power between themselves and the IDF forces. Consequently, the probability that the Egyptians intend to renew fighting is low.

Syria

41. There is no change in our estimate that the Syrian moves are caused by a fear, which even increased during the last day, of an Israeli action. The probability of a Syrian independent (without Egypt) action remains low.

Soviets

42. The exceptional development of the recent 24-hour period is the preparations for the evacuation of Soviet experts' families from Syria (and possibly also from Egypt) and the departure of Soviet naval units from Egyptian ports. These preparations include the sudden arrival of 11 Soviet passenger planes to the Middle East (5, with maximal capacity of 600 passengers, to Damascus; 6, with maximal capacity of 750 passengers, to Cairo), and the return of some of them back to the USSR.

43. The arrival of these planes both to Egypt and Syria, and the departure of the naval units from Egyptian ports, raises the possibility that the evacuation of the families from Syria was not caused by tension in the Soviet–Syrian relationship but because of Soviet apprehensions that an Egyptian–Syrian military initiative against Israel is expected. As stated, we estimate the probability of such initiated action as low.[59]

This summary reflects a combination of dogmas (which, by their nature, cannot be falsified), groundless interpretation that is incoherent with available information, and an exaggerated self-assurance. This is not a post facto critique. At the time that this review was written, many in the Research Department assessed that it presented a distorted picture of data and a farfetched assessment. But this was AMAN's official estimate, and it had not undergone any changes.

Paragraph 38 assessed that the unprecedented Egyptian deployment was possibly taken in the framework of the exercise. Since it did not suggest any alternative explanation, and since the writers of this paragraph could not admit that they had no idea what was standing behind the Egyptian layout, which included all the necessary preparations for war, the impression it must have left was that the reason for the heightened activity was Tahrir 41. However, when the document was written there were already considerable doubts whether such an exercise was really taking place. Even Zeira, one of the most prominent supporters of the calming thesis, admitted in Dayan's office that it was unclear whether there was an exercise at all. To explain, under such circumstances, the Egyptian war deployment by an exercise that probably was not taking place, was an irresponsible act.

Paragraph 39 presents a similar problem. As recalled, AMAN had no reliable information that indicated that the exceptional Egyptian activity was motivated by fear of an Israeli attack. And yet, the choice of words used here clearly creates the impression that new information had arrived, according to which the Egyptians were worried about an Israeli attack, especially since October 4 at noon. As in other cases, the assessment was phrased as information.

Paragraph 40 entered the Israeli annals when the Agranat Commission published it in its public report in 1975, to explain why it recommended preventing the head of Branch 6, Lt. Col. Yona Bandman, from working as an intelligence analyst.[60] Indeed, this paragraph vividly illustrates the atmosphere in AMAN's Research Department on the eve of the war—an atmosphere whose best representative was Yona Bandman. He himself testified in the Agranat Commission:

> ... I wrote the first version of this intelligence review without paragraph 40, and I felt before writing it that I have to add it.... I felt that if I did not add paragraph 40, I would not have been fulfilling my duty. In other words, I am not required to just come and point out the information; my assessment was that purely from a military perspective you have all the indicators that you can look for, for offensive intentions. As far as intentions, my estimate remained that they did not regard themselves as being capable of launching an attack. They attacked 24 hours later, but this is something else.[61]

Paragraph 41 was the only one among these six paragraphs that could stand the test of reasonable logic, for two reasons: first, since during the last days before the breakout of the war, the stream of Arab speculations about a possible Syrian–Israeli confrontation increased; and second, the thesis that Syria would not go to war without Egypt proved to be right. In contrast, the following two paragraphs presented a professional mentality similar to that of Bandman.

Paragraph 42 made an unusual use of the term "exceptional" when asserting that "the exceptional development of the recent 24-hour period" was the Soviet evacuation. This act, indeed, was highly irregular. And yet, the use of such phrasing could create the impression that all other developments in Syria and Egypt were regular. Obviously, whoever used this phrasing did not mean to deceive his consumers. And yet, intentionally or not, the writer must have done so.

Finally, paragraph 43 makes it clear that Zeira's remark that the Soviets were wrong if they thought that Egypt and Syria intended to launch war—a remark he had made during the discussion in the Prime Minister's office, approximately when the writing of the intelligence review was over—was an opinion that was shared also by other senior officers in AMAN. It reflected, more than everything else, a *Weltanschauung* of intellectual megalomania and hubris, and a pretension to know and understand, better than anyone else, what really happens in these two states.

* * *

The decision to call for an emergency and unplanned GHQ meeting was probably made during Friday's early-morning hours, following the arrival of information about the Soviet evacuation and the dimensions of the Egyptian disposition.[62] The meeting convened at around 1300. Following short opening remarks by the Chief of Staff, DMI Zeira described the present intelligence picture to the participants. Zeira's description of the situation is unavailable, but there is no reason to assume that it was different from the report that he gave at the meeting with the ministers at the Prime Minister's office, or the detailed intelligence review that was disseminated in the very same hour. Concluding his presentation, Zeira gave his assessment:

> Everything I counted so far does not change AMAN's basic estimate that the probability for a war initiated by Egypt and Syria is still very low. The Syrian action could be a small-scale attack in the Golan Heights, and if this succeeds, they might go deeper. As for Egypt—either opening fire, or a helicopter-borne raid. . . . The lowest probability—a large-scale attempt of crossing the Canal, aiming at taking over both banks, and trying to reach the [Gidi and Mitla] Passes. . . . In summary, I don't think that we go for war, but today we have more question marks than, I would say, 24 hours ago.[63]

Zeira's final words were that a coordinated Egyptian–Syrian attack was "in low probability, even lower than low."[64] These words, it should be pointed out now, would carry a heavy weight the next day. Despite a general war warning on Saturday morning, many of the IDF commanders, including the Commander of the Southern Command, continued focusing on a small-scale Arab initiative and acted accordingly.

The Chief of Staff, who spoke after Zeira, opened by saying that, in essence, he accepted AMAN's assessment. But, he added, "I see the danger that a war . . . will break out today or tomorrow as less probable than no war breaking out at all." This phrasing, which seriously considered the possibility that war might start in less than forty-eight hours, is clear evidence that Elazar saw such a development as a possible option. Certainly, he related to it a higher probability than the DMI did. In contrast to Zeira, furthermore, the Chief of Staff did not speak at all about small-scale attack scenarios, to which the DMI attributed a higher probability. By Elazar's consistent logic, such attacks were both less probable and less dangerous, and, hence, he continued to focus on the main threat. He then described his morning decisions with regard to raising the regular army state of alert to the maximum, and explained the logic behind it: As long as we do not have positive proofs that Egypt and Syria do not intend to launch war, we must prepare for such an option.[65]

Toward the end of his presentation, the Chief of Staff explained why he thought that the probability for war was relatively low: "Though we do not have a concrete warning on attack, I assume that if, indeed, they have an intention to simultaneously attack from Egypt and Syria—we will get a warning."[66] In other words, Elazar did not build his intelligence assessment on theoretical assumptions regarding Egyptian and Syrian considerations of whether or not to go to war (i.e., AMAN's conception), but on the assumption that if they went to war, the available means of collection would yield a good warning about it. Quite certainly, he assumed this since, as far as he knew, AMAN's special means of collection, which were prepared to give such a warning, were operational.

In any event, Elazar's apprehensions of war increased during the last hours. In the morning he hardly mentioned the possibility of mobilizing the reserve army. Later, he said that he was waiting with this step until additional warnings came. Now he was ready to consider the course of action even if war erupted without additional warning:

> I still assess that despite the fact that we do not have a warning, we might get one. If we have a positive warning, we will certainly mobilize the reserve and do all the additional preparations. If worst comes to worst, that is, a large-scale attack starts without any additional word, we will have to block it with the regular forces, that is, with the

Air Force and all the forces we have in the lines. To meet such a possibility, we do not only declare a C State of Alert, but also reinforce the lines by the regular forces we have. In case such a catastrophe takes place, we will have to make a rapid mobilization. In this sense, there is a certain limit since on Yom Kippur there is no radio. We will see what we can do. It is possible to hold Galei Zahal [IDF broadcast station] on alert, and in case of emergency to operate the telephone switchboards, to call citizens, and tell them to turn on the radio and inform their neighbors. If fire starts, or if we have a too short-time warning, for example, we know today at 4:00 p.m. that the H hour is 8:00 p.m.—we will have to conduct a very rapid mobilization.... I don't think that they intend to launch war, since I assume that we would have gotten better indications. I do not think that the H hour is this evening or tomorrow, and if they have such an intention and if they have an H hour, I hope we will receive a warning.... As you know, we do not want war, and I would not like it very much that it would start in total surprise. There will not be a total surprise. Even if it happened today, we can call it an almost-total surprise, not because I am worried about the final results, but [because] this is not the way we like to enter war. But, if we have a short warning and we know that it will start in twenty-four hours when we will be better organized, then I'm sure we'll do it very well and I'm sure we'll achieve all our future plans that we have in our drawers. Have a good holiday.[67]

These words were a far cry from Zeira's estimate that the probability for war was "lower than low." The impression is that between AMAN's assessment, which continued to serve as the basis of Dayan's estimate, and Dayan's words that he would enable the reserve mobilization only if the Arabs start moving toward war, stood a Chief of Staff with a strong gut feeling that war was in the gate, and that it might start without a warning—certainly not with a warning a number of days, as AMAN promised in the past. But, such a feeling could not justify a demand to mobilize the reserve at such a delicate time—on the eve of the most sacred day for the Jewish people. Consequently, Elazar prepared whatever he could with the regular army—his ex officio realm of independent command.

* * *

Shortly after the IDF GHQ meeting ended, Elazar's morning decisions were translated into the "Ashur 2" command—a continuation for the "Ashur 1" command that was issued by the Operations/G branch GHQ according to the Chief of Staff orders of October 1.[68] According to Ashur 2, the IDF was to enter a state of alert "Manul" ("lock") at 1100 on October 5. In this framework, three tank battalions—Battalions, 82 and 75, of Brigade 7, and Battalion 71 of Brigade 460 (the tank corps school brigade)—were to reinforce the Northern Command. Their teams were to be flown to a nearby airfield and man the ready tanks of reserve Brigade 179. They were to be accompanied by Brigade 7's headquarters and an additional artillery battalion. In the Southern Command, three tank brigades—Brigades 14 and 401 of Division 252, and Brigade 460 of Reserve Division 162 (which now replaced Brigade 7 that had been deployed in the north) were to deploy between the Bir Gafgafa area and the canal front. According to Ashur 2 two artillery battalions and one 175mm battery were to reinforce these tanks. Additional artillery batteries were put on alert and were advanced toward the front line. The order also organized the deployment of forces in the Sharm el Sheik sector. The Air Force and the Navy were to raise their state of alert to "Manul." Later, the Deputy Chief of Staff issued an order to organize the means to facilitate a public mobilization call of the reserve in the big cities and to put the IDF radio station on a state of alert. The IDF Supreme Command Control Center (also known as "the pit") became operational at 1230.

The Manul command was a general alert command and did not involve the execution of any specific war plan. Additional orders would be given only on the next day. At this stage, however, the Chief of Staff decided to make a highly irregular move. Following a talk with IAF Commander Benny Peled—who estimated by now that the probability for war was high[69]—Elazar checked how many reservists the Air Force would need in order to be in a full state of alert. The figure Peled gave was a few thousand. Without getting an approval from the Minister of Defense, Elazar decided to mobilize them. The orders were issued immediately, and the mobilization started within hours—without the knowledge of the political echelon.[70]

* * *

During the noon hours, when the traffic in Tel Aviv slowed down, soldiers and officers also left the IDF headquarters at the heart of the city. AMAN's Research Department was no exception. While all over the country noncombatant soldiers and women soldiers remained in their bases, most of AMAN's analysts—the experienced bright minds, whose most important task was to warn Israel if war comes—left home, to prepare for Yom Kippur and to rest after sleepless nights and ongoing lengthy discussions. Maj. Ilan Tehila, the newly appointed head of the Soviet political section in Branch 3, was the duty officer. With him was a duty officer from AMAN's dissemination section. Some officers remained in their offices, summarizing the intelligence picture on the basis of the information that had been received that morning. Maj. Yekutiel Mor, the head of the Syrian military affairs section, intended to spend that afternoon at the air-photograph interpretation center, in order to get, as soon as possible, the results of the sortie that took place a few hours earlier.

The Chief of Staff was working in his office, taking care of various aspects of the state-of-readiness and war plans. The IAF provided him with a purchasing list that should be submitted to the Americans. It included air-to-air and air-to-ground missiles, sophisticated bombs, and mobile Chaparral SAM batteries. Others requests involved weapon systems for the ground forces, including a large quantity of personal antitank "LAW" missiles. Elazar also conducted a talk with the Commander of the Southern Command about the counterattack plans in the canal sector. Gonen told him that he wanted to replace the large-scale "Desert Cat" plan with a new one—"Knights of the Heart." The Chief of Staff stayed in his office till 2100.[71] The Minister of Defense and DMI Zeira left home a few hours earlier. The Prime Minister left her office in the *Kiria* after her meeting with the ministers and went to console Simcha Dinitz, the Israeli ambassador to the United States, who was mourning his father who had passed away. Later she went back to her home but remained restless. The fear of war continued to trouble her.[72]

According to Dayan's decision that was made in the morning's discussion, moves were take in order to update the United States of Israel's apprehensions and to make use of her good services in order to inform the Soviets, and through them the Arabs, that Israel had no offensive plans but was ready to meet an Arab attack. Accordingly, at 1140 a cable was sent to Mordechai Shalev, the charge d'affaires in the embassy in Washington, who was standing in for the ambassador while he was in Israel. Shalev was told that he would soon get another cable that would demand an urgent meeting with Secretary of State Henry Kissinger. He was to arrange for such a meeting. Since Israel's Foreign Minister, Abba Eban, was in New York for the annual meeting of the UN General Assembly, Shalev was told that if Kissinger was in New York he was to meet him with Eban, but that if he was in Washington he would meet him alone.[73]

Following an inquiry Shalev made with Eban, it was found that Kissinger was in New York and it was arranged to meet with him as soon as the cable from Israel arrived. However, sending the cable involved new problems that delayed it. Mordechai Gazit, the Prime Minister's Office General Manager, prepared the text of the cable according to Golda Meir's instructions, but it was delivered—despite Gazit's objection—for comments by AMAN.[74] This led to a major delay in its dispatch and to a significant change in its content. It was finally sent to Shalev at 1810 local time (1210 eastern standard time). Another delay took place in processing it in the Israeli embassy. Shalev finally got it at 1630 and Eban received it one hour later.[75]

The message was comprised of two parts. The first was a personal note from Golda Meir to Kissinger. The second contained AMAN's intelligence estimate. The personal note, which Eban and Shalev were instructed to convey word by word, was as follows:

> (1) The accumulated information we collected required us to take into consideration that the enemy's deployment derives from one of two causes: a. a genuine estimation by one of the two states that we want to attack one of them or both; b. intention of both, or one of them, to attack us.
> (2) If these developments are the result of their fear of our action, these fears are totally baseless. We want to ensure him [Kissinger] personally, that Israel has no intention to start a military action against Syria or Egypt, and that to the contrary, we aspire to contribute to relax the regional military tension. Therefore, we, by his [Kissinger's] courteous help, want to inform the Arabs and the Soviets about our approach, in order to lessen their suspicions and return tranquility to the region.
> (3) If Syria and Egypt intend to attack, it is important to make it clear to them in advance that Israel would react strongly and vehemently. We would like to bring this to the knowledge of the Arabs and the Soviets by his [Kissinger's] available channels.[76]

At the same time that this cable was sent, an intelligence estimate that was to go together with it was dispatched to the embassy. After describing the main elements of the Arab deployment, it said:

> We estimate that the moves of alert taken by Egypt and Syria are partially connected to the exercise (in Egypt), and in part to fear of offensive steps by Israel.
> We relate low probability to the possibility of the initiation of a military operation against Israel by the two armies. The possible Soviet evacuation by civilian planes and the anticipated departure of most of the Soviet vessels from the ports of Alexandria and Port Said can be the outcome of a crisis in [the] Soviet relationship with Egypt and Syria or a result of a Soviet estimate that hostilities are to break out in the Middle East.[77]

When Eban received this message, Kissinger's assistants informed him that he was not available and suggested that it would be delivered to his assistant, Brent Scowcroft. According to Eban, even prior to that, a cable from Gazit informed him that there was no need to bother Kissinger with a personal meeting after all. Now, after hearing from the charge d'affaires in Washington the content of the message, he also understood why. His impression was that "the main weight in Golda Meir's message was in the enclosed intelligence report.... [and this] concluded with AMAN's official estimate that 'the probability for war was low.'" Eban added in his memoirs:

> I understood in strict logic why it had been decided by Jerusalem to cancel my proposed talk with Kissinger. He was a busy man whose closest friends have never praised him for monumental patience. He would not be liked to be asked for an emergency meeting twice in two days simply to be told that our government in Jerusalem did not see very much to worry about.[78]

The Agranat Commission concluded that Eban had at least to call Kissinger, in order to add a personal dimension to the meeting between Shalev and Scowcroft. But it also found a reason for this behavior—"the intelligence briefing that was basically calming, and gave no sense of urgency and immediate concern, neither to Dr. Kissinger nor to Minister Eban."[79]

Golda Meir was probably unaware of these developments when they took place. Gazit, claimed afterward that he understood that "the corrections" inserted by the IDF officers into the original message would "spoil" the Prime Minister's cable and neutralize its warning value. But, he did not attempt to withstand their pressure.[80] Indeed, this was precisely the impact that the cable had on the Secretary of State. His assistant, Gen. Scowcroft, delivered it to him at about 2000 (0200 of October 6, Israel's time).[81] But Kissinger, who was busy, was impressed by the calming tone of AMAN's estimate. A check Scowcroft did with the CIA yielded a similar estimate: The tension was the outcome of an Israeli fear of Arab action and Arab fear of an Israeli attack. "The military preparations that have occured," the CIA estimated, "do not indicate that any party intends to initiate hostilities." Accordingly, Kissinger decided to delay delivering the Israeli message to the Soviets and Arabs until the next day—October 6.[82] On that day, at 0640, about 80 minutes before the outbreak of hostilities, and after Golda Meir summoned the American ambassador to inform him that war is beginning and that Israel will not launch a preemptive strike, Kissinger called the Soviet ambassador in the United States, Anatoly Dobrynin, and delivered a message that still reflected doubts about the probability of war:

> The Israelis are telling us that Egypt and Syria are planning an attack very shortly and that your people are evacuating from Damascus and Cairo.... If the reason for your evacuation ... is the fear of an Israeli attack, then the Israelis are asking us to tell you, as well as asking us to tell the Arabs ... they have no plans whatever to attack.... But if the Egyptians and Syrians do attack, the Israeli response will be extremely

strong.... But the Israelis will be prepared to cooperate in an easing of military tension.... The President [Nixon] believes that you and we have a special responsibility to restrain our respective friends.... If this keeps up ... there is going to be a war....[83]

The next talk between Kissinger and Dobrynin took place after hostilities started.[84]

* * *

Although the rate of activity at the Israeli decision-making centers slowed down toward the beginning of Yom Kippur, in some places intensive action continued. One of them was Unit 848. At 1700, Lt. Col. Reuven Yardor, the unit's most senior code breaker, finished solving a message that he had received only a short time earlier. Known as "yakhmur" ("fallow deer") message, it came from a source with a good access to the information he provided. It reported that the cause for the evacuation of Soviet citizens from Syria and Egypt was the shared intention of the two states to launch war. The message was immediately brought to the attention of 848's commander, who was still in his office. Ben-Porat called the head of the Research Department, who was at home, and read him—on an unsecured line—its content. At the same time it was sent to the Research Department. It arrived there at 1715.[85]

Maj. Ilan Tehila, the Research Department's duty officer, was one among a number of officers who for days now had felt inconvenienced because of the department's dominant thesis. He did not receive a prewarning from Unit 848 that a highly important message was on its way. But, as soon as it arrived, he started drafting a short document for immediate widespread dissemination ("red" intelligence review in AMAN's terminology), in which he reported the new and dramatic information. According to the Research Department's rules, this type of document was to be disseminated within thirty minutes to one hour after the arrival of the critical information. But, this time, it was delayed.

While writing the document, Tehila started consultations with others. The first he turned to were his colleague, Maj. Meir Elran, the head of the Soviet military section, and Lt. Col. Chaim Yavetz, the head of Branch 3. Yavetz, one of the most orthodox believers in AMAN's dominant thesis, was far from enthusiastic about the distribution of a document that might shake the basis of AMAN's official estimate. He instructed Tehila to consult a higher echelon, and Tehila called Col. Gideon Gera, the deputy head of the Research Department. Tehila woke him up, but Gera did not help. Consequently, Tehila called the head of the Research Department, Arie Shalev.[86]

While Tehila was trying to obtain an approval for the dissemination of the document, a telephone debate about its phrasing was developing between the heads of Branches 3, 5, and 6. The head of Branch 5, Avi Yaari, who was waiting for the results of the interpretation of the aerial photography sortie conducted earlier of the Syrian front, demanded an immediate dissemination of the document with minimal analysis. Yona Bandman, the head of Branch 6, took a precisely opposite stand. The head of Branch 3 had difficulties making up his mind. Finally, toward 2300, almost six hours after the message arrived in the Research Department, Tehila called DMI Zeira. Zeira knew already about the latest information. He told the duty officer to delay the report's dissemination, explaining that he was waiting for another piece of information—presumably, the message that the head of the Mossad was to deliver from Europe.[87] When asked by the members of the Agranat Commission why he gave this instruction, Zeira replied:

> There was no need, in my opinion, to alert the Chief of Staff at 11:00 p.m. and to tell him: there is such a message, and add what we wrote later, that the source was not reliable enough and that there are mistakes and we also think so. And, it should be remembered that I know and the Chief of Staff knows that the whole IDF is at the highest state of alert [. . .] and we all stand ready to shoot. This was my feeling that night and so, I assume, was also the Chief of Staff's feeling. It was not a situation that came "out of the blue" where everyone went home, a regular Yom Kippur and [then] you have to call into action. So, the Chief of Staff would have seen it, and I assume that he would have said: Fine, but Gorodish [Gonen, the Southern Command Commander] has [300 tanks], Benny Peled holds all the pilots in the bases, Haka [Hofi, the Northern Command Commander] has [177 tanks], and everyone stands ready to shoot? Fine.[88]

Zeira's words present, in the clearest manner, his rather unique perception of his role. Throughout the day he heard the Chief of Staff repeatedly say that he was waiting with a demand to mobilize the reserve army until further indications for war arrived. He himself estimated that the Soviet evacuation was the most dramatic development in recent days. Moreover, he had no clear answer to why it was taken, but he had to admit that it casts doubt on AMAN's thesis that war was unlikely. Then a message from a source that checked the matter categorically said that the reason for the evacuation was the Soviet knowledge that Syria and Egypt plan to go to war—and yet Zeira decided to avoid disseminating this information to its most relevant consumers.

Why Zeira acted this way is a matter of speculation. It seems, however, that here again he was motivated by two factors: his confidence that Egypt did not perceive itself as being capable of launching a war, and certain personal traits that led him to believe that he both understood the situation better than others and knew better than them what should be done in Israel's most fateful matters. Zeira's explanation for his behavior was farfetched and unacceptable as demonstrated by the Chief of Staff's reaction upon learning about these events from the commander of Unit 848, a few weeks after the war:

> I was in my office until 9:00 p.m. and the whole GHQ staff was in the office until about 7:00 p.m. We could do everything. I went home at 9:00 p.m. thinking to myself that everything that had to be done according to the intelligence information was done, not knowing that four hours earlier, war information arrived on the floor above me [in AMAN's Research Department] and nobody showed it to me. . . . Had I seen the information at 5:00, 5:30, or 6:00 p.m. — I would have issued a mobilization order for the reserve army. Because we were already under grade C State of Alert since the morning, the mobilization offices were opened. Everything could have been done fast. The cabinet ended its Friday meeting deciding that if mobilization of the reserve army was required, I and the Minister of Defense had the authority to do it — without additional cabinet approval. Had we done so on Friday at 6:00 p.m., the reserve units of the Northern Command would have reached the front line before the beginning of the war, and the Syrians could not have broken through the front. The reserve forces of the Southern Command would not have arrived [on time], but at least they could have moved to the front in an orderly fashion and not a tank here and there, like crazy, unequipped, and not on tank transporters. Moreover, I would have had a whole night for the regular army. . . . According to the "dove cote" plan [the defense of the Canal line by the regular army] that was exercised a few times, I would have flown a paratroop brigade to the [Bar-Lev] strongholds and we would have taken them all, including the empty ones. Thirteen artillery batteries could have been deployed on the Canal. The regular division of Sinai would have been deployed at the front. The Egyptians would not have crossed the Canal. Perhaps they could have succeeded in the gaps, between the strongholds, but not along the whole line, without casualties, and as if they were on parade.[89]

Zeira's decision to delay the document's dissemination ended the telephone debate about its phrasing. It was distributed, ultimately, on October 6, at 0635. By then, Zamir's report, on the basis of his talk with Marwan, that war would start the same day had arrived, and the policy-makers were already discussing the necessary moves to meet the coming war — completely unaware of this intelligence review, which by now lost all its warning value. But the document has, nevertheless, some historical and educational value, since the way it was phrased and the estimate it contained constituted another example to the destructive effect of cognitive obstructions. The relevant paragraphs of the document were as follows:

> 2. A reliable source gave a message according to which the regime in Damascus decided to expel by air the Soviet military experts, including their families, from Syria. According to these sources, the Syrians explained their move by claiming that they and Egypt intend to launch a war against Israel.
> 3. Although the general line of the information, as given to the source, reflects the course of events, certain inaccuracies that can be derived from the source's reliability or the tendentiousness of the sources of the information, should be taken into account.
> 4. This message raises two basic possibilities:
>   a. That the Soviets learned that the Egyptians and the Syrians take military moves in order to initiate war, a development that according to Soviet estimate implies a grave danger, and a self-made dynamics that might lead to an uncontrolled escalation. If this was the case, it is reasonable to assume that Moscow demanded a more realistic and constrained behavior from Egypt and Syria. When it became clear to Moscow that the Arabs continue to prepare for war, they decided to evacuate, in an inclusive manner, their presence from these states, both in order to deter their clients from a disastrous miscalculation, and in order to demonstrate their resentment and decisive objection to this irresponsible Arab behavior.
>   b. That on the background of the Soviet objection to military moves taken by the Egyptians and the Syrians, a sharp disagreement that might even have involved exceptional/extortive Arab demands, erupted. Under such circumstances, it is possible that the Egyptians and the Syrians, on their own initiative, demanded the Soviet evacuation and used the war issue as a cause to expel them.[90]

The speculative estimates presented in this document—the outcome of an intensive debate among the leading analysts of the Research Department—aimed, primarily, to neutralize from the original message its alarmist components. It was done in three different ways. First, though the original message is unavailable, we can nevertheless conclude from Ben-Porat's and Tehila's testimonies that the way it was phrased in the document distorted its original meaning. Then, an attempt was made to kill the messenger by faulting the reliability of its source and by casting doubts about the Soviet explanation for the evacuation by speculating that Moscow might have had a hidden agenda that led her to indulge in deception. Finally, raising wild speculations, as if AMAN had any real information about Moscow's true relations with her clients, amounted to no more than an irresponsible attempt to settle the tension between the dogmatic belief that Arab war initiation was still out of the question, and the incoming solid information that said that such an initiative was precisely the cause for the sudden Soviet evacuation.

* * *

While the dispute concerning the document that Maj. Tehila wrote was still going on, new details of the Syrian disposition had become available through air photographs taken in a sortie a few hours earlier. The head of the military section of Branch 5, Maj. Yekutiel Mor, who joined the interpreters in order to get the results as soon as possible, had no doubts that, according to the Soviet doctrine, the layout was an offensive one.[91] The intelligence review that was written rather hastily, said, among others things:

1. Another reinforcement by 5–6 medium artillery corps battalions took place (altogether, 130 artillery batteries are deployed now in the first defense line and its rear).
2. Part of the medium artillery was advanced to more forward positions; about 8 medium artillery battalions had been advanced to a distance of 6–8 kilometers from the cease fire line.
3. A 240mm mortar battery (3 pieces) was localized in the front's central sector. It is possible, though with lesser probability, that it is heavy artillery 203/180mm. . . .
5. Part of the tank battalions of the infantry brigades was advanced to dispositions near the line of the front strongholds. In the oil-axis area in the southern sector of the front, part of the brigade's tank battalion was placed in fire positions behind a dirt embankment.
6. An addition of about 2 tank battalions was localized in the rear of the first defense line in the front's southern sector.[92]

The analysts of Branch 5 were cautious and avoided ruling categorically that the Syrian disposition was offensive. This was the result of an ongoing debate between Yaari and his analysts, and the command of the Research Department, primarily its head, Arie Shalev.[93] And yet, the estimate they added to the data was rather clear:

The present disposition indicates, in our estimate, a high degree of readiness in the units deployed in the front. In this framework the following should be noted:

1. The increase of medium artillery (5–6 battalions) that was localized in the sortie, draws, in our opinion, from the advancement of an additional GHQ medium artillery group and also reserve artillery battalions (one GHQ artillery group is already deployed in the front).
2. The advancement of some of the medium artillery battalions frontal positions in the first defense line (6–7 kilometers from the frontal strongholds line) enables the Syrians to cover by fire all the Golan Heights, including the slopes climbing to it. This enables the Syrians to cover by fire, for defensive purposes, all the routes through which the Golan Heights can be reinforced. On the other hand, it enables—also according to the doctrine—to cover by fire maximal territory for an offensive initiative.
3. This is the first time heavy artillery was localized in the Syrian front. 240mm mortars are used, primarily, to pound the strongholds in the Golan Heights. As for the additional armored units that were localized at the rear of the first line of defense—we cannot decide its exact identity. We estimate, however, that, possibly, these are:
    a. Units from Armored Brigade 47, that might have had arrived recently at the front.
    b. Units from Armored Division 3.

In summary, what is remarkable in the Syrian forces' disposition in the first line of defense, as located in the present air photographs, is the high degree of war readiness. It is hard for us to decide if this is true only about this line, since we do not know the deployment situation at the second line of defense (where the armored brigades are supposed to deploy). Another deployment is the change in the defensive character that we saw, so far in the first line of defense, and whose main expression is the forwarding of the medium artillery battalions, in contrast to the past, where they were usually deployed in a longer distance from the front line, when their range covered mainly the Syrian territory.[94]

It is unclear why this report was disseminated only at 0340 of the next day. As far as it is known, it was ready for distribution in the late afternoon, when it could have had a major impact, especially on the Chief of Staff, who noted a few times in earlier discussions that he was waiting to see the results of Friday's sortie. But, at 0340 on Saturday, October 6, the telephone already rang at the house of the Military Secretary of the Prime Minister. On the other end of the line was Fredy Eini, the head of the Mossad bureau chief, who reported that Zamir had just called him to report on his meeting with Marwan. "This evening," Eini began, "they'll start firing."[95]

Friday, October 5, 1973

* * *

The head of the Mossad, Zvi Zamir, arrived in London before noon on October 5. The meeting itself was scheduled to take place at 2200 local time—2300 Israeli time. The participants included the head of the Mossad, Marwan's task officer, and Marwan himself. The meeting lasted about an hour, during which the task officer wrote down what Marwan had to say, including the details of the war plan that he gave.

Marwan's message was clear, though not entirely decisive. War, according to him, was to start the next day. He did not give any specific H-hour, but he pointed out that the intention was to start fire toward nightfall—timing that was already known from the recognized Egyptian war plans. And yet, when asked by the Mossad's officers if the fate of this warning would be similar to that of earlier warnings that he had provided, he gave no definite answer. He said repeatedly that Sadat could change his mind at the last minute.

The issue of earlier warnings that did not materialize—a classic case of the cry-wolf syndrome—annoyed both the source and his Israeli handlers. From Zamir's perspective, issuing a clear-cut warning that war would start the next day was a dangerous gamble. It was clear to him that once his report arrived in Israel, an immediate reserve mobilization would start. This, especially in the midst of Yom Kippur, would have far-reaching implications. Zamir, too, was thinking about the "duck night" trauma of April 1959, and he, too, was thinking about a situation in which a public mobilization starts but there is no war. But, because he was aware of the recent days' information concerning Arab war preparations, and since Marwan provided a highly concrete warning this time, including an immediate date of its start and a detailed and updated war plan, he decided to deliver the warning in its clearest form to Israel.

When the meeting was over, Zamir wrote the version of the report that he intended to deliver to his bureau chief, according to prearrangements they made before he left Israel. He called Eini's house through the international switchboard. The operator tried to convince him that he had no chance to get a response on the other end of the line, since it was a holiday in Israel, but she was wrong. Einy, who finally answered the phone, wrote Zamir's words and, then, translated the code words into an understandable message. The message was clear: The Egyptians plan to start fire toward the evening, according to the plans we already know. The source is not certain 100 percent that war will indeed start, but he is certain in 99.9 percent that this will be the case.

While Zamir called Einy, the other Mossad officer who was present in the meeting wrote a lengthy cable, which included all the details of the Egyptian war plan as reported by Marwan. This report would be delivered in the early-morning hours to the Mossad headquarters in Tel Aviv. When it would arrive there, it would add operational dimensions to the general warning. Zamir's warning itself was responsible for raising the Prime Minister, the Minister of Defense, the Chief of Staff, and many others from their night's sleep at about 0400. They would soon start a series of intensive discussions and preparations for war, which would end only when the firing started some ten hours later. Zamir himself returned to Israel only on Monday.[96]

Chapter 16

Saturday, October 6, 1973, 0400 –1400

The timetables of the events of Yom Kippur, October 6, show an unexplained one-hour gap between the time that the head of the Mossad's bureau chief received the warning from Zamir and the specific time at which the relevant policy-makers received it. Einy received the message at about 0230, and he needed a few minutes to translate it into a coherent and understandable message. Although, according to one source, a report about the outcome of Zamir's meeting with Marwan had already reached AMAN by 0240[1], the military secretary of Golda Meir, and other assistants who were to inform their bosses, received it only after 0340.[2] Unfortunately for the Israelis, this was not the only hour that was lost during the short time span that remained before firing started.

The information that Marwan gave to Zamir was that the Egyptians intended to start fire according to the plans that AMAN already had in its possession. According to these plans, H-hour was to be at "sunset"—a timing that was to enable the Egyptian army to use the last minutes of light in order to make a first wave of air strikes into the Sinai and to carry out an effective shelling of the Bar-Lev line, and, then, to cross the canal under the cover of darkness as a means to evade the IAF strikes. As described, this H-hour was changed to 1400 on October 3 as a compromise with the Syrian demand to start fire in the early morning hours. Marwan, who was not aware of this last-minute change, told Zamir only what he could have known.

"Sunset" on October 6 was at 1720 and last light (or, to use the astronomical term, "civil twilight ending") was at 1744. The Chief of Staff and his commanders were informed that war would start at 1800,[3] and there were other reports that war would start at "last light."[4] This three- to four-hour difference between the expected and the actual H-hour added another dimension of chaos to the hasty Israeli preparations.

At the focus of the following description of events during the last ten hours before war broke out, stands the question of how the Prime Minister, the Minister of Defense, the Chief of Staff, and the Director of Military Intelligence estimated the situation in these hours and what was the impact of their estimates on the decisions that they made. The next chapter will answer two additional questions: First, how were the IDF's preparations to meet the attack on the two fronts influenced by the short time span of the warning? And second, what was the impact of the insufficient warning on the IDF's fighting capability during the war's first days?

* * *

The available information about the reaction of Golda Meir, Dayan, Elazar, and Zeira to the warning delivered by Zamir and the additional information that followed indicates that only two of them—the Premier and the Chief of Staff—accepted the warning at face value, estimated that war would start that same day, and acted accordingly. In contrast, the Defense Minister, the DMI—and a number of senior IDF and AMAN officers—continued to doubt, until the very last moment, that war would break. In theory, Dayan and Zeira's doubts did not carry any practical implications since the military preparations during those hours were initiated and maintained on the basis of the assumption that war would start that same day. In actuality, however, Zeira's continued assessment about the war's low likelihood influenced Dayan's estimate. And, the latter's assessment was crucial since it determined his stand on the two central decisions that had to be made: the conduct of a preemptive air strike, and the mobilization of the reserve army.

Elazar's independent decision on Friday morning to raise the state of readiness of the regular army to the top is an indication that by that stage he had already doubted the validity of AMAN's calming assessment. While on Friday he avoided openly challenging this estimate, he repeatedly said that all he needed in order to demand a reserve mobilization was another indication for war. Two such indications—Unit 848's decrypted message that explained the Soviet evacuation, and the findings of the air photograph sortie over the Golan front—had been available since Friday afternoon but were not disseminated. The warning that was delivered by Zamir—this time as a raw material and without AMAN's calming assessment—enabled him to re-estimate the situation and conclude that war was either certain or, at least, highly likely. Once he reached this conclusion, he ceased assessing the war probability and started acting as if it were certain.

One indication of this approach was Elazar's rapid and efficient rate of work. Ten minutes after receiving the telephone call about the coming war, he spoke with the IAF commander and instructed him to prepare his planes for a preemptive air strike in the afternoon hours. They agreed that the strike could be against Egypt or Syria, against their air force or SAM layout, and any other combination. Maj. Gen. Peled made it clear that the IAF would be ready to strike at 1100. At 0510, forty minutes after receiving the war warning, Elazar convened in his office with his deputy, Maj. Gen. Yisrael Tal to discuss a number of questions, including the launching of a preemptive strike, the mobilization of the reserve, deployment in the fronts and in the rear, and the partial evacuation of the civilian population of the Golan Heights. Ten minutes later, a GHQ meeting with a reduced number of participants started. During the discussion, the Chief of Staff authorized the IAF commander to mobilize all the reserve soldiers he needed for war. Simultaneously, he authorized the mobilization of an additional few thousand soldiers and issued instructions for full-scale mobilization once the political echelon approved it. All this was done within eighty minutes since Elazar received Marwan's warning.

This rate of activity stands in clear contrast to that of the Defense Minister. Dayan received the message about the incoming war at 0400, and it took him two hours to convene his assistants for a first discussion on preparations for war.[5] To the Prime Minister, who wanted to meet him immediately, Dayan explained that he would not be able to do this before 1000 or 1100. Their discussion was moved forward only after pressure was exerted by Meir's military secretary.[6]

The contradiction between the war assessments of the Chief of Staff and the Minister of Defense received an even more vivid expression in the discussion that started in the latter's office at 0600.[7] Dayan instructed at its beginning to prepare the civil defense layout for a possible strike by Egyptian Scud missiles on Tel Aviv. In addition, he suggested organizing a "trip" for the kids in the Golan's settlements in order to get them out of the range of the Syrian artillery. He later noted that the present situation did not justify a preemptive strike—certainly not against the Egyptians. On the other hand, if Egypt started fire, it would justify hitting the Syrians before they joined the war, because of the vulnerable settlements in the Golan. Later, Dayan raised the possibility of delivering a warning to the Arabs through the United States, both in order to deter them and in order to show the Americans that Israel was doing her best to prevent the war. He asked Elazar about what the Americans were saying. The latter said that the DMI believed that they did not see the situation clearly, that they were not aware of the Soviet evacuation, and that they had not assessed that the Arabs intended to attack.

Here, Elazar raised the issue of a preemptive air strike, as discussed earlier between him and the IAF commander. Though he did not say it explicitly, such a strike had become more critical now since Israel was caught unprepared for war. Only a successful air strike that would destroy the Egyptian or the Syrian air force, or the Syrian anti-aircraft defense layout, could have enabled the IAF to participate effectively in the defensive stage of the war. Elazar tended toward the Syrian option. He knew that the IAF commander assessed (as he would also say in a discussion at Dayan's office at 1100 that morning) that the destruction of the Syrian air force could take about an hour, and that the SAM layout between Damascus and the Golan could be destroyed within a few additional hours.[8]

Dayan fully rejected the option of a preemptive air strike. He was less concerned about the Chief of Staff's anxiety about a situation in which the IDF was caught unprepared for war at two fronts and more concerned about the White House's reaction to a situation in which Israel initiated fire while the Americans did not assess that the Arabs were planning to strike. Here, another dire result of AMAN's calming estimate manifested itself. A few days earlier, the CIA warned about Syrian preparations for war and AMAN explained to the Americans that the Syrian activity was for defensive purposes. Similar messages were delivered to Washington during the next few days. On Friday night another reassuring assessment accompanied the Prime Minister's urgent message to the Secretary of State. Consequently, the Americans became convinced that the Arabs did not intend to attack. But Dayan maintained that even if the Americans were absolutely certain that the Arabs planned to attack, they would not have given a green light for an Israeli preemptive strike. Under such conditions, so he assessed, Golda Meir would also object to this option.

It is possible that Dayan's decisive objection to the preemptive air strike option was based on a miscalculation of the risk that was involved in the Arab military initiative. But it is also likely that Dayan, who was not a risk-taking type of leader, categorically rejected this option and made it clear that he did not see a reason to approach the Americans about it, since he was still far from being certain that war would, indeed, break out. The way that he treated Elazar's next item on the agenda—the mobilization of the reserve—enhances this impression.

The dialogue between the Chief of Staff and the Defense Minister on the number of soldiers that should be mobilized reminded one of the participants in the discussion of the negotiations between God and Abraham on the minimal number of righteous that were needed to save the town of Sodom.[9] Their opening positions were clear: Elazar demanded the mobilization of the IDF's entire fighting force—about 200,000 reserve soldiers. Dayan agreed to the mobilization of one brigade, and then to 20,000 to 30,000. Explaining that the forces in Sinai did not need reinforcement, he added, "On the basis of messages from Zvika [Zamir] you do not mobilize the whole army."[10] The Chief of Staff, who knew that on the issue of mobilization he held a stronger position than in the question of preemptive strike, did not give up and maintained that the massive mobilization by itself could deter Egypt and Syria. Dayan responded by saying that even a limited mobilization for defensive purposes could cause panic in Damascus. Here, nevertheless, he was ready to compromise and expressed a readiness to mobilize the force that was needed for defense. He asked what the size of such a force would be. Elazar said that the reinforcement of the Golan front demanded one division and, altogether, 50,000 reserve soldiers were needed for defensive purposes on all the fronts. Specifically, he told Dayan, he wanted to mobilize one division and another partial division for the Northern Command, one division for the Southern Command, and one GHQ reserve division for the Central Command.

Now, the Defense Minister noted that a general mobilization would have public implications. Obviously, he weighed two factors here: On the one hand, if war erupted, the IDF would need to be at maximal force. On the other hand, a dramatic general mobilization—in the midst of Yom Kippur and an election campaign whose main theme was that Israel had never been safer—without the outbreak of war, might cause him (personally) and his Labor Party (politically) to suffer a considerable amount of damage. And, since Dayan was an experienced and prudent military man who knew the potential military consequences of an Arab surprise attack on two fronts, it is quite obvious that at this stage he did not attach a very high probability to the possibility that war was imminent.

The Chief of Staff, whose main concern was to create optimal conditions for a quick military victory, made it clear, again, that he wanted to mobilize maximal power. He claimed that under the conditions in which war was about to start—conditions that would enable the Egyptians and the Syrians to occupy some territories that were held by Israel—the distinction between offense and defense had lost its significance, since counterattacks would be needed anyhow in order to return to the territorial status quo. A counter attack in the Golan Heights would require two divisions. Here, Dayan asked what would be the difference between an immediate mobilization and a mobilization that would start only when war broke out. Elazar said that the difference would be twelve hours and Dayan responded, "The Chief of Staff wants to mobilize forces for a counterattack in a war that did not start?" Consequently, he agreed to the mobilization of the force that was needed for defense, but rejected the request to mobilize for a counter offensive—a request that he would accept, "only after the first shot."[11]

In light of this compromise, the Defense Minister suggested that the Prime Minister be asked to authorize the mobilization of one division for the north, one for the south, and the whole air force—altogether about 50,000 to 60,000 soldiers. His military secretary, Brig. Gen. Raviv went out of the office in order to call Golda Meir. Meanwhile, the debate between Elazar, who demanded the mobilization of a double figure, and Dayan, who refused it, continued. Raviv failed to communicate the message to the Prime Minister and, in light of the gap between the relative stands of the Defense Minister and the Chief of Staff, no further action was taken. According to Dayan, he understood that at this stage there was no reason to avoid the mobilization of the two divisions and the air force. To the members of the Agranat Commission, he said, "Either he [the Chief of Staff] thought he had the authority to mobilize on the basis of what I said, or that he thought there was no urgency...."[12] Elazar saw the situation differently: "At a certain stage in the discussion, the Defense Minister ordered his military secretary to ask, by telephone, the Prime Minister's authorization to mobilize two divisions. I made it clear that this was not enough. The Defense Minister cancelled his order ... and summarized that both suggestions would be brought for the Prime Minister's decision. I have to emphasize that the Defense Minister gave me no authorization to mobilize 50,000 to 60,000 men on his own responsibility, without waiting for the Prime Minister's decision but only suggested 'to ask the Prime Minister for an authorization to mobilize.'"[13] Elazar added that since preparations for a general mobilization continued anyhow, the loss of time was only partial.[14]

It is possible that a further discussion would have saved precious time. However, at this stage, DMI Zeira joined the discussion and provided an updated intelligence picture. He reported that the Americans knew (in contrast to his previous assessment) about the Soviet aerial evacuation, but that they did not know about the naval movements, and that they continued to claim that war was not going to take place. He also reported a number of worrisome pieces of information: The Soviet evacuation had been accelerated and it included not only women and children but also men, including non-Soviet citizens; air photographs indicated that the Syrian layout was more offensive than defensive, though the same could not be said about the Egyptian disposition; the chief of Jordan's intelligence service had arrived unexpectedly in Damascus; and Arab and Soviet media had reported on the mobilization of forces in Israel. Here, he also reported that according to a message decrypted by Unit 848 (Friday afternoon's "yakhmar"message), the Soviets were conducting the evacuation because they knew the Arabs intended to attack. Zeira did not forget to add that the reliability of the source was not high.

The DMI estimated that fear of an Israeli attack was not the reason for the Soviet evacuation. If this was the case, he maintained, the Soviets would have approached the Americans with a demand to restrain Israel. Instead, he raised three possible explanations for the tension: Egyptian and Syrian military exercises; a coordinated Egyptian-Syrian exercise; and a coordinated war. Despite incoming warning information, Zeira continued to claim that politically Sadat had no need to go to war, but admitted that he could not bridge the gap between this estimate and the gathering information. In response to the Defense Minister's question about whether all of AMAN's means of collection were operating, he answered in the affirmative. At this stage, the special means were, indeed, operational.

Following Zeira's intelligence review, the Chief of Staff asked for a reconnaissance flight by a remote piloted vehicle, which had started entering IAF operational service, on both fronts. Fearing that a shooting down of the plane over Arab territory might raise the tension and give the Arabs an excuse to attack, Dayan authorized a sortie only on the Israeli side of the border.

The discussion ended with Zeira's brief description of the Arab war plans, mentioning also an Egyptian intention to attack the Sharm el Sheik region. Consequently, Dayan ordered to evacuate families from Abu Rudies. According to the meeting's protocol that was used by the Agranat Commission, the Defense Minister closed the session by telling the Chief of Staff: "You have an agreement [on the mobilization] of the air force, one division for the north and one division for the south."[15]

* * *

When the discussion at the Defense Minister's office ended, the Chief of Staff convened, at 0715, a GHQ meeting. The intelligence picture that Zeira presented at its opening was similar to the one that he presented a short while earlier at Dayan's office, though here he mentioned Marwan's warning as one among a number of others. Before providing details about the Arab war plans, he made it clear that although it appeared that it was highly unlikely that the Egyptians and the Syrians thought themselves capable of launching a war, the accumulating warning indicators made this option a real possibility and that it should be regarded as such.

The Chief of Staff, who spoke after Zeira, elaborated on Marwan's warning and said that according to this information war would start at 1800. He noted that Dayan objected to a preemptive air strike and a massive mobilization and added that the IAF should, nevertheless, make preparations for a preemptive strike. Here, he estimated that once it became clear to everyone that the war was imminent, the dominant consideration would become how to win it as quickly and efficiently as possible. Implicitly, Elazar hinted here that the main obstacle to a preemptive strike was not fear of American reaction but the fact that Dayan still estimated that war was not certain.

Next, the Chief of Staff described the course of the coming war as he perceived it: During its first day, the IAF would carry much of the burden of fighting; the mobilization and the deployment of the reserve army would take another three days and, then, the IDF would launch its counterattack. Elazar issued the G branch GHQ an order to check the war plans with the Northern and Southern Commands. At the end of the meeting, he convened for a couple of minutes with the commanders of both Commands and discussed with them their war plans. In contrast to the Northern Command, which had been on a high state of alert for ten days now, the war plans of the Southern Command had not been refreshed for quite some time. As a result of this and some additional reasons, the Northern Command was better prepared for war than the Southern Command. Moreover, the commander in the north, Maj. Gen. Yitzhak Hofi clearly understood Elazar's message that war would break out at 1800. As we shall see later, his colleague in the south, Maj. Gen. Shmuel Gonen, understood it differently.[16] To the members of the Agranat Commission, who asked him why he did not enter into the details of the deployment in the south, the Chief of Staff gave an answer that reflected his state of mind and his order of priorities during these critical hours: "'Dove cote' is not a *critical issue* for me this morning. I have many more issues of graver concern than 'dove cote.' What did I have that morning? What concerned me? I am concerned about the air force preemptive strike; if I can get it, this is significant. What do we want to achieve...."[17]

Indeed, the impression is that prior to the discussion with the Prime Minister—whom he found out to be an ally in the issue of mobilization (though not the preemptive strike)—the Chief of Staff was preparing for war with one hand tied behind his back. Dayan's veto on a preemptive air strike, which Elazar deemed as essential, and his objection to a large-scale mobilization, further disrupted the Chief of Staff's ability to enter war in a reasonable manner. The surprise, which introduced a chaotic dimension to the usually highly organized staff work of the supreme command, also hampered Elazar's ability to function efficiently. He told the members of the Agranat Commission:

> What I'm trying to explain, and this is already unusual—is the atmosphere at the GHQ on Saturday morning, when suddenly one becomes aware that in 10–12 hours there is going to be a big war and now one has to do many things: Everyone is running and we carry out many activities in parallel. I never brief a Command Commander without having an audience and entourage and everyone writes down. On Saturday morning I have a mad house, where everyone is doing something different. So I let the Deputy Chief of Staff go, in order that he can take care of mobilization, the Chief of the General-Staff Branch prepares the "pit" for war, while maps are to be hung up ... so others run to hang them. And, this is what happened in the morning.[18]

In contrast to the intensive activity in the IDF GHQ, the atmosphere around the Minister of Defense was more relaxed. Dayan's concerns during these hours involved, primarily, the maintenance of order in the occupied territories and the evacuation of civilians from war zones. He also instructed his assistant, Zvi Zur, to check what would be the impact of a mobilization of 100,000 reserve soldiers on Israel's economy—another expression of his fear of what could turn out to be an unnecessary massive mobilization. Unlike his usual modus operandi, he did not get into the details of the operational plans of the IDF air and ground forces.

A low activity profile also characterized the Prime Minister's office. But although Golda Meir, unlike Dayan, deemed the war to be unavoidable now, it took her three hours to get from her residence in northern Tel Aviv to her office at the center of the town. Upon arrival she induced an atmosphere of sadness and concern, impatience and nervousness—but not a hasty mood of action. She ordered her cabinet ministers to gather within three to four hours, and to invite the American ambassador, Kenneth Keating, for an immediate meeting. Essentially, she wanted to hear from Dayan and Elazar, but avoided, at this stage, intervening in their discussions—including the issue of mobilization. The atmosphere around her was depressing as well. Her assistants, according to her military secretary, "walked in the dark, as if the Temple had been destroyed. Some of them did not speak even one word, walking around, totally shocked." At least in part, this atmosphere was the result of a sense that the Prime Minister and her assistants had no significant role to play at this stage. Thus, for example, the military secretary was mainly busy during these critical hours in organizing the means to bring the Deputy Prime Minister, Yigal Allon, from his Kibbutz in the north to the cabinet meeting in Tel Aviv.[19] But the atmosphere also reflected a feeling shared by all—that a war that no one wanted would start in a few hours.

* * *

The Prime Minister's isolation from the decision-making centers ended at 0805, when the meeting in which the main decisions were to be made, started in her office. In addition to Golda Meir, the participants included Dayan, Elazar, Yisrael Galili, Chaim Bar-Lev, and Yigal Allon, who joined in at a later stage.[20]

Dayan opened the discussion with some minor issues—the policy in the territories and the evacuation of civilians from war zones. The fact that he did not start with the more severe problems—the preemptive air strike and the mobilization—is another indication of his estimate regarding the probability of war. The way that he treated the evacuation of the settlers from the Golan Heights, is another: Instead of ordering the immediate evacuation of the civilians, he suggested the thirty children that lived there would be evacuated in the afternoon or toward the evening under the guise of a trip, while the women could stay. The Prime Minister suggested that evacuation of the children would start immediately "and not on the eve of action" and Elazar had to interfere in order to make it clear that "we are already on the eve of action." This discussion ended with the Prime Minister's note that the settlers would probably refuse the evacuation order.[21]

Then, Dayan mentioned the possibility that Jordanian radars would provide the Syrians with information about the activity in the IAF base at Ramat David in northern Israel. He suggested that if this became the case, the IAF should be given a green light to destroy the Jordanian installations without a prior warning to King Hussein.

At this stage, DMI Zeira started describing the intelligence picture. He estimated that the rushed Soviet evacuation was caused by a Syrian and Egyptian intention to launch war soon, and he noted that the recent changes in Syrian deployment indicated offensive intentions. Yet, he still maintained that war was not certain: Though Egypt and Syria were technically and operationally ready to launch it, Sadat was not in a situation where he had to start hostilities, and he knew that if he did, he would be defeated. Hence, he might be deterred from war at the last minute—and, if not, he might be deterred by a warning through the United States that Israel was ready for war.[22] As Zeira's analysis shows, at this stage he already accepted that the Arab military preparations aimed at the initiation of war. But he was not ready yet to forgo his belief that Sadat did not perceive himself as capable of winning it, and, hence, he added his reservations about its certainty.

Following Zeira's presentation, the discussion turned to the more critical problems. Dayan admitted that, operationally, the preemptive strike option was preferable to an Arab initiative, but added, "On the basis of the information we have now, it is impossible. Principally, we cannot open fire before they do." He also related to the mobilization issue, describing to the Prime Minister the argument between himself and the Chief of Staff. He repeated his stand that he was ready to mobilize the whole air force, one division for the north and one for the south, adding, "If the situation gets worse at night, if fire starts, we'll mobilize the rest in the night. Otherwise it [i.e., an immediate complete mobilization] would signal that we go for war."

The Chief of Staff presented the causes that made a preemptive strike and a massive mobilization, of 200,000 soldiers, so necessary now. From his perspective, Marwan's warning undoubtedly indicated that war was certain. Hence, the distinction between a limited or a massive mobilization, as far as its impact on world public opinion was concerned, had become quite irrelevant. In any event, Israel would be blamed for mobilizing the reserve army for the offensive.

The Prime Minister made it clear that she could not allow a preemptive air strike and pondered the pros and the cons of the overall and limited mobilization options. Here, the Chief of Staff understood that he had a green light for the mobilization of two divisions and the whole air force, and his bureau chief got out of the room at 0900 to inform the Deputy Chief of Staff that he could start this limited action. About twenty minutes later, after Dayan had made it clear that he would not fully object to a larger mobilization, the Prime Minister authorized the mobilization of 100,000 to 120,000 soldiers, including the four divisions that the Chief of Staff had demanded to mobilize from the start.

Thus, this critical discussion ended. Notably, Golda Meir rejected the option of a preemptive strike on viable grounds—primarily the American estimate that the Arabs did not intend to attack (which, by itself, was mainly the outcome of AMAN's calming assessment). And yet, it can be assumed that had Dayan been more supportive of this option, the Prime Minister would have probably accepted it. Ex post facto, Dayan and his assistants tried to mitigate the value of a preemptive strike by claiming that weather conditions prevented the bombing of the Syrian air defense layout in the Golan.[23] But, at least once Dayan was quoted as saying, "if I was hundred percent certain that war would break out, I would have asked to start with a counter strike. But, to count on a piece of information that says that war is going to start does not mean that there is certainty that this would happen."[24] Taken at face value, Dayan indicated here that his objection to an Israeli military initiative was primarily based on his estimate about the likelihood of war, rather than on diplomatic or operational considerations. This assumption got an additional impetus from an exchange between Dayan and the Chief of Staff at a discussion at the latter's office at 1100. Elazar described the IDF war plans and added that, so far, the mobilization of 70,000 soldiers had started. Here, the following exchange took place:

> DEFENSE MINISTER: And, if the Arabs won't start fire—when will all the reserve soldiers go home?
> CHIEF OF STAFF: If the matter won't be delayed by a day or two, but totally cancelled—we will send the soldiers back home.
> DEPUTY CHIEF OF STAFF: The process of their demobilization might take three to four days.
> DEFENSE MINISTER: But, what happens if, when Yom Kippur is over, at midnight, we find out that there is no war?
> CHIEF OF STAFF: Demobilizing the reserve soldiers won't start before forty-eight hours are over.
> DEFENSE MINISTER: One hundred thousand men will walk around a whole day before being sent home?
> CHIEF OF STAFF: They won't only walk around; they'll also go to the front. If it turns out that there is no war, we'll let them go within forty-eight hours.[25]

* * *

Since the dissemination, at 0340, of the intelligence review that described the Syrian deployment of the previous day, AMAN continued the distribution of information about growing Arab readiness to start the firing. However, the various written and verbal reports lacked one major component: a clear assessment by AMAN that the military preparations in Syria and Egypt were for war—which would start in a few hours.

At 0730, Branch 6 of the Research Department disseminated a review, based primarily on Marwan's warning, about the Egyptian–Syrian intention to renew fighting toward the last light of October 6. It presented an outdated version of the Egyptian war plan as it had been known by AMAN for quite some time. Its operational goal was "the takeover of the east bank of the Canal, the front of the Sinai till (and including) the [Gidi and Mitla] passes, and the occupation of Sharm el Sheik."[26] As recalled, this was the operational goal of Egypt's limited military plan up until October 1972. Toward April 1973, the Egyptians defined it as the operational goal of the "Updated Granite 2" plan, which was built in order to convince the Syrians to join the war.[27]

Another intelligence document, based on first details from a reconnaissance sortie that took place earlier that morning, was disseminated at 1140. In contrast to previous reviews, three out of six items in this document were based on information from ground observation posts along the canal. The review reported on the removal of covers in part of the Egyptian artillery, the advancement of 203mm guns[28] to positions at the front, the location of short-range rockets in positions in the Shaluffa and Ismailia regions, and the advancement of crossing equipment in the Shaluffa region.[29] An additional review that was disseminated by the IAF intelligence department, reported on an air-photograph sortie that had been carried out by Egyptian planes at 1100 the same morning. It mentioned similar sorties on October 3 and 4.[30]

At 1345, only fifteen minutes before firing started, the Research Department issued its last intelligence review. It was of immense importance since it described the updated (and real) version of Egypt's war plan, as given by Marwan during his meeting with Zamir. The main change in comparison with the report that had been disseminated about six hours earlier involved the Egyptian operational goal. Instead of defining it as the occupation of the eastern part of the Sinai, including the Gidi and Mitla Passes and the Sharm El Sheik area, the new document accurately defined it now as "the occupation of the eastern bank of the canal, and an effort to take over a territory to its east at the depth of 10 kilometers. The continuation [of the war] would be determined according to the results [of the first stage]. In any event, there is no intention to reach the passes at the first stage." The rest of the document reported additional details of the war plan, which, within hours, proved to be highly accurate.[31]

The messages that AMAN delivered to its consumers during these last hours could have been far more effective if, in addition to providing war indicators and information about Egypt's war intentions, it would have included a clear-cut estimate that war was just around the corner. But they all lacked the component that was so dominant in AMAN's documents of the previous days—an assessment, sometimes disguised as information, about the likelihood of war. This was no accident. Even during the ten hours that passed between the arrival of Marwan's warning and the outbreak of the war, the head of Branch 6 and DMI Zeira continued to doubt its certainty. Bandman assessed that from an Egyptian perspective there was no need to go to war and, hence, its likelihood was not too high. Faithful to his professional principles, he refused to add to AMAN's documents on Saturday morning an estimate that Egypt, indeed, intended to start war soon. At a certain stage, after he refused an instruction that had been given by the head of the Research

Department to do it, a head of another branch had to write an estimate that reflected the volume and the quality of the available warning indicators.[32]

DMI Zeira continued to be influenced by Bandman's estimate, despite the new consensus that now dominated the Research Department. While he was prudent enough to avoid adopting Bandman's assessment in the senior forums, he nevertheless expressed there a similar estimate to that of the head of Branch 6 (i.e., that there was no need for Sadat to take such a risky move). It is possible that Zeira's skepticism about the war derived from another source as well: The head of the Research Department tended to accept by then the Egyptian initiative as a fact and, yet, he estimated that Syria would join it only if it succeeded. All these factors probably influenced Zeira, when, about two hours before war, he received an intelligence document that had been prepared by Bandman, on his own initiative, which assessed the likelihood of war as low. In his office was also his predecessor, Aharon Yariv. Zeira pondered with Yariv on whether to authorize the dissemination of this report. Yariv suggested that he avoid it and Zeira accepted his advice. However, his readiness to consider authorizing the dissemination of another "low probability" estimate less than two hours before the outbreak of the war, constitutes a proof that he did not see it, even at that stage, as something totally out of order.[33]

The duality between the presentation of information according to which war was imminent and the avoidance of estimating its likelihood had no impact on the Chief of Staff. For him, the message received at 0430 was the sword that enabled him to cut the Gordian knot that had been created during the previous week, as a result of contradiction between the alarming information that AMAN had presented and the calming way in which it had been assessed. This split message did not stop the Prime Minister either. For days she had felt inconvenience with the situation that reminded her of the period before the 1967 war. And, since both assessed war to be rather likely, even before Marwan's warning had been received, it was easier for them to ignore AMAN's assessments and to focus on the information.

This was not the situation with the Defense Minister. Although Dayan was known to rely on his own intelligence estimates, in this specific case he seems to have leaned less on his own instincts and more on Zeira's assessments. Combined with the memory of the costly state of alert in the spring, which (so it seemed then) was needless, and the potential cost of another increase in the IDF's state of readiness, Dayan had become more skeptical about the war certainty and more certain about the negative impact of needless mobilization. The outcome was his objection to the massive mobilization and a preemptive air strike—a decision whose cost would become clear within less than twenty-four hours.

Chapter 17

Surprise

i. The Cabinet

Golda Meir's cabinet convened in her office at the Kiria in Tel Aviv at 12:00 at noon. The ministers—most of whom had no clue about the recent days' events—got a partial briefing from the Defense Minister about the situation and the possibility that Egypt and Syria would start war soon. The Prime Minister spoke next, explaining why she did not authorize a preemptive air strike. The discussion that followed focused on a hypothetical question: Should Israel attack Syria if only Egypt initiated hostilities? This also raised the issue of whether Golda Meir could make this decision purely on her own initiative or whether a cabinet approval was required. Finance Minister Pinhas Sapir expressed his frustration about the fact that the cabinet had not been informed about the recent developments and that critical decisions had to be taken now under severe time constraints and considerable emotional pressure. He finished by saying, "I don't understand why it is so difficult to wait a little bit longer and avoid making the decision precisely at this moment." In her answer, Golda Meir explained that it was not clear if war would start at 1800 and that there was a possibility that it could start earlier. But, if the cabinet decided not to attack Syria, then the problem would cease to exist. "I don't mind," she added "and in any event I will not get out of here [her office]. If the colleagues want to stay—fine, but I can tell you that we will meet here at 4:30 p.m. If then it would happen. . . ."

At this moment sirens were heard outside, but the Prime Minster continued, "If they don't start war by 4:30, we can vote again. I would like to know the situation and if by 4:30 they start . . ." Here, additional sirens were heard. According to the protocol of the meeting, the Prime Minister asked: "What is this?" The Cabinet's stenographer, who sat next to her, replied, "It seems that the war has begun." Golda Meir's reaction was typical. In Yiddish she said: *"nor dos felt mir...."* ("this is all that I lack....").

At this moment of confusion, the Prime Minister's military secretary entered the room and gave a brief report that Syrian airplanes had been detected taking off and that the Syrian army had started firing. The cabinet meeting ended within minutes. The decisions that were taken before the end of its session constitute a clear proof that Golda Meir and her ministers did not yet understand the situation. They decided that Israel would not launch a preemptive strike, and that the cabinet would have to approve any action against Syria if Egypt alone initiated hostilities.[1]

However, at this stage, the confusion in the cabinet was less critical to Israel's future than the situation at the fronts. And, as it soon became evident, the soldiers along the Suez Canal and in the Golan Heights were even less ready for war.

ii. The Canal Front

The Commander of the Sinai Division (Division 252), Maj. Gen. Albert Mendler believed, during the week before the war began, that hostilities were going to break out. On October 1 he noted in his personal diary: "This is fantastic. 0515 — intelligence — tomorrow war. The exchange of command has gone."[2] It seems that, like the intelligence officer of the Northern Command, Mendler also received through informal channels the warning that arrived in AMAN on the night of September 30–October 1, which said that the exercise that was to start on October 1 would develop into war. His source was the head of Branch 5 in the Research Department, Lt. Col. Avi Yaari, who served as Mendler's intelligence officer when the latter was the commander of Brigade 8, and who had continued to maintain good contact with him since then.

On receiving this warning, Mendler took measures to raise his Division's state of alert. Inter alia, he gave instructions to raise the state of readiness in the Bar-Lev strongholds and in the front-line tank units, to limit the number of furloughs, and to invigorate the "dove-cote" defense plan and the "Zfania" offense plan. His requests from the Southern Command to receive the forces that were needed to carry out these plans were rejected, since they involved the mobilization of reserve forces. All he could get was the Command's Reconnaissance Battalion, also known as Unit 424 (or "Sayeret Shaked"). On October 7, Mendler was scheduled to become the Commander of the Armored Corps, but on the last days of that week he made it clear that because of the growing tension he would not be able to leave his present command.[3]

On the night of October 4–5, Mendler received the results of the air-photograph sortie of Thursday. This, combined with information about the sudden Soviet evacuation that he had received from the head of Branch 5, led him to estimate that war was now highly likely. On Saturday morning, at 0720, the Commander of the Southern Command, Maj. Gen. Shmuel Gonen, informed him by telephone about the radical change in the Chief of Staff's estimate of the probability of war, and instructed him to start preparations for the execution of the dove cote plan, but to avoid any movement of forces.[4] Indeed, the magnitude of the threat was unclear yet at this stage, as reflected by the message of the Operations Officer in the Command's communications network: "... something serious is possible today. There is a need to be more alert, with bulletproof vests and helmets. ... an ABC State of Alert. Anti-aircraft defense should be increased in rear camps."[5]

Mendler's Division's battle procedure started at 0830, with an order group that refreshed the dove cote defense plan. During the discussion, at about 1000, Gonen called Mendler again to report that the expected H-hour was 1800. But, he did not say that this was war. The Divisional Operations Officer testified after the war that:

> Albert returned to the discussion room and reported to us what he had just heard: Information according to which the Egyptian H-hour was to be at 1800 in the evening, but its meaning was not clear at this stage—was it to be the end of the big exercise? Opening fire? The renewal of the War of Attrition? Perhaps a general war—though this was not considered to be reasonable.[6]

If, indeed, these were the instructions that Gonen gave to Mendler—and in light of Gonen's other activities on the eve of the war, there is no reason to doubt it—one can hardly avoid the conclusion that the Commander of the Southern Command had utterly distorted the orders that he had received a few hours earlier from the Chief of Staff. At the GHQ meeting that ended at 0800 that morning, Elazar made it clear that he was preparing the IDF for a war that would break out at 1800. One can hardly understand why Gonen conveyed his orders in a manner that made war a rather remote possibility. By his own account, he was influenced by an estimate that he heard from DMI Zeira in the corridor, prior to the beginning of that morning's GHQ meeting. According to Gonen, Zeira said that he still did not believe that war would break out. It is possible that he was also influenced by Zeira's estimate during Friday's GHQ meeting. Then, as recalled, the DMI said that even if Egypt initiated hostilities, it was more probable that it would be a limited move (commando raids, artillery fire) rather than a general crossing of the Suez Canal.

The confusing message that Gonen gave Mendler was not the only distorted message that he conveyed. During the short meeting that he held with the Chief of Staff at about 0745, Elazar instructed him to immediately deploy his forces (i.e., Division 252) for war and to return for another discussion at noon. But, Gonen decided to delay the immediate execution of the dove cote plan. His orders, as delivered to Col. Amnon Reshef, the Commander of Brigade 14 (the front-line brigade of Division 252), and to Col. Pinhas Noi, the Commander of Territorial Brigade 275 in charge of the Canal Zone, was: "Avoid breaking routine activity until 1600." After this hour, the observation posts along the Suez water line were to get back, and the observers on towers in the strongholds were to get down. Other instructions involved an increased state of alert in the strongholds, the evacuation of a number of strongholds that were held by a small number of soldiers, and an increased state of readiness of tank companies at the Suez second line of defense, about 8–10 kilometers east of the Canal. Division 252's two additional brigades—Brigade 401 under the command of Col. Dan Shomron and Brigade 460 under the command of Col. Gabi Amir—were instructed to be ready to move, but did not receive deployment orders.[7]

Following an additional telephone conversation between Gonen and Mendler, another alert command was issued. The new command detailed various preparations for the conduct of dove cote, ordering that all front-line forces were to enter a state of alert against enemy artillery fire at 1700.[8]

The first time the front-line battalion commanders heard that war might break out that same day was at 1200. At 1225, after a message "special time check"—a known code word for an alert against shelling—was transmitted by a UN observation post along the canal, the Division received an order to enter a state of readiness immediately. By 1300 the orders had begun making their way to the strongholds, and orders to perform a small dove cote plan by 1700 were given half an hour later. Some of the strongholds received these orders only upon start of fire. At 1330 the Operations Officer of the Southern Command issued a new order that summarized all previous ones. But, even this order—the most inclusive that had been given so far—avoided an instruction to execute the dove cote plan according to any specific timing. Instead, it instructed the Command's units to enter "a state of readiness to execute a complete dove cote."[9]

At this chaotic moment, fire broke out.

* * *

The poor level of readiness of the Bar-Lev line when the war started was the result of an ongoing neglect of the role of the strongholds as a means to block the Egyptian army from crossing the canal. A large number of the strongholds that were to be fully manned in readiness for war remained considerably undermanned. In other strongholds the number of fighting soldiers was well below the standard, varying between seven and twenty-four soldiers. In most strongholds there was only one officer, and in many there was no physician. The total number of soldiers in the Bar-Lev line on Yom Kippur at noon reached 451, of which 331 were fighting soldiers.[10] And this small fighting force was of a rather low quality. Battalion 68, whose soldiers manned most of the line, belonged to the Jerusalem Territorial Brigade — a second-rate reserve force by IDF standards. Many of its soldiers were hardly trained, and most of them did not have combat experience. Prior to entering their service, they received only a few days' instruction instead of the one week training that they were supposed to get. The Commander of Brigade 275 testified that the unit that had been replaced by Battalion 68 was far better. The NAHAL regular service company that held a few strongholds in Bar-Lev's southern sector was not a cohesive unit either. Although the quality of its soldiers was better than that of the soldiers of Battalion 68, it was nevertheless a far cry from the quality of the paratrooper units that were supposed to man the line in case of war. Given this opening situation, not much could have been done to improve the ability of the strongholds in order to repel the attack — even if the dove cote order had been issued a few hours earlier.

In contrast, had the order been issued in the morning, the ability of Tank Brigade 14 to confront the crossing Egyptian forces would have improved significantly. According to the dove cote plan, two tank brigades of Division 252 were to deploy between the water line and the second line, about 8–10 kilometers east of the canal. A third brigade was to deploy behind. As was noted earlier, on the morning of Yom Kippur the Commander of the Southern Command decided to deploy the forces according to "small dove cote" — a plan that was improvised at the divisional level — that called for the deployment of one brigade at the front and two behind. He reported to the Chief of Staff about it during the late morning hours. It is unclear whether Elazar understood this plan and authorized it, but it seems that he assumed that by 1800 Division 252 would be deployed according to the "regular" dove cote plan (i.e., two brigades on the water line and one behind).[11]

Gonen explained his decision to delay the deployment of Division 252 according to two reasons. First, the concern (whose source is unclear, but it is probable that he heard it in his "corridor talks" with DMI Zeira) that an early massive deployment in the front line a few hours before H-hour might increase the tension and bring the Egyptians to start a war even if they did not mean it from the start.[12] Second, an early deployment of the tanks might expose them and enable the Egyptians to effectively hit them. At around noon, the Commander of Division 252 pressured Gonen to initiate an earlier deployment. Gonen refused at first but then agreed to allow it one hour earlier.[13]

Theoretically, Gonen's decision to deploy one brigade at the front and two behind was logical, since it enabled him to use two tank brigades against the main efforts of the crossing forces. Indeed, during the war's first hours, locating these efforts became his main concern.[14] But, he was not aware enough of the fact that the intelligence files at his Command headquarters already answered this critical question. The Egyptian war plan, as studied and processed by AMAN's analysts, had no main effort. From the start, the crossing was designated to take place along the whole of the canal, at the five sectors of the five infantry brigades that had been deployed there since the end of the War of Attrition. This was the plan that was executed on October 6 at noon.

Odd as it might seem, the Commander of the Southern Command, whose main task was to defend the Suez Front against an Egyptian attack, was not aware of the fact that AMAN had already been in possession of the blueprints of this attack for approximately eighteen months. To the members of the Agranat Commission, who presented the plan to him—as distributed by AMAN in April 1972—he said that he was not familiar with this document or others like it. All that he had been aware about, he maintained, was the enemy's courses of action, as they had been presented to him by the Command's intelligence officer, Lt. Col. David Gdalia. According to Gdalia, the Egyptians were to employ one main and one secondary effort in the southern and central sectors of the canal. Being rather ignorant of the Egyptian plan, Gonen also estimated that the preparatory bombardment before the start of the actual crossing of the canal would last for a few hours. According to the plan that AMAN had, it was to take only forty-five minutes and, in reality, its duration was, indeed, thirty to forty-five minutes.[15]

Gonen's lack of knowledge also stemmed from a malfunction of his intelligence officer. AMAN's documents about Egypt's war plans had been disseminated to him, but they were filed without being properly considered. Gdalia himself argued that he accepted AMAN's estimate, according to which the Egyptian military preparations during the week before the war were connected to the Tahrir 41 exercise. Hence, even on the afternoon of October 5—when the dimensions of the Egyptian disposition were known, and after the Chief of Staff raised the IDF's state of alert to the highest since the war of 1967—he did not find it necessary to describe to his commander the Egyptian courses of action or the crossing plans.[16] A vivid expression of this behavior is found in an exchange between Gonen and Gdalia during a discussion on Friday evening. At a certain stage, the subject of the deployment of "wolfs"—Israeli-made short-range unguided rockets with a payload of 500 kilograms—was raised. Gonen suggested deploying them in front of the al-Balah island, since he was told that crossing equipment was in evidence there. Gdalia confirmed that he received such a report, and then the following dialogue took place:

GONEN: Where is the crossing equipment [?]
GDALIA: In principle, along the whole line.
GONEN: Where are the concentrations [?] You told me [about] two concentrations in front of the two infantry divisions. Where? Excuse me, you will decide on the two points where you assume that the crossing may take place and only there you will deploy ["wolfs"].

The clear impression that stems from this dialogue is that Gonen had no clue what the Egyptian war plans were and that his intelligence officer showed little interest in providing this information to him. Gonen, according to the protocol of that discussion, devoted more attention and time to the operational status of a single gun than to find out what the Egyptian operational plans or courses of action were. Gdalia, on his behalf, had never tried to brief his commander with this information. Such an interaction is very rare in the relationship between intelligence producers and consumers—a realm which is usually highly problematic. But these problems mostly stem from the decision-maker's frustration about the quality of the available intelligence information or the intelligence officer's interest to influence the policy-maker's decisions. The dialogue between Gonen and Gdalia, a few hours before the outbreak of the war, was not even a dialogue between the deaf. It was a dialogue between two persons without even minimal interest in the available intelligence that was so relevant for the decisions that were to be made. One can hardly explain it. But, certainly, an assessment of both men's views that war was still rather unlikely, combined with a deep disrespect of Egyptian war capabilities, explains some of it.

* * *

The results of this dialogue came into expression a few hours later. The fact that Division 252 did not deploy with two brigades at the front and one behind, made the Egyptian crossing of the canal far easier. The fire power that the Division could produce against the crossing forces was cut by half, precisely at the stage where they were in the water and highly vulnerable. But, because of Gonen's second mistake, the significance of the first became rather negligible. Since he decided to delay the deployment of the Division until the last moment, and since war started four hours before the expected H-hour, even the forces of Brigade 14 were still far behind when fire commenced. The only tank force—three out of 300 tanks—that was deployed in its position at 1400, October 6, was one tank platoon that deployed constantly in the "Orkal" strongholds on the northern part of the Bar-Lev line. The rest of Brigade 14 was deployed as follows: In the northern sector, Battalion 9 in two concentrations—a bi-company force at "Katya" near Baluza, and a company force in "Churchill," a few kilometers westward. In the central sector, one company of Battalion 184

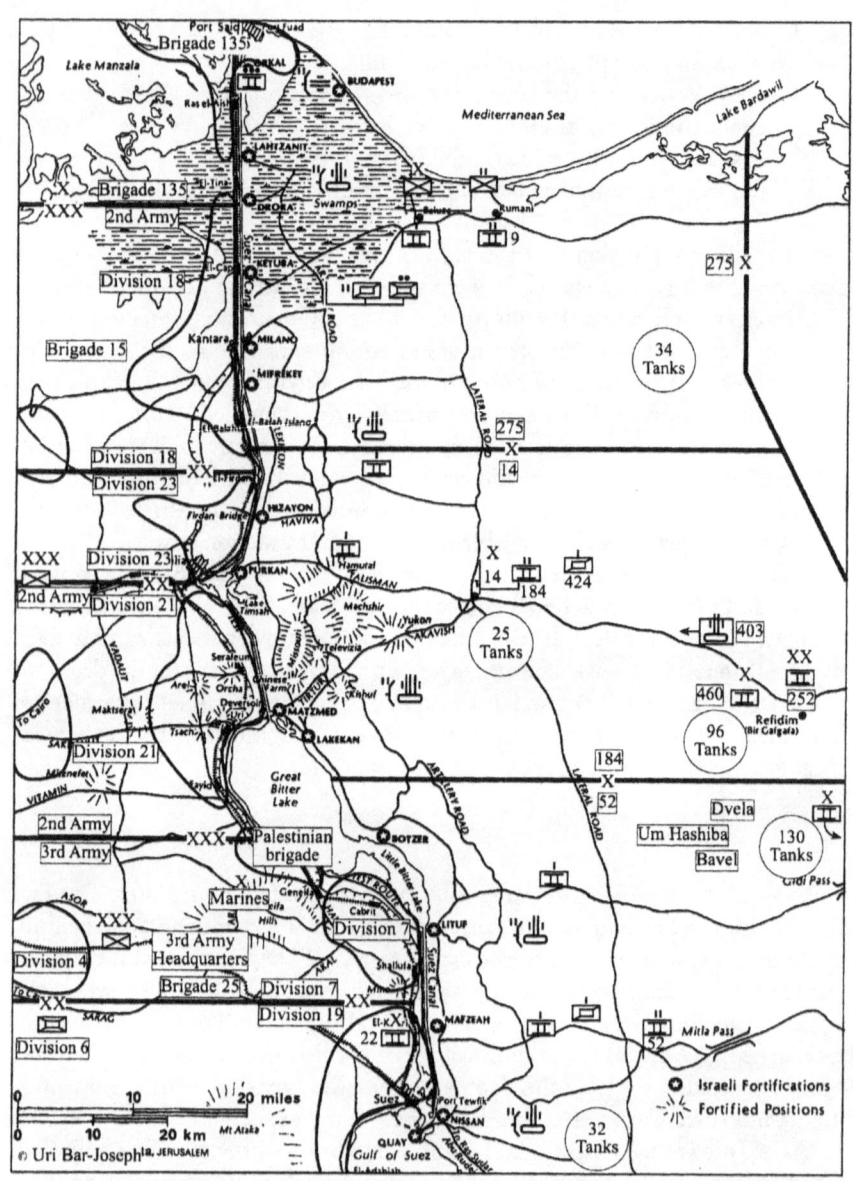

Military Deployment on the Suez Front, October 6, 1973 1400

was deployed near the "Havraga" second-line stronghold, and two additional companies were preparing to move. The tank companies of Battalion 52 were deployed near the second-line strongholds of "Mitzva," "Tseidar," and "Noza," about 10 kilometers from their fire positions by the water line.[17] Brigades 401 and 460 were still under preparation to move to their frontal assembly areas.

The strongholds in the Bar-Lev line received no warning. The Commander of Battalion 68 said a few days after the war started:

> The practical first warning was given to us at 1200. We were informed that at 1800 artillery fire and, perhaps, tank fire, would start along the line. I made a quick calculation—would I have enough time to run with a Jeep to all the strongholds? In fact, I climbed on the Jeep, but precisely then it broke down. I ran to the telephone. I succeeded calling all the strongholds to warn them. I ordered them to be at their maximal state of readiness for war at 1700. While I was still briefing them I received at around 1330 the codeword "dove cote"—to enter immediately into war deployment. While we were still thinking about how to get organized immediately, and the tanks were running to the strongholds, war started with air attacks against bases in the rear and some of the strongholds, and, in addition, extensive artillery bombardment of all the strongholds was under way.[18]

The Agranat Report summarized the IDF deployment as follows:

> Altogether, the front line [between the Bar-Lev line and the second-defense line, about 10 kilometers eastwards] deployment included 75 tanks and 50 artillery pieces. Additionally, 201 tanks were deployed at the rear.
>
> The deployment at the front line did not differ from a usual current security deployment. The routine security activity in the line (patrols, observations, occupation of "diluted" strongholds) continued on October 6 and was increased a little. . . .
>
> All this means that most of the forces, which enforced the Southern Command [Brigade 460], and the forces that were held in the rear area of Division 252 [Brigade 401], remained concentrated and not deployed.[19]

Dove cote, as recalled, was not the IDF main defense plan for the canal. Originally, it was developed in order to meet limited Egyptian moves, such as the renewal of the static war or commando raids along the canal and in the depth of Sinai. Only in early 1973 a decision was made to use it as a defense plan against an all-out Egyptian crossing attempt. But, even in the case of such a situation, the IDF's working assumption was that a strategic warning would be provided twenty-four to forty-eight hours before the outbreak of war. This time span sufficed to deploy Division 252 with two brigades at the front and one behind. According to this plan, the Egyptian crossing forces were to be met by 200 tanks, which were scheduled to be in their pre-prepared positions, some on the water line and others in positions about 1,000 meters from the canal. This force was to be backed up by eighty-eight artillery pieces. Well-trained paratrooper units were to man the Bar-Lev line strongholds and participate in the repelling effort.

As a result of the low-quality strategic warning and the mistaken decisions made by Gonen, "the Egyptians received the best opening conditions, which they could not have dreamed about even in their most optimistic dreams."[20] Brigade 14 was the only force that was deployed, very partially though, according to the dove cote plan. But, even this brigade's tanks were not in their positions when fire started. When they started moving to the ramps in order to meet the crossing forces, they found that many of their fire positions were by then occupied by Egyptian tank hunter teams of the first and the second waves that crossed the canal without meeting any Israeli resistance.[21] Consequently, some of the tanks were hit before they had even fired a single shot. The rest had to defend themselves rather than fire at the crossing forces. The strongholds, which were planned to cover narrow sectors of the canal by fire and report information concerning the Egyptian movements, had become, from the first moments of the war, a heavy liability rather than an asset. Since the infantry that met the first crossing units were not of high quality, their main activity had become urgent demands for assistance and rescue. These requests were met by the tank teams of Brigade 14 and, later, the other two brigades and by the IAF planes. And, since the evacuation of the line was not approved by the high command, the main effort of the tank force in the south during the critical first hours of the war had become the defense of the Bar-Lev line strongholds, rather than destroying the invading forces.

The reports that arrived from the fighting zone were of contradictory nature. The true gravity of the situation had become clear only on the early morning hours of Sunday, October 7. Then, it became known that out of the 300 tanks that Division 252 had had at the beginning of the war, only 103 were left. The IDF remained without any significant force to block the Egyptian army in its move eastward, into the heart of the Sinai.

iii. The Golan Front

The situation in the Golan front during the war's first hours was somewhat better, but it also deteriorated during the night. The fact that since New Year's Eve this front had received the attention of the decision-makers—primarily that of Dayan—made it more defendable than in regular times. But, since at the focus of attention was the fear of a Syrian small-scale act, the forces there were deployed to meet this particular type of challenge rather than an all-out attack to occupy the Heights.

According to the Syrian war plan that was disseminated by AMAN on April 27, 1973, the attack was to be carried out by three infantry divisions (numbers 5, 7, and 9) along the whole line. During the night, the three divisions were to complete the occupation of a strip 8 kilometers wide along the front line. On the war's second day, Armored Division 3 was to exploit this success in order to advance from the Rapid area to the center of the Heights and westward to the bridge of Bnot Yaacov ("Daughters of Jacob"), on the Jordan River.[22] An update of this plan, on the basis of the information that the CIA provided a week before the war, was disseminated by AMAN on October 2. The first stage of the offensive—a simultaneous attack by the three infantry divisions—was identical to the April plan. The second now involved two armored divisions: Division 1 was planned to break from the Rapid region in the direction of Bnot Yaacov bridge; at the same time, or a little bit later, Division 3 was to develop a main effort in the central/northern sector of the front (the sector of Division 7). But, if Israel developed a counteroffensive through Jordan, Division 3 was to stay in place and block the Israeli effort.[23]

About six months before the war, the Northern Command's Intelligence Officer presented the Syrian war plan along similar lines to the plan that was disseminated in April. Implicitly, he maintained that it was too ambitious and unrealistic. Hence, he devoted much of the presentation to a scenario according to which, if the Egyptians initiated a war of attrition in the canal, the Syrians might initiate a similar move in the Golan, primarily by artillery bombardments. According to this scenario, the Syrians could even attempt to carry out small-scale local attacks against civilian or military targets.[24] Two weeks later, on May 9, when the IDF war plans were presented to Golda Meir in the framework of blue-white state of readiness, DMI Zeira reviewed the Syrian war plan and estimated its feasibility:

> The Syrian plan is to start with an artillery attack at dark, and they have to reach a line 8 kilometers from the border with the [infantry] divisions. In the morning, Armored Division 3 has to exploit success in order to reach Mishmar Hayarden [the Israel side of the Bnot Yaacov bridge]. This is their intention. The Syrian Air Force has to attack airfields in Israel, [but] it is not ready and does not make preparations, in any case not at night. We do not see the Syrian army attacks at night with three divisions, but they might do it. The plan we

are talking about is a not a good plan from the military perspective, especially in the air. We regard it as having a very low probability.[25]

According to both plans that AMAN disseminated, the Syrians regarded the Rapid area as the main area from which the breakthrough westward should take place. This was clearly evident in intelligence summaries for the Sela defense plan and additional orders. On this basis, the Northern Command prepared a suitable defensive response. And yet, as post-war evidence shows, the Command maintained that the main Syrian effort would be at the Kuneitra area, about 15 kilometers north of Rapid,[26] ignoring the intelligence input as approved in the Command's defense plan. There are two explanations for this behavior: First, the Command officers believed that the Syrian advancement would be blocked on the border, in the first line of defense. Hence, the question of where the main effort would come from became less relevant. Second, though the topography of the area allowed for two areas of main effort, a breakthrough in the Kuneitra region was considered to be more dangerous, since it meant the possible conquest of Kuneitra, and since it was the shorter route to the Bnot Yaacov bridge. Consequently, the Northern Command estimated that the main Syrian effort would take place at the Kuneitra region.[27]

As it happened in so many cases in the story of the Yom Kippur surprise, even good intelligence information failed to change perceptions. In this case, since the estimate that came together with AMAN's review of the Syrian plan of early October 1973 was that the likelihood of a Syrian attack was low and that the plan was not very feasible—its ability to change the dominant belief was even smaller. Furthermore, it seems that there was not any real awareness in the Northern Command about the Syrian plans as reported in AMAN's documents. Lt. Col. Hagai Mann, the Command's Intelligence Officer, testified that he had not been aware of the Syrian plan according to the April review, since he had entered office only in mid-August. Lt. Col. Uri Simchoni, the Command's Operations Officer, told the Agranat Commission that he was not allowed to see this type of intelligence document because of their sensitivity. Therefore, he was not aware of the Syrian plan as described by AMAN in both April and in early October. Maj. Gen. Hofi said that he learned only after the war that AMAN had the Syrian war plans that indicated that the main effort would be in the south.[28]

Despite this shortcoming, the IDF was better prepared for combat in the north than in the south. The canal front had been quiet for more than three years, ever since the August 1970 cease-fire agreement that had ended the War of Attrition. In the north, in contrast, operational activity lasted throughout this period. The most recent major clash with the Syrians had taken place in January 1973, and routine operations were conducted even later, against Palestinian guerillas in southern Lebanon. As a result, the level of combat readiness in the north was better maintained than in the south. And yet, since the Northern Command focused only on current security missions, its ability to adapt to a very different type of threat—that of an all-out war—was somewhat hampered.

* * *

On October 6 the three Syrian infantry divisions were fully deployed in the first line of defense of the Syrian army. Each of the divisions was reinforced, in line with the attack plan, by an additional armored brigade: Infantry Division 5, at the front's southern sector, by Independent Armored Brigade 47; Infantry Division 7, at the central sector, by Armored Brigade 81 from Armored Division 3; and Infantry Division 9, in the northern sector of the front, by Independent Armored Brigade 51. Armored Division 1 remained in its camps in the Kiswa area, and did not deploy—in contrast to plans—in the second line of defense. Armored Division 3 was deployed in the Katana region and the Rifa'at Asad task force (one tank brigade and two commando battalions) was deployed in and around Damascus. The Syrian order of battle included 1,500 tanks: 930 tanks in the first line of defense, 470 tanks in the Katana and Kiswa regions, and another 100 in the Capital area. In addition, the Syrians deployed 115 artillery batteries—close to 800 pieces, including heavy mortars. Their anti-aircraft layout was made, primarily, of thirty-one SAM batteries—out of which fifteen were of the SA-6 mobile type—and 400 anti-aircraft guns, which were deployed between Damascus and the Golan Heights.[29]

The IDF's order of battle on Yom Kippur at noon did not meet, in size or the way in which it was deployed, any operational planning for war.[30] It mainly corresponded with Dayan's ongoing fears since the last week of September—that the Syrians might use their military superiority to raid a civilian settlement in the Golan. The main difference in the IDF deployment was that instead of only one tank battalion that was routinely deployed in the front, Armored Brigade 188 now deployed its two battalions—Battalion 74 and Battalion 53—in the front line. Two regular service infantry battalions—Battalion 50 (the paratrooper battalion of the Nahal Brigade) and Battalion 13 of the Golani Brigade—manned the eleven strongholds along the front line. On the morning of Yom Kippur, Hofi ordered reinforcements for the strongholds of four to six soldiers each, so the order of battle of each, when fire commenced, was about twenty fighting soldiers. Armored Brigade 7 with about 100 tanks—the main reinforcement force—was deployed in the rear, in order to respond to the main threat that was expected: "A massive artillery bombardment and a local small-scale ground attack to take over some territory or a settlement." The defending force also included eleven artillery batteries.[31] The Ashur order, which was issued by the Command on Friday at noon, instructed a "Lock" situation.

"Generally speaking," the Agranat Commission concluded, "this order fitted in with current security conditions" and not a threat of war.[32] Even post factum, the Commander of the Northern Command thought that this was the better way to deploy. While he regarded the border line as the best rear defense line, he had to leave it relatively powerless in light of the insufficient forces in the Golan on Yom Kippur. Hence, he preferred to keep a strong reserve, capable of carrying out counterattacks against any Syrian breakthroughs.[33]

Within a few fighting hours, it became evident that this deployment had two fundamental faults. The first involved preparations for war. The Chief of Staff's order "war today" was not translated by the Command into concrete orders of defense—the partition of the front into defense sectors, the allocation of forces, the allocation of local reserves, and the setting of a rear defense line. In the orders group of 1000, the two defense plans—"Gir" and "Sela"—were not discussed at all, although the order of battle of the Command that morning came close to the order of battle of the Gir plan. Instead, the forces were still organized to counter Syrian local attacks, with Brigade 188, which had only two battalions, at the front, and Brigade 7 at the rear.

The central headquarters that was to control the fighting was situated in Nafah, at the center of the Golan Heights, in a form that was suitable for small-scale fighting but not a general war. The latter form demanded the partition of the front into sectors and the establishment of two or more junior headquarters, so that each would have the capability to receive the massive information from the front, analyze it, and deliver the necessary information to the central headquarters. Here was the second mistake. Shortly after the war started, the central headquarters at Nafah was flooded with information that it could not analyze and translate into concrete orders. As a result, the Command's decision-making process was disrupted. The gravest result was the decision to send Brigade 7—that was to serve as the Command's reserve force—to the northern sector of the Golan at 1445, about forty-five minutes after the war started, without having a clear picture of the situation in the north. Later, it became clear that at around 1530 the Syrians were blocked there without the intervention of the Brigade in the fighting.

At least in one aspect, though, the situation in the Golan was better than in the canal. While the Bar-Lev line was manned by second-rate manpower that became a liability once fighting started, the strongholds in the Golan were manned by regular high-quality soldiers that participated effectively in the fighting, even when they were surrounded by the Syrian army.

Altogether, then, in the Northern Command, very much like in the south, the Chief of Staff's instructions to prepare for war had not been translated into concrete preparations. The failure in the south was, to a very large extent, a personal failure of the Command's Commander. In the north, the situation was less clear. The Northern Command's Commander testified that

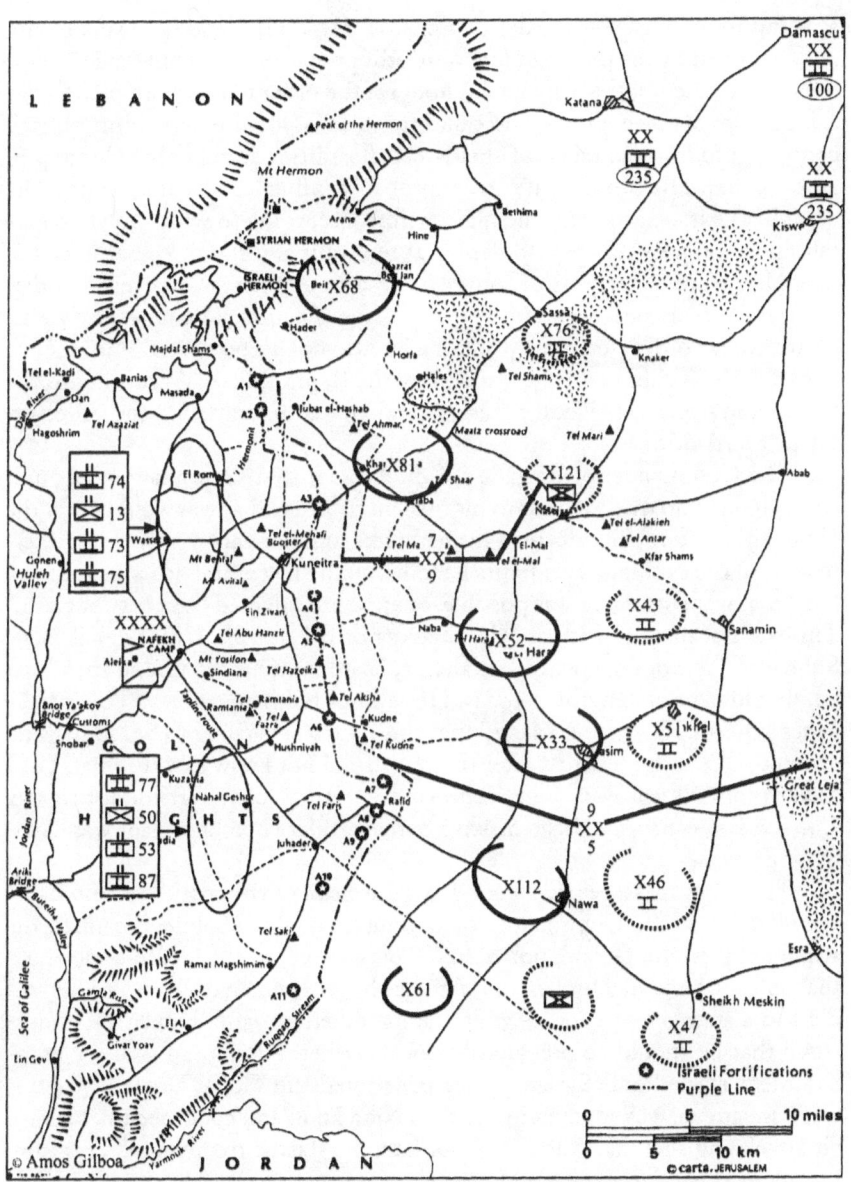

Military Deployment on the Golan Front, October 6, 1973 1400

at about 1000 he gave the order to prepare for war. He could not explain why, at 1400, most of his commanders were still preparing for small-scale hostilities.[34] It is also unclear why he did not give the order to carry out plan Gir — the parallel of dove cote at the canal front. It is possible that Hofi himself continued to think in terms of small-scale hostilities despite his order to prepare for war. His subordinates were probably influenced by the original orders that he issued to them the night before, according to which the two battalions of Brigade 188 were to deploy at the front and the three battalions of Brigade 7 were to serve as a Command reserve at the rear. During that discussion, Hofi also analyzed the Syrian courses of action. The most likely plan of attack, according to him, would be an attempt to take over a number of knolls at the Kuneitra area, or to occupy the Rapid salient. According to the Command's plans, Brigade 7 was to carry out counterattacks and reoccupy the lost territories.[35]

The Commander of Brigade 7, Col. Avigdor Ben-Gal, was the only unit commander who made it clear to his men on Saturday that war would erupt the same day. At 1000, he informed his battalion commanders that war was likely to start in the evening. Two hours later, his company commanders heard from him "that war with Syria was possible, or an unprecedented large border clash." This was not the case with the Commander of Brigade 188, Col. Yitzhak Ben-Shoham. The Commander of Battalion 53 heard from him at around 1030 "that we should expect something today. He did not tell me war. . . ." The intelligence officer of Brigade 188 heard that this time it was going to be "something serious." But, as he testified after the war, "I did not know exactly what, but I did not think it was war." The Commander of the Golan Territorial Brigade, Col. Zvi Bar, estimated that a massive Syrian artillery bombardment was likely, but not a war.[36]

The vague messages that went down the chain of command were probably the reason why the Commander of Battalion 13, whose soldiers manned the strongholds in the Golan's northern sector, was one of the last to understand that an actual war had broken out. At 1130, he received an order to put his soldiers in a state of alert for a Syrian bombardment at 1300. Hence, he understood that he should be prepared for local clashes. At 1345, an artillery bombardment started and Syrian planes penetrated the Golan airspace. At this stage already he was situated in the Abu Nida knoll and could see the massive air attack and shelling. About an hour later, he started receiving reports from his soldiers that Syrian ground forces were moving toward the border — an advancement that he himself could observe from his post. Only then he started thinking that this was something bigger than a local clash. In order to know more about the situation, he turned on the radio and heard a news report that the Egyptian army was crossing the Suez Canal. "Only then I understood it was war. No one had told me yet. But I understood it was war."[37]

* * *

During the first hours of the war in the Golan, the situation did not seem to be too grave, with most of the Syrian forces being blocked. The main damage during these hours was the loss of the IDF's biggest stronghold and the center of intelligence collection on Mount Hermon, on the northern part of the Heights. It fell, quite easily, to the hands of Syrian commando units that moved by foot from a nearby Syrian stronghold. Only eleven hours after the beginning of the war, the Northern Command started realizing that it had made a grave mistake in assuming that the main effort of the Syrian breakthrough would be in the Kuneitra area. As AMAN had accurately reported, it took place in the Rapid salient. At this stage, however, the Golan front was divided into two sectors. The three battalions of Brigade 7 defended the north, while the weaker Brigade 188, with only two battalions, defended the southern sector, where the breakthrough took place.

Toward midnight, the Commander of the Northern Command decided to move his command post from Nafah, a few kilometers from the front line, to Mount Canaan near the town of Safed, well within the Israeli hinterland. The Commander of Division 36, Brig. Gen. Raphael Eitan, received the command of the Golan front. Shortly after midnight, it became clear that Armored Divisions 1 and 3 started moving from the Kiswa and Katana at the rear, to the front. At about 0100, the Commander of Brigade 188, now located in the area of Ma'ale Gamla, reported that he observed Syrian tanks standing over the Sea of Galilee basin. Within a few hours it became clear that since there were no Israeli tanks between the Syrian forces and the Jordan River, the Syrian breakthrough now posed a threat to both the Golan's southern and central sectors. At 0200, the Commander of the Golan Territorial Brigade received instructions to prepare the demolition of the six bridges over the Jordan River. "This," he testified, "was the most difficult moment of the Golan Heights . . . the feeling was that we were facing a disaster." Then came instructions to burn sensitive documents in the Golan's camps and military posts in preparation for a retreat. At 0445, the magnitude of the military disaster became rather clear in the IDF headquarters in Tel Aviv: The Syrian forces broke the Israeli defense line at three points, and the local command remained with a very small number of tanks.[38]

This was the background for the Defense Minister's decision to go to the north, "to watch the situation closely, if we are going to lose the Golan Heights. . . ." At 0530, even before Dayan arrived there, the Chief of Staff instructed the Commander of the IAF to provide the Northern Command maximal air support. Upon Dayan's arrival to Mount Canaan, he heard from Hofi and his staff that the situation in the Golan was very grave and that "the fighting in the Height's southern sector ended and we lost. We don't have the force to stop them."[39]

Dayan was, no doubt, under extreme mental pressure now. Only twenty hours earlier, he objected to a massive mobilization and rejected any form of a preemptive air strike against Syria. While he was still busy giving orders to build a second defense line in the Jordan Valley, he made a direct call to the Commander of the IAF, Maj. Gen. Benny Peled. His message, as Peled vividly remembered it, was clear: "The Third Temple was in danger. If the air force would not transfer all its power to block the Syrian forces in the southern sector of the Golan Heights—Syrian tanks would enter Israel soon."[40]

iv. The Air Force

On Yom Kippur at noon, the IAF was well prepared for war. And yet, upon its start, it was surprised as well and in three different dimensions. The first involved the dimensions of the war. The IAF was prepared for a war on the Syrian front, but not in Egypt. On Friday at noon, it made preparations to carry out the "Dugman 5" operation—the destruction of the Syrian anti-aircraft disposition between the Golan and Damascus—but hardly related to the need to destroy the similar Egyptian layout along the canal. The fighting on two fronts divided the efforts of the IAF from the war's first moment—making it difficult to establish where to concentrate its main effort.

The second dimension of surprise involved the H-hour—1400—not sunset, about four hours later. Here, at least, the damage was somewhat smaller, since the IAF Commander had estimated, on the basis of professional considerations, that war might start earlier. In a discussion that he held at 1230, after the preemptive air strike was called off, he instructed that H-hour in the air should be expected between 1500 and "last light." Consequently, he said after the war, "I gave an instruction to cancel preparations to attack airfields, to replace ammunition, to download ammunition from the planes that had been allocated for defense, and the IAF started taking off at around 1330, in various places, including Ophir [Sharm el Sheik], a place where I had grave concerns."[41] The quick change of instructions was in place. Many IAF planes were not yet ready for interception when fire started, and yet those that did take off shot down thirty-seven Egyptian attack planes and helicopters, and five Syrian planes during the war's first hours.[42] This success disrupted the Egyptian efforts to lay commando ambushes on the main roads leading to the front line in order to isolate the small forces that were fighting near the Bar-Lev line. This success also prevented additional air attacks in the Sinai.

The third dimension of surprise—and it seems that this was the gravest one—was neither caused by the Syrian nor by the Egyptians. Rather, it was Dayan's decisive objection to the launching of a preemptive air strike on Saturday morning. This decision clearly contradicted earlier understandings on the basis of which the IAF had built its operational plans for war.

Less than four months earlier, on June 13, the IAF presented the Minister of Defense, the Chief of Staff and the IDF high command, its plans for a coming war. The plans included "Negiha" ("Butt"), the attack of Egyptian and Syrian airfields; "Tagar" ("Challenge"), the attack of Egypt's anti-aircraft layout along the Suez Canal; "Dugman" ("model")—the attack of the Syrian air defense layout between the Golan Heights and Damascus; "Dominique," attacks against strategic installations in Syria and Egypt; and "Srita" ("Scratch"), air support for the ground forces even before air superiority was achieved.[43] During the discussion, the newly appointed IAF Commander, Benny Peled, made it clear that the success of these attack operations depended upon a number of factors. Only an Israeli initiative, which might guarantee minimal uncertainty, especially an attack in suitable weather conditions, could ensure success. Peled stated:

> I told the forum that if we are not allowed to choose the day in which we make it, then there is grave doubt [whether we will succeed] and the plans would not suffer this disruption.... There was silence, and, then, the Minister of Defense told me: "Dear Benny, do you really think that if we had even a shred of doubt that we are going to be attacked, the air force would not receive the order to attack first?[44]

Peled responded by saying that in light of the Israeli claim that the newly occupied territories reduced the necessity of a preemptive strike, one could doubt this commitment. And yet, on the morning of Yom Kippur he was shocked when the Chief of Staff informed him, at about 1030, that the Prime Minister did not authorize the air strike.[45]

Dayan's veto on preemption hindered an effective participation of the IAF in the war's first hours. But during the night, the Chief of Staff and Benny Peled decided that at sunrise the next morning (October 7), the IAF would launch operation Tagar—the destruction of the Egyptian air defense layout near the canal. The first wave of Tagar included a preparation attack—the destruction of anti-aircraft guns and other forces—by eighty Skyhawk planes. This was to be immediately followed by an attack of eight airfields near the front, from which the main activity of the EAF in the war zone was taking place. The attack's goal was to prevent enemy planes from disrupting the bombing of the SAM sites. Three hours after the completion of this stage, the IAF was scheduled to carry out the operation's main stage: the attack of half of the SAM sites, in order to allow aerial freedom of action in a wide sector of the front.[46]

Tagar's opening stage was successful. The eighty attacking Skyhawks achieved good results and only two of them were hit. Four out of the seven (rather than eight) airfields that were attacked by Phantom F-4 planes, ceased to be operational. According to the Chief of Staff's report to the cabinet, six Mig planes were shot down during this attack, and others crashed on the runways. The Phantoms suffered no casualties.[47]

These initial achievements, however, bore no relevance to Tagar's ultimate success. The massive Syrian pressure and the threat of a Syrian breakthrough into Galilee and the Jordan Valley, led Dayan to make his direct talk with Peled, in which he made it clear that "the Third Temple" was in danger if the whole air force did not block the Syrian advancement. The Chief of Staff agreed. At 0630, when the planes of Tagar's first wave were already under way, the IAF Commander gave instructions to cease the operation and to divert the aerial efforts to the north. In addition, he ordered preparations for the execution of Dugman 5—the destruction of the Syrian anti-aircraft layout—at 1130.[48]

Peled's orders surprised and angered senior officers in the IAF underground commanding post in Tel Aviv.[49] Their objection came from three sources. The first was the need to exploit the success of the first stage of Tagar. Under the conditions of that early Sunday morning, when the chances of Tagar's success seemed to be high,[50] to stop it seemed like a grave mistake. In retrospect, this, indeed, was the case: Throughout the rest of the war, the IAF had to operate in this sector in a ground to air missile defended zone. Consequently, it lost not only more planes but also much of its operational effectiveness.

Second, to call off Tagar was not necessary. The small compartment of terrain in the southern sector of the Golan Heights did not allow a massive use of the IAF. Indeed, since the early-morning hours, the former Commander of the IAF, Maj. Gen. (res.) Mordechai Hod, improvised the operation of a Skyhawk squadron from the base of Ramat David against the Syrian tanks in the southern Golan front. These planes succeeded in delaying the Syrian movement westward, until the first IDF reserve forces arrived and pushed back the Syrian tanks. Altogether, that day the IAF conducted 129 ground support sorties[51]—a limited number that did not necessitate the halting of Tagar. The Commander of the Northern Command testified after the war that with only one exception, the ground forces did not feel the IAF support even after its activity was diverted from the south to the north.[52] Moreover, during the five hours that elapsed between Peled's order to carry out Dugman 5 and the start of the operation, the situation at the front improved. At 0630, the impression was that only the air force stood between the Syrian tanks and the civilian population of the Jordan Valley. By 0930, the Northern Command assessed that the Syrian pressure was decreasing and reports to this effect were delivered to the Chief of Staff. This recovery was the outcome of a number of factors. The most important one was the delay in the advancement of Armored Division 1 to the Tel Phares-Hushniya combat area and of Armored Brigade 47 to the Juhader-Ramat Magshimim zone at the southern flank of the Golan, because of ongoing IAF attacks in these areas. These forces crossed the border only at 1000. The second factor involved the rapid reinforcement of the Golan front with reserve forces. Reserve Brigade 679, under the command of Col. Ori Or, started climbing the Golan slopes in the early morning hours and its first tanks arrived at the Nafah area at 0700. Reserve Brigade 179, under the command of Colonel Ran Sarig, crossed the Jordan Valley at first light, and its tanks started climbing toward the area of Katzabiya and El Al. The command of Division 210, under Maj. Gen. (res.) Dan Laner, started climbing the Golan Heights on Sunday morning, and by 1100 the Golan front was divided into two sectors: the north under the command of Division 36 and the south under the command of Division 210. In addition, earlier that morning the Chief of Staff decided to assign Reserve Division 146—the main GHQ reserve force that was to defend the border with Jordan—to the Golan front. Since the morning hours, the Division was moving, on chains, from its bases in the south of the Jordan Valley to the north.

At 1000, a note "there is a recovery" was recorded in the unit-log of Division 36. Fifteen minutes later, the Commander of Division 36, Brig. Gen. Raphael Eitan and his staff returned to their headquarters in the camp of Nafah. At around 1100 three Syrian tank brigades developed an attack at the Hushniya-Nafah Zone. It was blocked at around 1500. This battle marked a strategic shift in the fighting. If until this stage the IDF had conducted only defensive battles, from now on it would take the initiative. The next morning, it started its counterattacks.[53]

Altogether then, the impression is that though the situation in the early morning hours of October 7 was highly dangerous and might have justified the decision to divert the IAF main effort from the south to the north, by 1000, about ninety minutes before operation Dugman 5 was to start, the situation improved and a second consideration of the necessity of the operation was in place. But it was not implemented, and this was the third and most critical mistake.

The rushed manner in which the operation to destroy the Syrian anti-aircraft layout was prepared that morning created an unbridgeable gap between planning and execution: a preparatory attack, like the one carried out by the Skyhawks and the Phantoms five hours earlier at the canal front, was not performed in the Golan; most of the electronic warfare layout that was deployed to assist Tagar could not be brought up in time to provide support for Dugman 5; ground artillery support was not provided; and lack of time also prevented the extensive use of chaff. Most important, in contrast to any earlier planning, a reconnaissance flight to pinpoint the location of the fifteen mobile SA-6 batteries was not taken. This was such a critical element of the operation, since locating the batteries while flying at low altitude in a g/a missile defended zone was both highly risky and unlikely to succeed.[54] And, since an SA-6 battery could start moving within ten minutes from order and start shooting twelve minutes after stopping at a new firing position—having the most updated information about the location of the fifteen batteries had become critical. On top of all these deficiencies, the last-minute improvisation of the operation prevented a proper briefing of many of the pilots who had just returned from the first attack wave of Tagar.

Lt. Col. Yiftah Spector, the commander of a Phantom squadron at the IAF base in Hatzor, expressed his frustration literally upon returning from the attack against the Egyptian airfields and revealing, to his great surprise, that while he was in the air the mission was changed and, now, he had to attack the Syrian SAM layout:

> To Syria?! And, with such urgency! What the hell was going on up there in the North? Has the situation turned so serious that they're scrambling off this way, sent to shut down missile batteries. The Squadrons in the Northern Theater of Israel, facing the Syrian-led assault from the Golan Heights supported by the Syrian Air Force and SAMs, must have taken a beating, but there were no loss numbers reported in the intelligence traffic; there was no time perhaps, and nobody wanted to overstate such things.
>
> Scrambling to a missile attack? No!! This is too wild. Have the generals at HQ thought this through? No one pounces onto missile batteries just like that, out of the blue. SAMs have proven to be a terrible enemy in the years since the Six-Day War. Built with all the sneaky wisdom of Soviet technology and given to the Arabs as a means of trapping and annihilating the Israeli Air Force. In every past encounter with them along the Suez Canal and above the Golan Heights, the missiles won most of the time and the IAF suffered severe losses—in planes, in prisoners of war, in casualties, in prestige, in self-confidence. This caused the IAF to fall back; it withdrew into itself to lick its wounds, hesitated, and reassessed the situation finding that it could not evade the problem.
>
> A great effort was made over the years to develop methods to fight the missiles—secret methods, complex and sophisticated. The fighter squadrons were trained with new tactics that were polished down to the finest details. Aircraft in the formations were geared to work together as one machine, with "pure precision," to attain perfect coordination between hundreds of planes, so that each plane would arrive at the right place and at the right time to cover for one another. On some of the aircraft would be newly arrived U.S. countermeasure jamming pods that would attempt to break the lock-on of the tracking SAM radars. The relatively rigid formations were designed for the optimal output of these electronic pods against the SAM radars, not for the comfort of the pilots who would instinctively prefer more

dynamic entries. Thus, the concept was established and the tactical details absorbed by the pilots. The mission orders were constructed, under the assumption that only such a "Swiss watch" approach would be able to cope with overlapping SAM batteries controlled from a central command point.

Now that the hour has come, for some reason the entire plan lies shattered. Had the American pods not worked? Did the Arabs get a counter-countermeasure from the Russians? Who cares now—the Squadron Commander is sending his people out to grab maps and rush to the planes, to start up and launch, in a "catch as catch can" style. There would be no briefing, no mission preparations, just a total disregard for the hundreds of details crucial to the successful performance of an "air operation." Pilots would be left to their instincts.

Has Headquarters completely lost its mind?[55]

Spector's gut feeling, like the pessimistic assessments of some of the officers who commanded the operation from the IAF headquarters in the "pit" in Tel Aviv, proved to be right. Out of thirty-one Syrian batteries that were attacked, only one was destroyed and another was damaged. The cost paid for this failure was high: six Phantom F-4 and three Skyhawk A-4 planes were shot down. The failure of Dugman 5 led Dayan to pressure the IAF to avoid additional attacks against the Syrian and the Egyptian SAM layouts. Rather, the air force was required now to support the ground fighting, especially in Sinai, where it became clear now that Division 252, with only a third of its original force, could not block an Egyptian breakthrough toward the Gidi and Mitla Passes. Now, that the situation in the Golan had improved, the focus of concern returned to the south. At its center was the fear that Egypt's Armored Divisions 4 and 21 would cross the canal and develop a massive attack towards the passes before the IDF first reserve forces could arrive to establish a new defense line. The Chief of Staff ordered the IAF to cease all attacks against the SAM sites. And, since the situation in the north was perceived now, in the afternoon of October 7, as less dangerous than in the morning, the IAF redirected its main efforts to the south.[56]

The chain of decisions that were taken on Sunday morning led to a situation in which the anti-aircraft threat remained effective in the northern as well as the southern front throughout most of the war. As a result, the freedom of action of the IAF remained significantly limited—a factor that delayed the Israeli success in the war, raised its cost, and prevented a clear-cut victory at its end. In the years before the war, Israel invested about half of its defense budget in the IAF. Now, when it had to pay back the return, it could not deliver the goods—not because of any fundamental weakness or because it was improperly prepared for the coming war, but because it was not operated correctly.[57]

This chain of mistakes was not a coincidental outcome of a normal decision-making process that took place under the uncertainty of the fog of war. It was not the only one of its kind either. To a large extent, it was the result of the shock of surprise to Israel's decision-makers when they found themselves fighting without earlier preparation the all-out war that broke out on Yom Kippur at noon.

Chapter 18

The Cost of Being Caught Unprepared

From the victim's perspective, surprise involves two heavy consequences. The first is the loss of strategic assets—weapon systems, vital areas, airfields, ports, avenues of approach, or means of communication—that are essential for the achievement of a military victory. The second is the destabilization of the victim's decision-making system, as a result of the combined appearance of the three factors that turn a normal situation into a crisis: the shock of surprise, the threat to central values, and a limited time response.[1] The surprise of Yom Kippur constitutes a good example for both.

i. The Material Losses

We cannot know what the course of the war would have been had the surprise been averted. Hence, no definite estimation of the IDF losses as a direct result of the surprise can be ascertained. The best that can be done is to estimate the IDF's losses in the war's first three days—until the end of its failed counterattack in Sinai, and the more successful counterattack in the Golan. These losses had been the direct outcome of surprise. And yet, it should be remembered that the heavy losses the IDF suffered throughout the rest of the war were also the direct outcome of the way the war started.

The IDF has never provided an official figure of the number of soldiers that were killed in the war's first phase. The best figure we have, from a simple count, is 724 soldiers killed until the end of October 8.[2] This figure does not include soldiers who were wounded and died later, or prisoners of war (most of whom were captured during the war's first three days), who died in Syrian or Egyptian prisons.

The IDF was involved in heavy battles before, but throughout its history it had never paid so dearly for such minor achievements as it did on the war's first day. In the morning of October 7, less than sixteen hours after fire started, Division 252—the main regular force that was supposed to hold back the Egyptian crossing force—was left with 103 tanks out of the 290 tanks it had when war started.[3] The Egyptians, on the other hand, succeeded during these hours to cross the canal with 90,000 soldiers, 850 tanks, and 11,000 additional vehicles. The price they claim to have paid for this achievement was twenty tanks, five fighters, and 280 soldiers killed.[4] If accepted at face value, this loss ratio means that for each destroyed Egyptian tank the IDF lost nine of its own. Such a loss ratio did not reflect a significant improvement in the performance of the Egyptian army or deterioration in the operational capabilities of the IDF's tank teams. Eight days later, the Egyptian army launched its second offensive in the war. It lost about 250 tanks without any territorial gains. The Israelis lost 10–12 tanks.[5] Only the shock of surprise, the confusion, the improper deployment, and the misunderstanding of the Egyptian war plan at the operational and strategic levels can explain the IDF's initial failure. This combination of factors led to a situation in which many of the tanks of Division 252 were hit by Egyptian teams of tank hunters when they were on their way to their firing positions—the same positions they were supposed to hold when the war started. Many additional tanks were hit when they tried to assist the strongholds in response to desperate calls for help from the reserve soldiers that were not supposed to man them from the start.

The loss ratio in the north was entirely different. The IDF suffered heavy losses here as well—Brigade 188 lost in the war's first sixteen hours fifty-two out of the seventy-seven tanks[6] and Brigade 7 was left on October 9 with thirty-two out of its 105 tanks.[7] But here the Syrians' losses were heavier by far, amounting to 700 tanks in the war's first three days. Brigade 7 alone destroyed about 500 armored vehicles, including 260 tanks.[8]

In this sense the price Israel paid for being caught unprepared varied from one front to another. In the Sinai, the IDF lost most of its defense force without causing significant casualties to the attacker. The fact that the Egyptian army avoided exploiting its success on the morning of October 7 and did not advance into the depth of Sinai was the product of Israel's deterrent posture that convinced the Egyptian war planners to adopt modest territorial goals from the start. It was also the outcome of the tendency of Egypt's high command to stick to existing plans and avoid improvisations. The Syrians, in contrast, attempted to exploit the surprise in order to occupy the entire Golan Heights. Paradoxically, their relative success was also the source of their failure, since the desperate fighting of Brigades 188 and 7 destroyed most of the Syrian attacking force. In this sense, the high price the Syrians paid for their initial achievements enabled the IDF to decide the war in the north at a far earlier stage than in the Sinai.

Beyond its human and material losses, the cost the IDF paid for being caught unprepared involved the state of combat readiness of the reserve forces upon their arrival at the front. In light of the chaotic way in which the war started, there were many claims that the reserve store units were poorly organized—allegedly proof of the fundamental neglect that contributed independently to the military failure. But as Adan pointed out, in 1973 the IDF was better prepared for war than in 1967. Still, in 1967 the IDF went to war better prepared since it had three weeks to get organized for the fighting.[9] In Yom Kippur some of the reserve forces started their way to the front within a few hours from the time of mobilization, and in a number of cases they got into battle within twelve hours from call. As a result they fought in an unorganized manner and, in many cases, without being properly equipped. Moreover, out of 1,741 tanks that entered combat service in both fronts during the war's first three days, only 309 arrived in the combat zone on transporters. The rest made their way on chains; 168 of them suffered various technical problems. The rest entered combat in a low state of technical fitness due to the long drive on chains. The hasty manner in which the armor brigades were mobilized caused some of them to equip themselves with tanks and kits from other brigades and to fight in unrecognized sectors. For example, Brigade 7 used the tanks of Reserve Brigade 179, and Brigade 179 was equipped with the tanks of Brigade 164, whose reserve store units were located in lower Galilee. The tank teams of Brigade 164, who were supposed to fight in the north, had been delivered to the south and there they were equipped with the tanks and kits of Brigade 7. These tanks had been in a low state of fitness since they were hurriedly left in the stores of Brigade 7 two weeks earlier.[10]

There is no way to estimate the cost paid for entering combat in such a hasty manner, but it was certainly high.[11] But given the magnitude of the surprise, the ability to get all the IDF tanks to the front line within seventy-two hours—even if not perfectly fitted for fighting—was a remarkable achievement. It shows that the IDF logistical layout had been properly built for the war. It also constitutes proof of both the excellent ability of the reserve soldiers at all ranks to improvise in order to overcome unexpected problems and their high motivation to get into combat as soon as possible.

The IAF also paid dearly for being surprised. According to official figures, it lost 7.2 percent of its forces, or about thirty planes during the first thirty-four hours of the war. According to a different source, it lost thirty-five planes by the end of the second day.[12] These figures represent heavy losses indeed, but they were not exceptional. During the first three hours of the Six-Day War, the IAF lost close to 10 percent of its combat planes (19 out of 205) and until the end of the first day the number increased.[13] But in 1967 this cost was paid in order to reach a decisive victory with the destruction of the air forces Israel fought against. In 1973 the IAF was used in a unorganized manner and, therefore, the damage it caused was relatively minor—about eighty fighter planes and helicopters had been shot down by the end of the second day of the war.[14] Although it was not its own fault, the IAF completely failed in its prime mission at the beginning of the war: the destruction of the Egyptian and Syrian anti-aircraft layouts and the achievement of freedom of action over the war zone. In this sense, though the IAF was well prepared for the war, Israel's desperate situation on the ground prevented it from properly exploiting its real potential.

ii. The Psychological Impact of Surprise

The decisions taken in the framework of the war had been analyzed by Michael Brecher with Benjamin Geist, who identified twenty major Israeli decisions between October 5 and 26.[15] But their study focused on the decisions taken by the political echelon—Golda Meir alone, her kitchen cabinet, or the government—while the relevant decisions for this study are the ones that were taken when the impact of surprise and its outcomes reached its height, (i.e., during the war's first days). The most critical decisions were taken during the war's second day, October 7. This was also the day in which the most devastating impact of the three elements that make a crisis—high levels of surprise, threat perception, and time pressure—were felt.

The impact of surprise on the war's second day was made up of two elements. The first was that the war started with hardly any strategic warning and Israel was ill-prepared for it. The second involved the results of the fighting during the war's first hours: the Syrian breakthrough in the Golan and the threat it created to the Jordan Valley and the collapse of the Bar Lev line and the destruction of Division 252, which paved the way for an Egyptian advance into the Sinai. During October 7, two additional surprises were added—the IAF's failure to destroy the Egyptian and Syrian air defense layouts, and a better than expected Arab fighting performance.

As a result of the high magnitude of surprise, the threat that was created on October 7 was the gravest of the war. On the morning of October 7, only the IAF's Skyhawks stood between the tanks of Armored Division 5 and the Sea of Galilee. In the south, the broken formations of about one hundred tanks separated between the masses of the Egyptian army and the depth of the Sinai. At this stage of the war, moreover, two out of Israel's three pillars of national security—the ability to deter the Arabs from launching a war, and the ability to receive a high-quality strategic warning of an impending attack—had collapsed. A failure to win a decisive victory could have had a devastating effect on Israel's ability to cope with the Arab challenge, not only in the short run but also long-term.

The time-pressure element was also the most grave on the morning of October 7. It was clear that without a considerable reinforcement in the north, the whole of the Golan Heights might fall within a few hours and the Syrian army would be able to break into the Galilee and the Jordan Valley. Hence, the urgent problem in the Golan was the regular forces' ability to hold back for another few hours. In the Sinai, the problem was of a similar nature, though here an advancement of the Egyptian army eastward did not imply a threat to Israel within the pre–1967 borders. And yet, two factors intensified the volume of the time pressure at this front: the fear for the fate of the Bar Lev line strongholds with approximately 450 soldiers that manned them, and the estimation that Armored Divisions 4 and 21 were about to cross the canal—a move that would make the reoccupation of the territory lost already far more difficult.

The main burden of decision-making during October 7 rested on the shoulders of five persons: Prime Minister Golda Meir; Defense Minister Moshe Dayan; Chief of Staff David Elazar; Commander of the Southern Command, Maj. Gen. Shmuel Gonen; and Commander of the Northern Command, Maj. Gen. Yitzhak Hofi. Two of the five—Dayan and Gonen—functioned very badly under the stress. Two—Meir and Elazar—functioned very well. And while Hofi had difficulties in coping with the situation, his personal conduct had no major bearing upon the war in the Golan. Consequently, this section focuses on the way Dayan and Gonen functioned and the impact it had on the course of the war.

For Moshe Dayan, October 7 started at about 0400, when he was awakened from two hours' sleep to be informed about the difficult situation in the Golan. He decided to go to observe the situation there himself, and he arrived at Mount Canaan, near the city of Safed—where the command post of the Northern Command was located—at about 0600. There Dayan was influenced not only by the dire situation at the front but also by the atmosphere and the way Maj. Gen. Hofi and his close aides functioned. With this background, he called the commander of the IAF, Benny Peled. In his memoirs Dayan described the talk in an undertone: "This was the first time that I had spoken to the Air Force Commander in this way and on such a matter. This [Dayan's demand to direct all the IAF's efforts to the north] was not an order. I had to issue orders through the Chief of Staff. This was very much more than an order—and so was the positive response."[16]

What Dayan avoided describing in his memoirs was the shock he caused to the IAF Commander when he used the term "the Third Temple [i.e., the state of Israel] is under threat."[17] Implicitly, he laid the responsibility for the fate of the country on Peled's shoulders. Hence, Peled's protests that operation Tagar was already under way and that the success in the south should be exploited before turning the main effort to the north had become useless.[18] Dayan's anxiety was infectious. On the morning of October 7, he was still

Israel's highest authority in security affairs. His distress must have had a decisive impact on the way the Chief of Staff and the Commander of the IAF considered the situation as well as their acceptance of his demand.

The faults of Dayan's decision to call off Tagar and to launch Dugman have already been discussed. It is important to emphasize here, again, that given that the IAF had never tried to launch similar operations until the end of the war and as a result, it could not provide the ground forces with an effective air support, the significance of this decision cannot be overestimated. It was, probably, the most important decision taken by the Israelis after war started.

Dayan's apocalyptic mood continued to be expressed during the coming hours. Following his visit to the command post in the north, he continued to the south to observe the situation first hand there. Upon arriving at Um Hashiba, an attack by Egyptian Mig-17s began. The pilot of his helicopter ran to him and urged him to take shelter. Dayan ignored the pilot and continued walking slowly and apathetically, "as if he was not there."[19] Maj. Gen. Gonen testified later that "the impression Dayan left on him was difficult. He was highly excited and clasped his hands." Gonen's radio operator said that Dayan "looked gloomy, almost miserable."[20]

Dayan's estimate of the situation reflected his anxiety level as well. With only partial information about the situation in the front, he gave Gonen "a ministerial advice" to abandon the soldiers in the Bar Lev line, to take a deep withdrawal into the Sinai, and to continue fighting from the new line. The extent of the suggested withdrawal was unclear. In his memoirs he maintained that he referred to the line of the Gidi and the Mitla Passes, although he did not specify it. He did so after Gonen informed him that he had no ability to hold to the second defense line—about 10 kilometers east of the Bar Lev line.[21] According to Herzog, Dayan showed on the map a withdrawal line that went deeper into the Sinai, from east of Bir Gafgafa, to Jebel Ma'ara and Jebel Yalek, to Abu Rudeis on the Gulf of Suez. The Chief of Staff understood a few hours later that Dayan's withdrawal plan included Bir Gafgafa and Um Hashiba.[22]

The extent of Dayan's pessimism—perhaps even depression—during these hours is evident from the testimony of Maj. Gen. Rehavam Zeevi, who retired from active service on October 1 and now accompanied Dayan. Zeevi heard from him on their way back from Um Hashiba that "between Tel Aviv and Abu Ageila [in the Sinai] there isn't even a single tank and this is the destruction of the 'Third Temple.'"[23] In his memoirs Dayan described his way of thinking during these hours:

> The Arabs have forces and a lot of equipment. Behind them—the USSR and the Arab peoples, a source for reinforcement of soldiers and equipment. Our main danger at the moment is not only a loss of territory but, mainly, the erosion of our forces. We have a very limited

and constant number of tanks and planes, of tank teams and pilots. If these forces would be exhausted without bringing the war to a decision, Israel would remain exposed to the advancement of the Arab armies from Egypt, Syria, and, perhaps, Jordan. This is the main threat, and it demands an answer—immediately.[24]

Dayan also described, though in a reserved tone, his personal state of mind:

Indeed, as I flew back from Sinai to Tel Aviv, I could recall no moment in the past when I had felt such anxiety. If I had been in a physical strait, involved in personal danger, it would have been simpler. I knew this from experience. But now I had quite a different feeling. Israel was in danger, and the results could be fatal if we did not recognize and understand the situation in time and if we failed to suit our warfare to the new methods.[25]

This was Dayan's mood when he met, upon returning to Tel Aviv, Golda Meir, her close aide Yisrael Galili, and her deputy Yigal Allon. He suggested that the IDF withdraw into the depth of Sinai.[26] The advantage of the new line he proposed was that it was defensible. Its disadvantages were three: First, the second line of defense, which the IDF still held, set on a ridge of hills and controlled the area that was held at this stage by the Egyptians. A unilateral withdrawal into the Sinai would have given them, without any fighting, significant achievements that were beyond their initial expectations. Second, the withdrawal suggested by Dayan could prevent the IDF from launching a counteroffensive and regain the lost territory. Third, a deep withdrawal could have turned the Egyptian initial achievements—at the stage when the balance of forces favored them radically—into the final results of the war, especially since there was a good chance that the UN would attempt to reach a cease fire "in place." In other words, if Dayan's proposal was accepted, the tactical defeat of the war's first day could have become a strategic defeat in the war as a whole.

Yisrael Galili defined the picture portrayed by Dayan as "sad and desperate," and one that created "an atmosphere of a threat of destruction." His proposals could lead to "fatalistic results."[27] Golda Meir noted in her memoirs that she listened to him in "horror."[28] Her secretary testified that during the discussion she came out and told her that "Dayan wants to talk about the terms of surrender."[29]

The participants in the discussion accepted at its end the proposal set by the Chief of Staff—who was called to join in order to counterbalance Dayan's apocalyptic estimation—that he will go to Um Hashiba to see if the situation at the front was really so desperate. Shortly after arriving there, at about 1900, Elazar became convinced that there was no need for retreat. Moreover, the fast accumulation of the reserve forces made feasible the launching of the counteroffensive on the next morning. The discussion he conducted in the Southern Command's war room and the decisions he made annulled Dayan's earlier proposals.

Dayan himself came after the afternoon discussion to Golda Meir and offered her his resignation. This was his personal admission that he failed in his duty. The Prime Minister rejected the offer for her own reasons.[30] From Dayan's perspective, the offer to resign must have been the climax of the most difficult day of his career—the day in which he lost forever his status as Israel's highest security authority.

* * *

The second person that functioned poorly under the sudden stress of the war was the commander of the Southern Command, Maj. Gen. Shmuel Gonen. During the first ten hours of the war he was in Beer Sheba—the location of his Command—where he received only partial information about the fighting and remained rather calm. At about midnight he arrived at Um Hashiba, where the dire situation in the front had become more clear. His deputy, Brig. Gen. Uri Ben-Ari testified after the war:

> When we arrived at Um Hashiba the behavior of the commander of the Command completely changed. Until then he was relatively calm, [but] after we arrived in Um Hashiba he lost, in many cases, his self control. His attitude toward the staff officers in the war room did not allow anyone to function because of concern and even fear to do the smallest thing, [and they were] prohibited from expressing their opinion freely. In fact, as a result of the Commander's behavior, no staff work could be done.... When views had been expressed, it was under the pressure of personal fear. Consequently, one of the problems was that the Command's Commander had difficulties crystallizing a view or any estimate of the situation, since the atmosphere in the war room was one of fear and terror, which did not allow for any normal [staff] work.[31]

On another occasion, Ben-Ari compared Gonen's managerial style to that of Lt. Gen. (res.) Chaim Bar-Lev, who replaced him on October 9. "During the war's first days," he said, "the Command was in an unacceptable moral, organizational, and disciplinary situation. Once Chaim [Bar Lev] arrived, the Command became calm. After he came, communication sets ceased flying in the air, officers were not fired or replaced, and a normal functioning of a front was established."[32]

Maj. Gen. Avraham Adan, the commander of the IDF Armored Corps, who headed Division 162—one of the three divisions in the Suez sector—estimated that Gonen's first "sober order" was given only on the morning of October 7, when he ordered the remains of Division 252 to withdraw and keep a distance from the Egyptian forces. But the dire situation in the front did not prevent him from cultivating:

> ... optimistic hopes that were clearly unrealistic and irrelevant to the situation. He lacked patience and he had an urge to change his difficult situation and soon! It seems that he did not comprehend the difficult situation as a situation that is significant for the past and the future but as a temporary accident that could easily be fixed. Any fragment of piece of information that added to the positive side of the balance sheet ... breaded his optimism.... Under an optimistic mood he neglected a realistic approach and did not take the measures required for the relevant situation.[33]

In the days before the war, Gonen did not assess that large-scale fighting was possible. Since October 1, he visited the Bar Lev line only once. On the night of October 4–5 he was unavailable—visiting friends in the northern town of Haifa, as he later claimed. He demonstrated no interest in the intelligence information available on the Egyptian war plan, and on the morning of October 6 he distorted the Chief of Staff's order to prepare for a war the same day by instructing the commander of Division 252 to prepare for an unspecified act, "perhaps a general war—though this was not considered to be reasonable." His order to deploy the tanks of Division 252 in a small dove-cote formation rather than the original plan, cut in half the number of tanks that could fire at the crossing forces. But his additional mistaken order—to delay the deployment until late the afternoon—annulled the significance of the first and led to a situation where only three tanks were in their positions when war started.

Gonen's deputy testified after the war that during its first hours he "tried all the time to find the Egyptian main effort.... Only after the war, I learned that it was known exactly how the Egyptians would cross and that there was no main effort but that their effort would go along the whole length of the canal."[34] Gonen's futile search for a nonexistent main effort was the direct outcome of his lack of interest in the available intelligence. This led to a situation where the crossing forces met no effective opposition while the defending forces suffered the heaviest losses the IDF had ever suffered in such a short period of time.

Later, on October 7 at noon, Gonen concluded that the Egyptian armored divisions had started crossing the canal. Consequently, and counting on Dayan's "ministerial advice" he ordered to prepare for a withdrawal to the Gidi and the Mitla Passes. Less than an hour later, upon receiving a message from

Maj. Gen. (res.) Ariel Sharon that his reserve Division 143 would be ready for attack toward nightfall, he called off the withdrawal and instead instructed Sharon to prepare to cross the canal.[35] The same pattern, of a swift transition from deep pessimism to groundless optimism was reflected in Gonen's behavior on October 8 — the day on which the IDF launched its futile counteroffensive. On the basis of partial reports of an initial success of Division 162, Gonen changed the original plan as authorized by the Chief of Staff and ordered Division 143 to start advancing to the south. At 1240 he asked Elazar to authorize the occupation of the town of Suez in four hours.[36] Only after it became evident that Division 162 failed in its mission, was the improvised offensive mission of Division 143 called off. Summarizing the course of events during that tragic day, Chief of Staff Elazar said of Gonen's note that asked for a "permission to occupy [the town of] Suez at 1600": "A normal man who did not yet leave Tassa [the deployment area of Division 143] does not usually ask for a permission to occupy Suez."[37]

The decisions taken by Dayan and Gonen on the eve of the war and during its initial stage contributed significantly to the IDF's setbacks during the war's first days. Although these two men were not the only ones influenced by the devastating impact of surprise, the combination of their personal conduct and their critical responsibilities single them out in comparison to others who also functioned poorly. Luckily for Israel, the Chief of Staff and the Prime Minister coped quite well with the pressure. Their ability to make the right decisions limited the damage that could have been caused had Dayan's proposals been automatically accepted. Toward the end of the war's initial stage, the personal impact of Dayan and Gonen was dramatically reduced. Gonen was replaced by the former Chief of Staff, Chaim Bar Lev, who was nominated as the de facto commander of the Southern Command on October 9; Dayan maintained his formal status but his "ministerial advices" were, from October 7 onward, almost always ignored.

Chapter 19

The Causes of the Intelligence Failure

The course of events that led Israel to pay so dearly for being caught unprepared for war has been described in the previous chapters. Now it is time to analyze the main causes of this failure. But before turning to this, three points should be emphasized.

First, the public atmosphere of self-assurance and complacence, which relied on the belief that Israel continued to maintain its military superiority, that its deterrent power remained effective, and that its intelligence community had the capability of providing a war warning under any circumstances, played a significant role in facilitating the intelligence failure since it created the milieu within which the estimation and policy-making processes took place. Its impact, however, cannot be measured. For many Israelis it constitutes a major cause of the failure—a sort of moral "crime and punishment." But a more sober analysis must take into account that such an atmosphere could have had only a limited impact on the professional conduct of experienced intelligence and military officers.

Second, AMAN's fiasco was not the failure to provide a clear war warning a few days before the outbreak of the war. Rather, it was the fact that despite receiving an ample amount of warnings that clearly indicated war, the organization continued telling its consumers until Friday morning that war was unlikely. By October 1, AMAN had sufficient information to assess that Arab preparation for war was one of three possible explanations for the situation—the other two being an exercise and a fear of an Israeli attack. Had it done so then, the information it collected later would have enabled it to turn the war explanation into the main one no later than the night of October 4–5.

Third, Israel's intelligence failure was not a failure of the intelligence system as a whole but of some of its critical elements. Most of the community's resources were invested in collection. Both AMAN and the Mossad's collection agencies provided high-quality warnings about the war preparations and the intention to launch it. Had Zeira approved the use of AMAN's special means of collection, the available information could have been of a higher quality. The chief of the Mossad was far more tuned to the possibility of war and in AMAN there was a number of high ranking officers—such as the head of the Collection Department, Col. Menahem Digli; the commander of Unit 848, Col. Yoel Ben-Porat; and, in the Research Department, the heads of Branches 2, 5, and 7 (technical/technological) as well as the heads of the Egyptian political and military sections—who assessed that the military preparations were for war.

The causes for the 1973 intelligence failure are grouped below in five clusters. Most of them have been identified already in the theoretical literature about strategic surprise and are applied here for the 1973 case. In conclusion, I will elaborate on what I regard to be the main explanation for this failure—an explanation that has not been identified yet as such in this literature.

1. Obstacles Unique to the Warning-Response Process

Cover and deception

The praise that the attempts to cover Arab war preparations and deceive Israel into believing that it was merely a regular exercise seem, in retrospect, exaggerated. The Egyptians, and even more so the Syrians, used tight compartmentation to keep the number of persons who knew about the coming war to the minimum, but, nevertheless, Israel received excellent information about their war plans, the nature of their preparations, and their intention to launch war in the first week of October. The Syrians, for their own reasons, avoided building a strategic deception plan at all and limited their action to a sporadic distribution, through the Arab press, of simple disinformation messages. The Egyptians prepared a more impressive deception plan—exercise Tahrir 41 as a cover for their logistical preparations—but this was a crude scheme that was carried out without sophistication. It did increase the volume of "noise," but any reasonable analysis of the information that was available could have shown that an exercise (that did not take place) could not explain Egypt's military preparations. In this sense, the Egyptian deception plan succeeded because of AMAN's weaknesses at the analytical level rather than because of its own strengths.

Cry-wolf syndrome

The cry-wolf syndrome had a devastating effect on Israel's war readiness. The syndrome's main effect derived from the fact that three times prior to the war—at the end of 1971, at the end of 1972, and in the spring of 1973—it seemed as if Egypt might launch a war, and, accordingly, measures to meet such a possibility were taken, but war did not take place.

As is known now, at the end of 1971 ("the year of decision") and in late 1972, Egypt had no intention to initiate hostilities. The war information that Israel received reflected false noise generated for domestic purposes or an Egyptian attempt to create a crisis in order to get out of the "no peace no war" limbo. In contrast, in spring 1973 there was, probably, a genuine intention to go to war, which did not materialize because of Syria's insufficient war readiness. In this sense, the three events were not the outcome of an intentional attempt aimed at reducing Israel's war awareness, though this was precisely their impact. By the same token, the various measures that Israel took to deter Sadat from launching a war in each of these instances had no impact on his decision to avoid war, since he did not intend to go to war from the start.

This, indeed, seems to be one of the reasons for the impact of the cry-wolf syndrome in the fall of 1973. Very much like any other organization, AMAN had no inclination to analyze its success. Consequently, the agency related the outcome of each of these three instances to an Egyptian bluff that failed to reach its target, without taking into account the possibility that at least once (spring 1973), this was not the case. When the clouds of war started gathering at the end of the summer, the tendency of AMAN's chief analysts to assess the warnings through the prism of the three previous events was already fixed. And the analysts who maintained earlier that Egypt was going for war started doubting the validity of their assessment. In the fall of 1973 they were already nicknamed "alarmists" and they were in a weaker position to challenge the dominant conception. The civilian and military policy-makers went through a similar process. This was clearly evident in the case of Dayan, who in May 1973 ordered the IDF to prepare for war in the second half of the summer. When the signs of war were not detected in the weeks that followed, he radically changed his mind: In July, as recalled, he forecasted that war was not likely to erupt in the coming decade.

The cry-wolf syndrome harmed also the effectiveness of a number of human sources since earlier warnings they provided did not materialize. It is possible that King Hussein would have acted more decisively had he not warned of war in May. The same is true with regard to Marwan. His warning came so late and, even then, involved some reservations, precisely because his earlier warnings—primarily of a war that should break in May—did not materialize. Consequently, he felt uneasy alerting his handlers again. This seems to be the reason why he hesitated to do so in October.[1]

Compartmentization

AMAN distributed certain types of sensitive information—primarily Marwan's—on a very strict basis. There is no evidence, however, that the use of this need-to-know principle caused difficulties in the estimation process. The only clear case in which compartmentization could have caused significant damage concerned King Hussein's warning about Syria's war preparations, which was not delivered to the head of Branch 5. In this case, as recalled, the relevant information was unofficially delivered to him by his colleague from Branch 2.

There were claims that compartmentization was used as a means to avoid alarmist analysts from receiving relevant information.[2] In addition, it was argued that the Northern Command's Operations Officer was not aware of the Syrian offense plans because of security considerations. The truth of this claim is doubtful. In any event, the Commander of the Northern Command and his intelligence officer were aware of these plans. There is no indication that the relevant commanders did not receive relevant information because of compartmentization. On the other hand, there were cases in which highly relevant information—such as certain high-quality warnings or observations reports from the canal—were not delivered to consumers. This, however, was not done because of the sources' sensitivity. Rather it was the product of some of AMAN's officers who decided that either the policy-makers did not need it or that it might confuse them.

Overconfidence in the quality of the intelligence sources

As recalled, according to some sources, the wealth of intelligence sources that were available to Israel on the eve of the war created an expectation that if Egypt and Syria intended to launch war, Israel would certainly know about it. Since such a warning did not arrive until the very last moment, the expectation for war remained low.[3] The empirical evidence calls into question the validity of this explanation. Marwan was, indeed, expected to provide a war warning. But even when he did, it did not cause a major shift in Zeira's and Bandman's war estimates. The same is true with Dayan, who continued doubting the imminence of war.

The wealth of intelligence sources had, however, another and more relevant effect. The combination between the belief of the Chief of Staff and the Minister of Defense that the special means of collection would yield a strategic warning in case of a real threat of war and the fact that they yielded none until war broke out strengthened their estimate that war was unlikely. It was only post factum that they learned that these means had not been activated. In this sense, their ability to reach a more realistic estimation was damaged, in this unique case, by the mere existence of the special sources.

The victim's structural inferiority

The nature of the interaction between the initiator of the surprise and its victim implies that the victim will always find itself in a weaker position. This is so because of the time gap (i.e., the time that the victim needs in order to digest the initiator's moves and to respond to them) and also because of the advantage involved in being able to postpone the initiation (i.e., the initiator's ability to decide whether or not to launch the attack). Theoretically, the initiator can avoid attacking whenever the victim is ready. In the long run, primarily because of the impact of the cry-wolf syndrome, the initiator is likely to catch the victim unprepared.

In 1973 the time factor was critical. Israel lagged behind not because of insufficient information but because of its misinterpretation. The partial understanding, in the early hours of October 6, that the preparations were for war, left the IDF with 24-48 hours lag needed to meet the Arab attack by the minimal force according to earlier plans. Since the ten hours' warning span was not used efficiently enough, Israel found itself in a very difficult situation when war started.

The initiation factor played a more minor role for three main reasons: First, there was not even one instance (including May 1973) when Egypt intended to launch war and was deterred by Israeli preparations. Second, the logistical preparations that Egypt and Syria had to take in order to be ready for war were greater than those of Israel. Consequently, if a cycle of Arab-Israeli war preparations had been created, it is rather possible that it would have had played into the hands of the Israelis. Third, in contrast to its doctrine, Israel avoided taking the initiative in 1973 by launching a preemptive strike. This decision, however, was an exception and to some extent it was rooted in the intelligence fiasco—the fact that Dayan was not convinced that the Arab war preparations were, indeed, for an immediate strike.

Fear of destabilizing the status quo

In the initiator-victim interaction, the victim strives to maintain the status quo and the initiator aims at its revision. This was well-reflected in the years that preceded the war. Since Golda Meir strived to maintain the status quo, any increase in the IDF state of alert or a call for the USA to restrain the Egyptians could have yielded an undesired crisis or pressure for a diplomatic solution. Given that this was a political consideration, one could expect the political echelon to use it in order to avoid mobilization. In reality, however, the opposite was true. Golda Meir and Moshe Dayan had never considered this factor as an obstacle to an increased state of IDF alert, and they themselves asked the White House in April and in October to cool Sadat down. Peculiarly, it was DMI Zeira who used this argument in order to play down the tense atmosphere. In spring 1973 he argued that the war noises from Cairo were merely futile noise and aimed at creating an artificial crisis that would lead the superpowers to pressure Israel into concessions. His war estimate in the fall was based, among others, on a similar assumption. As recalled, fear of an unnecessary escalation also played a role in the mistaken decision of the Southern Command's commander to delay the implementation of the dove cote plan until 1600 on October 6.

Political considerations

The Agranat Commission accepted at face value the declarations of the Prime Minister and the Minister of Defense "that they did not even think about putting partisan considerations above their national obligations in this crucial issue [of the reserve army mobilization]."[4] Indeed, there are no indications that Golda Meir had ever taken such considerations into account. The fact is that she immediately accepted the Chief of Staff's demand for a comprehensive mobilization on Saturday morning. Dayan, on the other hand, objected to such a drastic move and, initially, authorized the mobilization of only one brigade. Although it is obvious that his stand was primarily motivated by his estimate that war was not imminent, one cannot escape the impression that he also feared the embarrassment and the political cost to be paid—including the elections scheduled for the end of October—if a dramatic mobilization was to take place without the eruption of war. Except for Dayan, however, there are no indications that such considerations influenced any other participant of the decision-making process.

ii. Bureaucratic Obstacles

Standard Operational Procedures (SOP)

There are no indications that adherence to SOP had any impact on the estimation process, the decision-making process, or the preparations for war. To a certain extent, the opposite is true. The Israeli experience gained in many emergency situations, the awareness of the threat of Arab attack, and the Israeli tendency toward improvisation led to a situation in which the response to the warning was more efficient than expected. This was certainly the case with the mobilization of the reserve army being faster than expected. It also involved situations in which the use of common sense overcame destructive procedures, such as the decision of the head of Branch 2 to deliver, against orders, the essence of King Hussein's warning to his colleague in Branch 5, and the unauthorized warning about the possibility of war that the head of Branch 5 passed a few days later to the Northern Command. Notably, a deviation from the SOP could have also caused severe damage, as reflected in the way DMI Zeira handled the issue of the activation of the special means of collection and his reluctance to pass critical warnings to his superiors. The same is true with regard to the improper way the Chief of Staff's orders to prepare for war had been carried out in the Northern and, especially, in the Southern Commands.

Bureaucratic and inter-bureaucratic rivalry

This factor seems to have played a role in the process that led to the fiasco. The fact that the Mossad was in charge of HUMINT contributed to the tendency of some officers in AMAN to play down the value of the information that was received from these sources. This was highly significant, because most of the information about the intention to launch war came from these sources. In addition, there are indications that the Mossad's Chief, Zvi Zamir, did not participate in crucial discussions—such as the one at the Prime Minister's office on October 3—because of AMAN's interest in maintaining its monopoly in the domain of national intelligence estimates. Within AMAN, the lack of cooperation between Branch 6 and the intelligence officers of the Southern Command is relevant. This explains, to some extent, why warning indicators that had been collected in the field were not reported. Insufficient communication between the officers of Branch 6 and their colleagues in the Command contributed to the fact that the analysts in Tel Aviv were unaware of the fact that some officers in the Southern Command had assessed that the Egyptian preparations were for war. Lack of direct communication explains also why none of the officers of Branch 6 had personally visited the front line to observe the Egyptian war preparations. Post factum, some analysts estimated that this would have made a big difference.[5] Within the Research Department, a rivalry was created between the dominant group that adhered to the "conception" (the department's head, his two deputies, the head of the basic division, and the heads of Branches 3 and 6) and a group that regarded the probability of war as higher and included the heads of Branches 2, 5, and 7, as well as some other officers. Some of the "alarmists" sensed a threat to their personal status. They also maintained that—intentionally or not—they were distanced from the estimation process and did not receive certain relevant pieces of information. This certainly hampered the ability of the Research Department to conduct an objective assessment process.[6]

The "Research opinion"

According to the work format that was adopted by AMAN in the year that preceded the war—the "consensus" as titled by the Agranat Commission[7]—the discussions within the Research Department were open but they ultimately yielded a single dominant assessment that was passed to consumers without informing them about other views that were expressed in AMAN's internal debates. Consequently, AMAN's documents and verbal assessments created the impression that there was a consensus among the analysts that the Arab military preparations were not for war. It can be assumed that if the Chief of Staff or the Minister of Defense were aware of the fact that many analysts (including highly relevant ones) assessed that Egypt and Syria were gearing for war, their conclusion would have been different. This is especially relevant for the events of October 5. Most of the officers of the Research Department assessed by then that war was looming high. The written "research opinion," on the other hand, maintained that the probability of war was low and DMI Zeira, regarded it, verbally, as even "lower than low."

The Research Department's Monopoly of National Intelligence Estimate

Within AMAN the analysts of the Research Department were the only ones to receive top-secret reports. This was one of the reasons why their estimates were automatically considered to be superior to that of others, such as those of the IAF and the navy intelligence organs, or the intelligence officers of the Commands. Consequently, the Chief of Staff was completely dependent on the estimates of the Research Departments. Attempts to challenge them (e.g., by the Deputy Chief of Staff on September 30 or by the Commander of the Navy a day later) were met by a disparaging reaction—that the challengers lack either the information or the expertise (and usually both) to challenge the "research opinion." Within the intelligence community, AMAN had a monopoly over assessment since the Mossad and the Foreign Office lacked research organs. Policy-makers could, of course, develop their own intelligence estimates (and sometimes they did), but they were also dependent on AMAN's expertise and knowledge, especially in military affairs. The ultimate result of this situation was that on the eve of the war there was not a single person or agency that could present an alternative to AMAN's dominant estimates.[8]

iii. Groupthinking

Four forums in which certain components of groupthinking took place can be identified. In one forum out of the four, all the eight symptoms of groupthinking had been present.

The *first forum* and the most homogenous one was made up of the senior analysts. In addition to Arie Shalev; his two assistants, Aharon Levran and Gideon Gera; and the heads of Branch 6 (Yona Bandman), Branch 3 (Chaim Yavetz), and the Basic Division (Shlomo Marom), it included also DMI Zeira, and Col. Rafi Harlev and Lt. Col. Yehuda Porat from the IAF intelligence department. They all shared the estimation that Egypt and Syria did not perceive themselves as having the capability to launch war. Little is known about the internal dynamics within this group, which bore no official status. There is some evidence, however, of attempts to prevent other intelligence officers—who estimated that war was probable—from hindering the assessment process that was dominated by this group. For example, the head of the Egyptian political section, Mr. Albert Sudai, demanded on a number of occasions to participate in a discussion with DMI Zeira, so that he would be able to present his view that war was imminent. Though he was promised that he would be invited, he ultimately found out that the discussion took place without his participation. Similarly, the head of Branch 2, one of the more prominent "alarmists" (who served earlier as the acting head of the Egyptian Branch), was never invited to any of the central discussions about the likelihood of war.[9] The nickname "alarmists"—given by some of this group's members to their colleagues who believed that war was likely—reflects the groupthink's symptom of using out-group stereotypes.

It can be estimated that the dynamics of informal discussions between the members of this group helped strengthen their belief in the dominant conception. For example, DMI Zeira and Bandman maintained a lively dialogue not only because of Bandman's formal status as the prime estimator of Egypt's war intentions but also because Zeira regarded him as an excellent analyst. A similar dynamic was in play between Zeira and Levran, who admired Zeira.[10] Though we do not know exactly what was said in these informal exchanges, it can be assumed that Levran's unequivocal conclusion that war was unlikely strengthened Zeira's belief in this direction and vice versa.

A *second forum*, in which groupthink dynamics clearly took place, is the forum of the branch heads of the Research Department. This body, which was regarded very highly—some analysts referred to it, sincerely, as the "holy Synod"—was AMAN's most senior analysis forum. Taking part in it was considered to be highly prestigious, and its conclusions laid the bases for the national intelligence estimate. No protocols were taken during its discussions, and all that is available is the verbal evidence of its participants. Even this limited data is sufficient to identify the eight symptoms of groupthinking:

- *The illusion of invulnerability*, which creates a sense of over-optimism and leads to a high level of risk-taking: Some members of the group had reservations about the validity of the conception but in many cases these reservations were not expressed in the discussions. Some participants maintained later that they thought that even if they were mistaken, the regular IDF force sufficed to block the offensives in the Suez and the Golan.[11] Implicitly, they could make a mistake since its cost would not be too high.
- *Belief in the inherent group morality:* Even twenty-five years after the war, some of the group's members continue to doubt if any dogmatic thinking was present in its discussions. They objected to any hint that there was a motivated or unmotivated attempt to block any fresh thinking or an alternative to the dominant conception.[12]
- *Collective rationalization:* Even when information that was inconsistent with the dominant conception was raised (e.g., the advancement of vast quantities of live ammunition to the front line in the south, or of bridging tanks in the north), there was an attempt to explain it in a way that would not refute the thesis of an exercise in the south and readiness in the north. Ultimately, such information was ignored.[13] On Friday at noon, one of the more senior analysts raised the possibility that the whole conception was invalid. His tired colleagues (they did not sleep the night before), agreed to discuss this possibility, but only on Sunday morning, after they had rested on Yom Kippur.[14]
- *Out-group stereotypes:* Within this forum (but not only there) one can identify the tendency for underestimating Sadat and his leadership skills, as well as the Syrian–Egyptian ability to coordinate the initiation of war. It is important to note here that the stubborn belief that Sadat would not dare going to war without the necessary arms projected onto the Egyptian leader a simplistic, stereotypical, and unimaginative way of thinking that actually typified AMAN's analysts themselves.
- *Self-censorship*, as the outcome of the group's interest to avoid breaking the consensus: The head of the Research Department had, at least since Thursday, a sense of discomfort—a "short circuit" as he put it—concerning the information about Egypt's military preparations and its interpretation by his own analysts. But even he did not express it then in clear words.[15] Officers who participated in the discussions expressed reservations about the dominant view in the discussion room, but they did so only in informal talks with their colleagues, in the corridors, or in the restroom.[16] The representative of Unit 848, who participated in the daily discussions at Arie Shalev's office, did not express any reservations about the dominant explanation for Egypt's military

activity, although the experts of 848 had already concluded that it was not merely an exercise that was taking place.[17] And the head of Branch 5 decreased the tone of his criticism of the dominant thesis after the incident of October 1, in which he was rebuked for alerting the Northern Command to the possibility of war.[18]

- *Illusion of unanimity:* As far as known, such a collective illusion did not fully exist. It is apparent, however, that the level of objection to the dominant thesis was not clearly known because of the mechanism of self-censorship.
- *Direct pressure on dissident views:* Such informal pressure was certainly felt by the head of Branch 5 and caused him to somewhat play down his branch's estimate that war was highly likely. It is possible that such pressure led the head of Branch 10 in Unit 848 to avoid expressing the assessment that it was not an Egyptian exercise that was taking place. The head of the Research Department demanded that the head of Branch 2 avoid criticizing Bandman's thesis that war was unlikely — he did this at least once, though half a year before the war.[19]
- *Self-appointed mindguards:* The mere use of the term "alarmists" or "panickers" to point to anyone who threatened the calming atmosphere was an expression of the existence of this symptom. Another was given by Bandman who, in the aftermath of the discussion of October 1 about the warning that a war might start that same day, said, as recalled, that the only benefit from this discussion and the excitement the warning created was that there would be no further debates about the possibility of war. On other occasions, he demonstrated by body language his objection to any opposition to the dominant conception.[20]

A *third forum* in which some elements of groupthink took place was the decision-making forum in which the Chief of Staff and DMI Zeira participated. Here, one must be prudent. On the one hand, in light of the tense relationship between some members of this group as well as Dayan's individualistic character, this was not a typical forum in which groupthink could be nurtured. On the other hand, the protocols of the discussions reveal that in some instances the members of this group did not raise fundamental questions. It took external members to raise them. Thus, for example, during the discussions of April 18 and October 3, it was Golda Meir who asked the right questions. Similarly, the note by Dayan's assistant, Maj. Gen. (res.) Zvi Zur, at the Defense Minister's forum on October 5, which suggested that the forum should discuss the possibility that the Arabs were preparing for war and that concrete measures should be taken to meet such a possibility, diverted the discussion, although temporarily, from futile issues to the main problem at hand.

Finally, the *last forum* in which certain symptoms of groupthink can be detected is the IDF GHQ forum. With the two exceptions that have already been mentioned, the IDF generals did not try to challenge the intelligence thesis that was presented by Zeira. Even when Tal challenged this thesis, the fact that he avoided taking a similar action later as well as the explanation that he gave for his behavior—that presenting opposition to the stand of the Chief of Staff "contradicts norms of subordinate's behavior to his commander"—indicate that he wanted to avoid additional pressure on the Chief of Staff, who was a close friend of his.[21] It is quite likely that the rest of the GHQ members accepted Zeira's estimation at face value because of their professional respect for AMAN and its director. And yet, it is interesting to note that reserve generals, such as Aharon Yariv, Ariel Sharon, and Rehavam Zeevi, who did not participate in the GHQ discussions prior to the war and were exposed to the air photographs of the Egyptian and Syrian layouts only on Saturday morning, concluded immediately and unequivocally that the available evidence indicated war preparations.[22]

iv. Psychological Obstacles at the Individual Level

Confirmation bias

The human tendency to notice and to look for information that confirms one's beliefs, and to ignore, not look for, or undervalue the relevance of information that contradicts it, is the most known bias in the social psychology professional literature.[23]

The effects of confirmation bias in the 1973 case is evident in each element of the estimation process and in the behavior of each of the participants—intelligence officers and policy-makers alike. Thus, for example, all the threatening information about an unprecedented Syrian layout could not alter Dayan's fundamental belief that the main threat in the north was not an isolated action but an all-out offensive for the capture of the whole of the Golan. He continued believing so until the very last moment, as reflected by his stand concerning the evacuation of the Golan settlers on the morning of Yom Kippur. Another example is the way that the head of the Research Department used information, such as the start of registration of Egyptian soldiers for the haj, or preparations to return to routine activity in the Egyptian army, in order to calm apprehension about war during the discussion at the Prime Minister's office on October 3. Any thorough analysis could have shown that such pieces of information could be merely the product of deception while the emergency Egyptian activity along the canal or the advancement to the front of vast quantities of live ammunition could not fit the patterns of a routine exercise.

But this information was mostly ignored. A lively example of the impact of confirmation bias was given on Friday, when information that Egyptian soldiers were ordered to break the Ramadan fast arrived. Senior analysts who were asked how they could fit this highly irregular order with the exercise thesis merely ignored the question.[24] In some cases, the human tendency to act according to this bias received an official seal. Bandman's clarification in the intelligence report of September 30, that the irregular military activity that would be observed in Egypt in the coming days was merely connected to the planned exercise, enabled senior officers in the Southern Command to ignore the reports of the observations posts about activity that could only coincide with war and explain it, with the approval of the highest professional authority, as a part of Tahrir 41.

Cognitive dissonance

Very much like confirmation bias, the theory of cognitive dissonance explains why humans tend to prefer information that confirms existing belief to information that refutes it. Since both lead to similar results, it is difficult to trace the mistaken assessment to any one of these two sources. Nevertheless, it seems that the effect of cognitive dissonance is more prominent when the discrepancy between one's beliefs about reality and the information received about it is clear and cannot be ignored. Under such circumstances, the discrepancy is resolved by entailing heavier weight to information or interpretation that coincides with the present belief and underestimating the evidence that contradicts it.

A typical example of the probable impact of cognitive dissonance is the interpretation that AMAN's intelligence experts gave to the sudden Soviet evacuation that started on October 4. As recalled, they offered three explanations—two that coincided with the dominant thesis and a third that explained the Soviets' belief that Egypt and Syria planned to attack Israel. At the discussion in Dayan's office the next morning, a consensus was reached that the calming interpretations were invalid. Here, DMI Zeira added another component, which, nevertheless, enabled him to hold to the calming conception: The Soviets, he said, may think that the Egyptians and the Syrians intend to attack, but they do so "since they do not know the Arabs well."[25] In the case of the head of Branch 6, the impact of cognitive dissonance continued to be felt even after the war. When asked why he ignored the information that said that Egypt's military preparations were for war rather than an exercise, Bandman explained that he did not attach much value to junior field sources who saw preparations for an exercise and explained it as preparations for war.[26]

Heuristic judgment

The use of a number mechanisms of heuristic judgment to simplify complicated estimation tasks was evident in a number of cases. Fundamentally, the dominant conception that war was unlikely, despite the alarming information, was based to a large extent on a heuristic of representativeness (i.e., the fact that similar events occurred in the past, especially in April–May 1973 without culminating in war). Heuristic of representativeness also helped some analysts to dismiss war warnings from HUMINT sources by claiming that the same sources warned of war in the past. Bandman's statement on September 30 that the warning indicators that would be collected in the coming week were connected in actuality to the Tahrir 41 exercise, was also based on the experience that was gained in similar events and ended without war.

The use of heuristic of availability was evident when possible explanations for the sudden Soviet evacuation were to be given. Although there were no prior indications for a tension in Moscow's relations with her two clients, the first explanation that AMAN's analysts came up with was a crisis in this relationship. This explanation relied on the July 1972 crisis, which led to the expulsion of Soviet personnel from Egypt. The fact that the patterns of the 1972 evacuation were very different from the pattern of the present one played only a limited role, primarily since the alternative explanation could create a discrepancy between the dominant thesis and the new information. Thus, the heuristic of availability served as a convenient outlet from an inconvenient situation.

v. The Human Factor

The general explanations that have been suggested so far help to understand the causes for the 1973 intelligence fiasco but they do not suffice to bridge the gap between the exceptional quality of the war information that Israel had prior to the war and the low quality of AMAN's warning. To bridge this gap, one needs one more type of explanation—one that focuses on the structure and the personal characteristics of Israel's top analysts in 1973. Though this explanation is idiosyncratic, it also involves implications of a more general nature.

The prime source of Israel's costly intelligence fiasco was the way the Director of Military Intelligence, Maj. Gen. Eli Zeira, and the head of Branch 6, Lt. Col. Yona Bandman functioned since Zeira's nomination for DMI in October 1, 1972. The combination of an extremely self-assured DMI who perceived himself more as a policy-maker than an information and assessments provider, and a chief estimator of Egyptian affairs, whose way of analyzing the likelihood of war was typified by extreme fixation, was the main source of

Israel's intelligence failure. This was so since both men, though mainly Zeira, erred not only professionally but also ethically, by consciously conducting acts that were clearly beyond their realm of responsibility.

Zeira's decision to lie to his superiors with regard to the activation of the special means of collection is the clearest act of this kind. By acting this way, the DMI prevented Israel from receiving excellent information on the coming war, and, at the same time, distorted the intelligence picture as perceived by Dayan and Elazar, intentionally causing them to believe that the likelihood of war was smaller than it really was. The members of the Agranat Commission related significant importance to this issue and acquitted Dayan from responsibility for the fiasco, among others, because his confidence that the conception was valid was strengthened after he heard from the DMI that all of AMAN's means of collection were operating.[27] For unknown reasons, the Commission avoided relating the same standards to the Chief of Staff, who, as recalled, asked Zeira the same question and received the same answer. After the war, Elazar said that the DMI's answer "confused me even more, since I knew their [the special means] capability and if there was no war information from them, it was a sign that all was in order. Now it is clear to me that I was not told the truth."[28] In 1993, the then-Chief of Staff, Maj. Gen. Ehud Barak, confirmed that AMAN did not use all its means of collection until the last minute.[29]

Other acts by Zeira were highly destructive as well. Estimating the war probability, in contrast to AMAN's doctrine, on the basis of intentions rather than early-warning indicators, was one such act. Another was the fact that he unnecessarily delayed critical warnings from reaching his superiors. The most devastating case here was his decision on Friday afternoon to avoid dispatching the message that confirmed that the cause of the Soviet evacuation was that Syria and Egypt had informed the Kremlin that they intended to launch war. As recalled, the Chief of Staff said when learning about this message that if he had received it on time the course of the whole war would have been different. By acting the way he did, Zeira breached norms of proper professional behavior. He behaved as if the information collected by AMAN was his own private property and not a most-critical component on which Israel's security was based.

Bandman's destructive role was expressed in a number of ways: the unequivocal tone of his written estimates; his total ignorance of assessments by other analysts—including his two assistants—that war was highly probable; his silencing of any opposition to his estimates in internal discussions in the Research Department; his stubbornness in preventing any change in the written documents that he produced; and, above all, his disregard for any piece of information that contradicted the thesis he had cultivated for such a long time—that Egypt perceived itself as incapable of launching war and that war, therefore, was utterly unlikely. Because of his high formal and informal status within the Research Department, and since Zeira regarded him and his assessments so highly, Bandman had became extremely authoritative in shaping and maintaining the conception that war was, in fact, impossible.

Other analysts erred professionally but not ethically. Arie Shalev, the head of the Research Department, lacked the decisiveness that typified the estimates of Bandman and Zeira. And yet, throughout the process, he did not cast any doubts on the validity of the conception. He acted in this way, because, as he put it, the available information did not justify a different approach.[30] In this sense—very much like other dogmatic supporters of the dominant thesis—he had fallen victim to the previously discussed pathologies that caused him to adhere to the calming information and to reject the warnings. Other supporters of the dominant conception—such as Shalev's two assistants, the head of Branch 3, and the heads of the IAF Intelligence Department—contributed significantly to immunizing the main thesis against any challenge. But, unlike Zeira, Bandman, and Shalev, who determined the national estimate, the others could only influence its shape.

The key to bridging the gap between the excellent war information that was available and the poor level of strategic warning that AMAN produced, remains, then, the way Zeira and Bandman functioned in the weeks before war broke out. The available information we have on their patterns of behavior and their beliefs about their professional duties suggests that the two were authoritarian and dogmatic types. Traditional explanations for their behavior would focus, then, as the main mechanisms to explain their behavior, on their closed minds, "which, as their names suggests, resolutely resist taking in anything that conflicts with their preconceptions and treasured beliefs."[31] But recent findings in the field of cognitive psychology offer a more pinpointed explanation for their behavior and, thus, to the intelligence debacle as a whole.

According to Arie Kruglanski's theory of lay epistemics, an individual's judgment formation processes (i.e., the process of hypothesis-testing and evidence-gathering) is a function of the individual's need for cognitive closure. The need for cognitive closure has been defined as the desire for a confident judgment on an issue, any confident judgment, as compared to confusion and ambiguity. Under the pressure of a high need for closure, an individual may desire two things: to have closure as quickly as possible, and to keep it for as long as possible. The sense of urgency under a heightened need for closure prompts the "seizing" on early closure-providing cues. The quest for permanence prompts a "freezing" on a closure once it is attained, and the tendency to stay impervious to subsequent, potentially relevant, information.

The need for cognitive closure may vary as a function of situation and personality. Situational variables that produce a high need for cognitive closure include high levels of time pressure, noise, fatigue, and dullness of the information-processing task.[32] General tendencies of "seizing" and "freezing" have been found to express themselves in a variety of concrete behavioral phenomena, including (1) reluctance to consider novel information (particularly inconsistent with one's prior notions) once a given conception has been adopted, (2) denial and reinterpretation of inconsistent information in terms that match one's prior conception, (3) placing particular premium on clarity, order, and coherence, (4) poor appreciation of perspectives different from one's own, (5) considerable confidence and self-assuredness, (6) intolerance of pluralism of opinions and rejection of opinion deviates, and (7) authoritarian style of leadership and decision-making.[33]

The available evidence on the personal traits of Zeira and Bandman shows that their conduct since entering office in 1972, as well as their own definitions of their professional tasks, suited each of the individual behavioral phenomena that are set above very well. In this sense, it is clear that both of them had a high need for cognitive closure, and that this personal tendency led them to (a) quickly seize on the conception that Egypt could not go to war (both men believed this was the case long before entering office), and (b) stubbornly "freeze" this belief and easily ignore the new information, which indicated that their thesis might be wrong.[34] Other officers, such as the intelligence officer of the navy, the operations officer of Unit 848, or the head of Branch 5, who estimated the situation correctly, showed very different behavioral patterns. And many analysts of the Research Department, who related a low probability to war in late September, changed their estimate in light of the new information and regarded war as highly likely or even certain, on October 5. Certainly, Zeira and Bandman were not the only officers with a high need for cognitive closure, but they were the most prominent ones among them. This was merely a matter of bad luck. Though one cannot conclusively prove it, it is very probable that if other officers—such as Aharon Yariv, who preceded Zeira, or Shlomo Gazit, who replaced him—were serving in the position of DMI, the surprise would have been averted. The same is highly likely if Lt. Col. Meir Meir (who served as the head of Branch 6 before Bandman) or if Lt. Col. Zusia Kaniazher (who replaced him during the war) had been Israel's chief estimators for Egyptian affairs.[35]

In this sense, it was Israel's misfortune that Zeira and Bandman manned the most critical analytical positions on the eve of the war. And for the fact that its watchmen fell asleep, the Jewish country paid a dear price.

Notes

Introduction

1. *Yezekiel*, 33: 1–6 (New International Version).

2. In a poll conducted among 5,603 Israelis who were asked what were the best and the worst decisions in Israel's history, 64 percent chose the decision to delay the mobilization of the reserve army on the eve of the Yom Kippur War as the worst decision (*Yedioth Ahronot*, April 26, 2002).

3. Roberta Wohlstetter, *Pearl Harbor: Warning and Decision* (Stanford: Stanford University Press, 1962).

4. *Ibid.*, 397.

5. See, for example: U.S. Select Committee on Intelligence and U.S. House Permanent Select Committee on Intelligence, Together with Additional Views. *Joint Inquiry Into Intelligence Community Activities Before and After the Terrorist Attacks of September 11, 2001.* 107th Cong., 2nd sess., December 2002; Bill Gratz, *Breakdown: How America's Intelligence Failure Led to September 11* (Washington, D.C.: Regnery, 2002).

6. For a discussion of these pathologies, see: Richard K. Betts, *Surprise Attack: Lessons for Defense Planning* (Washington, D.C.: The Brookings Institution, 1982), 95–110; Ephraim Kam, *Surprise Attack: The Victim's Perspective* (Cambridge: Harvard University Press, 1988), 176–86.

7. Uri Bar-Joseph, *Intelligence Intervention in the Politics of Democratic States: The USA, Israel, and Britain* (University Park: Penn State University Press, 1995); Kam, 199–212; Michael I. Handel, "The Politics of Intelligence," *Intelligence and National Security* 2 (1987): 5–46; Richard K. Betts, "Intelligence for Policymaking," *Washington Quarterly* 3 (1980): 118–29; Yehoshafat Harkabi, "The Intelligence-Policymaker Tangle," *Jerusalem Quarterly* 30 (1984): 125–31; Glenn P. Hastedt, "The New Context of Intelligence Estimation: Politization or Publicizing?" in *Intelligence and Intelligence Policy in a Democratic Society*, ed. Stephen J. Cimbala (New York: Transnational Publishers, 1987), 47–67; Arthur S. Hulnick, "Controlling Intelligence Estimates" in *Controlling Intelligence*, ed. Glenn P. Hastedt (London: Frank Cass, 1991) 81–96; Thomas L. Houghs, *The Fate of Facts in the World of Men: Foreign Policy and Intelligence Making* (New York: Foreign Policy Association, 1976).

8. Leon Festinger, *Theory of Cognitive Dissonance* (Stanford: Stanford University Press, 1957) and *Conflict, Decision and Dissonance* (Stanford: Stanford University Press, 1964). For a good discussion of the impact of cognitive dissonance on foreign policy decision-making, see: Robert Jervis, *Perception and Misperception in International Politics* (Princeton: Princeton University Press, 1976) 382–406.

9. Jonathan St. B. T. Evans, *Bias in Human Reasoning: Causes and Consequences* (London: Lawrence Erlbaum Associates, 1989).

10. Daniel Kahneman and Amos Tversky, "Subjective Probability: A Judgment of Representativeness," *Cognitive Psychology* 3 (1972): 430–51; Amos Tversky and Daniel Kahneman, "Availability: A Heuristic for Judging Frequency and Probability," *Cognitive Psychology* 5 (1973): 207–32; Amos Tversky and Daniel Kahneman, "Judgment Under Uncertainty: Heuristics and Biases," *Science* 185 (1974): 1124–31.

11. Irving Janis, *Victims of Groupthink* (Houghton Mifflin: Boston, 1972); Paul T. Hart, *Groupthink in Government: A Study of Small Groups and Policy Failure* (Baltimore: The John Hopkins University Press, 1990).

12. Among the many works in this field, some of the more relevant ones for the subject of intelligence failures are: Harold Wilensky, *Organizational Intelligence* (New York: Basic Books, 1967); Graham T. Allison, *Essence of Decision* (Boston: Little Brown, 1971); Morton Halperin, *Bureaucratic Politics and Foreign Policy* (Washington, D.C.: The Brookings Institution, 1974); and John Steinbruner, *The Cybernetic Theory of Decision* (Princeton: Princeton University Press, 1974). For a discussion of the impact of these features on the performance of intelligence agencies' on the eve of sudden attacks, see: Betts 1982, 92–95, and *Kam*, 176–86.

13. Viktor Suvorov, *Icebreaker: Who Started the Second World War?* (New York: Viking, 1990).

14. The only exception is an article that was published shortly after the war and before many of the details of the intelligence blunder became known. According to this piece, the Israelis knew about the impending attack but decided to avoid military preparations in order to draw the Arabs to attack, defeat them, and dictate a new political settlement in the Middle East. However, once it became clear that the IDF suffered defeats, Dayan and Golda Meir decided to explain this embarrassing outcome by surprise. (Zvi Klein, "The Surprise of Yom Kippur," *State and Government* 6 (1974): 127–41).

15. Michael I. Handel, *Perception, Deception, and Surprise: The Case of the Yom Kippur War*, Jerusalem Papers on Peace Problems No. 19 (Hebrew University of Jerusalem, Leonard Davis Institute for International Relations, 1976), 7–8.

16. *Ibid.*

17. Michael I. Handel, "War, Strategy and Intelligence: An Overview," in *War, Strategy and Intelligence*, ed. Michael I. Handel (London: Frank Cass, 1989), 34.

18. Abraham Ben-Zvi, "Hindsight and Foresight: A Conceptual Framework for the Analysis of Surprise Attacks," *World Politics*, 28 (1976): 381–95; Abraham Ben-Zvi, "Threat Perception and Surprise: In Search of the Intervening Variable," in *Conflict in*

World Politics: Advances in the Study of Crisis, War and Peace, eds. Frank P. Harvey and Ben D. Mor (New York: St. Martin's Press, 1998), 241–71.

19. Betts, 1982, 68–69. The main source of the American estimate—especially of the CIA and the DIA—that war was unlikely, was the overreliance on AMAN's war assessment.

20. Avi Shlaim, "Failures in National Intelligence Estimates: The Case of the Yom Kippur War," *World Politics,* 28 (1976): 348–80.

21. Hanoch Bartov, *Daddo—48 Years and 20 More Days* (Hebrew, Tel Aviv: Maariv, 1978).

22. Janice Stein Gross, "The 1973 Intelligence Failure: A Reconsideration," *The Jerusalem Quarterly,* 24 (1982): 41–46; "Calculation, Miscalculation, and Conventional Deterrence II: The View from Jerusalem," in *Psychology & Deterrence,* eds. Robert Jervis et al. (Baltimore: John Hopkins University Press, 1985), 60–88, 79.

23. Zvi Lanir, *Fundamental Surprise: The National Intelligence Crisis* (Hebrew, Tel Aviv: Hakibutz Hameuchad, 1983), 54–57.

24. Yoel Ben-Porat, "Intelligence Estimates—Why Do They Collapse?" in *Intelligence and National Security,* eds. Zvi Offer and Avi Kober (Hebrew, Tel Aviv: Maarachot, 1987), 223–50.

25. Alouph Hareven, "Disturbed Hierarchies: Israeli Intelligence in 1954 and 1973," *Jerusalem Quarterly,* 9 (1978), 3–19.

26. Alex Roberto Hybel, *The Logic of Surprise in International Conflict* (Lexington, Mass: Lexington Books, 1986), 100.

27. Yossi Melman, "Double Trouble." *Haaretz,* January 20, 2003; Abraham Rabinovich, "Historian Dr. Ahron Bregman Exposes Top Mossad Spy Ashraf Marwan."*Jerusalem Post,* 25 February, 2003.

28. Aharon Levran, "Surprise and Warning—Considerations of Fundamental Questions," *Maarachot,* 276–277 (1980), 17–21; Levran's Interview in *Yedioth Ahronot,* September 24, 1999.

29. Eliot Cohen and John Gooch, *Military Misfortunes: The Anatomy of Failure in War* (New York: Vintage Books, 1991), 126–27.

30. Levran, 1980, 18.

31. Eli Zeira, *Myth Versus Reality, The October 1973 War: Failures and Lessons* (Hebrew, Tel Aviv: Yedioth Ahronot, 2004), 116–20, 151–63.

32. Ibid., 159.

33. Amos John, "Deception and the 1973 Middle East War," in *Strategic Military Deception,* eds. Donald C. Daniel. and Katherine L. Herbig (New York: Pergamon Press, 1981), 317–34, 326.

34. Aharon Zeevi, "The Egyptian Deception Plan," in *Intelligence and National Security,* eds. Zvi Offer and Avi Kober (Hebrew, Tel Aviv: Maarachot, 1987), 432–38, 431.

Chapter 1. The Egyptian War Decision and Its Implementation

1. The best description of this crucial meeting is available in the war memoirs of Egypt's two highest ranking officers at the war—the Chief of Staff, Lt. Gen. Saad el Shazly (Saad el Shazly, *The Crossing of the Suez*. San Francisco: American Mideast Research, 1980, 173–81), and his Chief of Operations, Gen. Abdel Ghani Gamasy (Mohamed Abdel Ghani Gamasy, *The October War: Memoirs of Field Marshal Gamasy of Egypt*. Cairo: The American University of Cairo Press, 1993, 149–52). Sadat's memoirs (Anwar Sadat, *In Search of Identity: An Autobiography*. New York: Harper and Row, 1978, 234–37) provide a sketchy and unreliable description of this event, including the meeting's date, which, according to Sadat, was October 28, while by all other accounts it was four days earlier.

2. *Gamasy*, 150.

3. *Ibid.*, 177–80.

4. *Ibid.*, 181.

5. The animosity between Ismail and Shazly had a small impact on the management of the war. As one student of the subject put it, it was "a proper chain of command at the highest level and an example ... for the rest of the High Command (George W. Gawrych, "The Egyptian High Command in the 1973 War," *Armed Forces and Society*, 13 (1987): 535–59, 550).

6. *Shazly*, 180.

7. *Gamasy*, 134.

8. Fuad Ajami, The *Arab Predicament: Arab Political Thought and Practice Since 1967*. (London: Cambridge University Press, 1981), 5.

Chapter 2. Planning the Next War

1. Lt. Gen. Chaim Bar-Lev, A Summary Report: 1968–1971 (unpublished).

2. *Shazly*, 195.

3. Mohamed Heikal, *The Road to Ramadan* (New York: Ballantine, 1975), 77.

4. Trevor N. Dupuy, *Elusive Victory: The Arab-Israeli Wars, 1947–1974*. New York: Harper & Row, 1978, 369. Given that by Egyptian sources the losses in spring 1970 amounted to 4,000, Dupuy seems to have underestimated the number of Egyptian casualties.

5. According to these reports, between March 1969 and August 1970 Egypt lost 98 planes and Israel 14. Egyptian figures (which according to the Egyptians themselves are highly unreliable) are 190 Israeli lost planes and 11 Egyptians (Dan Schueftan, *Attrition: Egypt's Post-War Political Strategy, 1967-1970*, Hebrew, Tel Aviv: Maarachot, 1989, 439).

6. *Shazly*, 20.

7. Abdel Magid Farid, *Nasser: The Final Years* (Reading: Itacha Press, 1994), 189–90.

8. *Heikal*, 110. The Soviet reluctance to participate in an Egyptian war initiative was increased since the Kremlin regarded Sadat—as Brezhnev told Communist leaders in a top secret report—as an "impulsive," "instable," and "rash" leader (Report of Comrade Leonid Ilych Brezhnev at the meeting of the leaders of the socialist countries' communist and working parties in Crimea, July 30–31, 1973 (*Central State Archive*, Sofia, Fond 1-B, Record 35, File 4300).

9. Fawzi Mahmoud, *The Three Years War*, Arabic (Cairo: Dar al Mustakbal al Arabi, 1984), 375–76; *Gamasy*, 123–25.

10. Asher, Dani. "All Out War Limited in Its Dimensions: The Egyptian Military-Doctrinal Solution to the Problems Presented By the Israeli Defence System in the Sinai Front Prior to the Yom Kippur War." (Ph.D. diss., Haifa University, 2002), 120; Shmuel Bar, *The Yom Kippur War in the Eyes of the Arabs*. (Hebrew, Tel Aviv: Maarachot, 1986), 22; *Shazly*, 23.

11. Yona Bandman, The War of Yom Kippur, Egypt—The Goals of the War and the Attack Plan (IDF, General Staff Branch GHQ–Instruction Division–History Department, Study of Enemy Team, 1981), 38 (unpublished); an interview with Yona Bandman. This exercise was the basis for the claim made by General Muhammad Fawzi, Egypt's War Minister in 1970, that in late August 1970 his army reached the actual ability to cross the Canal and develop an offense into the Sinai. According to Fawzi, Nasser was about to authorize the plans that included also a simultaneous Syrian offense in the north and only his death prevented the implementation of these plans (*Fawzi*, 190, 199, 210–12, 375–76). These claims had not been supported by other Egyptian sources.

12. *Heikal*, 156–57; *Asher*, 81.

13. "The Instruction of the Chief of Staff of the Armed Forces, No. 41: Infantry Division in the Crossing of a Water Obstacle," The War Office (Egypt), March 20, 1973 (from herein, Instruction 41). In Enemy Documents—Egypt, *The Library of the Center for the Memorialization of the Intelligence Community* (MALAM), Glilot, Israel (from herein, MALAM). This document summarizes the detailed Egyptian crossing plan. For a somewhat more dramatic description of the challenge involved in the crossing phase, see *Shazly*, 7–9.

14. Maj. Gen. Avraham Adan, who was the head of the team that planned the Bar-Lev line, explained in an IDF GHQ meeting in December 1968:

> We have here a first-class water obstacle, which, unlike rivers, is very linear. In all its 160 kilometers, there are only six bridging areas and bridging points—where the widest is six kilometers and the narrowest is a kilometer and a half. The rest can be crossed by rafts or something similar. Accordingly, the system we selected is a defense in place on the water line and the use of armored forces to obtain surprise. In order to meet any possibility, our goal is to

build a system of warning and control throughout the Canal—an objective that becomes highly feasible because of the linear lines.

"Maoz [stronghold] Plan, December 19, 1968." Protocol of an operational discussion in the IDF GHQ War Room, unpublished.

15. "The IDF defense system in the canal and the use of offensive forces in order to overcome it." Enemy document—Egypt 805/7, *MALAM*.

16. *Asher*, 177.

17. Bar-Lev's A Summary Report.

18. *Gamasy*, 179–82.

19. *Instruction 41*.

20. During the war the Egyptians used three types of Soviet-made bridges: TPP and Unifloat, on which 120 tanks or 200 vehicles could cross within one hour; and PMP, which could carry 240 tanks or 300–400 vehicles per hour *(Instruction 41)*.

21. *Gamasy*, 154–58; *Shazly*, 44–48.

22. *Instruction 41*.

23. "Memorandum on Air Activity of the Enemy on 18 September 1971" in Enemy documents—Egypt, *MALAM*.

24. Bar-Lev's Summary Report.

25. *Shazly*, 81.

26. The source for these figures is the IAF intelligence department as presented in Lt. Col. (res.) Yossi Abudi, "The Israeli Air Force in the War," *A series of lectures in the framework of a seminar on the Yom Kippur War, Ramat Efal, 4 May 2000*. Abudi served as the head of the IAF history department.

27. *Shazly*, 82–83.

28. *Ibid.*, 83.

29. *Ibid.*, 82. The Kremlin regarded the ending of the active Soviet role in Egypt's defense as a positive development "because the risk of involving the Soviet Union in direct military confrontation with the USA as a result of some irresponsible actions of that same Sadat was diminished" (Brezhnev's secret report in the Crimea, 30–31 July 1973.)

30. Bar-Lev's Summary Report.

31. *Shazly*, 196.

32. *Farid*, 11–12.

33. *Shazly*, 128. Parenthesis in original.

34. Lon Nordeen and Nicole David, *Phoenix Over the Nile: A History of Egyptian Air Power—1932-1994* (Washington: Smithsonian Institution Press, 1996), 186–87, 267–68, 273.

35. *Ibid.*, 269–70; *Shazly*, 147.

36. The technical data of the Kelt and the Scud-B is mainly from Ronald T. Pretty (ed.), *Jane's Weapon Systems* (London: Jane's, 1979), 45–46; 160.

37. Brezhnev's secret report in the Crimea, 30–31 July 1973.

38. *Sadat*, 220; *Nordeen and Nicolle*, 262–63, *Heikal*, 117.

39. *Sadat*, 226–27.

40. *Shazly*, 309.

41. *Ibid*, 198–99.

42. *Ibid.*, 27–28.

43. *Nordeen and Nicolle*, 267, 272.

44. *Shazly*, 32. Shazly does not indicate what the term "crossing" means operationally. It could be the start of the preparatory bombardment (which lasted 30–45 minutes), the actual start of the crossing by the hundreds of boats, or the stage where the crossing forces reached a fighting ability on the Israeli bank of the canal after crossing. Since the timing of the Israeli response was measured by minutes, this distinction is highly relevant.

45. *Ibid.*, 33–34.

46. IDF GHQ Discussion, November 21, 1968.

47. Notably, during the war, the reserve force counter attack in Sinai was indeed launched about 48 hours after the mobilization started.

48. *Shazly*, 35

49. *Ibid.*, 34.

50. Dani Asher, "The Anti-Tank Weapons as an Answer: The Planning of the Operation of Anti-Tank Means by the Egyptians in the War of Yom Kippur," *Maarachot*, No. 346, 6–10; Dani Asher, *Breaking the Concept* (Hebrew, Tel Aviv: Maarachot, 2003), 214–18; *Shazly*, 34.

51. *Ibid.*

Chapter 3. The Egyptian Deception Plan

1. *Shazly*, 33, 202.

2. For example, a recent study of the Syrian deception plan in the war of Yom Kippur found it to be "an elaborate deception scheme, similar to the Egyptian effort along the Suez." (Kenneth M. Pollack, *Arabs at War: Military Effectiveness, 1948-1991* (Lincoln: University of Nebraska Press, 2002), 481.

3. *Heikal*, 24. Shazly notes in this connection that on Thursday evening, "to our amazement, the enemy had not guessed the truth" (*Shazly*, 213).

4. Amos John, "Deception and the 1973 Middle East War," in Daniel Donald C. and Herbig Katherine L. (eds.) *Strategic Military Deception* (New York: Pergamon Press, 1981), 317–34, 317–319.

5. For an excellent analysis of this subject, see Michael I. Handel, "Intelligence and the Problem of Strategic Surprise," *The Journal of Strategic Studies*, 7, no.3 (September 1984): 229–81.

6. *Shazly*, 211; *Zeira*, 145–46. Despite these extreme measures, some leaks took place. Thus, for example, from a personal diary of a junior infantry officer, it is evident that by October 1 he knew that he was going to war and not an exercise. Consequently, he wrote farewell letters to his fiancé and to his family ("The personal diary of Naqib Mahmud Fuad Muhammad." Enemy documents—Egypt. 308/12, December 13, 1973) (*MALAM*).

7. *Gamasy*, 185.

8. *Heikal*, 15–16.

9. The commander of [Syrian] Brigade 12 to the commander of Battalion 203. October 6, 1973. Enemy documents—Syria, 25/10, October 13, 1973 (*MALAM*).

10. Sayigh Yazid, *Armed Struggle and the Search for State: The Palestinian National Movement, 1949-1993* (Washington, D.C: Oxford University Press, 1997), 331.

11. Israelyan Victor, *Inside the Kremlin During the Yom Kippur War* (University Park: Penn State University Press, 1995), 1–2; An interview with the Soviet Ambassador in Cairo in 1973, *Yedioth Ahronot*, September 24, 1993.

12. Kirpichenko Vadim, *From Intelligence Man's Archive* (Russian, Moskva: Mezhdunarodnye Otnosheniia, 1998), 118–19.

13. Zeevi Aharon, "The Egyptian 'Deception' in the Plan of the Yom Kippur War." *MA Thesis, Tel Aviv University, the Faculty of Humanities, School of History, Middle Eastern and African Studies* (September 1980), 30–33 (from herein *Zeevi 1980*); Zeevi Aharon, "The Egyptian Deception Plan," in: Kober Avi and Offer Zvi (eds.) *Intelligence and National Security* (Tel Aviv: Maarachot, 1987, Hebrew), 431–38, 432–33; *Shazly* 206–7; *Gamasy*, 194–95.

14. *Zeevi 1980*, 33; *Shazly*, 75, 206–7; *Gamasy*, 194.

15. Sheffi Gabai, "The Egyptian Surprise," *Maariv*, September 24, 1993.

16. *Zeevi 1980*, 34–35.

17. *Gamasy*, 194–95.

18. *Shazly*, 206–7.

19. *Gamasy*, 195.

20. *Zeevi 1980*, 35–36, 44.

21. *Shazly*, 206–7, 209.

22. *Zeevi 1980*, 44; *Sadat*, 244.

23. *Zeevi 1980*, 44; *Heikal*, 25; *Gamasy*, 195.

24. *Amos*, 321.

25. "The War of Yom Kippur," in: Oded Granot, *The Intelligence Corps* in the series *The IDF in Its Arms*, vol. 6 (Hebrew, Tel Aviv: Maariv, 1981), 136.

26. *Heikal*, 7.

27. *Ibid.*, 42–43.

28. *Shazly*, 209.

29. *Zeevi 1980*, 40.

30. *Sadat*, 236.

31. A speech by Egypt's War Minister, October 13, 1974. Quoted in *Zeevi 1980*, 40.

32. Interview with Yona Bandman.

Chapter 4. The Egyptian–Syrian War Coordination

1. Seale Patrick, *Asad: The Struggle for the Middle East* (Berkeley: University of California Press, 1988), 185.

2. *Ibid.*, 191.

3. *Gamasy*, 157.

4. "Battle Order No. 1 of the artillery commander of Brigade 68 in defense." September 23, 1972. Enemy documents—Syria 236/11. *MALAM*.

5. "Instruction of military intelligence of Brigade 58." August 10, 1972. Enemy documents—Syria 23/10. *MALAM*.

6. "Operation order of Brigade 58, Operation Salah-a-Din." August 16, 1973. Enemy documents—Syria 24/10. *MALAM*.

7. "Instruction for Brigade 85—Air Defense." Enemy documents—Syria 75/10. *MALAM*.

8. For details of these deals, see Maoz Moshe, *Asad the Sphinx of Damascus: A Political Biography* (London: Wiedenfeld and Nicholson, 1988), 85–86; Jon D. Glassman, *Arms for the Arabs: The Soviet Union and War in the Middle East* (Baltimore: Johns Hopkins University Press, 1975), 115–16; Maoz Moshe, *Israel and Syria: The End of the Conflict?* (Hebrew, Or Yehuda: Maariv, 1996), 111–12.

9. *Dupuy*, 608.

10. *Maoz 1988*, 87–88.

11. *Seale* 197. The Syrian territorial goals did not include the crossing of the Jordan River into Israel in its pre–1967 borders. According to a rather rare Syrian expression on this issue, Asad estimated that he could occupy the Golan within 48 hours but feared an Israeli nuclear response. Consequently he ordered to stop the progress of his forces on October 7 in order to signal Jerusalem that there was no reason for panic and

that there was no need to get the nuclear genie out of the bottle (Richard B. Parker (ed.) *The October War—A Retrospective* (Gainsville: University of Florida Press, 2001), 102–3; 119).

12. *Seale*, 197. The validity of this claim is dubious, however. Asad, who was the commander of the Syrian Air Force in the late 1960s, was probably aware of the problem involved in launching a war to occupy the Golan without an effective air defense. The Syrian intensive effort to build such a system before the war is a good indication that this and not the Egyptian state of combat readiness was the main cause of the delay.

13. *Sadat*, 241–42.

14. *Shazly*, 20–203; *Gamasy*, 182–83; *Seale*, 193–94.

15. *Seale*, 194.

16. *Shazly*, 38–39, 205–6; *Heikal*, 20–23.

Chapter 5. The Balance of Forces—the Israeli View

1. Bar-Lev's Summary Report.

2. *Ibid.*

3. Interview with Yehuda Porat.

4. A lecture by Yosef Abudy, *The IAF in the Yom Kippur War*. Ramat Efal, May 4, 2000.

5. *Jane's Weapon Systems 1976*, 92. According to this source, the use of optical means could enable the SA-6 to hit targets flying at 150 feet.

6. Harlev's interview.

7. Gur Mordechai, *From the North and from the West* (Hebrew, Tel Aviv: Maarachot, 1998), 192. Gur had been the IDF Military Attaché in Washington since 1972; after the Yom Kippur War he replaced Elazar as the IDF Chief of Staff.

8. Harlev's interview.

9. *Abudy's lecture*; Ran Ronen, *Hawk in the Sky* (Hebrew, Tel Aviv: Hemed, 2002), 335.

10. Harlev's interview; Porat's interview; *Ronen*, 339.

11. Bar-Lev's Summary Report.

12. Karmit Gai, *Bar-Lev* (Hebrew, Tel Aviv: Am Oved, 1998), 209.

13. For a good discussion of the development of American-Israeli military relationship, see: Abraham Ben-Zvi, *The United States and Israel: The Limits of the Special Relationship* (New York: Columbia UP, 1993), Abraham Ben-Zvi, *Decade of Transition* (New York: Columbia UP, 1998), and Abraham Ben-Zvi, *John F. Kennedy and the Politics of Arms Sales to Israel* (London: Cass, 2002).

14. *Gai*, 175, 208–9.

15. *Gur*, 97–107; Arie Hashavia, *The Armor Corps*, in: *The IDF in Its Arms* (Hebrew, Tel Aviv: Revivim, 1981), 138–45; Moshe Bar-Kochva, "Operation 'Kiton-10': Tanks Breakthrough into Syria," in: *Chariots of Steel* (Hebrew, Tel Aviv: Maarachot, 1981), 263–77.

16. For a good and concise discussion of this subject see: Shlaim Avi, *The Iron Wall: Israel and the Arab World* (London: Penguin, 2000), 250–318.

17. *Maariv*, July 20, 1973.

18. *Ibid.*

Chapter 6. The Intelligence Conception and Its Sources

1. Agranat Commission, *The Agranat Report* (Hebrew, Tel Aviv, Am Oved, 1975), 19 (from herein *Agranat 1975*).

2. The Investigation Committee, *The Yom Kippur War, An Additional Partial Report: Reasoning and Completion to the Partial Report of April 1, 1974*, 7 Volumes (Hebrew, Jerusalem, 1974), 64 (from herein, *Agranat*).

3. Protocol of the IDF GHQ discussion. November 21, 1968.

4. Interviews with Arie Shalev and Yehuda Porat.

5. Interviews with Zvi Zamir, Albert Sudai, Arie Shalev, Yona Bandman, Aharon Levran, Rafi Harlev, Yehuda Porat.

6. *Agaranat 1975*, 19; interview with Avieezer Yaari.

7. Gad Yaacobi, *On the Razor's Edge* (Hebrew, Tel Aviv: Edanim, 1989), 160.

8. Eli Zeira, *The October 73 War: Myth Against Reality* (Hebrew, Tel Aviv: Edanim, 1993), 84 (from herein, *Zeira 1993*). In the Hebrew edition of my book on the surprise of Yom Kippur I labeled the source "Bavel," (Babylon), using this label from an article about him by Ronen Bregman (*Haaretz*, September 17, 1999). Since then, Dr. Ahron Bregman, an Israeli historian in London revealed—probably on the basis of information he received from Zeira—that the source was Dr. Ashraf Marwan. This had also been confirmed by members of the American intelligence community. See: Howard Blum, *The Eve of Destruction: The Untold Story of the Yom Kippur War* (New York: HarperCollins, 2003), 330–32. In late 2004 Zeira republished his book and this time he confirmed (pp. 159–63) that the label "information" that he used in the 1993 edition of his book referred, indeed, to Dr. Ashraf Marwan.

9. *Shazly*, 148, 149, 185.

10. *Haaretz*, January 20, 2003.

11. Ahron Bregman, *A History of Israel* (Houndmills: Palgrave Macmillan, 2003), 143. Years later, so it seems, Marwan shared these protocols with academicians as well.

In a book published in 1999 on Soviet policy in the Middle East, the author, Talal Nizameddin, quoted "transcripts of conversations" between the Egyptian and the Soviet leadership in October 1971 and April 1972 (Talal Nizameddin, *Russia and the Middle East: Towards a New Foreign Policy*. London: Hurst & Company, 1999, 31–32). In his introduction, the author thanks "Dr. Ahmad Ashraf Marwan, who was chief of national security in the early 1970s under President Anwar Sadat, for providing vital documents of the meetings between the Egyptian and Soviet leaderships from 1971–72" (*Ibid.*, iii).

12. *Zeira*, 155.

13. *Zeira*, 155–56; interviews with Arie Shalev, Albert Sudai, Zvi Zamir, Yona Bandman, Aharon Levran.

14. Interview with Zvi Zamir.

15. Interviews with Arie Shalev, Albert Sudai, and Zvi Zamir.

16. *Zeira*, 157–63; *Bregman 2003*, 142–48; Ahron Bregman and Jihan El-Tahri, *The Fifty Years' War: Israel and the Arabs* (New York: TV Books, 1999); Ahron Bregman, *Israel's Wars, 1947-93* (London: Routledge, 2000), 112–17.

17. *Bregman 2003*, 143–44.

18. *Zeira*, 161 *Bregman 2003*, 144–45.

19. *Zeira*, 161–62.

20. *Ibid.*

21. *Shazly*, 213. The first Egyptian intelligence estimate that Israel knew about the impending threat was distributed on October 5 at noon, about 24 hours before the outbreak of the war (an interview with Gen. Ahmed Fuad Huwaidi, the head of the Israeli desk in the Egyptian intelligence, *Maariv*, September 24, 1993).

Chapter 7. The Strategic Warning and Its Role in Israel's War Plans

1. For a discussion of this subject, see: Avner Yaniv, *Deterrence Without the Bomb: The Politics of Israeli Strategy* (Lexington, MA: 1987); Yoav Ben Horin and Bary Posen, *Israel's Strategic Doctrine* (Santa Monica: 1981); and Michael I. Handel, *Israel's Political-Military Doctrine (C*ambridge, MA: 1973).

2. For a discussion of this crisis, see: Uri Bar-Joseph, "Rotem: The Forgotten Crisis on the Road to the 1967 War," *Journal of Contemporary History*, vol. 31 (1996), 547–66, and "Israel Caught Unaware: Egypt's Sinai Surprise of 1960," *International Journal of Intelligence and Counterintelligence*, vol. 8, no. 2 (Summer 1995), 203–19.

3. The Chief of Staff Review, IDF GHQ meeting 1/68 (January 1, 1968).

4. From DMI Major General Aharon Yariv, to the Chief of Staff, re: "Warning." October 3, 1968. In: Grundman Moshe, *Cautious Assessment: Writings by Aharon Yariv* (Hebrew, Tel Aviv: 1998, Maarachot), 41–42.

5. *Ibid.*

6. From DMI Major General Aharon Yariv, to the Chief of Staff, re: "The state of the warning cover." October 1969. *Ibid.*, 44.

7. Interview with Rafi Harlev, Yehuda Porat, Arie Shalev.

8. IDF GHQ meeting, November 21, 1968.

9. An operational discussion in the IDF GHQ War Room, December 19, 1968.

10. AMAN's document, June 16, 1972.

11. "A stenographic protocol of a consultation at the house of the Prime Minister on 18 April 1973," (unpublished); *Agranat*, 69; Arie Braun, *Moshe Dayan and the Yom Kippur War* (Hebrew; Tel Aviv: Edanim, 1992), 21–22; Zeira, 101–2.

12. *Agranat*, 69.

13. Golda Meir, *My Life: The Autobiography of Golda Meir* (London: Futora, 1976), 354.

14. *Braun*, 20–21.

15. *Agranat*, 274.

16. *Agranat 1975*, 40.

17. Hanoch Bartov, *Daddo: 48 Years and 20 More Days* (Hebrew, Or Yehuda: Dvir, 2002), 284.

18. *Agranat*, 196.

19. *Ibid.*, 195, 196; Uri Milstein, *The Lesson of the Collapse* (Hebrew, Kiron: Sridut, 1993), 236.

20. *Agranat*, 229; Bartov, 264.

21. *Agranat*, 191.

22. *Ibid.*, 192.

23. Bartov, 275–77; *Agranat*, 191–95; Avraham Adan, *On Both Banks of the Suez* (Hebrew, Jerusalem: Edanim, 1979), 54–55.

24. *Agranat*, 195.

25. *Ibid.*, 195.

26. *Ibid.*, 251.

27. *Ibid.*, 232.

28. *Ibid.*, 228.

29. Good examples are AMAN's success to get excellent warnings from SIGINT sources on the Egyptian army's intention to deploy in the Sinai in February 1960 (the "Rotem" crisis) and in May 1967. In 1960, AMAN intercepted the command to the Egyptian army to deploy in the Sinai (*Bar-Joseph 1995*, 209–10). In 1967, AMAN intercepted the cable sent by the Syrian Chief of Staff to his Egyptian counterpart, in which he reported on IDF concentrations near the Syrian border and an

Israeli intention to launch an attack on the Golan Heights between May 15 and 22 (*Grundman*, 162).

Chapter 8. The Next War Scenarios

1. Intelligence Summary for Operation "Dove Cote," December 17, 1972. This summary presents the main elements of the intelligence review of April 1972, which is not available yet.

Chapter 9. The War Estimate: October 1972–August 1973

1. *Yaacobi*, 161.
2. AMAN's annual estimate, May–June 1972.
3. *Braun*, 17–18.
4. *Ibid.*, 19.
5. *Agranat 1975*, 34.
6. For a detailed analysis of the behavior of Zeira and Bandman during this period, and psychological explanations for it, see: Uri Bar-Joseph and Arie W. Kruglanski, "Intelligence Failure and the Need for Cognitive Closure: On the Psychology of the Yom Kippur Surprise," *Political Psychology*, vol. 24, no.1, March 2003, 75–99.
7. Semiannual Intelligence Estimate, January 23, 1973.
8. *Ibid.*
9. The heaviest attacks took place on January 8, 1973, when the IAF hit military and civilian targets in Latakia and Tartus in northern Syria. About 400–500 soldiers and civilians had been killed in these raids. They were the culmination of an ongoing military operation that started after the massacre of the Israeli athletes in the Munich Olympic games (summer 1972), to compel Damascus to restrain its involvement in Palestinian terror activity against Israel (*Maoz, 1996*, 113).
10. Semiannual Intelligence Estimate, January 23, 1973.
11. Interviews with Aviezer Yaari and Arie Shalev.
12. The sources for the war information and its assessment: *Bartov*, 250–51; *Braun*, 19–30; *Maariv*, April 10-May 10, 1973; *Agranat*, 69–72; interviews with Avner Shalev, Yona Bandman, Rafi Harlev, Aharon Levran, Yehuda Porat, Arie Shalev, Albert Sudai, Yaacov Rosenfeld, Zvi Zamir, and Aviezer Yaari.
13. *Braun*, 19.
14. *Ibid.*, 19–20.

15. AMAN's document, April 18, 1973.

16. *Ibid.*

17. The description of this meeting is based on a "stenographic protocol of a consultation at the Prime Minister's residence on 18.4.74" (unpublished). *Agranat* (69–70, 149–50) and *Braun* (21–23) include some elements of this protocol.

18. In contrast to Sadat and Asad, who defined the war's goal as the regaining of the territories lost in the 1967 war, Gadhafi maintained that its goal should be the destruction of Israel. This would require far more intensive preparations, including the unification of the Arab world. As he viewed it, war too early might be disastrous and might make the goal of Israel's destruction far less feasible.

19. *Bartov*, 263; *Haaretz*, April 20, 1973; *Maariv*, April 24, 1973.

20. *Bartov*, 279–81.

21. *Ibid.*, 281.

22. AMAN's document, May 11, 1973.

23. Interviews with Yona Bandman, Zvi Zamir, Albert Sudai, and Arie Shalev.

24. *Braun*, 26–27.

25. *Braun*, 28.

26. *Ibid.*, 29. Dayan's confidence that Jordan would avoid participation in the war relied on a meeting that he and Golda Meir held with King Hussein and his Prime Minister, Zeid Al Rifai, on May 9. During the meeting the King warned that the Egyptians and the Syrians had decided to go to war, but he did not specify a concrete date. Dayan and Meir responded that Sadat was aware of the fact that he had no military option but that he may act illogically (Gai Gavra, *The Hussein–Golda Meeting on the Eve of the Yom Kippur War*, Seminar paper, Tel Aviv University, the Social Sciences Faculty, Security Program Studies, September 2000). The main source for Gavra's information is the original, unsanitized version of Braun's book.

27. Yisrael Tal, *National Security: A Few Against Many* (Hebrew, Tel Aviv: Dvir, 1996), 168.

28. *Adan*, 67.

29. *Braun*, 30; *Bartov*, 288.

30. Elazar's Military Assistant, Avner Shalev, could not recall a specific date on which blue-white ended (Shalev's interview). Dayan's adjutant maintained that the Defense Minister did not receive a report about the end of the state of readiness (*Braun*, 30).

31. *Braun*, 30, 32.

32. *Ibid.*, 33.

33. *Ibid.*, 32.

34. *Maariv*, June 25, 1973.

35. *Bartov*, 288.

36. *Maariv*, August 10, 1973.

37. *Ibid.*

38. *Time*, July 30, 1973.

39. Ben-Porat et al., *The Failure ('HaMehdal')* (Hebrew, Tel Aviv: special publishing, 1974), 117. In his testimony before the Agranat Commission, Dayan said that he did not remember that in the months between May and October he ever said that war was unlikely in the coming years (*Agranat*, 173). For unclear reasons, committee members accepted his testimony at face value.

40. *Parker*, 144.

41. *Haaretz*, September 10, 1973.

42. Uzi Benziman, *Sharon, an Israeli Caesar* (Hebrew, Tel Aviv: Adam, 1985), 135.

43. Beilin Yossi, *The Cost of Unity: The Labor Party and the War of Yom Kippur* (Hebrew, Tel Aviv: Revivim, 1985), 145.

Chapter 10. August–September 1973

1. *Braun*, 33. On the eve of the war, Syria had thirty-six SAM batteries, of which twenty-five (including fifteen SA-6 batteries) had been deployed in the front (*Abudi's lecture*).

2. Interview with Shabtai Brill.

3. *Braun*, 33.

4. Interviews with Rafi Harlev and Yehuda Porat.

5. Yisrael Tal's lecture, "Warning in the Yom Kippur War." It should be mentioned that the commander of the Northern Command, Maj. Gen. Yitzhak Hofi, and the Chief of Staff Military Assistant, Lt. Col. Avner Shalev, who were present in the meeting, do not remember that Tal said what he claims to have said (interviews with Hofi and Shalev). The protocol of the meeting confirms that Tal did say it. (*Háaretz*, December 18, 2002).

6. *Agranat*, 187.

7. *Braun*, 34–35; an interview with Arie Shalev.

8. *Braun*, 34; *Bartov*, 296.

9. Eliezer Cohen and Zvi Lavie, *Sky Is Not the Limit* (Hebrew, Tel Aviv: Maariv, 1990), 444; *Braun*, 35; *Bartov*, 298–99.

10. Interview with Yaari; *Braun*, 35, 36.

11. AMAN's document, September 17, 1973, 1–2.

12. *Ibid.*, 2–4.

13. *Ibid.*, 6.

14. *Ibid.*

15. *Ibid.*, 7.

16. *Bartov*, 302. Braun, who as Dayan's Military Assistant tried to portray his boss as one who continued to be worried about war even after June 1973, reports that "from the Defense Minister's body language and remarks he made, it was evident that he rejected Zeira's assessment" (*Braun*, 36). But Braun did not use the protocol to prove his point, and body language was not recorded in the meeting. Hence, one cannot count on this evidence.

17. Interviews with Albert Sudai, Yaacov Rosenfeld, and Zusia Kaniazher.

18. *Bartov*, 304–5.

19. *Braun*, 35, 36.

20. A combination of Hofi's words in this meeting on the basis of: *Agranat*, 263; *Braun*, 38; *Bartov*, 305; interview with Hofi.

21. *Braun*, 39. The IDF GHQ was aware of the situation. In a GHQ meeting on July 10, 1972, Maj. Gen. Shmuel Gonen warned that a surprise attack could take place, adding, "In the case of Syria, we all agree that the Syrian army can attack without any prior warning." (*Agranat*, 39).

22. Hofi's interview.

23. *Agranat*, 263. For a slightly different version of Dayan's words, see *Braun*, 38.

24. A combination of quotes from *Agranat*, 264, and *Braun*, 39.

25. Interview with Avner Shalev; *Bartov*, 307.

26. Naphtali Lau-Lavi, *Nation as a Lion* (Hebrew, Tel Aviv: Maariv, 1993), 265; *Haber*, 17.

27. *Gavra*, 31–32. The main source for these reports is the draft (uncensored) version of Braun's book.

28. Interviews with Lou Kedar and Eli Mizrahi (the Prime Minister's Aide de Camp), conducted by Gavra and a draft of Braun's book as quoted in *Gavra*, 46–56; Gai Gavra, *Yedioth Ahronot*, October 8, 2000.

29. Bregman and el Tahri, 118–19.

30. *Seale*, 199. Seale, who probably received the information from Syrian sources, did not mention Jordan but merely "an Arab state." According to Seale, the information was delivered to two persons—Dayan and Kissinger—but they both took it as an Arab disinformation exercise.

31. *Haber*, 17–18. When this book, based on the papers of the Prime Minister's military assistant, was published in 1987, the censorship forbade any information about the Hussein–Meir meeting. Hence, Haber conceived it as taking place between Golda Meir and the head of the Mossad, Zvi Zamir.

32. Interview with Zvi Zamir; interview with Aharon Levran.

33. Aviezer Yaari, *The Road from Merhavia* (Hebrew, Or Yehuda: Zmora-Bitan-Dvir, 2003), 173–74; Zusia Kaniazher, "The Directorship of AMAN and the Research Department—Mistakes in Estimating Warning Intelligence," a seminar paper, MA studies, Haifa University, February 1999; a talk with Kaniazher, October 17, 1999; Kaniazher's remarks to a draft of the Hebrew version of *The Watchman Fell Asleep*, March 15, 2000; Yaari interview.

34. Interview with Yaari; interview with Kaniazher.

35. *Yaari*, 173–74; Interview with Shalev; interview with Yaari.

36. A talk with Kaniazher; Kaniazher's remarks to a draft of the Hebrew version of *The Watchman Fell Asleep*. Arie Shalev did not remember this incident.

37. A talk with Kaniazher; Kaniazher's remarks.

38. Interview with Yitzhak Hofi.

39. Interview with Arie Shalev.

40. *Bartov*, 310–11; *Braun*, 40.

41. Levran's interview in *Gavra*, 61

42. *Agranat*, 264.

43. This, at least, was the impression of Elazar's military assistant, Lt. Col. Avner Shalev, who participated in the meeting (Shalev's interview).

44. *Braun*, 40.

45. Stern interview to Gavra, *Gavra*, 61. According to Kaniazher, Stern did not listen to the exchange between Golda Meir and the King; his English was not good enough to understand the nuances in the King's warning, and he was not aware of its crucial meaning (a talk with Kaniazher).

46. *Braun*, 40.

47. *Dayan*, 572; *Braun*, 41; *Bartov*, 294.

48. *Braun*, 41.

49. *Haaretz*, September 30, 1973.

50. Indeed, two days later the Syrian daily *A 'Thaura*, assessed that Dayan's warning was aimed at providing Israel a new pretext to attack Syria.

51. *Yedioth Ahronot*, September 30, 1973.

52. AMAN document, September 29, 1973.

53. Interview with Albert Sudai.

54. *Braun*, 45; *Zeira*, 185–86; interview with Avi Yaari.

55. AMAN document, September 30, 1973.

56. *Ibid*.

57. *Braun*, 44–45; *Bartov*, 296–98; Yair Sheleg, "The Lieutenant Colonel that adhered to the conception of high probability," *Kol Ha'ir*, September 24, 1993.

58. *Agranat,* 170–71; *Bartov,* 297–98. Shalev did not remember this incident (Shalev's interview) and Zeira did not mention it in his book.

59. Interview with Rami Luntz; Amos Gilboa, "Naval Intelligence Warned: There will be War. Nobody Listened," *Maariv,* September 25, 1998.

60. Interview with Shabtai Brill; Ronit Zach, "The Last and Final War," *Kol Ha'ir,* July 25, 1997; *Kol Ha'ir,* September 25, 1993. Ben Porat has a different account in his memoirs of the war, but following a libel suit presented by Brill, he had to admit that the latter was right (Yoel Ben Porat, "An apology to our friend, Lieutenant Colonel (res.) Shabtai Brill, *"A letter to AMAN's reserve officers at the rank of lieutenant colonel and higher,"* August 10, 1997).

61. Interview with Brill; *Ben Porat,* 72.

62. AMAN document, September 30, 1973 (21:45); *Braun,* 45.

Chapter 11. Monday, October 1, 1973

1. *Bartov,* 299; *Ben Porat,* 23.

2. On October 4, the manager of Egypt Air decided to stop the flights of his airline and disperse its planes in order to protect them from incoming Israeli air strikes. He started doing so, without any approval, on the evening hours of October 4. When the war planners in Cairo learned about it, they immediately ordered him to return to normal activity. Egypt Air returned to regular operation on the early morning hours of October 5 (*Shazly,* 213–14; *Gamasy,* 197). There is no evidence in AMAN's reports that the agency was aware of this incident.

3. Interviews with Arie Shalev and Yehuda Porat.

4. *Yaari,* 174. Interview with Avi Yaari.

5. Interview with Arie Shalev.

6. Interview with Avner Shalev; *Braun,* 45. According to Braun, Zeira reported the warning to Elazar and Elazar reported it to Dayan.

7. Interviews with Yitzhak Hofi and Avner Shalev.

8. Interviews with Avi Yaari, Yitzhak Hofi and Avner Shalev; *Agranat,* 159; *Yaari,* 174–75.

9. Interviews with Avi Yaari, Arie Shalev; *Agranat,* pp 159–60.

10. *Braun,* 46.

11. *Ibid.,* 23–24.

12. According to Mizrahi, Allon took a look at the cable and explained him that there was no reason for panic, since the IDF knew about the situation and the probability for was low (Eli Mizrahi's interview to *Yedioth Ahronot,* September 6, 1991).

13. This was Brigade 47, which was regularly deployed at Homs. AMAN knew that according to Syria's plans in case of war, the brigade was to team with Division 5,

which deployed on southern flank of the Golan Front. The analysts of Branch 5, who regarded the departure of the brigade a clear warning indicator, did not know at this stage if it was moving toward the southern sector of the Golan or to another destination (Interviews with Avi Yaari and Zusia Kaniazher).

14. *Agranat*, 265.

15. *Braun*, 46–47; *Bartov*, 300. In light of the problem, an attempt was made to tap the Syrian wire communication in the line of forward localities. The Syrians found out about it immediately (interview with Yitzhak Hofi).

16. *Agranat*, 197–98.

17. *Ben-Porat*, 26–28; interview with Shabtai Brill. Brill's account was sustained by other senior officers in 848.

18. *Agranat*, 309–10.

19. *Braun*, 46.

20. *Agranat*, 310.

21. *Braun*, 48.

22. Interviews with Yona Bandman, Albert Sudai, Yaacov Rosenfeld.

23. Interview with Yona Bandman.

Chapter 12. Tuesday, October 2, 1973

1. *Braun*, 49.

2. AMAN document, October 2, 1973.

3. AMAN document, October 2, 1973.

4. AMAN document, October 2, 1973; interview with Avi Yaari; *Braun*, 49

5. Interviews with Arie Shalev, Albert Sudai, Yaacov Rosenfeld, Avi Yaari, Shabtai Brill.

6. *Ben-Porat*, 62; interview with Shabtai Brill.

7. *Agranat*, 266; *Braun*, 49.

8. Interview with Avner Shalev. According to the account by the commander of Unit 848, Elazar, who spoke with him about these means, implied that he asked Zeira about them on October 1 (*Ben-Porat*, 103). According to Bartov, probably a better source about Elazar's timetable prior to the war, the talk was held on October 2 (*Bartov*, 322).

9. *Braun*, 49.

10. *Ibid.*, 50.

11. *Ibid.*

12. *Bartov*, 323.

13. *Agranat*, 267.

Chapter 13. Wednesday, October 3, 1973

1. *Heikal 1975*, 29–31.

2. *Ibid.*, 30. This account, however, is somewhat problematic, since according to *Gamasy* (183), Sadat and Asad had already decided during Sadat's visit in Damascus, in late August, to start the war on October 6, and according to Shazly (149) they had informed their war ministers and chiefs of staff about it on September 22.

3. See, for example, *Shazly*, 51.

4. *Heikal*, 22.

5. *Ibid.*, 19, 21.

6. *Shazly*, 151–152; *Heikal*, 22.

7. *Heikal*, 1, 21.

8. *Haaretz*, October 3, 1973.

9. *Braun*, 51; *Agranat*, 14.

10. The description of this meeting relies on three partial protocols. The first, which was written by the prime minister's military secretary, Brigadier General Yisrael Lior, is in the *Agranat Commission* report. It is the most authorized one but is highly fragmented. *Braun* presents certain parts of the discussion—primarily those that positively portray the Defense Minister. *Zeira* presents, in a selective manner, the parts of the protocol that mitigate AMAN's responsibility to the mistaken intelligence estimate. My description integrates these three sources in an attempt to present the most comprehensive account.

11. *Agranat*, 14–15.

12. *Zeira*, 166. Zeira is the only source that notes that Shalev mentioned Hussein's warning.

13. *Braun*, 52.

14. *Zeira*, 166, integrated with *Braun*, 52.

15. *Braun*, 52.

16. *Ibid.*

17. *Agranat*, 16.

18. *Ibid.*, 17.

19. *Zeira*, 169.

20. *Agranat*, 268.

21. *Zeira,* 169; *Braun,* 53.

22. *Zeira,* 170–71.

23. *Braun,* 53.

24. *Zeira,* 172–73.

25. *Agranat,* 19; *Zeira,* 174.

26. *Agranat,* 19–20.

27. *Braun,* 54.

28. *Meir,* 354–55.

29. *Bartov,* 325–26; *Janice Gross Stein* (1982), 41–45.

30. For the classic study of the impact of groupthink on the decision-making process during the Bay of Pigs situation, see: *Janis 1972,* 14–49. For the CIA–White House dynamics in this affair and the way the relevant intelligence information was filtered to meet the CIA need for White House approval, see: Bar-Joseph 1995, *Intelligence Intervention,* 76–148.

31. Interview with Zvi Zamir; *Haber,* 21.

32. *Braun,* 54; *Haber,* 21.

33. Interview with Zamir.

34. *Braun,* 54–55.

35. *Ben-Porat,* 62; Interview with Shabtai Brill; 848 other officers sustain Brill's evidence.

Chapter 14. Thursday, October 4, 1973

1. *Braun,* 55

2. *Agranat,* 310–11.

3. *Ibid.,* 311.

4. *Ibid.,* 378.

5. *Ibid.,* 417, 422.

6. *Ibid.,* 372–75. The Agranat Commission praised Siman-Tov's initiative and regarded him, and rightly so, as one of the sole distinguished figures in the intelligence community on the eve of the war. This does not mean, however, that the dissemination of his document in its original form would have had any impact. After all, the heads of the military and political sections in Branch 6—who were more senior and experienced than Siman-Tov, and who conducted a daily dialogue with Bandman—assessed that war was highly likely, but, nevertheless, failed to change his (and, thus, AMAN's) estimate.

7. *Ibid.,* 415, 420.

8. *Ibid.*, 418–19; interviews with Bandman, Sudai, Rosenfeld.

9. *Agranat*, 378.

10. Brezhnev's secret report in the Crimea, 30–31 July 1973.

11. *Kirpichenko*, 118–19.

12. Vinogradov, Vladimir M., *Diplomacy; People and Events: From Ambassador's Notes* (Russian, Moskva: ROSSPEN 1998), 238.

13. *Israelyan*, 9; *Vinogradov*, 239.

14. *Vinogradov*, 239–40; *Israelyan*, 9; *Sadat*, 246–47. According to *Heikal* (14–15), another meeting between the two took place on October 1.

15. *Shazly*, 212.

16. *Sadat*, 246.

17. *Israelyan*, 1–2.

18. *Shazly*, 213.

19. *Gamasy*, 196–97.

20. *Parker* 2001, 45.

21. *Sadat*, 247; *Vinogradov*, 239.

22. AMAN document, October 5, 1973; *Ben-Porat*, 60–61.

23. AMAN document, October 5, 1973.

24. *Ben Porat*, 59.

25. Interview with Shabtai Brill.

26. *Ben-Porat*, 60–63.

Chapter 15. Friday, October 5, 1973

1. Zamir's interview. Zeira's account of that night's events (*Zeira*, 118–20) is, essentially, the same.

2. Zamir's interview; *Braun*, 58–59.

3. AMAN's document, October 5, 1973.

4. Interview with Yaacov Rosenfeld.

5. *Braun*, 67.

6. *Zeira*, 137; *Yaari*, 176–77.

7. The meeting was not mentioned in the books by Zeira and Braun, and the Agranat Commission also ignored it.

8. *Bartov*, 332–33.

9. *Ibid.*

10. *Zeira,* 180; *Braun,* 58. According to the transcript they present, Elazar said, "There is proof that this is a diplomatic rift." But in the context in which it was said, Elazar obviously meant "There is no proof that this is a diplomatic rift."

11. *Zeira,* 180–81.

12. *Zeira,* 180; *Braun,* 58.

13. *Zeira,* 180; *Braun,* 58.

14. AMAN's document, September 17, 1973.

15. Moshe Zonder, "The Mishap Architect," *Maariv,* September 25, 1993; Alex Fishman, "Until Today He Does Not Believe that War Broke Out," *Hadashot,* September 25, 1993; *Ben-Porat,* 62; Shalev's interview.

16. *Braun,* 58–59; *Zeira,* 182.

17. *Agranat 1975,* 46. Notably, the members of the commission regarded Zeira's behavior in this matter as a reason to ease Dayan's responsibility for the fiasco but did not do so with regard to Elazar, who heard this dialogue and who, earlier that week, asked Zeira similar questions and received similar answers.

18. *Ibid.,* 46–47. In his 2004 book on the Yom Kippur surprise, Zeira responded to this claim that was originally raised in the 2001 Hebrew version of my book. Zeira maintained that Dayan did not ask specifically about the "special means" and that the means were activated the night before (*Zeira,* 178). After rechecking the subject with a person who in October 1973 played a crucial role in the activation of this means, I insist that my original claim, as presented here and in the Hebrew edition of this book, is true.

19. *Fishman,* September 24, 1993; *Ben-Porat,* 103.

20. *Fishman,* September 24, 1993; *Ben-Porat,* 71.

21. Interviews with Yona Bandman, Yaacov Rosenfeld, Arie Shalev, Albert Sudai, and Shabtai Brill.

22. For example, Col. Ben-Porat, whose unit was the main source of information about the exercise, told the head of the Research Department on Friday morning that there was no exercise. Shalev did not argue to the contrary (*Ben-Porat,* 64). Notably, during the Soviet preparations for the invasion of Czechoslovakia, CIA analysts responded in a similar manner. As a declassified CIA study shows, there were no indications for a Warsaw Pact exercise on the eve of the invasion. And yet, "a majority of the analysts were reluctant to say that these were not exercises, or to draw the conclusion that the *only* thing that was in progress was a mobilization and deployment.... And it may be noted that even in retrospect, some analysts have persisted in referring to the 'exercises'" (Cynthya M. Garbo, "Soviet Deception in the Czechoslovak Crisis," *Studies in Intelligence,* 10 (2000): 71–86, 82).

23. Interview with Avner Shalev.

24. *Zeira,* 183.

25. *Interview with Avner Shalev.*

26. *Zeira,* 184.

27. *Braun,* 60. One can hardly understand why Zeira assessed that the US intelligence community would fail detecting a sudden Soviet airlift to Syria and Egypt or irregular Soviet naval movements in the Mediterranean.

28. *Ibid.*

29. *Zeira,* 185.

30. *Ibid,* 185, 187.

31. *Agranat,* 76.

32. It is not clear why none of the participants in this discussion paid attention to the contradiction between Zeira's words in the earlier discussion that it was unclear if an exercise was taking place at all, and these words that put the exercise, again, as a prime explanation for the Egyptian deployment.

33. *Agranat,* 76–77.

34. *Braun,* 61.

35. Zeira's remark was not incidental. A similar phrase regarding the Soviet motivation appeared in the Research Department's intelligence review that was written at the very same hours and was distributed at 1315. [AMAN document, October 5, 1973 (1315)].

36. *Braun,* 61.

37. *Ibid.*; *Agranat,* 282; *Bartov,* 335. The results of the air-photograph sortie that became available that evening showed that the Syrian Army deployed in an offensive layout according to Soviet doctrine. Elazar heard about it only on Saturday morning.

38. *Braun,* 61.

39. *Ibid.*

40. AMAN document, October 5, 1973 (1210).

41. *Ibid.*

42. *Agranat,* 26; *Zeira,* 195.

43. *Agranat,* 78–79; *Zeira,* 196–97.

44. *Zeira,* 197–98.

45. *Ibid.,* 200–1.

46. *Ibid.,* 201.

47. *Agranat,* 28, 77.

48. *Zeira,* 201–2.

49. AMAN's document, October 5, 1973 (1315).

50. *Ibid.*

51. *Ibid.*

52. *Agranat*, 401–6; Moty Ashkenazy, *A War Will Break Out at Six p.m.* (Hebrew, Tel Aviv: Am Oved, 2003), 48–51.

53. *Agranat*, 407–8.

54. *Ibid.*, 408–9.

55. AMAN document, October 5 (1315).

56. *Ibid.*

57. *Ibid.*

58. *Ibid.*

59. *Ibid.*

60. *Agranat 1975*, 36–37.

61. *Ibid.*, 36.

62. *Agranat*, 311.

63. *Braun*, 64.

64. *Agranat*, 283.

65. *Ibid.*

66. *Ibid.*

67. *Agranat*, 283–84; *Bartov*, 338–39.

68. *Agranat*, 198.

69. Interview with Harlev. Harlev still estimated at this stage that the probability for war was low (Amos Amir, *Flames in the Sky* (Hebrew, Tel Aviv: The Ministry of Defense Publishing House, 2000), 225).

70. Interview with Avner Shalev.

71. *Bartov*, 341.

72. Meyron Medzini, *The Proud Jewess: Golda Meir and Israel's Vision* (Hebrew, Jerusalem: Edanim, 1990), 422.

73. *Agranat*, 56.

74. *Ibid.*; Shlomo Nakdimon, *Low Probability* (Hebrew, Tel Aviv: Revivim, 1982), 96.

75. *Agranat*, 57.

76. *Ibid.*

77. *Ibid.*, 80.

78. Abba Eban, *Personal Witness: Israel through My Eyes* (New York: G.P. Putnam's Sons, 1992), 525.

79. *Agranat*, 59.

80. *Nakdimon*, 96.

81. *Braun*, 66.

82. Henry Kissinger, *Years of Upheaval* (Boston: Little Brown & Co., 1982), 465. His words to Eban after the war, in: *Agranat*, 59.

83. Henry Kissinger, *Crisis: The Anatomy of Two Major Foreign Policy Crises: Based on the Record of Henry Kissinger's Hitherto Secret Telephone Conversations* (New York, Simon & Schuster, digital edition, 2003), 27.

84. Anatoly Dobrynin, *In Confidence: Moscow's Ambassador to America's Six Cold War Presidents (1962-1986)* (New York: Times Books, 1995), 289-90.

85. *Ben Porat*, 65; Yitzhak Letz, "This is the Code Breaker," *Maariv*, September 13, 1995.

86. Interviews with Tehila and Arie Shalev.

87. Interviews with Tehila, Arie Shalev, and Yaari.

88. *Agranat*, 157.

89. *Ben-Porat*, 103. According to his biographer, Elazar testified in the Agranat Commission that had he received the information in time, he would have demanded, immediately, the mobilization of the reserve army (*Bartov*, 340).

90. AMAN's document, October 6, 1973 (06:35).

91. Interview with Avi Yaari.

92. AMAN document, October 6, 1973 (03:40).

93. Interview with Avi Yaari.

94. AMAN's document, October 6, 1973 (03:40).

95. *Haber*, 11; Zamir's interview.

96. Zamir's interview.

Chapter 16. Saturday, October 6, 1973, 0400–1400

1. *Nakdimon*, 105.

2. Golda Meir's military secretary reported that he received the message at 0340 (*Haber*, 11). By all accounts he was the first to whom Einy called. Dayan notes in his memoirs (*Dayan*, 463) that he received it at 0400. Golda Meir wrote in her account of the events (*Meir*, 358) that she received it at around 0400, and the Chief of Staff received it at 0430 (*Bartov*, 367).

3. Interview with Avner Shalev. Shalev received 1800 as H-hour from Dayan's Military Secretary, Yishayahu Raviv, who probably got it from AMAN.

4. *Braun*, 69.

5. *Agranat*, 31; *Bartov*, part 2, 367-70; *Braun*, 68-69; *Nakdimon*, 108-9.

6. *Haber*, 14, 21.

7. The description of this discussion is based mainly on the following sources: *Bartov*, 370–73; *Braun*, 69–71; *Nakdimon*, 109–11; *Haber*, 24; *Dayan* (Hebrew), 575–78 (Dayan's memoirs in English does not refer to this discussion); interview with Avner Shalev.

8. *Agranat*, 217.

9. *Genesis*, chapter 18, 22–33.

10. The text of the discussion, as written by Maj. Gen. Shlomo Gazit (*Haaretz*, January 1, 1999).

11. *Bartov*, 372.

12. *Agranat*, 35.

13. David Elazar, A Memorandum in the Subject of the Investigation Commission on the Yom Kippur War, submitted to Yizthak Rabin, the Prime Minister (Tel Aviv, May 1975), 11–12 (unpublished).

14. *Agranat*, 37.

15. This protocol was written by Dayan's adjutant, Arie Braun. Dayan and his assistants quoted it in their war memoirs (*Dayan (Hebrew)*, 576, *Braun*, 71, *Lavi*, 270) in order to show that the Defense Minister was not responsible for the delay in the mobilization. According to Elazar's bureau chief, certain changes were inserted into these protocols (Avner Shalev's interview). Given that Elazar pressured for an immediate mobilization, one can hardly understand why he did not use this permission—if indeed it was given—in order to mobilize the force he was allowed to. Elazar himself denied categorically that he was given this permission, and he quoted Dayan who said to the Agranat Commission that "if someone would say differently [i.e., that there was no authorization at the end of the meeting to mobilize 50,000–60,000 reserve soldiers], if the Chief of Staff would say differently, I will not argue that he misleads." (*Elazar's 1975 memorandum*, 12).

16. *Bartov*, 375–76; *Agranat*, 285–90; interviews with Avner Shalev and Hofi.

17. *Agranat*, 292–93 (emphasis in original).

18. *Ibid.*, 296.

19. *Haber*, 23–25.

20. The description of this meeting is based on the following sources: "Summary of a consultation with the Prime Minister, Tel Aviv, Yom Kippur, 6.10.73 at 0805"; *Bartov*, 378–82; *Haber*, 25–27; *Nakdimon*, 111–15; *Braun*, 73–76; interview with Avner Shalev.

21. The Investigation Commission—*The Yom Kippur War, A Third and Final Report* (Jerusalem, 1975) (from herein, *Agranat Third and Last*), 1187–88. Golda Meir was right when asserting that the Golan settlers would object to the evacuation of children. The commander of the Golan Territorial Brigade, Col. Zvi Bar, testified after the war that on the hours before fire started he had to go to the settlements in order to convince, without success, the settlers to agree to the children's evacuation (*Ibid.*, 1190–91).

22. *Braun*, 72, 73.

23. For example, *Dayan (Hebrew)*, 576; *Braun*, 76.

24. *Nakdimon*, 114.

25. *Bartov*, 386. An almost identical exchange in *Nakdimon*, 122.

26. AMAN's document, October 6, 1973, 07:30.

27. *Shazly*, 36–37.

28. This was a mistake. The Egyptians had no 203mm guns. The only Arab army that used them was the Jordanian army.

29. AMAN's document, October 6, 1973, 11:40. The rockets that were identified were the operational version of the "al Kaher" and "al Zaafer" ground-to-ground missiles that had been developed by German scientists in Egypt in the early 1960s. Following the project's failure, the Egyptians were left with a number of short-range and highly inaccurate (800 meters CEP at a range of 7.5km) missiles. The al Zaafer rockets had been put in positions during the last three days before the war and the bigger, al Kaher missiles were positioned only on the night of October 5–6. They were used without any impact (*Shazly*, 78–80).

30. An IAF intelligence document, October 6, 1973 (1200).

31. AMAN's document, October 6, 1974 (13:45). Unfortunately, AMAN's analysts did not use this excellent information and continued to assess the Egyptian moves on the basis of the more familiar but outdated Egyptian war plan that was distributed as an AMAN document in April 1972. According to that plan, following the crossing of the canal and the occupation of the Bar-Lev line by five infantry divisions, Egypt's two armored divisions (4 and 21) were to cross the canal and initiate, on D+2 or D+3, the second stage of the plan—an attack toward the mountain passes. During the first hours of the war, Branch 6 estimated that the Egyptians planned to move their armored divisions eastward, so that "they will carry the momentum of the offensive to the east" (*Agranat, Third and last*, 1213). Apprehension shortly turned into information. About five or six hours after war broke out, the head of Branch 6 and DMI Zeira reported to the Chief of Staff that Divisions 4 and 21 were crossing the canal. They thus created anticipations for a large-scale tank offensive during the next day. About twelve hours after war started, AMAN estimated, again, that Division 21 was about to cross (*Bartov*, 402; *Braun*, 92). In reality, first elements of these divisions crossed the canal only a week later and large segments of the divisions remained on the western side of the canal until the end of the war. The analysts of Branch 6 started understanding that the way the Egyptians actually acted in the war was different from the plan that they worked with, only on the night of October 8–9. It is possible that this change was influenced not only by reports from the front that showed that the divisions did not cross, but also by the return of the head of the Mossad to Israel. Upon his return, Zamir participated in a meeting at the Prime Minister's office, and there he made it clear that the Egyptian operational plan was to take a strip of 10–12 kilometers wide along the canal (*Agranat Third and Last*, 465–67; interview with Zvi Zamir). It is also possible that the removal of the head of Branch 6 from his position on the night of October 8–9 enabled a better understanding of the situation.

32. Alex Fishman, "Until Today He Does Not Believe that War Broke Out," *Hadashot*, September 24, 1993; interviews with Kanizher and Sudai.

33. Interviews with Zusia Kaniazher and Avi Yaari.

Chapter 17. Surprise

1. *Nakdimon*, 124–31.

2. Aviezar Golan, *Albert* (Hebrew, Tel Aviv: Yedioth Ahronot, 1977), 192.

3. *Ibid.*, 191–95.

4. *Ibid.*, 197–200.

5. Amir Rappaport and Yotam Yarkoni, "Leave the Wounded to be POWs," *Maariv*, August 8, 2003.

6. *Golan*, 201.

7. *Agranat*, 205–8.

8. *Ibid.*, 208–10.

9. *Ibid.*, 210–11, 323–28; *Bartov*, 391–92; *Golan*, 202.

10. *Bartov*, 376.

11. *Ibid.*, 386–87.

12. This reasoning, as well as the orders given by Gonen that morning, bring into memory Stalin's fear, on the eve of the German attack of June 1941, that any increase in Soviet state of readiness might cause the situation to deteriorate. An hour before operation Barbarossa started, a warning to prepare for war was finally issued to the Soviet army. The second of the three warning paragraphs said: "The task of our forces is to refrain from any kind of provocative action that might result in serious complications" (Gabriel Gorodetsky, *Grand Delusion: Stalin and the German Invasion of Russia* (New Haven: Yale University Press, 1999), 310.

13. *Agranat*, 321, 330–31.

14. *Ibid.*, 321.

15. *Ibid.*, 317–22.

16. *Ibid.*, 379–80.

17. *Ibid.*, 212.

18. *Bartov*, 392.

19. *Agranat*, 214.

20. This was the estimate of the commander of Reserve Division 143, Maj. Gen. Avraham Adan, as quoted in *Braun*, 83.

21. *Agranat*, 212–13.

22. *Agranat Third and Last*, 904.

23. AMAN's document, October 2, 1973; interview with Avi Yaari. See also the Syrian plan according to King Hussein, in his meeting with Golda Meir on September 24.

24. *Agranat Third and Last*, 908–9.

25. *Ibid.*, 909.

26. *Ibid.*, 905.

27. Interview with Yitzhak Hofi.

28. *Agranat Third and Last*, 910–16; Interview with Yitzhak Hofi; *Milstein*, 234.

29. *Agranat Third and Last*, 929–30; *Dupuy*, 441.

30. In the summer of 1973, the Northern Command's Commander, Maj. Gen. Hofi, presented the Minister of Defense with the Command's plans for a variety of challenges. The only plan for an all-out Syrian attack that was presented was the Sela plan—a full mobilization of two divisions, about 600 tanks. According to this plan, Division 36 was to deploy in the Golan, and the other division, under the command of Maj. Gen. Dan Laner, was to deploy at the rear for counterattacks or in order to carry out an outflanking through the Baka'a in Lebanon toward Damascus (interview with Hofi).

31. *Agranat*, 204; *Agranat Third and Last*, 928.

32. *Agranat*, 251–52.

33. Interview with Hofi.

34. *Agranat Third and Last*, 941; A talk with Hofi, December 2 1999.

35. The testimony of the intelligence officer of Brigade 7, in *Milstein*, 209.

36. *Agranat*, 253–57. According to Kahalani, the Commander of Battalion 77 of Brigade 7, Ben-Gal's estimate that war would break out the same day was even more decisive (Kahalani Avigdor, *Courage 77* (Hebrew, Tel Aviv: Shoken, 1975), 42–44).

37. *Agranat Third and Last*, 936–37.

38. Chaim Herzog, *The War of Atonement* (Tel Aviv: Steimatzky, 1975), 101; *Agranat Third and Last*, 1021–25.

39. *Dayan* (Hebrew), 595

40. Maj. Gen. (res.) Benny Peled, "The Israeli Air Force in the War of Yom Kippur" *A lecture in the framework of a seminar on the Yom Kippur War*. Ramat Efal. December 2, 1999; *Bartov*, part b, 50–51; Ehud Yonai, *No Margin for Error: The Making of the Israeli Air Force* (Hebrew, Jerusalem: Keter, 1995), 254–55.

41. *Agranat*, 218, 219.

42. *Yonai*, 244–47.

43. *Yossi Abudy's* lecture.

44. *Peled's* lecture. According to *Abudy's* lecture, all those who were present in the discussion of June 13 understood that the IAF would, if the need arose, get permission to shoot first in order to obtain air superiority.

45. *Peled's* lecture.

46. *Agranat Third and Last*, 1086–87.

47. *Ibid.*, 1087; *Abudy's* lecture; *Cohen and Lavie*, 472–74.

48. *Peled's* lecture; *Dayan*, 596; *Bartov*, part b, 53; *Yonai*, 255.

49. *Yonai*, 255.

50. The head of the IAF intelligence department in 1973, Brig. Gen. Rafi Harlev, estimated that the continuation of Tagar could have yielded 70 to 80 percent success and, as a result, the whole course of the war in the south would have been different (Harlev's interview).

51. Shmuel Gordon, "The Paradox of October 7," Hebrew *Maaracot*, 361 (1998): 45–67, 52. The source of the figure of 129 sorties is the history branch of the IAF.

52. Hofi's lecture, December 2, 1999.

53. *Agranat Third and Last*, 1090–93.

54. Abudy's lecture.

55. Yiftah Spector, *A Dream in Blue and Black* (Jerusalem: Keter, 1991), 11–12. The English translation is from the author's unpublished edition.

56. *Agranat Third and Last*, 1090–93; *Cohen and Lavie*, 474–76; *Yonai*, 258–56; *Amir*, 229; *Dayan*, 594–95.

57. *Gordon*, 55–57.

Chapter 18. The Cost of Being Caught Unprepared

1. Charles F. Hermann, "International Crisis as a Situational Variable," in *International Politics and Foreign Policy*, ed. James N. Rosenau (New York: Free Press, 1969), 409–21.

2. "And These Are the Names," *Yedioth Ahronot*, April 28, 1998, 32–33. According to one source, the IDF losses, including MIA's numbering 345 by the morning of October 7 (Ronen Bergman and Gil Meltzer, "120 Hours in October," *Yedioth Ahronot*, 8 August 2003).

3. *Bartov*, 412.

4. *Shazly*, 232–33. Notably, the number of EAF losses was by far higher than five planes, but the figures for the ground force losses seem to reflect reality.

5. Avi Kober, *Military decision in the Arab-Israeli wars, 1948-1982* (Hebrew, Tel Aviv: Maarachot, 1995), 359. According to Dupuy (whose sources were not as good as

Kober's), the Egyptians lost 260 tanks and 200 armored vehicles, while the IDF losses amounted to 40 tanks (*Dupuy*, 487).

6. Eitan Haber, *Barak—The War of Yom Kippur, the Golan Heights*, October 1973 (Hebrew, Tel Aviv: The Publication of the Bereaved Families, 1979), 163.

7. Arie Hashavia, The Armored Corps, vol. 7, in: Erez Yaacov and Kfir Ilan (eds.) *The IDF in Its Arms: An Encyclopedia for Army and Security* (Hebrew, Tel Aviv: Revivim, 1981) 187.

8. *Kober*, 341, *Herzog*, 113.

9. *Adan*, 67.

10. Roland Aloni, "The Ground Forces' Logistics in the War of Yom Kippur," Hebrew *Maarachot* 361 (1998): 28–37.

11. A typical example is the literary description, based on a real-war experience, of a tank team's desperate fighting in the Golan in a tank whose sights had not been adjusted because of the need to rush to the battlefield. See: Chaim Sabbato, *Adjustment of Sights* (Hebrew, Tel Aviv: Yedioth Ahronot: 2002).

12. *Gordon*, 52; *Yonai*, 258. According to Bartov, the IAF lost thirty planes in the first twenty-seven hours of the war and forty-four planes until October 8 at 2000 (*Bartov*, 427, 464).

13. *Dupuy*, 246.

14. *Gordon*, 34.

15. Brecher Michael with Geist Benjamin, *Decisions in Crisis: Israel, 1967 and 1973* (Berkeley: California University Press, 1980).

16. *Dayan* (in English), 483.

17. In his memoirs, Dayan did not mention this term at all, nor did he directly relate to his belief that Israel was under an existential threat during this stage of the war.

18. *Yonai*, 254–55. Yonai's description of this episode is based on an interview with Peled.

19. *Cohen and Lavie*, 469.

20. Bergman Ronen and Meltzer Gil, *The Yom Kippur War—Moment of Truth* (Hebrew, Tel Aviv: Yedioth Ahronot, 2003), 73.

21. *Dayan*, 597.

22. *Herzog*, 182–83; *Bartov*, 423.

23. Michael Shashar, *Talks with Rechav'am-'Gandi'-Ze'evi* (Hebrew, Tel Aviv: Yedioth Ahronot, 1992), 169.

24. *Dayan*, 598.

25. *Dayan* (in English), 494.

26. *Dayan*, 599.

27. Yesha`yahu Ben-Porat, *Dialogues* (Hebrew, Jerusalem: Yedioth Ahronot, 1981), 124–25.

28. *Meir*, 360.

29. *Medzini*, 434.

30. *Meir*, 361.

31. The testimony of Brig. Gen. Uri Ban-Ari for the IDF History Division, January 29, 1975, *Yedioth Ahronot*, August 8, 2003.

32. *Gai*, 255.

33. *Adan*, 87–88.

34. Ben-Ari testimony, *Yedioth Ahronot*, August 8, 2003.

35. *Yedioth Ahronot*, August 8, 2003.

36. *Bartov*, 467.

37. *Yedioth Ahronot*, August 8, 2003.

Chapter 19. The Causes of the Intelligence Failure

1. Interviews with Levran and Zamir.

2. A talk with Kaniazher, October 17, 1999.

3. *Cohen and Gooch*, 126–27; *Levran 1980;* Levran's interview, September 24, 1999.

4. *Agranat 1975,* 48.

5. Interviews with Yaacov Rosenfeld and Rafi Harlev.

6. Interview with Albert Sudai; a talk with Zusia Kaniazher on October 17, 1999.

7. *Agranat*, 157–59.

8. *Ibid*, 160–75.

9. Interviews with Sudai and Kaniazher.

10. Twenty-five years after the war, Levran still considered Zeira as AMAN's best DMI (Levran's interview).

11. *Ben Porat 1987,* 237; interviews with Levran and Sudai.

12. Interviews with Arie Shalev, Bandman, and Levran.

13. Interviews with Arie Shalev, Bandman, and Yaari.

14. Interview with Levran.

15. Interview with Arie Shalev.

16. Interviews with Ilan Tehila and Yaacov Rosenfeld.

17. *Ben Porat*, 118–19.

18. *Agranat*, 159; interview with Yaari.

19. Interviews with Gilboa and Brill; Kaniazher's seminar paper; a talk with Kaniazher.

20. Interviews with Levran and Yaari.

21. Interview with Avner Shalev.

22. *Shashar,* 168; Fishman, *Hadashot,* September 24, 1993; Ariel Sharon with David Chanoff, *Warrior: the Autobiography of Ariel Sharon* (New York: Simon & Schuster, 2001), 288.

23. Evans, Jonathan T., *Bias in Human Reasoning: Causes and Consequences* (London: Lawrence Erlbaum Associates, 1989), 41.

24. Interview with Albert Sudai.

25. *Braun,* 61.

26. Interview with Yona Bandman.

27. *Agranat 1975,* 46.

28. Moshe Zonder, *Tel Aviv,* October 4, 1991; *Ben-Porat,* 103; interview with Avner Shalev.

29. *Israeli TV,* September 19, 1993.

30. Interview with Arie Shalev.

31. Norman F. Dixon, *The Psychology of Military Incompetence* (London: Futura, 1985), 262.

32. Kruglanski, A.W., & Webster, D.M. (1996). Motivated closing of the mind: "Seizing" and "freezing." *Psychological Review,* 103, 263–28; Webster, D.M., Richter, L., & Kruglanski, A.W. (1996). On leaping to conclusions when feeling tired: Mental fatigue effects on impressional primacy. *Journal of Experimental Social Psychology,* 32, 181–95; Webster, D.M. (1993). Motivated augmentation and reduction of the overattribution bias. *Journal of Personality and Social Psychology,* 65, 261–71.

33. Kruglanski & Webster, 1996; Webster, D.M. & Kruglanski, A.W. (1998). Cognitive and social consequences of the need for cognitive closure. In W. Stroebe & M. Hewstone (eds.), *European Review of Social Psychology,* 8, 133–41.

34. For a detailed discussion of how the behavior of Zeira and Bandman suited each of these behavioral phenomena, see: *Bar-Joseph and Kruglanski,* 82–89.

35. The role of a high need for cognitive closure as a cause for intelligence failure had not been recognized yet in the theoretical literature. Initial evidence shows, however, that this factor had its impact in facilitating this type of fiasco. Thus, for example, studies of the case of Pearl Harbor debacle show that the Chief of the War Plans Division in the Navy Department, Rear Admiral Richmond Kelly Turner, was "one of the most important persons responsible if not the man mainly responsible" for the disaster

(Prange, G.W. with Goldstein, D.M. & Dillon K.V, *Pearl Harbor: The Verdict of History* (New York: Penguin, 1991), 295). Turner was described by one colleague as a "man of inflexible mental habits, a man who wanted it all simplified ... [who] wanted all answers quickly and in black and white and no difficult mental process to go through, by all means no thinking, just machine-gun answers—bang, bang, bang!" Another officer described him as "rigid, narrow, intolerant." (*Ibid.*, 294), all characteristics prototypical of an individual with a high need for closure.

Bibliography

Official Documents

Agranat Commission, *The Agranat Report* (Hebrew, Tel Aviv, Am Oved, 1975) (*Agranat 1975*).

The Investigation Committee, *The Yom Kippur War, An Additional Partial Report: Reasoning and Completion to the Partial Report of April 1, 1974*, 7 volumes (Hebrew, Jerusalem, 1974) (*Agranat*).

The Investigation Commission ("The Agranat Commission") — *The Yom Kippur War, A Third and Final Report*. Hebrew, Jerusalem, 1975 (*Agranat Third and Last*).

U.S. Select Committee on Intelligence and U.S. House Permanent Select Committee on Intelligence, Together with Additional Views. *Joint Inquiry Into Intelligence Community Activities Before and After the Terrorist Attacks of September 11, 2001*. 107th Cong., 2nd sess., December 2002.

Unpublished Academic Works

Asher, Dani. "All-Out War Limited in Its Dimensions: The Egyptian Military-Doctrinal Solution to the Problems Presented By the Israeli Defence System in the Sinai Front Prior to the Yom Kippur War." Ph.D. diss., Haifa University, 2002.

Gavra, Gai. *The Hussein–Golda Meeting on the Eve of the Yom Kippur War*. Seminar paper, Tel Aviv University, 2000.

Kaniazher, Zusia. "The Directorship of AMAN and the Research Department — Mistakes in Estimating Warning Intelligence." Seminar paper, Haifa University, 1999.

Zeevi, Aharon. "The Egyptian 'Deception' in the Plan of the Yom Kippur War." *MA Thesis, Tel Aviv University*, 1980.

Other Unpublished Works

Bandman, Yona. *The War of Yom Kippur, Egypt—the Goals of the War and the Attack Plan*. IDF, General Staff Branch GHQ–Instruction Division–History Department, Study of Enemy Team, 1981.

Lectures

Lieutenant Colonel (res.) Yossi Abudi. "The Israeli Air Force in the War." *A lecture in the framework of a seminar on the Yom Kippur War*. Ramat Efal, May 4, 2000.

Major General (res.) Benny Peled, "The Israeli Air Force in the War of Yom Kippur." *A lecture in the framework of a seminar on the Yom Kippur War*. Ramat Efal. December 2, 1999.

Tal, Yisrael. "The Warning in the Yom Kippur War." A lecture to AMAN's officers, July 12, 1993, in the framework of *A Series of Symposiums to Summarize the Role of Intelligence in "The Yom Kippur War."* Hebrew, Glilot: Bahad, July 15, 1994.

Interviews (in parentheses, the interviewee's role in 1973)

Bandman Yona (head of Branch 6 in AMAN's Research Department) Tel Aviv, August 17, 1998.

Brill Shabtai (Operations Officer, Unit 848) Tel Aviv, May 4, 2000.

Eini Yumi (head of AMAN's distribution system) Tel Aviv, August 22, 2000.

Gazit Shlomo (Coordinator of Government Operations in the Administered Territories, replaced Zeira as DMI) Tel Aviv, July 10, 2000.

Gilboa Amos (head of Basic Branch in Basic Division in AMAN's Research Department) Tel Aviv, July 11, 2000.

Harlev Rafi (head of the Intelligence Division of the IAF) July 29, 1999.

Hofi Yitzhak (Commander of the Northern Command), Ramat Gan, June 25, 2000.

Kaniazher Zusia (Head of Branch 2 of the Research Department), various unrecorded talks in Haifa and Tel Aviv.

Levran Aharon (DMI Zeira's assistant for operations) Kfar Saba, March 8, 1999.

Lunz Rami (head of the Intelligence Division of the Israeli Navy) Kfar Saba, June 19, 1999.

Porat Yehuda (head of the Research Branch, the Intelligence Division of the IAF) Shfayim, July 25, 1999.

Rosenfeld Yaacov (head of the Military Section in Branch 6) Tel Aviv, September 14, 1998.

Shalev Arie (head of AMAN's Research Department) Tel Aviv, August 27, 1998.

Shalev Avner (the Chief of Staff Military Assistant) Neve Magen, May 4, 1999; October 29, 1999.

Sudai Albert (head of the Political Section of Branch 6) Neve Savion, April 12, 1999.

Tehila Ilan (head of Soviet Political Section in AMAN's Research Department) Herzlia, August 10, 1998.

Yaari Aviezer (head of Branch 5 in AMAN's Research Department) August 10, 1998.

Zamir Zvi (head of the Mossad) August 13, 1998; August 19, 1998.

Books

Adan, Avraham. *On Both Banks of the Suez*. Hebrew, Jerusalem: Edanim, 1979.

Ajami, Fuad. The *Arab Predicament: Arab Political Thought and Practice Since 1967*. London: Cambridge University Press, 1981.

Allison, Graham T. *Essence of Decision*. Boston: Little Brown, 1971.

Amir, Amos. *Flames in the Sky*. Hebrew, Tel Aviv: The Ministry of Defense Publishing House, 2000.

Asher, Dani. *Breaking the Concept*. Hebrew, Tel Aviv: Maarachot, 2003.

Ashkenazy, Moty. *A War Will Break Out at Six p.m.* Hebrew, Tel Aviv: Am Oved, 2003.

Bar, Shmuel. *The Yom Kippur War in the Eyes of the Arabs*. Hebrew, Tel Aviv: Maarachot, 1986.

Bar-Joseph, Uri. *Intelligence Intervention in the Politics of Democratic States: The USA, Israel, and Britain*. University Park: Penn State Press, 1995.

Bartov, Hanoch. *Daddo—48 Years and 20 More Days*. Hebrew, Tel Aviv: Maariv, 1978.

Bartov, Hanoch, *Daddo—48 Years and 20 More Days* (an expanded and footnoted edition). Hebrew, Or Yehuda: Dvir, 2002.

Beilin, Yossi. *The Cost of Unity: The Labor Party and the War of Yom Kippur*. Hebrew, Tel Aviv: Revivim, 1985.

Ben Horin, Yoav and Posen Bary. *Israel's Strategic Doctrine*. Santa Monica, CA: Rand, 1981.

Ben-Porat, Yoel *Neila, Locked-on*. Hebrew, Tel Aviv: Idanim, 1991.

Ben Porat, Yishayahu, Gefen Jonathan, Dan Uri, Haber Eitan, Carmel Hezi, Landau Eli, and Tavor Eli, *The Failure ('HaMehdal')*. Hebrew, Tel Aviv: Special Publishing, 1974.

Ben-Zvi, Abraham. *The United States and Israel: The Limits of the Special Relationship.* New York: Columbia University Press, 1993.

Ben-Zvi, Abraham. *Decade of Transition.* New York: Columbia University Press, 1998.

Ben-Zvi, Abraham. *John F. Kennedy and the Politics of Arms Sales to Israel.* London: Cass, 2002.

Benziman, Uzi. *Sharon, an Israeli Caesar.* Hebrew, Tel Aviv: Adam, 1985.

Bergman, Ronen and Meltzer, Gil, *The Yom Kippur War—Moment of Truth.* Hebrew, Tel Aviv: Yedioth Ahronoth, 2003.

Betts, Richard K. *Surprise Attack: Lessons for Defense Planning.* Washington, D.C.: The Brookings Institution, 1982.

Blum, Howard. *The Eve of Destruction: The Untold Story of the Yom Kippur War.* New York: HarperCollins, 2003.

Braun, Arie. *Moshe Dayan and the Yom Kippur War.* Hebrew, Tel Aviv: Edanim, 1992.

Brecher Michael with Geist Benjamin, *Decisions in Crisis: Israel, 1967 and 1973* Berkeley: California University Press, 1980.

Bregman, Ahron and El-Tahri Jihan. *The Fifty Years' War : Israel and the Arabs.* New York : TV Books, 1999.

Bregman, Ahron. *Israel's Wars, 1947–93.* London: Routledge, 2000.

Bregman, Ahron. *A History of Israel.* Houndmills: Palgrave Macmillan, 2003.

Cohen, Eliezer and Lavie Zvi. *Sky is Not the Limit.* Hebrew, Tel Aviv: Maariv, 1990.

Cohen, Eliot, and Gooch John. *Military Misfortunes: The Anatomy of Failure in War.* New York: Vintage Books, 1991.

Dayan, Moshe. *Story of My Life.* Hebrew, Jerusalem: Edanim, 1976.

Dixon, Norman F. *The Psychology of Military Incompetence.* London: Futura, 1985.

Dobrynin, Anatoly. *In Confidence: Moscow's Ambassador to America's Six Cold War Presidents (1962–1986).* New York: Times Books, 1995.

Dupuy, Trevor N. *Elusive Victory: The Arab-Israeli Wars, 1947–1974.* New York: Harper & Row, 1978.

Eban, Abba. *Personal Witness: Israel Through My Eyes.* New York: G.P. Putnam's Sons, 1992.

Evans, Jonathan St. B. T. *Bias in Human Reasoning: Causes and Consequences.* London: Lawrence Erlbaum Associates, 1989.

Farid Abdel Magid, *Nasser: The Final Years.* Reading: Itacha Press, 1994.

Fawzi, Mahmoud. *The Three Years War.* Arabic, Cairo: Dar Al-Mustakbal Al-Arabi, 1984.

Festinger Leon. *A Theory of Cognitive Dissonance.* Stanford: Stanford University Press, 1957.

Festinger, Leon. *Conflict, Decision and Dissonance.* Stanford: Stanford University Press, 1964.

Gai, Karmit. *Bar-Lev.* Hebrew, Tel Aviv: Am Oved, 1998.

Gamasy, Mohamed Abdel Ghani el, *The October War: Memoirs of Field Marshal Gamasy of Egypt.* Cairo: The American University of Cairo Press, 1993.

Glassman, Jon D. *Arms for the Arabs: The Soviet Union and War in the Middle East.* Baltimore: The John Hopkins University Press, 1975.

Golan, Aviezar. *Albert.* Hebrew. Tel Aviv: Yedioth Ahronot, 1977.

Gorodetsky, Gabriel. *Grand Delusion: Stalin and the German Invasion of Russia.* New Haven: Yale University Press, 1999.

Granot, Oded. *The Intelligence Corps.* Volume 6 in the series *The IDF in Its Arms.* Hebrew, Tel Aviv: Maariv, 1981.

Gratz, Bill. *Breakdown: How America's intelligence Failure Led to September 11.* Washington, D.C.: Regnery, 2002.

Grundman, Moshe. (ed.) *Cautious Assessment: Writings by Aharon Yariv.* Hebrew, Tel Aviv: Maarachot, 1998.

Gur, Mordechai. *From the North and from the West.* Hebrew, Tel Aviv: Maarachot, 1998.

Haber, Eitan. *Today War Will Break Out.* Hebrew Tel Aviv: Yedioth Ahronot, 1987.

Halperin, Morton. *Bureaucratic Politics and Foreign Policy.* Washington D.C.: The Brookings Institution, 1974.

Handel, Michael I. *Perception, Deception, and Surprise: The Case of the Yom Kippur War.* Hebrew University of Jerusalem, Leonard Davis Institute for International Relations. Jerusalem Papers on Peace Problems. 19 (1976).

Handel, Michael I. *War, Strategy and Intelligence.* London: Frank Cass, 1989.

Handel, Michael I. *Israel's Political-Military Doctrine.* Cambridge, Mass.: Center for International Affairs, Harvard University, 1973.

Hart, Paul T. *Groupthink in Government: A Study of Small groups and Policy Failures.* Baltimore: John Hopkins University Press, 1990.

Hashavia, Arie. *The Armor Corps.* Volume 7 in the series *The IDF in Its Arm.* Hebrew, Tel Aviv: Revivim, 1981.

Heikal, Mohamed, *The Road to Ramadan.* New York: Ballantine, 1975.

Herzog Chaim, *The War of Atonement,* Tel Aviv: Steimatzky, 1975.

Houghs, Thomas L. *The Fate of Facts in the World of Men: Foreign Policy and Intelligence Making.* New York: Foreign Policy Association, 1976.

Hybel, Alex Roberto. *The Logic of Surprise in International Conflict.* Lexington, Mass: Lexington Books, 1986.

Israelyan, Victor. *Inside the Kremlin During the Yom Kippur War.* University Park: Penn State Press, 1995.

Janis, Irving. *Victims of Groupthink.* Boston: Houghton Mifflin, 1972.

Jervis, Robert. *Perception and Misperception in International Politics*. Princeton: Princeton University Press, 1976.

Kahalani, Avigdor. *Courage 77*. Hebrew, Tel Aviv: Shoken, 1975.

Kam, Ephraim. *Surprise Attack: The Victim's Perspective*. Cambridge: Harvard University Press, 1988.

Kirpichenko, Vadim. *From Intelligence Man's Archive*. Russian, Moskva: Mezhdunarodnie Otnoshenija, 1998.

Kissinger, Henry. *Years of Upheaval*. Boston: Little Brown, 1982.

Lanir, Zvi. *Fundamental Surprise: The National Intelligence Crisis*. Hebrew, Tel Aviv: Hakibutz Hameuchad, 1983.

Lau-Lavi, Naphtali. *Nation as a Lion*. Hebrew, Tel Aviv: Maariv, 1993.

Maoz, Moshe. *Asad the Sphinx of Damascus: A Political Biography*. London: Wiedenfeld and Nicholson, 1988.

Maoz, Moshe. *Israel and Syria: The End of the Conflict?* Hebrew, Or Yehuda: Maariv, 1996.

Medzini, Meyron *The Proud Jewess: Golda Meir and Israel's Vision*. Hebrew, Jerusalem: Edanim, 1990.

Meir, Golda. *My Life: The Autobiography of Golda Meir*. London: Futora, 1976.

Milstein, Uri. *The Lesson of the Collapse*. Hebrew, Kiron: Sridut, 1993.

Nakdimon, Shlomo. *Low Probability*. Hebrew, Tel Aviv: Revivim, 1982.

Nizameddin Talal, *Russia and the Middle East: Towards a New Foreign Policy*. London: Hurst & Company, 1999.

Nordeen, Lon and Nicole David. *Phoenix Over the Nile: A History of Egyptian Air Power—1932-1994*. Washington: Smithsonian Institution Press, 1996.

Parker, Richaed B. (ed.) *The October War—A Retrospective*. Gainsville: The University of Florida Press, 2001.

Pollack Kenneth M., *Arabs at War: Military Effectiveness, 1948-1991*. Lincoln: University of Nebraska Press, 2002.

Prange, Gordon W. with Goldstein, Donald M. and Dillon Katherine V. *Pearl Harbor: The Verdict of History*. New York: Penguin, 1991.

Pretty, Ronald T. ed. *Jane's Weapon Systems*. London: Jane's, 1979.

Ronen, Ran. *Hawk in the Sky*. Hebrew, Tel Aviv: Hemed, 2002.

Sabbato, Chaim. *Adjustment of Sights*. Hebrew, Tel Aviv: Yedioth Ahronot: 2002.

Sadat, Anwar. *In Search of Identity: An Autobiography*. New York: Harper and Row, 1978.

Schueftan, Dan. *Attrition: Egypt's Post-War Political Strategy, 1967-1970*. Hebrew, Tel Aviv: Maarachot, 1989.

Seale, Patrick. *Asad: The Struggle for the Middle East*. Berkeley: University of California Press, 1988.

Sharon, Ariel with David Chanoff. *Warrior: the Autobiography of Ariel Sharon*. New York: Simon & Schuster, 2001.

Shashar, Michael. *Talks with Rechav'am-Gandi'-Ze'evi*. Hebrew, Tel Aviv: Yedioth Ahronot, 1992.

Shazly, Saad el. *The Crossing of the Suez*. San Francisco: American Mideast Research, 1980.

Shlaim, Avi. *The Iron Wall: Israel and the Arab World*. London: Penguin, 2000.

Steinbruner, John. *The Cybernetic Theory of Decision*. Princeton: Princeton University Press, 1974.

Suvorov, Victor. *Icebreaker: Who Started the Second World War?* New York: Viking, 1990.

Tal, Yisrael. *National Security: A Few Against Many*. Hebrew, Tel Aviv: Dvir, 1996.

Vinogradov, Vladimir M. *Diplomacy, People and Events: From Ambassador's Notes*. Russian, Moskva: ROSSPEN 1998.

Wohlstetter, Roberta. *Pearl Harbor: Warning and Decision*. Stanford: Stanford University Press, 1962

Wilensky, Harold. *Organizational Intelligence*. New York: Basic, 1967.

Yaacobi, Gad. *On the Razor's Edge*. Hebrew, Tel Aviv: Yedioth Ahronot, 1989.

Yaari, Aviezer. *The Road from Merhavia*. Hebrew, Or Yehuda: Zmora-Bitan-Dvir, 2003.

Yaniv, Avner. *Deterrence Without the Bomb: The Politics of Israeli Strategy*. Lexington, Mass.: Lexington Books, 1987.

Yazid, Sayigh. *Armed Struggle and the Search for State: The Palestinian National Movement, 1949-1993*. Washington, D.C.: Oxford University Press, 1997.

Yonai, Ehud. *No Margin for Error: The Making of the Israeli Air Force*. Hebrew, Jerusalem: Keter, 1995.

Zeira, Eli. *The October 73 War: Myth Against Reality*. Hebrew, Tel Aviv: Yedioth Ahronot, 1993.

Zeira, Eli. *Myth versus Reality, The October 1973 War: Failures and Lessons*. Hebrew, Tel Aviv: Yedioth Ahronot, 2004.

Articles and Published Chapters

Amos, John. "Deception and the 1973 Middle East War." In: *Strategic Military Deception*, edited by Donald C. Daniel and Katherine L. Herbig, 317–34. New York: Pergamon Press, 1981.

Asher, Dani. "The Anti-Tank Weapons as an Answer: The Planning of the Operation of Anti-Tank Means by the Egyptians in the War of Yom Kippur." (Hebrew) *Maarachot*, 346 (1994): 6–10.

Bar-Joseph, Uri. "Israel Caught Unaware: Egypt's Sinai Surprise of 1960." *International Journal of Intelligence and Counterintelligence,* 8 (1995): 203–19.

Bar-Joseph, Uri. "Rotem: The Forgotten Crisis on the Road to the 1967 War." *Journal of Contemporary History,* 31 (1996): 547–66.

Bar-Joseph, Uri and Arie W. Kruglanski. "Intelligence Failure and the Need for Cognitive Closure: On the Psychology of the Yom Kippur Surprise," *Political Psychology,* 24 (2003): 75–99.

Bar-Kochva, Moshe. "Operation 'Kiton-10': Tanks Breakthrough into Syria." In *Chariots of Steel,* edited by Moshe Bar-Kochva. 263–77. Hebrew, Tel Aviv: Maarachot, 1981.

Ben-Porat, Yoel. "Intelligence Estimates—Why Do They Collapse?" In *Intelligence and National Security,* edited by Zvi Offer and Avi Kober, 223–50. Hebrew, Tel Aviv: Maarachot, 1987.

Ben-Zvi, Abraham. "Hindsight and Foresight: A Conceptual Framework for the Analysis of Surprise Attacks." *World Politics* 28 (1976): 381–95.

Ben-Zvi, Abraham. "Threat Perception and Surprise: In Search of the Intervening Variable." In *Conflict in World Politics: Advances in the Study of Crisis, War and Peace,* edited by Frank P. Harvey and Ben D. Mor, 241–71. New York: St. Martin's Press, 1998.

Betts, Richard K. "Intelligence for Policymaking." *Washington Quarterly* 3 (1980): 118–29.

Garbo, Cynthya M. "Soviet Deception in the Czechoslovak Crisis." *Studies in Intelligence,* 10 (2000): 71–86.

Gawrych, George W. "The Egyptian High Command in the 1973 War." *Armed Forces and Society* 13 (1987): 535–59.

Gordon, Shmuel. "The Paradox of October 7." *Maaracot,* 361 (1998): 45–67.

Gross Stein, Janice. "The 1973 Intelligence Failure: A Reconsideration." *The Jerusalem Quarterly* 24 (1982): 41–46.

Gross Stein, Janice. "Calculation, Miscalculation, and Conventional Deterrence II: The View from Jerusalem." In *Psychology & Deterrence,* edited by Robert Jervis, Richard Ned Lebow, and Janice Stein Gross, 60–88. Baltimore: Johns Hopkins University Press, 1985.

Handel, Michael I. "Intelligence and the Problem of Strategic Surprise." *The Journal of Strategic Studies* 7 (1984): 229–81.

Handel, Michael I. "The Politics of Intelligence." *Intelligence and National Security* 2 (1987): 5–46.

Hareven, Alouph. "Disturbed Hierarchies: Israeli Intelligence in 1954 and 1973." Jerusalem Quarterly 9 (1978): 3–19.

Harkabi, Yehoshafat. "The Intelligence-Policymaker Tangle." *Jerusalem Quarterly.* 30 (1984): 125–31.

Hastedt, Glenn P. "The New Context of Intelligence Estimation: Politization or Publicizing?" In *Intelligence and Intelligence Policy in a Democratic Society*, edited by Stephen J. Cimbala, 47–67. New York: Transnational, 1987.

Hulnick, Arthur S. "Controlling Intelligence Estimates." In *Controlling Intelligence*, edited by Glenn P. Hastedt. 81–96. London: Cass, 1991.

Kahneman, Daniel and Tversky, Amos. "Subjective Probability: A Judgment of Representativeness." *Cognitive Psychology* 3 (1972):430–51.

Klein, Zvi. "The Surprise of Yom Kippur." (in Hebrew) *State and Government* 6 (1974): 127–41.

Kruglanski, Arie W. and Webster Donna M. "Motivated Closing of the Mind: Its Cognitive and Social Effects." *Psychological Review*, 103 (1996): 263–83.

Levran, Aharon. "Surprise and Warning—Considerations of Fundamental Questions." (Hebrew) *Maarachot*, 276–77 (1980): 17–21.

Shlaim, Avi. "Failures in National Intelligence Estimates: The Case of the Yom Kippur War." *World Politics* 28 (1976): 348–80.

Tversky, Amos and Kahneman, Daniel. "Availability: A Heuristic for Judging Frequency and Probability." *Cognitive Psychology* 5 (1973): 207–32.

Tversky, Amos and Kahneman, Daniel. "Judgment Under Uncertainty: Heuristics and Biases." *Science* 185 (1980): 1124–31.

Webster, Donna M., Richter L., and Kruglanski, Arie W. "On Leaping to Conclusions When Feeling Tired: Mental Fatigue Effects on Impressional Primacy." *Journal of Experimental Social Psychology*, 32 (1996): 181–95.

Webster, Donna M. "Motivated Augmentation and Reduction of the Overattribution Bias." *Journal of Personality and Social Psychology*, 65 (1993): 261–71.

Webster, Donna M. and Kruglanski, Arie W. "Cognitive and Social Consequences of the Need for Cognitive Closure." In *European Review of Social Psychology*, edited by Wolfgang Stroebe and Miles Hewstone, 133–41. Tailor and Francis, 1998.

Zeevi, Aharon. "The Egyptian Deception Plan." In *Intelligence and National Security*, edited by Zvi Offer and Avi Kober, 431–38. Hebrew, Tel Aviv: Maarachot, 1987.

Index

Abu Ageila, 230
Abu Nida, 216
Abu Rudeis, 193, 230
Abu Zweir, 144
Adan, Avraham, 74, 227, 233, 257 (note 14), 282 (note 20)
Aden, 29
Aeroflot, 138, 168
Agranat Commission, 7, 45, 56, 118, 125, 142, 146, 149, 151, 166, 171, 178, 180, 192, 193, 194, 206, 209, 212, 214, 240, 242, 249
al Ahram, 28, 163
al Balah island, 206
'alarmists', 111, 237, 241, 243, 245
Alexandria, 22, 28, 34, 81, 90, 119, 156, 158, 169, 177
Algeria, 83
Allon, Yigal, 77, 106, 122, 129, 195, 231, 271 (note 12)
AMAN (Military Intelligence) estimates: Egypt, 45–46, 49, 59–61, 63–65, 68–70, 71, 75, 84–87, 96, 97–98, 109–10, 113–14, 115–16, 118, 122–24, 138–39, 144–45, 146–47, 148, 153–54, 157–59, 162–63, 165–72, 172–73, 176–77, 182, 188, 192–93, 195–96, 197–99, 203, 205, 237, 243–48, 249–50; Jordan, 47, 195; Syria, 46–47, 65–66, 67, 72, 81–84, 92–94, 96–97, 98, 101, 107, 110, 114–15, 118, 122–24, 138–39, 144–45, 146–47, 153–54, 157–59, 164–65, 170, 172–73, 176–77, 182, 183–84, 188, 192–93, 195–96, 211–13, 243–48; the Soviet Union, 41, 69, 96, 138–39, 146–47, 153–54, 156, 158–59, 164–65, 168–70, 177, 179–80, 182–83, 192, 248, 276, 277; the United States, 69, 86, 151, 189, 192, 276
Amir, Gabi, 204
Asad, Hafez, 5, 26, 29, 33–35, 46, 66, 67, 68, 81, 82–83, 90, 98, 120, 124, 137, 213, 261 (note 11), 262 (note 12), 267 (note 18), 273 (note 2)
Ashrafi island, 168
Associated Press (AP), 121
Austria, 95

Bab el Mandab, 66
"Babylon" (848 base in Um Hashiba), 108–9, 131
Baluza, 207
Bandman, Yona: general, 6, 48, 64, 104, 198–99, 243, 245, 248–51, 266 (note 6), 274 (note 6), 287 (note 34); intelligence estimate, 64–65, 92, 97–98, 104, 109–10, 136, 139, 165–72, 180, 198–99, 247
Bar-Lev, Chaim, 15, 18, 39, 42, 43, 53, 54, 157, 195, 232, 234
Bar-Lev line, 17–19, 39, 56–57, 59, 60, 66, 187, 204–5, 207, 209–11, 214, 218, 257 (note 14), 281 (note 31)
Barak, Ehud, 249
Barbarossa, 2, 4, 282
Bartov, Hanoch, 272 (note 8)
Bay of Pigs, 130, 280 (note 30)
Ben-Ari, Uri, 232, 282 (note 6)
Ben-Gal, Avigdor, 216
Ben-Porat, Yoel, 5, 100, 106, 108–9, 116, 131, 139, 148, 179, 236, 271 (note 60)
Ben-Shoham, Yitzhak, 216

Ben-Zvi, Avraham, 4
Betts, Richard, 4
Bilbays air base, 167
Bir Gafgafa ("Refidim"), 230
Blay air base, 114
'blue-white' state of readiness, 73–74, 148, 211, 267 (note 30)
Bnot Yaacov bridge, 211–13
"Botzer" stronghold, 166
Branches in AMAN's Research Department: Branch 2 (Jordan, and the Arab Peninsula), 86, 91, 238, 241, 243, 251; Branch 3 (international), 48, 69, 138, 175, 179, 180, 243, 256; Branch 5 (Syria, Lebanon and Iraq), 47, 66, 91, 96–97, 101, 104, 105, 115, 145, 164, 180, 183, 202, 203, 238, 245, 251, 271 (note 13); Branch 6 (Egypt, Sudan and North Africa), 47, 48, 59, 64, 86, 91, 92, 96, 97, 104, 105, 110, 114, 125, 135–36, 143, 147, 165, 166, 171, 180, 197, 198, 199, 241, 243, 247, 248, 251, 274 (note 6), 281 (note 31)
Braun, Arie, 269 (note 16), 273 (note 10), 280 (note 15)
Brecher, Michael, 228
Brezhnev, Leonid, 21, 48, 49, 75, 136, 137, 257 (note 8)
Brill, Shabtai, 100, 115, 134, 271 (note 60)
Britain, 31, 77
"Budapest" stronghold, 166
Burg el Arab, 34

Cairo, 21, 26, 28, 29, 35, 43, 72, 90, 93, 96, 109, 113, 115, 121, 136, 137, 138, 144, 156, 166, 169, 170, 178
Cairo international airport, 168
Canaan mount, 217, 229
Central Intelligence Agency (CIA), 96, 98, 110, 115, 125, 130, 152, 160, 178, 189, 190, 206, 249, 274
"Churchill", 207
cognitive dissonance, 3, 247, 254 (note 8)
Cohen, Eliot, 5
'conceptzia' (intelligence conception), 45–47, 63–65, 68, 69, 71, 75, 84–85, 92–93, 94, 96, 98, 107, 115, 117, 124, 135, 139, 147–8, 159, 162–63, 170, 172–73, 177, 196, 198–99, 242
confirmation bias, 3, 246–47
cry-wolf syndrome, 2, 27, 49, 50, 185, 237, 237, 239
Czechoslovakia, 26, 95, 108, 276 (note 22)

D-day, 25, 26, 35, 49, 67, 81, 109, 124, 125, 137, 142
Damascus, 26, 33, 34, 42, 66, 72, 82, 84, 98, 118, 119, 121, 122, 123, 126, 128, 136, 137, 164, 168–69, 170, 178, 190, 192, 213, 218, 219, 273 (note 2), 283 (note 30)
Dar'a, 81
Dayan, Moshe: general, 1, 6, 49, 50, 63, 67, 68, 69–71, 72–73, 74, 86, 88–89, 90, 91, 93, 95, 96, 104, 105–6, 113, 116, 117, 118, 121, 122, 124, 130, 133–34, 135, 142, 143, 144, 145–53, 154–55, 157, 175, 176, 181, 186, 188, 189–93, 194, 195–97, 201, 211, 217–18, 219, 220, 223, 229–32, 234, 240, 254 (note 14), 268 (note 39), 269 (note 30), 271 (note 6), 273 (note 10), 276 (note 18), 279 (note 2), 280 (note 15), 283 (note 30), 285 (note 17); Intelligence estimate, 47, 68, 70–71, 72–73, 76–77, 83, 94, 108, 117, 123, 128–29, 133–34, 146, 148, 149, 154–55, 157, 162, 188, 196–97, 199, 237, 238, 239, 242, 249, 267 (note 26)
Deception, 2, 5–6, 25–32, 40, 49–51, 75, 96, 149–50, 164, 166, 182, 236–7, 246, 259, 276
Détente, 137
Digli, Menahem, 101, 106, 148, 236
Dinitz, Simcha, 155, 176
Dobrynin, Anatoly, 178–79
'duck night', 150–51
Dumair air base, 81, 100, 144

Eban, Abba, 176–78
Egypt: air-defense, 16, 19–23; Air Force (EAF), 16, 19–23; and Iraq, 21; and Jordan, 91; and Libya, 21; and the USSR, 20–21, 136–38; impact of the War of Attrition, 15–16, 19–20; quest for "de-

terring weapons", 21–22, 50, 65, 85, 86; strategic cooperation with Syria, 33–35, 81, 119–20; war conception, 12, 22, 23; war decision, 11–13, 16; war plans: general, 17–24, 25–26, 84, 126; Granite, 17, 61, 67, 103; Instruction 41, 18, 19, 257 (note 13), 258 (note 20); Tahrir exercises (including 'Tahrir 41'), 50–51, 97, 98, 101, 103–4, 105, 107, 109, 166, 120, 135, 149, 160, 166, 171, 206, 236, 247, 248

Egypt Air, 277

Ein Zivan, 95

Einy, Freddy, 142, 185, 187, 279 (note 2)

Eitan, Raphael, 217, 221

Ekron air base, 120

El Al, 221

El Arish, 77

Elazar, David, 5, 43, 49, 55–56, 57, 67, 89, 93, 96, 104–5, 117–18, 126–27, 141, 150, 153, 157, 175–76, 188–89, 190–94, 195–97, 203, 203, 204, 205, 229, 231–32, 234, 249, 262 (note 7), 271 (note 6), 272 (note 8), 280 (note 15); Intelligence estimate: 6, 50, 68, 70, 72, 75–76, 88, 91, 92, 94, 99, 107–8, 116–17, 118, 124–26, 135, 146, 149, 154, 160–61, 173–74, 249, 275 (note 10), 276 (note 17), 277 (note 37), 279 (note 89)

Elran, Meir, 179

Etzion air base, 39

Fahmy, Ali, 11

Fawzi, Mahmoud, 257 (note 11)

"Fortitude", 31

Gadhafi, Muammar, 33, 70, 75, 267 (note 18)

Galili, Yisrael, 49, 69, 122, 129, 157, 162, 195, 231

Gamasy, Mohamed Abdel Ghani, 18, 256 (note 1)

Gaza Strip, 17, 77

Gazit, Mordechai, 157, 176, 177, 178

Gazit, Shlomo, 251, 279 (note 10)

Gdalya, David, 135–36, 206–7

Geist, Benjamin, 228

Gera, Gideon, 179, 243

Gidi Pass, 17, 23, 34, 60–61, 66, 103, 109, 162, 172, 197, 198, 223, 230, 233

Gilboa, Amos, 115

Golan Heights, 1, 34, 46, 67, 70, 81–83, 87–88, 93, 96, 107, 123, 126, 128, 134, 153, 154, 158, 159, 162, 163, 172, 184, 189, 191, 195, 202, 211–18, 219, 220–21, 222, 227, 265 (note 29)

Gonen (Gorodish), Shmuel, 109, 135, 136, 176, 180, 193, 203–4, 205–6, 207, 210, 229, 230, 232–34, 269 (note 20), 282 (note 12)

Gooch, John, 5–6

Great Bitter Lake, 60, 166

Gromyko, Andrei, 137

groupthink, 3, 5, 129–30, 152, 243–46, 274 (note 30)

H-hour, 26, 50, 51, 119–20, 147, 185, 187, 203, 205, 207, 218, 279 (note 3)

Haaretz, 121

Haber, Eitan, 269 (note 31)

Handel, Michael, 4

Harkabi, Yehoshafat, 151

Harlev, Rafi, 243, 278 (note 69), 284 (note 50)

Hatzor air base, 222

"Havraga" stronghold, 209

Hazani, Michael, 157

Heikal, Mohamed, 119, 120, 121

Helwan air base, 167

Helwan, 113

Hermon Mount, 217

Herzog, Chaim, 230

heuristic judgment, 3, 254

Hillel, Shlomo, 157

Hod, Mordechai, 220

Hofi, Yitzhak, 87, 88, 94, 98–99, 105, 193, 212, 213, 216, 217, 229, 268 (note 5), 283 (note 30)

Homs, 98, 114, 115, 164, 271 (note 13)

Hungary, 156

Hushniya, 220, 221

Hussein, King, 35, 47, 50, 89–91, 92, 93, 96, 98, 107, 125, 160, 195, 237, 238, 241, 267 (note 26), 270 (note 45), 282 (note 23)

Huwaidi, Ahmed Fuad, 264 (note 21)
Hybel, Alex Roberto, 5

Iraq, 3, 31, 47, 68, 73, 91
Ismail, Ahmed, 12, 28, 30, 33, 34, 48, 103, 113, 119, 120, 121, 123, 256 (note 5)
Ismailia, 198
Israel: balance of forces, 39–43; elections in 1973, 77, 151, 240; Foreign Affairs and Defense Committee of the Parliament, 55, 64, 67, 75; and Jordan, 73, 89–91, 195; nuclear capability, 261–62 (note 11); war conception, 41–42, 43
Israeli Air Force (IAF), 16, 19–23, 24, 28, 29, 34, 40–41, 45–46, 47, 57, 58, 60, 69, 82, 85, 87, 93, 109, 120, 122, 134, 145, 175, 176, 187, 188–89, 190, 192, 193, 195, 198, 210, 217, 218–24, 227–28, 299–30, 242, 243, 250, 258 (note 26), 266 (note 9), 283 (note 44), 284 (note 50), 285 (note 12)
Israeli Air Force Intelligence Division, 82, 104, 242, 243
Israel Defense Force (IDF): force buildup, 20, 39–40, 41, 73–74, 176; losses, 225–28, 284 (note 2), 284 (note 5); Units: Battalion 13 (Golani Brigade), 213, 216; Battalion 50 (NAHAL Brigade), 213; Battalion 68 (Brigade 16), 205, 210; Battalion 424 (Sayeret Shaked), 213; Brigade 7, 93, 99, 108, 175, 213, 214, 216, 217, 226, 227; Brigade 8, 202; Brigade 14, 204, 205, 207, 210; Brigade 164, 227; Brigade 179, 105, 108, 117, 153, 175, 221, 227; Brigade 188, 42, 93, 213, 214, 216, 217, 226; Brigade 401, 204, 209; Brigade 460, 175, 204, 209; Division 36, 217, 221, 283 (note 30); Division 143, 234; Division 146, 221; Division 162, 74, 175, 233, 234; Division 209, 221; Division 252 ('Ugdat Sinai'), 18, 56, 57, 74, 175, 202, 204, 205, 207, 209, 210, 223, 226, 228, 233; Divisional headquarters 440, 74; war plans: general, 6–58, 71, 72, 128, 174–75, 176, 181, 188–89, 190, 193–94, 201, 202, 203, 204, 209–11, 211–13, 213–15, 218, 219–23, 229–31; "Abirei Lev" (Knights of the Heart), 248; "Assur" (Assyria), 108, 174–75, 213; "Dominique", 219; "Dugman" (Model), 41, 218, 219, 220, 221–23, 230; "Gir" (Chalk), 57, 214, 216; "Hatul Hamidbar" (Desert Cat), 176; "Kayitz/Horef" (Summer/Winter SOP), 108; "Manul" (Lock), 175; "Negiha" (Butt), 219; "Sela" (Rock), 56, 212, 214, 283 (note 30); "Shovach Yonim" (Dovecote), 57, 181, 194, 202, 203–5, 209–11, 216, 233, 240; "Srita" (Scrach), 219 "Tagar" (Challenge), 41, 219–20, 221, 222, 229, 230, 284 (note 50); "Zfania", 202
Israeli Navy Intelligence Department, 99–100
Israelyan, Victor, 137

Jerusalem, 69, 77, 122, 205
Jordan, 20, 34, 35, 42, 47, 53, 66, 73, 76, 89, 91, 96, 122, 158, 164, 211, 221, 231, 267 (note 26), 269 (note 30)
Jordan River, 68, 96, 128, 211, 217, 261 (note 11)
Juhader, 220

Kanizher, Zusia, 91–92, 94, 251
Kantara, 166
Katana, 213, 217
"Katya", 207
Katzabiya, 221
"Kavkaz" (Caucasus) operation, 20
Keating, Kenneth, 195
Kedar, Lou, 89, 269 (note 28)
Kennedy, John, 130
Kirpichenko, Vadim, 136
Kissinger, Henry, 151, 155, 176, 178–79, 269 (note 30)
Kiswa, 213, 217
Kober, Avi, 284 (note 5)
Kornienko, Georgi, 137
Kreisky, Bruno, 95
Kteifa, 114
Kuneitra, 34, 212, 216, 217
Kuznetsov, Vasilii, 137

Labor Party, 77, 89, 191, 240
Laner, Dan, 221, 283 (note 30)
Lanir, Zvi, 5
Laskov, Chaim, 108–9
Latakiya, 138
Lebanon, 26, 47, 83, 212, 283 (note 30)
Levran, Aharon, 5–6, 90, 93–94, 96, 243
Libya, 21, 68, 73, 75, 85, 167
Lidor, Zvi, 100–1, 134
Likud Party, 77
Lillehammer, 78
Lior, Yisrael, 142, 273 (note 10)
"Lituf" stronghold, 166
London, 48, 142, 195
Luntz, Rami, 99–100

Ma'ale Gamla, 217
"Mafzea'ch" stronghold, 165
Mamoun, Saad, 11
Mann, Hagai, 105, 212
Marsa Matruch, 156, 169
Marwan Ashraf, 5–6, 47–51, 141–43, 184–86, 187, 198, 237, 238, 263 (note 8), 263–64 (note 11); and theory of 'double-agent', 6, 49–51
'maskirovka', 25
Mecca, 28, 31, 113, 123
Meir, Golda, 43, 48, 55, 57, 64, 69–71, 72, 89–91, 94, 95, 113, 117, 122, 124, 126, 129, 130, 142, 143, 145, 150, 151, 152, 153–55, 157, 162, 163, 176, 177–78, 184, 186, 187, 188, 189, 190, 191, 194–98, 199, 201–2, 211, 219, 228, 229, 231–32, 234, 239–40, 245, 254 (note 14), 267 (note 26), 269 (note 31), 270 (note 45), 279 (note 2), 280 (note 21)
Meir, Meir, 251
Mendler, Albert, 202–4
Middle East News Agency, 29, 120, 121
'mikreh hakol' ("the case of all"), 53
Mitla Pass, 17, 23, 34, 60, 61, 66, 103, 109, 128, 162, 172, 197, 198, 223, 230, 233
"Mitzva" stronghold, 209
Mizrahi, Eli, 106, 271 (note 12)
Mor, Yekutiel, 181, 183
Morgan oil field, 28, 31

Moscow, 22, 48, 49
Mossad (Institute for Intelligence and Special Tasks), 32, 47–48, 50, 55, 64, 66, 68, 69, 72, 78, 89–90, 104, 106, 121, 130, 133, 141–43, 145, 150, 154, 180, 184, 185–86, 236, 241, 242 (see also: Zamir Zvi)
Mubarak, Husni, 35

Nafah, 214, 217, 221
Nasser, Fuad, 25
Nasser, Gamal Abdel, 15, 16, 17, 46, 47–48, 50, 257 (note 11)
Naufal, Bahi al-Din, 119
need for cognitive closure, 250–51, 266 (note 6), 287 (note 35)
Nixon, Richard, 69, 75, 179
Noi, Pinhas, 204
Normandy, 31
"Noza" stronghold, 209
Nuzha air base, 167

oil embargo, 12, 71
Ophir air base, 218
"Orkal" stronghold, 207

Palestine Liberation Organization (PLO), 26
Pas de Calais, 31
Pearl Harbor, 2, 4, 5, 287 (note 35)
Peled, Benny, 45, 145, 175, 180, 189, 218, 219, 220, 229
Peres, Shimon, 157
Porat, Yehuda, 104, 243
Port Said, 113, 143, 156, 166, 169, 177
Port Sudan, 29
preemptive strike, 178, 189–90, 193, 194, 196, 202, 218–19, 239
"Purkan" stronghold, 166

Rabin, Yitzhak, 280 (note 13)
Rafah, 221
Ramadan feast, 56, 98, 165, 167, 169, 170, 247
Ramat David air base, 120, 195, 220
Ramat Magshimim, 220
Rapid, 211, 212, 216, 217

R'ar'daka, 168
Raviv, Yishayahu, 191, 279 (note 3)
'research opinion', 242
Revivim, 95
Rifai, Zeid al, 267 (note 26)
Rogers plan, 39
Romani, 60
Rosenfeld, Yaacov, 110
'Rotem' crisis, 59, 265 (note 29)

Sa'asa, 34
Sadat, Anwar, 5, 11–13, 16, 18, 22, 25, 26, 28, 29, 33, 34–35, 41, 46, 48, 49, 50, 61, 63, 64, 65, 67, 68, 69, 70, 76, 81, 82, 86, 87, 90, 98, 137, 138, 185, 192, 196, 197, 237, 240, 244, 256 (note 1), 257 (note 8), 258 (note 29), 264 (note 11), 267 (note 18), 267 (note 26), 273 (note 2)
Sadiq, Mohamed Ahmed, 12, 17, 22
Salah a-Din operation, 261 (note 6)
Sapir, Pinhas, 201
Sarig, Ran, 221
Schannau, 95
Scowcroft, Brent, 223
Seale, Patrick, 269 (note 30)
Shaduwan island, 168
Shakour, Yusuf, 119
Shalev, Arie, 47, 91–92, 94, 98, 99, 101, 104, 105, 106, 115–16, 118, 122–24, 129, 179, 183, 243, 250, 270 (note 36), 270 (note 58), 273 (note 12), 276 (note 22)
Shalev, Avner, 118, 267 (note 30), 268 (note 5), 270 (note 43), 279 (note 3)
Shalev, Mordechai, 155, 176–77, 178
Shaluffa, 204
Sharm el Sheik, 66, 95, 175, 193, 197, 198, 218
Sharon, Ariel, 43, 77, 234, 246
Shazly, Saad el, 12, 15, 17, 18, 20, 23, 48, 256 (note 1), 256 (note 5), 259 (note 44), 259 (note 3)
Shlaim, Avi, 5
Shomron, Dan, 204
Siman-Tov, Benyamin, 135, 274 (note 6)
Simchoni, Uri, 212

Six Days' (1967) War, 11, 12, 19, 21, 42, 43, 46, 47, 49, 65, 86, 100, 162, 163, 199, 206, 227, 267 (note 18)
Soviet Union: general, 69, 98, 108, 126, 159, 160, 178, 222, 264, 276 (note 22), 282; military deployment in Egypt, 16, 20, 39, 41, 48, 156, 258 (note 29); relations with Egypt, 21–22, 26, 41, 48, 136–38, 154; relations with Syria, 26, 82, 83, 154, 164–65; emergency evacuation, 131, 133, 136–39, 141, 142, 143, 145–47, 148, 152, 153, 154, 156–57, 158–59, 164, 168–69, 170, 177, 179–80, 188, 192, 195, 247, 248, 249, 276
special means of collection, 116–17, 144–45, 148–49, 161, 173, 192, 236, 238, 241, 249, 276 (note 17), 276 (note 18)
Spector, Yiftah, 222–23
Stein Gross, Janis, 5
Stern, Yaacov, 94, 96, 109, 270 (note 45)
strategic surprise: psychological aspects, 218, 225, 228–34; situational and fundamental, 5; theory of, 2–4
strategic warning in Israel's national security doctrine, 7, 53–58, 88, 99, 107–8, 124–25, 126, 127, 133–34, 152–53, 154–55, 160–61, 173–74, 188, 239
strategic warnings prior to the war, 50–51, 66–67, 89–92, 96–97, 103–5, 107, 109, 141–43, 179–83, 185–86, 193, 236
Sudai, Albert, 110, 243
Sudan, 29, 48, 73
Suez Bay, 28, 168, 230
Suez Canal, 1, 12, 16, 17–19, 22, 53, 55, 94, 95, 99, 109, 121, 122, 128, 144, 147, 202, 203, 204, 209, 216, 219, 222
Suez town of, 143, 166, 234
"Sumud" (Joining) operation, 159
Sun Tzu, 25
Sweida, 114
Syria: air-defense layout, 33, 81–83, 87, 123, 126, 213; war plans: general, 33–34, 211–13, 213, 217; Operation Salah a-Din, 261 (note 6); "Sumud" (Joining), 159

T-4 air base, 98, 100, 114

Tal, Yisrael, 54, 57, 82, 99, 130–31, 145, 189, 246, 268 (note 5)
Tartus, 266 (note 9)
Tehila, Ilan, 175, 179–80, 183
Tel Aviv, 1, 89, 109, 141, 143, 152, 153, 157, 175, 185, 189, 195, 201, 217, 220, 223, 230, 231, 241
Tel Phares, 220
Telem, Benjamin, 100
Time magazine, 77
Timsah lake, 60
Tlas, Mustafa, 35, 119
"Tseidar" stronghold, 209
Turner, Richmond Kelly, 287 (note 35)
"Tzomet" ("juncture"), 54, 130, 160

Um Hashiba, 108, 230, 231, 232
Unit 848 (AMAN's SIGINT unit), 100, 106, 108, 115, 116, 138, 139, 148, 149, 160, 179, 181, 188, 192, 236, 245, 251
United States: general: 2, 6, 24, 39, 41, 42, 43, 46, 63, 65, 66, 67, 69, 71, 77, 84, 86, 137, 147, 151, 152, 155, 176–79, 189, 193, 195, 196, 223, 239, 258, 262, 286; intelligence estimates, 46, 96, 125, 152, 160, 178, 190, 192, 249, 268, 276

Vienna, 95
Vietnam War, 19
Vinogradov, Vladimir, 136, 137

War of Attrition, 11, 12, 15, 16, 17, 19, 20, 39–40, 41, 43, 45, 46, 48, 49, 54, 55, 206, 212
warning indicators: Egypt, 54, 55, 67, 68, 70, 72, 81, 93, 95–96, 97, 99–100, 103–4, 106, 113, 114, 115, 116, 118, 121, 123, 134–36, 138–39, 142, 143–44, 146–47, 156–57, 165–70, 192, 198; Syria, 67, 72, 81–83, 87, 92, 95, 98, 100, 101, 107, 114, 115–16, 118, 121, 122–23, 138–39, 142, 146–47, 157–58, 159, 164, 183–84, 192, 195–96; the USSR, 131, 133, 138–39, 141, 142, 143, 145–47, 148, 152, 153, 154, 156–57, 158–59, 164, 168–69, 170, 177, 179–83, 192, 195

Warsaw Pact, 32, 276
weapon systems—Egypt and Syria: al-Zaafer (al-Zeitun), 281; al-Kaher (al-Tin), 281; Dulphin, 167; Frog-7, 85; Kelt (AS-5), 21–22, 259; Mig-21, 20, 83, 96; Mirage 3E, V, 21–22, 67, 70; PMP assault bridge, 18, 258 (note 20) ; SA-2, 40, 81; SA-3, 20, 40, 81; SA-6, 20, 22, 34, 40–41, 81, 213, 221, 262, 268; SA-7, 22; Sagger (AT3), 24; Sukhoi SU-7, SU-17 (SU-20), 98, 100, 114, 123, 153, 158; Scud B (SS-1C), 21, 22, 50, 65, 85, 86, 189, 259; TPP assault bridge, 258 (note 20); Tupolev TU-16, 21, 22
weapon systems—Israel: C-97 Stratocruiser, 19; F-15, 87; LAW (AT4), 176; Mirage, 83; M-60, 42; Phantom F-4, 19, 20, 21, 40, 42, 83, 220, 222, 223; Shrike (AGM-45), 19, 41; Skyhawk A-4, 21, 219, 220, 223; "Zeev" ("Wolf"), 206, 207
Weitzman, Ezer, 45
Wohlstetter, Roberta, 2

Yaari, Aviezer (Avi), 47, 91–92, 104–5, 106, 180, 183, 202
Yardor, Reuven, 179
Yariv, Aharon, 53–54, 55, 63–64, 199, 246, 251
Yavetz, Chaim, 179, 243
'year of decision', 63, 237

Zamir, Zvi, 48–49, 50, 69–70, 90, 94, 130–31, 133, 141–43, 145, 148, 150, 154, 161, 180, 184, 185–86, 187, 188, 190, 198, 241, 269 (note 31), 281 (note 31)
Zeevi, Aharon, 30
Zeevi, Rehavam, 230, 246
Zeira, Eli, general: 6, 47, 48, 49, 55, 63–65, 67, 94, 99, 100, 118, 122, 130, 139, 142–43, 171, 176, 188, 240, 243, 245, 246, 247, 248–49, 250–51, 263 (note 18), 266 (note 6), 271 (note 6), 286 (note 10), 287 (note 34); intelligence estimates, 61, 64–65, 68, 69, 71–72, 75–76, 81, 83, 84–

Zeira, Eli, general *(continued)*
   87, 92–93, 98, 100, 101, 104–5, 107, 116, 143, 146–48, 152, 153–54, 157–60, 161, 162–63, 169, 173–74, 192, 193, 195–96, 198–99, 203, 205, 211–13, 242, 249, 250, 276 (note 27), 281 (note 31); perception of his professional duty, 55, 64, 99, 104–5, 106, 118, 154, 180–81, 249; unethical behavior, 104–5, 106–7, 116–17, 148–49, 162–63, 180–81, 199, 203, 205, 236, 241, 248–49, 263 (note 8), 272 (note 8), 276 (note 17), 276 (note 18)

Zeira, Yossi, 116, 149

Zur, Zvi, 93, 151, 152, 157, 194, 245

www.ingramcontent.com/pod-product-compliance
Lightning Source LLC
Chambersburg PA
CBHW030128240426
43672CB00005B/68